VERSION
2003

MICROSOFT®
VISUAL
C# .NET
STEP BY STEP

Microsoft®
.net™

John Sharp
Jon Jagger

PUBLISHED BY
Microsoft Press
A Division of Microsoft Corporation
One Microsoft Way
Redmond, Washington 98052-6399

Library of Congress Cataloging-in-Publication Data
Sharp, John, 1964-
    Microsoft Visual C# .NET Step by Step: Version 2003 / John Sharp, Jon Jagger.
       p. cm.
    Includes index.
    ISBN 0-7356-1909-3
    1. C# (Computer program language) 2. Microsoft .NET.   I. Jagger, Jon, 1966- II. Title.

    QA76.73.C154S53   2003
    005.2'768--dc21   2003041290

Printed and bound in the United States of America.

2 3 4 5 6 7 8 9   QWT   8 7 6 5 4 3

Distributed in Canada by H.B. Fenn and Company Ltd.

A CIP catalogue record for this book is available from the British Library.

Microsoft Press books are available through booksellers and distributors worldwide. For further information about international editions, contact your local Microsoft Corporation office or contact Microsoft Press International directly at fax (425) 936-7329. Visit our Web site at www.microsoft.com/mspress. Send comments to *mspinput@microsoft.com*.

Acquisitions Editor: Robin Van Steenburgh
Project Editor: Denise Bankaitis
Technical Editor: Jim Fuchs

Body Part No. X09-45406

Table of Contents

Acknowledgments

This is the first book I have written, but I hope it's not the last. In undertaking this project, I never realized how much hard work it would be or how many people would be involved. I am now enlightened! There are far too many to thank individually, but I would like to mention Karen Szall and Danielle Bird at Microsoft Press, and Joe Perez, Stephanie Edmundson, Elisabeth Knottingham, and Lonnon Foster, and thank them for their enduring patience with my endless typos, grammatical errors, and jargon. I would also like to thank Suzanne Carlino, my project manager at Content Master, who beat me up and made sure I stuck to the schedule, and Robert Burbidge, who stepped in at the last minute and spent many thankless hours reviewing my work—and we are still friends!

For the second edition of this book, I would also like to thank everyone who submitted reports to the Microsoft Press Web site identifying typos, mistakes, and making requests. I hope we have incorporated everything! Furthermore, I am indebted to David Glanville, my project manager at Content Master, who guided me though the process of performing these updates and made sure I had the necessary time available (mainly after midnight!).

Finally, I would like to acknowledge the support and help given to me by my family—to Diana, who had to put up with me creeping to bed at 2:00 in the morning on many occasions (at least some occurrences of which were related to my book-writing activities), to James, who kept asking "Is Daddy STILL on that computer?" and to Francesca, who just wants to see her name in a book.

And finally, finally, "Up the Gills!"

John Sharp

I'd like to dedicate this book to the five most important people in my life: my mother for having such a strong but gentle influence on me; my wife, Natalie, for making my life infinitely richer; and our three children, Ellie, Penny, and Patrick, who teach me important new things every day.

I'd also like to thank everyone who has helped me learn interesting things, particularly Douglas Adams, Christopher Alexander, Sean Corfield, Richard Gabriel, Kevlin Henney, John Holt, and David Pye.

Finally, I'd like to pay tribute to the elegance of the two-seater sports cars made by Marlin Engineering, the hilarity of the films made by Monty Python, the grass roots programming support provided by ACCU (*http://www.accu.org*), and the quality of life generated by the people of the village I live in.

Jon Jagger

Introduction

Microsoft Visual C# .NET is a powerful but simple language aimed primarily at developers creating applications for the Microsoft .NET platform. It inherits many of the best features of C++ and Microsoft Visual Basic but with some of the inconsistencies and anachronisms removed, resulting in a cleaner and more logical language. C# also contains a variety of useful features that accelerate application development, especially when used in conjunction with Microsoft Visual Studio .NET.

The aim of this book is to teach you the fundamentals of programming with C# using Visual Studio .NET and the .NET Framework. You will learn the features of the C# language, and then use them to build applications running the Microsoft Windows operating system. By the time you have completed this book, you will have a thorough understanding of C# and will have used it to build Windows Forms applications, manipulate XML, access SQL Server, control Windows services, develop ASP.NET applications, and build and consume a Web service.

Finding Your Best Starting Point in This Book

This book is designed to help you build skills in a number of essential areas. You can use this book if you are new to programming or you are switching from another programming language such as C, C++, Sun Microsystems's Java, or Microsoft Visual Basic 6. Use the following table to find your best starting point in this book.

If you are	Follow these steps
New	
To object-oriented programming	**1** Install the practice files as described in the next section of this chapter, "Installing and Using the Practice Files."
	2 Work through the chapters in Parts 1, 2, and 3 sequentially.
	3 Complete Parts 4, 5, and 6 as your level of experience and interest dictates.
New	
To C#	**1** Install the practice files as described in the next section of this chapter, "Installing and Using the Practice Files." Skim the first five chapters to get an overview of C# and Visual Studio .NET, and then concentrate on Chapters 6 through 17.
	2 Complete Parts 4, 5, and 6 as your level of experience and interest dictates.

If you are	Follow these steps
Migrating	
From C, C++, or Java	**1** Install the practice files as described in the next section of this chapter, "Installing and Using the Practice Files."
	2 Skim the first seven chapters to get an overview of C# and Visual Studio .NET, and then concentrate on Chapters 8 through 17.
	3 For information about building Windows applications and using a database, read Parts 4 and 5.
	4 For information about building Web applications and Web services, read Part 6.
Switching	
From Visual Basic 6	**1** Install the practice files as described in the next section of this chapter, "Installing and Using the Practice Files."
	2 Work through the chapters in Parts 1, 2, and 3 sequentially.
	3 For information about building Windows applications, read Part 4.
	4 For information about accessing a database, read Part 5.
	5 For information about creating Web applications and Web services, read Part 6.
	6 Read the Quick Reference sections at the end of the chapters for information about specific C# and Visual Studio .NET constructs.
Referencing	
The book after working through the exercises	**1** Use the index or the Table of Contents to find information about particular subjects.
	2 Read the Quick Reference sections at the end of each chapter to find a brief review of the syntax and techniques presented in the chapter.

Minimum System Requirements

You'll need the following hardware and software to complete the exercises in this book:

- Microsoft Windows XP Professional Edition, Microsoft Windows Server 2003, Microsoft Windows 2000 Professional, or Microsoft Windows 2000 Server with Service Pack 3

- Microsoft Visual Studio .NET 2003 Professional or Enterprise Edition (If you're using the Standard Edition of Visual C# .NET 2003 you can't create controls, but you can complete the other exercises in this book.)

- Microsoft Desktop Engine (MSDE) installed and configured, if you are running Microsoft Visual Studio .NET 2003 Professional or access to Microsoft SQL Server 2000 or later, if you are running Microsoft Visual Studio .NET 2003 Enterprise Edition
- Access to the Northwind Traders database running under MSDE or SQL Server
- Microsoft Internet Information Services 5 (or later) installed and running
- 450 MHz Pentium II-class or compatible processor (600 MHz Pentium III-class recommended)
- 3.25 GB available hard disk space minimum (5 GB recommended)
- 192 MB RAM (256 MB or more recommended)
- Super VGA Monitor (800 x 600 or higher resolution) monitor with at least 256 colors
- CD-ROM drive
- Microsoft Mouse or compatible pointing device

Installing and Using the Practice Files

The CD-ROM inside this book contains the practice files that you'll use as you perform the exercises in the book. For example, when you're learning about *if* statements, you'll use a pre-written project called *Selection*. By using the practice files, you won't waste time creating objects that aren't relevant to the exercise. Instead, you can concentrate on learning object-oriented programming with Visual C# .NET. The files and the step-by-step instructions in the lessons also let you learn by doing, which is an easy and effective way to acquire and remember new skills.

Installing the Practice Files

Follow these steps to install the practice files on your computer's hard disk so that you can use them with the exercises in this book.

1 Remove the CD-ROM from the package inside this book and insert it into your CD-ROM drive.

> ▶ **Note** A Starting menu should launch automatically. If this menu does not appear, double-click the My Computer icon on the desktop, double-click the icon for your CD-ROM drive, and then double-click StartCD.exe.

2 Click Install Practice Files.
3 Follow the onscreen instructions.

4   When the files have been installed, remove the CD-ROM from your CD-ROM drive and replace it in the package inside the book.

A folder named Microsoft Press\Visual C# Step by Step has been created in your My Documents folder on your hard disk, and the practice files have been placed in that folder.

Using the Practice Files

Each chapter in this book explains when and how to use any practice files for that chapter. When it's time to use a practice file, the book will list the instructions for how to open the file. The chapters are built around scenarios that simulate real programming projects, so you can easily apply the skills you learn to your own work.

For those of you who like to know all the details, here's a list of the Visual C# projects on the practice disk.

Project	Description
Chapter 1	
TextHello	This project gets you started. It steps through the creation of a simple program that displays a text-based greeting.
WinFormHello	This project displays the greeting in a window using Windows Forms.
Chapter 2	
PrimitiveDataTypes	This project demonstrates how to declare variables of each of the primitive types, how to assign values to these variables, and how to display their values in a window.
MathsOperators	This program introduces the arithmetic operators (+ - * / %).
Chapter 3	
Methods	In this project, you'll re-examine the code in the previous project and investigate how it is structured by using methods.
DailyRate	This project walks you through writing your own methods (both manually and by using a wizard), running the methods, and stepping through the method calls using the Visual Studio debugger.
Chapter 4	
Selection	This project shows how a cascading *if* statement is used to compare two dates.
switchStatement	This simple program uses a *switch* statement to convert characters into their XML representations.

Project	Description
Chapter 5	
Iteration	This project displays code fragments for each of the different iteration statements and the output that each generates.
whileStatement	This project uses a *while* statement to read the contents of a source file one line at a time and display each line in a Windows text box.
doStatement	This project uses a *do* statement to convert a number to its string representation.
Chapter 6	
MathsOperators	This project re-examines the MathsOperators project from Chapter 2 and causes various unhandled exceptions to make the program fail. The *try* and *catch* keywords then make the application more robust so that it no longer fails.
Chapter 7	
Classes	This project covers the basics of defining your own classes, complete with public constructors, methods, and private fields. It also covers creating class instances using the *new* keyword and static methods and fields.
Chapter 8	
Parameters	This program investigates the difference between value parameters and reference parameters. It demonstrates how to use the *ref* and *out* keywords.
Chapter 9	
StructsAndEnums	This project uses an *enum* to represent the four different suits of a playing card, and then uses a *struct* to represent a calendar date.
Chapter 10	
Aggregates	This project builds on the previous one by using the *ArrayList* collection class to group together playing cards in a hand.
Chapter 11	
ParamsArrays	This project demonstrates how to use the *params* keyword to create a single method that can accept any number of *int* arguments and find and return the one with the smallest value.
Chapter 12	
CSharp	This project uses a hierarchy of interfaces and classes to simulate both reading a C# source file and classifying its contents into various kinds of tokens (identifiers, keywords, operators, and so on). As an example of use, it also derives classes from the key interfaces to display the tokens in a rich text box in color syntax.

Project	Description
Chapter 13	
UsingStatement	This project revisits a small piece of code from the previous chapter and reveals that it is not exception-safe. It shows you how to make the code exception-safe with a *using* statement.
Chapter 14	
Properties	This project presents a simple Windows application that uses several properties to continually display the size of its main window.
Chapter 15	
Indexers	This project uses two indexers: one to look up a person's phone number when given a name, and the other to look up a person's name when given a phone number.
Chapter 16	
Delegates	This project displays the time in digital format using delegate callbacks. The code is then simplified by using events.
Chapter 17	
Operators	This project builds on the previous one by using three structs, called *Hour*, *Minute*, and *Second*, that contain user-defined operators. The code is then simplified by using a conversion operator.
Chapter 18	
BellRingers	This project is a Windows Forms application demonstrating basic Windows Forms controls.
Chapter 19	
BellRingers	This project is an extension of the application created in Chapter 18, but with drop-down and pop-up menus added to the user interface.
Chapter 20	
CustomerDetails	This project demonstrates how to validate user input using customer information as an example.
Chapter 21	
SplitterDemo	This project shows how to use the *Splitter* control, and shows how the *Dock* property of various controls can be used.
BellRingers	This project demonstrates how to use the *TreeView* and *ListView* controls.
Chapter 22	
MDIDemo	This project is a simple text editor that demonstrates how to build an MDI application and how to use common dialog controls.

Project	Description
Chapter 23	
LoginControl	This project is a Windows Control. It provides the logic for logging in to a system in a generic manner.
LoginTest	This project is a test harness for testing the LoginControl project.
SubclassedControls	This project uses inheritance to create a specialized version of the *CheckBox* class called *ToggleButton*.
ToggleButtonTest	This project is the test harness for *ToggleButton*.
Chapter 24	
ListProducts	This project implements a data link for accessing the Northwind Traders database.
DisplayProducts	This project uses the data link created in the ListProducts project to connect to the Northwind Traders database, and retrieve and modify information in the Products table using an *SqlDataAdapter* and a *DataSet* control.
ReportOrders	This project shows how to access a database using Microsoft ADO.NET code rather than a data link and data controls. The application retrieves information from the Orders table.
Chapter 25	
DataBindingDemo	This project shows how to use simple data binding to bind properties of controls to single values in various data sources.
ComplexBindingDemo	This project shows how to use complex data binding to display a list of values from a data source.
ManageTerritories	This project demonstrates how to use data binding and a disconnected *DataSet* to retrieve and maintain information from the Territories table in the Northwind Traders database.
Chapter 26	
RecordTimesheets	This project defines an XML schema and converts user input into XML using the schema.
AnalyzeTimesheets	This project validates and parses data in an XML file using the XML schema defined in the RecordTimesheets project.
Chapter 27	
EmployeeInfo	This project is a simple ASP.NET application that introduces Web forms and Server controls.
Chapter 28	
EmployeeInfo	This project is an extended version of the EmployeeInfo project from the previous chapter and shows how to validate user input in an ASP.NET Web application.

Project	Description
Chapter 29	
CustomerInfo	This project shows how to use Forms-based security for authenticating the user. The application also demonstrates how to use ADO.NET from an ASP.NET Web form, showing how to manipulate a database in a scalable manner.
Chapter 30	
SupplierInfo	This project shows how to sort data in a *DataGrid* and how to cache data in an ASP.NET Web application.
ProductInfo	This project shows how to use Column templates to tailor the appearance of columns in a *DataGrid* control.
ProductCategories	This project shows techniques for navigating between Web forms in an ASP.NET application, passing information from one Web form to another.
Chapter 31	
NorthwindServices	This project implements an XML Web service, providing remote access across the Internet to data in the Products table in the Northwind Traders database.
Chapter 32	
OrderCost	This project shows how to create a Windows application that consumes an XML Web service. It shows how to synchronously invoke the XML Web service created in Chapter 31.
ProductInfo	This project is another XML Web service consumer. It shows how to invoke a Web service asynchronously.

In addition to these projects, several projects have solutions available for the practice exercises. The solutions for each project are included on the CD-ROM in the folder for each chapter and are labeled Complete.

Uninstalling the Practice Files

Follow these steps to remove the practice files from your computer. These steps are written for Windows XP Professional operating system. If you are using a different version of Windows, refer to your Windows Help documentation for removing programs.

1   Click Start, and then click Control Panel.
2   Click Add/Remove Programs.
3   From the list of Currently Installed Programs, select Microsoft Visual C# .NET Step By Step (2003) Sample Files.
4   Click Change/Remove. The Confirm Uninstall dialog box opens.

5   Click OK to delete the practice files.

6   Click Finish to close the InstallShield Wizard dialog box.

7   Click Close to close the Add Or Remove Programs dialog box.

8   Close Control Panel.

Conventions and Features in This Book

This book presents information using conventions designed to make the information readable and easy to follow. Before you start the book, read the following list, which explains conventions you'll see throughout the book and points out helpful features in the book that you might want to use.

Conventions

- Each exercise is a series of tasks. Each task is presented as a series of numbered steps (1, 2, and so on). A round bullet (•) indicates an exercise that has only one step.
- Notes labeled "tip" provide additional information or alternative methods for completing a step successfully.
- Notes labeled "important" alert you to information you need to check before continuing.
- Text that you type appears in **bold**.
- A plus sign (+) between two key names means that you must press those keys at the same time. For example, "Press Alt+Tab" means that you hold down the Alt key while you press the Tab key.

Other Features

- Shaded sidebars throughout the book provide more in-depth information about the exercise. The sidebars might contain background information, design tips, or features related to the information being discussed.
- Each chapter ends with a Quick Reference section. The Quick Reference section contains quick reminders of how to perform the tasks you learned in the chapter.

Corrections, Comments, and Help

Every effort has been made to ensure the accuracy of this book and the contents of the practice files on the CD-ROM. Microsoft Press provides corrections and additional content for its books through the World Wide Web at this location:

http:/www.microsoft.com/mspress/support/

To connect directly to the Microsoft Press Knowledge Base and enter a query regarding a question or issue that you may have, go to *http://www.microsoft.com/ mspress/support/search.asp*.

If you have problems, comments, or ideas regarding this book or the CD-ROM, please send them to Microsoft Press.

Send e-mail to:

mspinput@microsoft.com

Or send postal mail to:

Microsoft Press

Attn: Step by Step Series Editor

One Microsoft Way

Redmond, WA 98052-6399

Please note that product support is not offered through these mail addresses. For further information regarding Microsoft software support options, please go to *http://support.microsoft.com/directory/* or call Microsoft Support Network Sales at (800) 936-3500.

Visit the Microsoft Press Web Site

You are also invited to visit the Microsoft Press World Wide Web site at the following location:

http://www.microsoft.com/mspress/

You'll find descriptions for the complete line of Microsoft Press books, information about ordering titles, notice of special features and events, additional content for Microsoft Press books, and much more.

You can also find out the latest in Microsoft .NET software developments and news from Microsoft Corporation by visiting the following Web site:

http://msdn.microsoft.com/net

Check it out!

Introducing Microsoft Visual C# and Visual Studio .NET

Chapter

1

Welcome to C#

In this chapter, you will learn how to:

- Start Microsoft Visual Studio .NET.

- Use the Visual Studio .NET programming environment.

- Create a C# console application.

- Create a C# Windows Forms application.

Microsoft Visual C# .NET is Microsoft's powerful, component-oriented language. C# plays an important role in the architecture of the Microsoft .NET Framework, and some people have drawn comparisons to the role that C played in the development of UNIX. C# uses curly brackets, so if you already know a curly bracket language such as C, C++, or Java, you'll find the syntax of C# reassuringly familiar.

In Part 1, you'll learn the fundamentals of C#. You'll discover how to declare variables and how to use operators such as the plus sign (+) and the minus sign (−) to create values. You'll see how to write methods and pass arguments to methods. You'll also learn how to use selection statements such as *if* and iteration statements such as *while*. Finally, you'll understand how C# uses exceptions to handle errors in a graceful, easy-to-use manner. These topics form the core of C#, and from this solid foundation you'll progress to more advanced features in Part 2 through Part 6.

Beginning Programming with the Visual Studio .NET Environment

Visual Studio .NET is a tool-rich programming environment containing all the functionality you'll need to create large or small C# projects. (You can even create projects that seamlessly combine modules from different languages.) In the first exercise, you'll start the Visual Studio .NET programming environment and learn how to create a console application.

Create a console application in Visual Studio .NET

1   In Microsoft Windows, click the Start button, point to All Programs, and then point to Microsoft Visual Studio .NET 2003.

2   Click the Microsoft Visual Studio .NET 2003 icon. Visual Studio .NET starts.

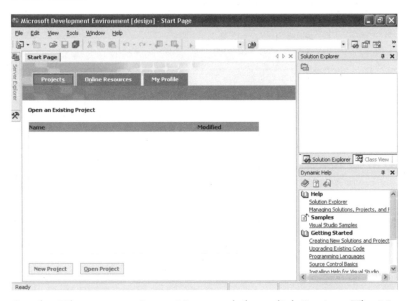

3   On the File menu, point to New, and then click Project. The New Project dialog box opens. This dialog box allows you to create a new project using various templates such as Windows Application, Class Library, and Console Application that specify the type of application you want to create.

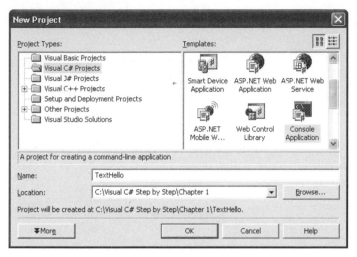

4 In the Project Types pane, click the Visual C# Projects folder.

5 In the Templates pane, click the Console Application icon. (You might need to use the Templates pane scrollbar to reveal this icon.)

6 In the Location field, type **C:\Visual C# Step by Step\Chapter 1**.

▶ **Note** If the folder you specify does not exist, Visual Studio .NET will create it for you.

7 In the Name field, type **TextHello**.

8 Click OK. The new project opens.

The *menu bar* provides access to the commands you'll use in the programming environment. You can use the keyboard or the mouse to access the menus and commands exactly as you can in all Windows-based programs. The *toolbar* is located beneath the menu bar and provides button shortcuts to run the most frequently used commands. The Code pane displays the source files. In a multi-file project, each source file has its own tab labeled with the name of the source file. You can click the tab once to bring the named source file to the foreground in the Code pane. The Solution Explorer displays the names of the files associated with the project. You can also double-click a filename in the Solution Explorer to bring that source file to the foreground in the Code pane. The Output pane lists the diagnostic messages generated from build commands.

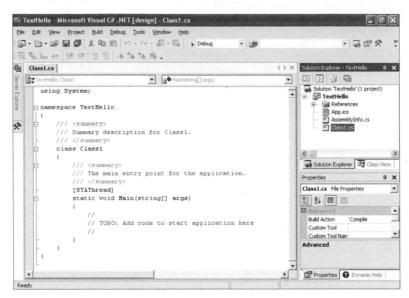

Before writing the code, examine the files listed in the Solution Explorer that Visual Studio .NET has created as part of your project:

- **TextHello.sln**   This is the top-level solution file, of which there is one per application. Each solution file contains one or more project files. In the file system, each solution file has the extension .sln. In the Solution Explorer, it appears with a name that is easier to read, such as "Solution 'TextHello'" in this project.

- **TextHello.csproj**   This is a C# project file. Each project file contains one or more source files. The source files in a single project must be written in the same programming language. This file type is displayed in the Solution Explorer using only the project's name; however, it is stored on the file system with the extension .csproj.

- **Class1.cs**   This is a C# source file. You will write your code in this file. It contains some code that Visual Studio .NET provides automatically, which you will examine shortly.

- **AssemblyInfo.cs**   This is another C# source file. You can use this file to add attributes to your program, such as the name of the author, the date the program was written, and so on. There are other more advanced attributes you can use to modify the way in which the program will run.

- **App.ico**   This is the icon that is associated with the application. All Windows applications that have a user interface have an icon that appears minimized on the taskbar when the application is running.

If you use Windows Explorer to navigate to the C:\Visual C# Step by Step\Chapter 1 folder specified as the project location, you'll find a folder named TextHello. (This folder might be hidden depending on your Windows settings.) This folder contains the files listed in the Solution Explorer.

Writing Your First Program

The Class1.cs file defines a class called *Class1* that contains a method called *Main*. All methods must be defined inside a class. The *Main* method is special—it designates the program's entry point. It must be a static method. (Methods are discussed in Chapter 3, static methods are discussed in Chapter 7, and the *Main* method is discussed in Chapter 11.)

▶ **Important**   C# is a case-sensitive language. You must spell *Main* with a capital *M*.

In the following exercises, you'll write the code to display Hello World to the console; you'll build and run your Hello World console application; you'll learn how namespaces are used to partition code elements; and you'll learn how to comment your code using XML and then view your XML comments as HTML documents.

Write the code using IntelliSense technology

1 Remove the TODO: comments (the lines starting with //) from the *Main* method in Class1.cs, and then delete the [STAThread] line just before *Main*.

   Main should look like this:

```
static void Main(string[] args)
{
}
```

2 Add a blank line after the opening brace and type **Console**.

   Main should look like this:

```
static void Main(string[] args)
{
    Console
}
```

▶ **Note**   *Console* is a built-in class that contains the methods for displaying messages on the screen and getting input from the keyboard.

3 Type a dot after *Console*. An IntelliSense list appears. This list contains all the methods, properties, and fields of the *Console* class.

4   Scroll down through the list by pressing the Down Arrow key repeatedly until *WriteLine* is selected, and then press Enter. Alternatively, you can use the mouse to scroll through the list, and then double-click *WriteLine*.

The IntelliSense list closes, and the *WriteLine* method is added to the source file. *Main* should now look like this:

```
static void Main(string[] args)
{
    Console.WriteLine
}
```

▶ **Tip**   When the IntelliSense list appears, you can press the *W* key to select the first *Console* member starting with the letter *w*.

5   Type a left parenthesis. An IntelliSense tip appears.

This tip displays the parameters of the *WriteLine* method. In fact, *WriteLine* is an *overloaded* method, meaning that *Console* contains more than one method named *WriteLine*. (Overloaded methods are discussed in Chapter 3.) *Main* should now look like this:

```
static void Main(string[] args)
{
    Console.WriteLine(
}
```

You can click the tip's up and down arrows to scroll through the overloaded versions of *WriteLine*.

6   Type the right parenthesis, followed by a semicolon.

Main should now look like this:

```
static void Main(string[] args)
{
    Console.WriteLine();
}
```

7   Type the string "Hello World" between the left and right parentheses. *Main* should now look like this:

```
static void Main(string[] args)
{
    Console.WriteLine("Hello World");
}
```

▶ **Tip**   Get into the habit of typing matched character pairs, such as (and) and { and }, *before* filling in their contents. It's easy to forget the closing character if you wait until after you've entered the contents.

IntelliSense Icons

IntelliSense displays the name of every member of a class. To the left of each member name is an icon that depicts the type of member. The icons and their types include the following:

Icon	Meaning
	method (discussed in Chapter 3)
	property (discussed in Chapter 14)
	class (discussed in Chapter 7)
	struct (discussed in Chapter 9)
	enum (discussed in Chapter 9)
	interface (discussed in Chapter 12)
	delegate (discussed in Chapter 16)
	namespace

Build and run your console application

1. On the Build menu, click Build Solution. The build succeeds and the following line is displayed in the Output pane:

```
Build: 1 succeeded, 0 failed, 0 skipped
```

▶ **Note** An asterisk after the filename in the Code pane indicates that the file has been changed since it was last saved. There is no need to manually save the file before building because the Build Solution command saves automatically.

2. On the Debug menu, click Start Without Debugging. The program runs in a Command window, writing Hello World to the console, as shown in the next illustration.

▶ **Note** Be sure to click Start Without Debugging and not Start. The Start command runs the program in a Command shell but does *not* pause at the end of the run.

3   Ensure the Command shell has the focus, and then press any key. The Command window closes and you return to the Visual Studio .NET programming environment.

4   In the Solution Explorer, click Show All Files. Entries named *bin* and *obj* appear above the C# source filenames.

These correspond directly to folders named bin and obj in the project folder. These folders are created when you build your application, and they contain the executable version of the program and other files used for debugging the program.

5   In the Solution Explorer, click the + to the left of the bin entry. A nested entry named Debug appears.

6   In the Solution Explorer, click the + to the left of the Debug entry. Two entries named TextHello.exe and TextHello.pdb appear.

These are files in the bin\Debug folder. The Solution Explorer should now look like the following illustration:

Command Line Compilation

You can also compile your source files into an executable file manually by using the csc command-line C# compiler. You must first complete the following steps to set up your environment:

1   Open the Command window and go to C:\Program Files\Microsoft Visual Studio .NET 2003\Vc7\Bin.

2   Run vcvars32.bat to modify the shell environment variables PATH, LIB, and INCLUDE, adding the folders that contain the various .NET libraries and utilities necessary for command-line compilation.

3   Go to the \Visual C# Step by Step\Chapter 1\TextHello project folder, and then enter the following command:

```
csc /out:Greeting.exe AssemblyInfo.cs Class1.cs
```

This creates the executable file Greeting.exe from both C# source files. If you don't use the *out* command-line option, the executable file will take its name from the name of the first source file.

Using Namespaces

Small programs and small children have one obvious thing in common: they grow. As a program grows, it creates two problems. First, more code is harder to understand and maintain than less code. Second, more code usually means more names, more named data, more named functions, and more named classes. As the number of names increases so does the likelihood of the project build failing because two or more names clash (especially when the program uses third-party libraries).

▶ **Tip**   Here's a handy way to open a Command window in a particular folder from within Windows Explorer: On the Tools menu, click Folder Options. When the Folder Options dialog box opens, click the File Types tab. Locate and select the Folder file type in the Registered File Types list, and then click Advanced. In the Edit File Type window, click New. In the New Action window, type **Command** in the Action text box, and type **C:\WINDOWS\System32\CMD.EXE** for the application to be used to perform the action. Click OK to close the New Action window. Click OK to close the Edit File Type window. Click OK once more to close the Folder Options dialog box. In Windows Explorer, right-click any folder. You will see the Command option appear in the pop-up menu. If you click Command, a Command window will open and make that folder active.

In the past, programmers tried to solve the name-clashing problem by prefixing names with a "subsystem" qualifier. This is not a good idea because it's not a scalable solution; names become longer and you spend less time writing software and more time typing (there is a difference), and more time reading and re-reading incomprehensibly long names.

Namespaces help to solve this problem by creating a named container for other identifiers. For example, rather than creating a class called *TextHelloGreeting*, you can create a class named *Greeting* inside the namespace named *TextHello*, like this:

```
namespace TextHello
{
    class Greeting
    {
        ⋮
    }
}
```

You can then refer to the *Greeting* class as *TextHello.Greeting*. If someone else also creates a *Greeting* class in his own namespace and installs it on your computer, your application will still work as expected.

The .NET Framework software development kit (SDK) documentation recommends defining all your classes in namespaces, and the Visual Studio .NET environment follows this recommendation, using the name of your project as the top-level namespace.

▶ **Tip**   Avoid name clashes between namespaces and types. In other words, don't create a class with the same name as a namespace. A namespace can contain multiple classes.

The .NET Framework SDK also adheres to this recommendation; every single class in the .NET Framework lives inside a namespace. For example, the *Console* class lives inside the *System* namespace. This means that its fully qualified name is actually *System.Console*. Of course, if you had to write the fully quali-fied name every time, it would be no better that just naming the class *System-Console*. Fortunately, you can solve this problem with a *using* directive:

```
using System;
```

You can add *using* directives to the top of a source file (or as the first statement inside a namespace). They effectively make the names of the classes inside the namespace visible outside the namespace in their shorthand form. In other words, they make long names short again, but only inside the source file (or namespace) in which the *using* directives appear. The following exercise demon-strates this concept.

Try longhand names

1   In the Code And Text Editor window, comment out the *using* direc-tive at the top of Class1.cs:

```
//using System;
```

2   On the Build menu, click Build Solution. The build fails and the Out-put pane displays the following diagnostic message:

```
The type or namespace 'Console' could not be found: (are you missing
a using directive or an assembly reference?)
```

▶   **Tip**   When you are learning a new language, making deliberate, controlled errors can be a useful technique. Later, when you make the error accidentally, the error message is familiar. An expert is simply someone who knows how to make all the errors in his or her field, and hence how to avoid or correct them!

3   In the Output pane, double-click the diagnostic message. The identi-fier that caused the error is selected in the Class1.cs source file.

▶   **Tip**   The first error can affect the reliability of subsequent diagnostic mes-sages. If your build has more than one diagnostic message, correct only the first one, ignore all the others, and then rebuild. This strategy works best if you keep your source files small and work iteratively, building frequently.

4   In the Code And Text Editor window, edit *Main* to use the fully qual-ified name *System.Console*.

Main should look like this:

```
static void Main(string[] args)
{
    System.Console.WriteLine("Hello World");
}
```

5   On the Build menu, click Build Solution. The build succeeds this time. If it doesn't, make sure *Main* is *exactly* as it appears in the preceding code, and then try building again. (Hopefully, this will not result in an infinite loop!)

6   In the Solution Explorer, click the + to the left of the References entry. This displays the assemblies referenced by the Solution Explorer (the other possible cause of the error in the diagnostic message).

Creating Documentation Using XML and Comments

As programs grow, so does the importance of up-to-date, easy-to-use, and informative documentation. Traditionally, programs have been quite poorly documented. One reason for this is the habit of writing the code and its documentation in separate files. This separation makes it very easy for the code and the documentation to get out of synchronization. It also creates a large amount of duplication because, ideally, the structure of the documentation should mirror the structure of the code it documents.

The .NET Framework solves this problem by specifying a set of XML tag names you can embed directly in your code comments. The .NET Framework also provides a command-line compiler option (/doc:) to extract code documentation, in XML format, directly from source files. This solves both problems at one time: There is no separation and, because the compiler already understands the grammar of the C# language, it can automatically replicate the structure of the code in the structure of the XML.

In the following exercise, you'll learn how to generate a structured, hyperlinked set of HTML files from XML tags in code comments.

Add XML comments to your code

1   On the View menu, click Class View. A Class View tab appears at the bottom of the Solution Explorer.

2   Click the Class View tab. The Solution Explorer displays the Class View window.

3   On the Class View tab, click the + to the left of the TextHello project to expand the entry to show the *TextHello* namespace. Click the + to the left of the *TextHello* namespace to show the *Class1* class. Right-click the Class1 entry. A pop-up menu appears.

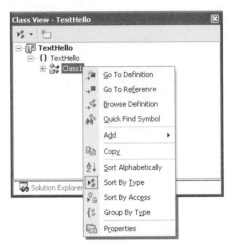

4   On the pop-up menu, click the Properties entry. The Properties window appears, displaying the properties of the class.

5   Double-click the *(Name)* property. The *(Name)* property and its value are selected.

6   Type **Greeting** and then press Enter. In the Code And Text Editor window, the name of the class changes to *Greeting*. Notice that the name also changes in the Types list at the top left of the Code pane.

7   In the Code pane, change the comment between the *<summary>* tags above the class to read "The obligatory Hello World in C#".

8   In the Code pane, add the following *<remarks>* comment after the *<summary>* comment:

```
/// <remarks>
/// This program writes out "Hello World"
/// using the WriteLine method of the
/// System.Console class.
/// </remarks>
```

The Code pane should look like the following illustration.

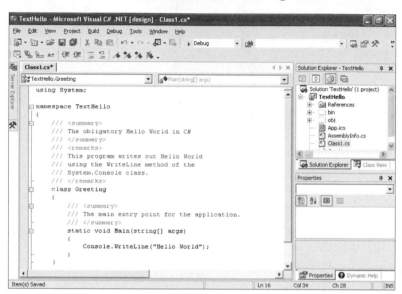

9   In the Solution Explorer, ensure that Class1.cs is selected on the Solution Explorer tab, and then click Properties. The Properties window appears.

10 In the Properties window, change the value of the *File Name* property from Class1.cs to Greeting.cs.

Notice the Code pane tab's name also changes from Class1.cs to Greeting.cs. If you view the TextHello folder using Windows Explorer, you can confirm that the name of the file has changed.

▶ **Tip**   Changing the name of a class does not change the name of the .cs file. It is common practice to name the .cs file after the class.

11 In the Properties window, click Close. The Properties window closes, and the Solution Explorer is displayed.

By default the Solution Explorer window and the Properties window are dockable. You can drag them around the development environment and resize them if you want to keep them both open at the same time.

12 On the Tools menu, click Build Comment Web Pages. The Build Comment Web Pages dialog box opens.

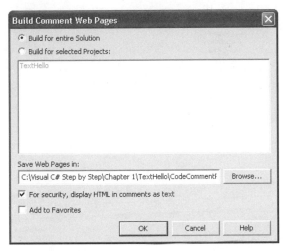

13 In the Build Comment Web Pages dialog box, click OK. Visual Studio .NET parses the source files, extracts the XML comments, creates a structured, hyperlinked set of HTML documents based on the XML, and displays the top-level HTML file in a pane in the Code And Text Editor windows. You can click the links in the Code pane to display the additional views available.

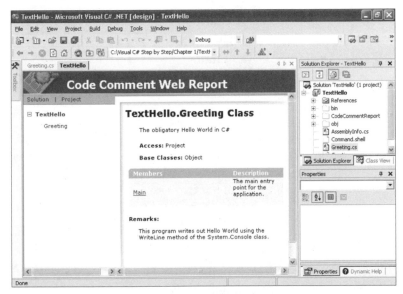

14 In the Solution Explorer, click Show All Files. A new entry named CodeCommentReport appears. This corresponds to a folder named CodeCommentReport that contains the HTML files created by the Build Comment Web Pages command.

15 In the Solution Explorer, click the + to the left of the CodeComment-Report entry. The CodeCommentReport entry expands to reveal a number of files and a TextHello subfolder.

16 In the Solution Explorer, click the + to the left of the TextHello entry below the CodeCommentReport entry. The TextHello entry expands to reveal a number of HTML files, including TextHello.htm, which is the top-level HTML file visible in the Code pane.

XML Tags

The following shows the most common XML tags and their intended purposes:

<summary>	Brief, one-line summary of a class, method, or property
<remarks>	Longer, more detailed information; can contain *<para>* and *<list>* formatting tags as well as *<cref>* for creating hyperlinks
<value>	Description of a property
<exception>	Exceptions arising from methods and properties
<param>	Method parameters

Creating a Windows Forms Application

The Visual Studio .NET programming environment also contains everything you'll need to create Windows applications. You will create the form-based user interface of your Windows application interactively by using the Visual Designer. Visual Studio .NET will generate the program statements to implement the user interface you've designed. This means there are two views of the application: the Design View and the Code View. The Code pane doubles as the Design View window, and you can switch between the two views whenever you want.

In the following set of exercises, you'll learn how to create a Windows program in Visual Studio .NET. This program will display a simple form containing a text box for entering your name and a button, which will display a personalized greeting in a message box. You will use the Visual Designer to create your user interface by placing controls on a form; inspect the code generated by Visual Studio .NET; use the Visual Designer to change the control properties; use the Visual Designer to resize the form; write the code to respond to a button click; and run your first Windows program.

Create a Windows project in Visual Studio .NET

1 On the File menu, point to New, and then click Project. The New Project dialog box opens.

2 In the Project Types pane, click the Visual C# Projects icon.

3 In the Templates pane, click the Windows Application icon.

4 In the Location field, type **C:\Visual C# Step by Step\Chapter 1**.

5 In the Name field, type **WinFormHello**.

6 Click OK. Visual Studio .NET creates and displays an empty Windows form in Design View.

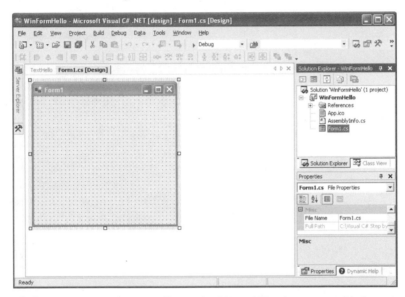

In the following exercise, you'll use the Visual Designer to add three controls to the Windows form and examine some of the C# code automatically generated by Visual Studio .NET to implement these controls.

Create the user interface

1 On the Visual Studio .NET toolbar, click Toolbox. The Toolbox appears to the left of the form.

2 In the Toolbox, click Label, and then click the top left of the form. A *Label* control is added to the form.

▶ **Tip** If the Toolbox obscures the form, click the Toolbox's Auto Hide button. This moves the form to the foreground.

3 In the Toolbox, click TextBox, and then click under the label on the form. A *TextBox* control is added to the form.

4   In the Toolbox, click Button, and then click to the right of the *Text-Box* control on the form. A *Button* control is added to the form. The form should now look similar to the one in the following illustration.

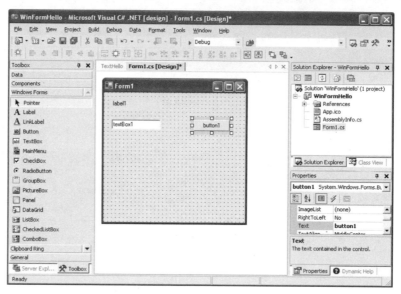

5   On the Visual Studio .NET toolbar, click Solution Explorer. The Solution Explorer window appears.

6   In the Solution Explorer, click View Code. The Form1.cs source file appears in the Code And Text Editor window.

There are now two tabs named Form1.cs in the Code/Design View window. You can click the one suffixed with [Design] to return to Design View at any time.

Form1.cs contains all the code automatically generated by Visual Studio .NET. Scroll through the contents of this Form1.cs and note the following elements:

■   *using* directives Visual Studio .NET has written a number of *using* directives at the top of the source file. For example:

```
using System.Windows.Forms;
```

■   A namespace Visual Studio .NET has used the name of the project as the name of the top-level namespace:

```
namespace WinFormHello
{
    ⋮
}
```

■   A class Visual Studio .NET has written a class called Form1 inside the WinFormHello namespace:

```
namespace WinFormHello
{
    public class Form1 ...
    {
        ⋮
    }
}
```

This class implements the form you created in the Design View. (Classes are discussed in Chapter 7.)

■ Three fields Visual Studio .NET has written three fields inside the Form1 class:

```
    ⋮
    public class Form1 ...
    {
        private System.Windows.Forms.Label label1;
        private System.Windows.Forms.TextBox textBox1;
        private System.Windows.Forms.Button button1;
        ⋮
    }
```

These fields implement the three controls you added to the form in Design View. (Fields are discussed in Chapter 7.)

■ A constructor Visual Studio .NET has written a constructor for the Form1 class:

```
    ⋮
    public class Form1 ...
    ⋮
    {
        ⋮
        public Form1()
        {
            ⋮
        }
        ⋮
    }
```

A *constructor* is a special method with the same name as the class. It is executed when the form is created and can contain code to initialize the form. (Constructors are discussed in Chapter 7.)

■ An InitializeComponent method Visual Studio .NET has written a method of the Form1 class called InitializeComponent. (This method is hidden in a collapsed region named Windows Form Designer Generated Code. Click the + to the left of this label to expand the region.)

```
    public class Form1 ...
⋮
```

```
    {
        ⋮
    private void InitializeComponent()
    {
        this.label1 = new System.Windows.Forms.Label();
        ⋮
        this.label1.Location = new System.Drawing.Point(32, 24);
        ⋮
    }
        ⋮
    }
```

The statements inside this method set the properties of the controls you added to the form in the Design View. (Methods are discussed in Chapter 3.)

▶ **Important**   Never modify the contents of the *InitializeComponent* method with the Code And Text Editor window. If you make changes to the properties of components in Design View or in the Properties window, your code modifications will be lost.

■   A *Main* method Visual Studio .NET has written a static method of the *Form1* class. It is called *Main*:

```
    ⋮
    public class Form1 ...
    {
        ⋮
    static void Main()
    {
        Application.Run(new Form1());
    }
    }
```

Main is the program entry point. It creates an instance of *Form1* and runs it.

In the following exercise, you'll learn how to change the properties of the three controls from Design View.

Change the control properties

1   On the Solution Explorer menu bar, click View Designer. Design View opens.

2   On the Standard menu bar, click Properties Window. The Solution Explorer closes and the Properties window opens.

3   Move the mouse pointer over the button on the form, and then select the button. As you move the mouse pointer over the button, the

mouse pointer changes to double-arrowed crosshairs. As you click, eight resize handles (small squares) appear equally spaced around the button, and the Properties window displays the selected button's properties.

4   In the Properties window, highlight the text in the *Text* property (the box to the right of the Text label).

5   Type **OK** and then press Enter. On the form, the button's text changes to OK.

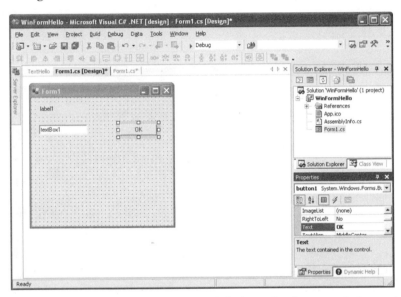

6   Move the mouse pointer over the label on the form, and then select the label.

7   The label is selected and the Properties window displays the selected label's properties.

8   In the Properties window, highlight the text in the *Text* property.

9   Type **Enter your name** and then press Enter. On the form, the label's text changes to Enter Your Name.

10 Move the mouse pointer over the text box on the form, and then select the text box. The text box is selected and the Properties window displays the selected text box's properties.

11 In the Properties window, highlight the text in the *Text* property.

12 Type **here** and then press Enter. On the form, the text box's text changes to Here.

13 In Design View, click the Form1.cs tab. The Form1.cs source file appears in the Code window.

14 Scroll through the statements of the *InitializeComponent* method. The property values entered in Design View appear to the right of three assignment statements:

```
private void InitializeComponent()
{
    ⋮
    this.button1.Text = "OK";
    ⋮
    this.textBox1.Text = "here";
    ⋮
    this.Label1.Text = "Enter your name";
    ⋮
}
```

In the following exercise, you'll learn how to resize the form.

Resize the form

1   Click the Form1.cs [Design] tab. The form appears in Design View.

2   Move the mouse pointer over the form, and then select the form. Eight resize handles (small squares) appear, spaced equally around the form. The Properties window displays the form's properties.

3   Move the mouse pointer over the resize handle in the lower-right corner. The mouse pointer changes to a diagonal double-headed arrow.

4   Hold down the left mouse button, and drag the mouse pointer to resize the form. Stop dragging and release the mouse button when the spacing around the controls is roughly equal.

> ▶ **Tip**   You can resize only by using a white resize handle. Gray resize handles are fixed.

In the following exercise, you'll learn how to add code that runs when the OK button is clicked.

Write the code for the OK button

1   Move the mouse pointer over the OK button on the form, and then double-click the button. The Form1.cs source file appears in the

Code window. Visual Studio .NET has added a method called *button1_Click* to the *Form1* class. It has also added a statement to the *InitializeComponent* method to automatically call *button1_Click* when the OK button is clicked. (It does this by using a *delegate* type; *delegates* are discussed in Chapter 16.)

2 Type the following *MessageBox* statement inside the *button1_Click* method:

```
private void button1_Click(object sender, System.EventArgs e)
{
    MessageBox.Show("Hello " + textBox1.Text);
}
```

Give this program code your closest attention. Make sure you type it exactly as shown, including the trailing semicolon. It is correct.

You're now ready to run your first Windows program.

Run the Windows program

1 On the Debug menu, click Start Without Debugging. Visual Studio .NET saves your work, builds your program, and runs it. The Windows form appears:

2 Enter your name, and then click OK. A message appears welcoming you by name.

3 Click OK. The message closes.

4 In the Form1 window, click Close. The Form1 window closes.

If you want to continue to the next chapter

■ Keep Visual Studio .NET running and turn to Chapter 2.

If you want to exit Visual Studio .NET now

■ On the File menu, click Exit. If you see a Save dialog box, click Yes.

Chapter 1 Quick Reference

To	Do this	Key combination
Create a new console application	On the File menu, point to New, and then click Project to open the New Project dialog box. For the project type, select the Visual C# Projects. For the template, select Console Application. Select a directory for the project files in the location box. Choose a name for the project. Click OK.	
Create a new Windows application	On the File menu, point to New, and then click Project to open the New Project dialog box. For the project type, select Visual C# Projects. For the template, select Windows Application. Select a directory for the project files in the location box. Choose a name for the project. Click OK.	
Build the application	On the Build menu, click Build.	Ctrl+Shift+B
Run the application	On the Debug menu, click Start Without Debugging.	Ctrl+F5
Create documentation using XML and comments	On the Tools menu, click Build Comment Web Pages to open the Build Comment Web Pages dialog box. Click OK.	

Working with Variables, Operators, and Expressions

> **In this chapter, you will learn how to:**
>
> ■ Use variables to store information.
>
> ■ Use arithmetic operators such as the plus sign (+) and the minus sign (–).
>
> ■ Combine two or more operators together.
>
> ■ Increment and decrement the value of a variable by one unit using the ++ and –– operators.

In Chapter 1, you learned how to use the Microsoft Visual Studio .NET programming environment to build and run a console program and a Windows Forms application. In this chapter, you'll be introduced to the elements of Microsoft Visual C# syntax and semantics, including statements, keywords, and identifiers. You'll study the primitive C# types (the types that are built into the C# language) and the characteristics of the values that each type holds. You'll also see how to declare and use local variables (variables that exist only within a function or other small section of code), learn about the arithmetic operators that C# provides, learn how to use operators to manipulate values, and learn how to control expressions containing two or more operators.

Understanding Statements

A *statement* is a command that performs an action. Statements are found inside methods. You'll learn more about methods in Chapter 3, but for now, think of a method as a named sequence of statements inside a class. *Main*, which was introduced in the previous chapter, is an example of a method. Statements in C# must follow a well-defined set of rules. These rules are collectively known as *syntax*. (In contrast, the specification of what statements *do* is collectively known as *semantics*.) One of the simplest and most important C# syntax rules is that you must terminate all statements with a semicolon. For example, without its terminating semicolon, the following statement won't compile:

```
Console.WriteLine("Hello World");
```

▶   **Tip**   C# is a "free format" language, which means that white space, such as a space character or a new line, is not significant except as a separator. In other words, you are free to lay out your statements in any style you choose. A simple, consistent layout style makes a program easier to read and understand.

The trick to programming well in any language is learning its syntax and semantics and then using the language in a natural and idiomatic way. This approach makes your programs readable and easy to modify. In the chapters throughout this book, you'll see examples of the most important C# statements.

Using Identifiers

Identifiers are the names you use to identify the elements in your programs. In C#, you must adhere to the following syntax rules when choosing identifiers:

- You can use only letters (uppercase and lowercase), digits, and underscore characters.
- An identifier must start with a letter (an underscore is considered a letter).

So, for example, *result*, *_score*, *fortyTwo*, and *plan9* are all valid identifiers, whereas *result%*, *fortyTwo$*, and *9plan* are not.

▶   **Important**   C# is a case-sensitive language: *fortyTwo* and *FortyTwo* are not the same identifier.

Identifying Keywords

The C# language reserves 76 identifiers for its own use. These identifiers are called *keywords*, and each has a particular meaning. Examples of keywords are *class*, *namespace*, and *using*. You'll learn the meaning of most of the keywords as you proceed through this book. The keywords are listed in the following table.

abstract	*as*	*base*	*Bool*
break	*byte*	*case*	*Catch*
char	*checked*	*class*	*Const*
continue	*decimal*	*default*	*Delegate*
do	*double*	*else*	*Enum*
event	*explicit*	*extern*	*false*
finally	*fixed*	*float*	*for*
foreach	*goto*	*if*	*implicit*
in	*int*	*interface*	*internal*
is	*lock*	*long*	*namespace*
new	*null*	*object*	*operator*
out	*override*	*params*	*private*
protected	*public*	*readonly*	*ref*
return	*sbyte*	*sealed*	*short*
sizeof	*stackalloc*	*static*	*string*
struct	*switch*	*this*	*throw*
true	*try*	*typeof*	*uint*
ulong	*unchecked*	*unsafe*	*ushort*
using	*virtual*	*void*	*while*

▶ **Note**   In the Visual Studio .NET Code pane, keywords are blue by default.

Using Variables

A *variable* is a storage location that holds a value. You can think of a variable as a box holding temporary information. You must give each variable in a program a unique name. You use a variable's name to refer to the value it holds.

Naming Variables

The Microsoft .NET Framework documentation makes several recommendations about variable naming:

■ Don't use underscores.

■ Don't create identifiers that differ only by case. For example, do not create one variable named *myVariable* and another named *MyVariable* for use at the same time.

■ Start the name with a lowercase letter.

- In a multiword identifier, start the second and each subsequent word with an uppercase letter. (This is called *camelCase* notation.)
- Don't use Hungarian notation. (Microsoft Visual C++ developers reading this book are probably familiar with Hungarian notation. If you don't know what Hungarian notation is, don't worry about it!)

▶ **Important**   You should treat the first two recommendations as compulsory because they relate to Common Language Specification (CLS) compliance. If you want to write programs that can interoperate with other languages, such as Microsoft Visual Basic .NET, you need to comply with these recommendations.

So, for example, *score*, *fortyTwo*, *_score*, and *FortyTwo* are all valid variable names, but only the first two are recommended.

Declaring Variables

Remember that variables are like boxes in memory that can hold a value. C# has many different types of values that it can process—integers, floating-point numbers, and strings of characters, to name three. When you declare a variable, you must specify what type of data it will hold.

You declare the type and name of a variable in a declaration statement. For example, the following statement declares that the variable named *age* holds *int* (integer) values. The semicolon is included, of course.

```
int age;
```

▶ **Important**   Microsoft Visual Basic programmers should note that C# does not allow implicit declarations. You must explicitly declare all variables before you can use them if you want your code to compile.

The variable type *int* is an example of a keyword. It is the name of one of the primitive C# types—integer. (An *integer* is a whole number. You'll learn about several primitive data types later in this chapter.) After you've declared your variable, you can assign it a value. The following statement assigns *age* the value 42. Again, you'll see that the semicolon is required.

```
age = 42;
```

The equal sign (=) is the *assignment* operator, which assigns the value at its right to the variable at its left. After this assignment, the *age* variable can be used in your code to refer to the value it holds. The next statement writes the value of the *age* variable, 42, to the console:

```
Console.WriteLine(age);
```

▶ **Tip**   If you leave the mouse pointer over a variable in the Visual Studio .NET
Code pane, a ToolTip appears telling you the type of the variable.

Working with Primitive Data Types

C# has a number of built-in types called *primitive data types*. The next table
lists the most commonly used primitive data types in C#. The *int* and *long* types
hold whole numbers (*long* can hold bigger numbers than *int* but requires more
memory); the *float* and *double* types hold numbers containing decimal points
(*double* holds the values to twice the precision of *float*, hence its name); the *decimal* type is designed for holding monetary values to 28 significant figures; the
char type holds individual characters (in Unicode representation); the *string*
type holds sequences of characters; and the *bool* type holds either *true* or *false*.

Unassigned Local Variables

When you declare a variable, it contains a random value until you assign a value
to it. This behavior was a rich source of bugs in C and C++ programs that created a variable and used it as a source of information before giving it a value.
C# does not allow you to use an unassigned variable. You must assign a value
to a variable before you can use it, otherwise your program will not compile. This
requirement is called the *Definite Assignment Rule*. For example, the following
statement will generate a compile-time error because *age* is unassigned:

```
int age;
Console.WriteLine(age); // compile time error
```

Data type	Description	Size (bits)	Range[*]	Sample usage
Int	Whole numbers	32	-2^{31} through 2^{31}-1	int count; count = 42;
Long	Whole numbers (bigger range)	64	-2^{63} through 2^{63}-1	long wait; wait = 42L;
float	Floating-point numbers	32	$\pm3.4 \times 1038$	float away; away = 0.42F;
double	Double precision (more accurate) floating-point numbers	64	$\pm1.7 \times 10308$	double trouble; trouble = 0.42;
decimal	Monetary values	128	28 significant figures	decimal coin; coin = 0.42M;
string	Sequence of characters	16 bits per character	Not applicable	string vest; vest = "42";

Data type	Description	Size (bits)	Range*	Sample usage
char	Single character	16	0 through 2^{16}-1	`char grill;` `grill = '4';`
bool	Boolean (*true* or *false*)	8	*true* or *false*	`bool teeth;` `teeth = false;`

*   The value of 2^{16} is 32,768; the value of 2^{31} is 2,147,483,648; and the value of 2^{63} is 9,223,372,036,854,775,808.

Displaying Primitive Data Type Values

In the following exercise, we'll use a C# program named PrimitiveDataTypes to demonstrate how several primitive data types work.

Display primitive data type values

1   Start Visual Studio .NET.

2   On the File menu, point to Open, and then click Project. The Open Project dialog box opens.

3   Open the PrimitiveDataTypes project, located in the \Microsoft Press\Visual C# Step by Step\Chapter 2\PrimitiveDataTypes folder in your My Documents folder.

4   On the Debug menu, click Start. The following application window appears.

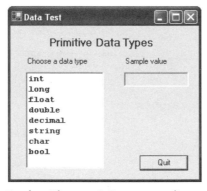

5   In the Choose A Data type list, select the *string* type. The value 42 appears in the Sample Value box.

6   Select the *int* type in the list. The value *to do* appears in the Sample Value box, indicating that the statements to display an *int* value still need to be written.

7 Select each data type in the list. Confirm that the code for the *double* and *bool* types also needs completing.

8 Click Quit to stop the program. Control returns to the Visual Studio .NET programming environment.

Use primitive data types in code

1 Click the Form1.cs tab in the Code pane. (Right-click the form and choose View Code if the Form1.cs tab isn't visible. If the form isn't visible, right-click on Form1.cs in the Solution Explorer and choose View Code.) The Code pane opens.

2 In the Code pane, find the *showFloatValue* method listed here:

```
private void showFloatValue()
{
    float var;
    var = 0.42F;
    value.Text = "0.42F";
}
```

▶ **Tip** To locate an item in your project, point to Find And Replace on the Edit menu and click Find Symbol. A dialog box opens asking what you want to search for. Type in the name of the item you're looking for, and then click Find. If you are not sure whether the item includes capital letters, clear the Match Case check box. You can experiment with the other options as well. If you want to know more about the options, click Help in the dialog box.

Visual Studio .NET lists any occurrence of the item in the Find Symbol Results pane. Double-click an item in the Find Symbol Results pane to jump to the corresponding location in the Code pane.

The *showFloatValue* method runs when you click the *float* type in the list box. This method contains three statements. The first statement declares a variable named *var* of type *float*. The second statement assigns *var* the value 0.42F. (The F is a type suffix specifying that 0.42 should be treated as a *float* value. If you forget the F, the value 0.42 will be treated as a *double* and your program will not compile because you cannot assign a value of one type to a variable of a different type in this way.) The third statement assigns to the *value.Text* property the string "*0.42F*". (You'll learn more about properties later, but for now, you can think of them as being like variables.) The *value* variable refers to the text box on the screen. This variable is declared elsewhere in the program.

3   In the Code pane, locate the *showIntValue* method listed here:

```
private void showIntValue()
{
    value.Text = "to do";
}
```

The *showIntValue* method is called when you click the *int* type in the list box. This method contains one statement.

4   Type the following two statements at the start of the *showIntValue* method:

```
int var;
var = 42;
```

The *showIntValue* method should now look like this:

```
private void showIntValue()
{
    int var;
    var = 42;
    value.Text = "to do";
}
```

5   On the Build menu, click Build. The build is successful.

6   In the original statement, change the string "*to do*" to "*42*". The method should now look exactly like this:

```
private void showIntValue()
{
    int var;
    var = 42;
    value.Text = "42";
}
```

7   On the Debug menu, click Start. The application window appears.

▶ **Note**   If you have edited the source code since the last build, the Start command automatically rebuilds the program before starting the application.

8   Select the *int* type in the list box. Confirm that the value 42 is displayed in the Sample Value box.

9   Click Quit to stop the program.

10   In the Code pane, find the *showDoubleValue* method.

11   Edit the *showDoubleValue* method exactly as follows:

```
private void showDoubleValue()
{
    double var;
    var = 0.42;
    value.Text = "0.42";
}
```

12 In the Code pane, locate the *showBoolValue* method.

13 Edit the *showBoolValue* method exactly as follows:

```
private void showBoolValue()
{
    bool var;
    var = false;
    value.Text = "false";
}
```

14 On the Debug menu, click Start. The application window appears.

15 In the list, select the *int*, *double*, and *bool* types. In each case, verify that the correct value is displayed in the Sample Value box.

16 Click Quit to stop the program.

Setting Arithmetic Operators

C# supports the regular arithmetic symbols you learned in your childhood: the plus sign (+) for addition, the minus sign (–) for subtraction, the asterisk (*) for multiplication, and the forward slash (/) for division. These symbols are called *operators*: they "operate" on values to create new values. In the following example, the variable *moneyPaidToConsultant* ends up holding the product of 500 (the daily rate) and 20 (the number of days):

```
long moneyPaidToConsultant;
moneyPaidToConsultant = 500 * 20;
```

> ▶ **Note** The values that an operator operates on are called *operands*. In the expression 500 * 20, the * is the operator and 500 and 20 are the operands.

Determining an Operator's Values

Whether you can use an operator on a value depends on the value's type. For example, you can use all the arithmetic operators on values of type *char*, *int*, *long*, *float*, *double*, and *decimal*. However, with one exception, you can't use the arithmetic operators on values of type *string* or *bool*. For example, the following statement is not allowed because the *string* type does not support the minus operator. Subtracting two strings would be meaningless.

```
// compile time error
Console.WriteLine("Gillingham" - "Manchester City");
```

The exception is that the + operator can be used to concatenate string values. The following statement writes 431 (not 44) to the console:

```
Console.WriteLine("43" + "1");
```

▶ **Tip**   You can use the method *Int32.Parse* to convert a string value to an integer if you need to perform arithmetic computations on values held as strings.

C# also supports one less familiar arithmetic operator: the remainder, or modulus, operator, which uses the percent symbol (%). The result of *x* % *y* is the remainder after dividing *x* by *y*. (In C and C++, you can't use the % operator on floating-point values, but you can use it in C#.)

Examining Arithmetic Operators

The following exercise demonstrates how to use the arithmetic operators on *int* values using a previously written C# program named MathsOperators.

Work with arithmetic operators

1   On the File menu, point to Open, and then click Project. The Open Project dialog box opens.

2   Open the MathsOperators project, located in the \Microsoft Press\Visual C# Step by Step\Chapter 2\MathsOperators folder in your My Documents folder.

3   On the Debug menu, click Start. The form for the application appears on the screen.

4   Type **54** in the Left Operand text box.

5   Type **13** in the Right Operand text box. You can now apply any of the operators to the values in the text boxes.

6   Select the –Subtraction option, and then click Calculate. The text in the Expression box changes to 54 –13, and 41 appears in the Result box, as shown in the following illustration.

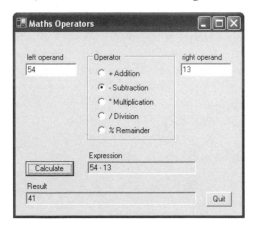

7   Select the / Division option, and then click Calculate. The text in the
Expression text box changes to 54 / 13, and the number 4 appears in
the Result box. In real life, 54 / 13 is 4.153846 recurring, but this is
not real life; this is C#! In C#, when you divide one integer by
another integer, the answer you get back is an integer.

8   Select the % Remainder option, and then click Calculate. The text in
the Expression text box changes to 54 % 13, and the number 2
appears in the Result box. This is because 54 − ((54 / 13) * 13) is 2.

9   Practice as much as you like. When you're finished, click Quit. The
program stops, and you return to the programming environment.

Now take a look at the MathsOperators program code.

Examine the MathsOperators program code

1   Click the Form1.cs tab in the Code pane. (Right-click the form and
choose View Code if the Form1.cs tab isn't visible. If the form isn't
visible, right-click on Form1.cs in the Solution Explorer and choose
View Code.) The Form1.cs source file appears in the Code pane.

2   In the Code pane, find the following two statements near the top:

```
private System.Windows.Forms.TextBox lhsOperand;
private System.Windows.Forms.TextBox rhsOperand;
```

These statements declare two variables, named *lhsOperand* and
rhsOperand, of type *TextBox*. The *Text* property of each of these
controls holds (as strings) the numeric values you enter. *TextBox* is a
nonprimitive type (it is not built in to C#), but it is a type defined in
one of the code libraries supplied by Microsoft. The *TextBox* type is
used in Windows applications for displaying a text box on a form.

▶ **Note**   The *lhsOperand* and *rhsOperand* variables are not declared in any particular method but rather in a class. Being declared in a class means that they
can be used by all the methods in the class. Variables that are declared as part
of a class rather than in a method are called *fields*.

3   In the Code pane, locate the following two statements, also near the
top:

```
private System.Windows.Forms.TextBox result;
...
private System.Windows.Forms.TextBox expression;
```

▶ **Note**   These fields were actually created by Visual Studio .NET, and their order
and position are determined by the development environment rather than by the
programmer.

The first statement declares a field named *result* of type *TextBox*. The *result.Text* property holds the value of the *result* control on the form. The second statement declares a field named *expression* of type *TextBox*. The *expression.Text* property holds the value of the *expression* control on the form.

4   In the Code pane, locate the *subtractValues* method:

```
private void subtractValues()
{
    int lhs = int.Parse(lhsOperand.Text);
    int rhs = int.Parse(rhsOperand.Text);
    int outcome;
    outcome = lhs - rhs;
    expression.Text = lhsOperand.Text + " - " +
        rhsOperand.Text;
    result.Text = outcome.ToString();
}
```

The first statement in this method declares an *int* variable called *lhs* and initializes it to the result of the explicit conversion of the *lhsOperand.Text* property to an *int*. The second statement declares an *int* variable called *rhs* and initializes it to the result of the explicit conversion of the *rhsOperand.Text* property to an *int*. The third statement declares an *int* variable called *outcome*. The fourth statement subtracts the value of the *rhs* variable from the value of the *lhs* variable, and the result is assigned to *outcome*. The fifth statement concatenates three strings and assigns the result to the *expression.Text* property. The sixth statement converts the *int* value of *outcome* to a *string*, using the *ToString* method, and assigns the string to the *result.Text* property.

The *Text* Property and the *ToString* Method

Text fields that are displayed on a form have a *Text* property that allows you to access the contents of the field. For example, the expression *result.Text* refers to the contents of the *result* field on the form. Text fields have many other properties as well, such as the location and size of the text field on the form. You will learn more about properties in Chapter 14.

Every class has a *ToString* method. The purpose of *ToString* is to convert an object into its string representation. In the previous example, the *ToString* method of the integer object, *outcome*, is used to convert the integer value of *outcome* into the equivalent string value. This conversion is necessary because the value is displayed in the *Text* property of the *result* field—the *Text* property can only contain strings. When you create your own classes, you can also define your own implementation of the *ToString* method. Methods are discussed in Chapter 3.

Controlling Precedence

Precedence is the order in which an expression's operators are evaluated. Consider the following expression that uses the + and * operators:

```
2 + 3 * 4
```

This expression is potentially ambiguous; does 3 bind to the + operator to its left or to the * operator to its right? The order of the operations matters because it changes the result.

- If the + operator takes precedence over the * operator, 3 binds to the + operator, the result of the addition (2 + 3) forms the left operand of the * operator, and the result of the whole expression is 5 * 4, which makes 20.

- If the * operator takes precedence over the + operator, 3 binds to the * operator, the result of the multiplication (3 * 4) forms the right operand of the + operator, and the result of the whole expression is 2 + 12, which makes 14.

In C#, the multiplicative operators (*, /, %) have precedence over the additive operators (+, –). The answer to 2 + 3 * 4 is therefore 14. As each new operator is discussed in later chapters, its precedence will be explained.

You can use parentheses to override precedence and force operands to bind to operators of your choice. For example, in the following expression, the parentheses force the 2 and the 3 to bind to the + operator (making 5), and the result of this addition forms the left operand of the * operator to produce the value 20:

```
(2 + 3) * 4
```

▶ **Note** The term "parentheses" or "round brackets" refers to ( ); "braces" or "curly brackets" refers to { }; and "square brackets" refers to [ ].

Using Associativity to Evaluate Expressions

Associativity is the direction (left or right) to which an expression's operators are bound. Consider the following expression that uses the / and the * operators:

```
2 / 3 * 4
```

This expression is still ambiguous. Does 3 bind to the / operator to its left or to the * operator to its right? The precedence of both operators is the same, but the order in which the expression is evaluated is important because you will get one of two possible results.

■ If the 3 binds to the / operator, the result of the division (2 / 3) forms the left hand operand of the * operator and the result of the whole expression is (2/3) * 4, or 8/3.

■ If the 3 binds to the * operator, the result of the multiplication (3 * 4) forms the right hand operand of the / operator and the result of the whole expression is 2/12.

It just so happens that the * and / operators have the same precedence, so you cannot use precedence to determine whether the 3 binds to the * operator or to the / operator. However, operators also have associativity to determine how they are evaluated. The * and / operators are both left-associative, which means the operands are evaluated from left to right. In this case, 2 / 3 will be evaluated before multiplying by 4, giving the result 8/3. As each new operator is discussed in later chapters, its associativity will also be covered.

▶ **Note**   Strictly speaking, the value returned by the expression 2 / 3 * 4 is 0 rather than 8/3. This result is due to the way in which the expression is evaluated using integer arithmetic; 2 / 3 evaluates to 0, and 0 * 4 is 0.

Incrementing and Decrementing Variables

If you want to add 1 to a variable, you could use the + operator:

```
count = count + 1;
```

However, it is unlikely that you will see an experienced programmer write this code. Adding 1 to a variable is so common that C# lets you do it with the ++ operator. To increment the variable *count* by 1, write the following statement:

```
count++;
```

Similarly, subtracting 1 from a variable is so common that C# lets you do it with the – – operator. To decrement the variable *count* by one, write this:

```
count--;
```

▶ **Note**   The ++ and − − operators are *unary* operators (they take only a single operand) and share the same precedence and left associativity as the ! unary operator, which is discussed in Chapter 4.

The following table shows you how to use these operators.

Don't write this	Write this
variable = variable + 1;	variable++;
variable = variable - 1;	variable--;

Prefix and Postfix

The increment (++) and decrement (− −) operators are unique in that you can place them either before or after the variable. Using the operator symbol before the variable is called the prefix form of the operator, and using the operator symbol after the variable is called the postfix form. Here is an example:

```
count++; // postfix increment
++count; // prefix increment
count--; // postfix decrement
--count; // prefix decrement
```

Whether you use the prefix or postfix form of the ++ or − − operator makes no difference to the variable being incremented or decremented. For example, if you write *count*++, the value of count increases by 1, and if you write ++*count*, the value of count also increases by 1. Knowing this, you're probably wondering why there are two ways to write the same thing. To understand the answer, you must remember that ++ (and − −) are operators and that all operators produce a value. The value produced by *count*++ is the value of count before the increment takes place, whereas the value produced by ++*count* is the value of count after the increment takes place. Here is an example:

```
int x;
x = 42;
Console.WriteLine(x++); // x is now 43, 42 written out
x = 42;
Console.WriteLine(++x); // x is now 43, 43 written out
```

This behavior is most commonly used in *while* and *do* statements, which will be presented in Chapter 5. If you are using the increment and decrement operators in isolation, stick to the postfix form and be consistent.

If you want to continue to the next chapter

■   Keep Visual Studio .NET running, and turn to Chapter 3.

If you want to exit Visual Studio .NET now

■   On the File menu, click Exit. If you see a Save dialog box, click Yes.

Chapter 2 Quick Reference

To	Do this
Declare a variable	Write the name of the type, followed by the name of the variable, followed by a semicolon. For example: `int outcome;`
Change the value of a variable	Write the name of the variable on the left, followed by the assignment operator, followed by the expression calculating the new value, followed by a semicolon. For example: `outcome = 42;`
Convert a *string* to an *int*	Call the *System.Int32.Parse* method. For example: `System.Int32.Parse("42")`
Override precedence	Use parentheses in the expression to force operands to bind to specific operators. For example: `(3 + 4) * 5`
Increment or decrement a variable	Use the ++ and -- operators. For example: `count++;`

2 Variables, Operators, Expressions

Writing Methods and Applying Scope

In this chapter, you will learn how to:

- Create and call methods.

- Pass information to a method.

- Return information from a method.

- Use the Microsoft Visual Studio .NET integrated debugger to step in and out of methods as they run.

In Chapter 2, you learned how to declare variables, how to create expressions using operators, and how precedence and associativity control expressions containing multiple operators. In this chapter, you'll learn all about methods. You'll also learn how to use arguments and parameters to pass information to a method and how to return information from a method using return statements. Finally, you'll see how to step in and out of methods using the Microsoft Visual Studio .NET integrated debugger. This information is useful when you need to trace the execution of your methods because they do not work quite as you expected.

Declaring Methods

A *method* is a named sequence of statements. Each method has a name and a body. The method body contains the actual statements to be run when the method is called. The method name should be a meaningful identifier that indicates the overall purpose of the method (*CalculateIncomeTax*, for example).

Most methods can be given some data, which they process, and can return information, which is usually the result of the processing. Methods are a fundamental and powerful mechanism.

Specifying the Method Declaration Syntax

The syntax of a Microsoft Visual C# method is as follows:

```
returnType  methodName ( parameterList )
{
    // method body statements go here
}
```

- The *returnType* is the name of a type and specifies what kind of information the method returns. This can be the name of any type, such as *int* or *string*. If you're writing a method that does not return a value, you must use the keyword *void* in place of the return type.

- The *methodName* is the name used to call the method. Method names must follow the same identifier rules as variable names. For example, *addValues* is a valid method name, whereas *add$Values* is not valid. For now, you should use camelCase for method names, and you should make method names descriptive—start with a verb, such as *displayCustomer*.

- The *parameterList* is optional and describes the types and names of the information that the method accepts. You write the parameters between the left and right parentheses as though you're declaring variables: name of the type, followed by the name of the parameter. If the method you're writing has two or more parameters, you must separate them with commas.

- The method body statements are the lines of code that are run when the method is called. They are enclosed in an opening curly brace ({) and a closing curly brace (}).

▶ **Important** C, C++, and Microsoft Visual Basic programmers should note that C# does not support global methods. You must write all your methods inside a class or your code will not compile.

Here's the definition of a method called *addValues* that returns an *int* and has two *int* parameters called *lhs* and *rhs* (short for left-hand side and right-hand side, respectively):

```
int addValues(int lhs, int rhs)
{
    // ...
    // method body statements go here
    // ...
}
```

Here's the definition of a method called *showResult* that does not return a value and has a single *int* parameter called *answer*:

```
void showResult(int answer)
{
    // ...
}
```

Notice that you use the keyword *void* to indicate that the method does not return anything.

▶ **Important** Visual Basic programmers should notice that C# does not use different keywords to distinguish between a method that returns a value (a function) and a method that does not return a value (a procedure or subroutine). You must always specify either a return type or *void*.

Writing *return* Statements

If you want your method to return information (in other words, its return type is not *void*), you must write a *return* statement inside the method. You do this using the keyword *return* followed by an expression that calculates the returned value and a semicolon. The type of expression must be the same as the type specified by the function. In other words, if a function returns an *int*, the *return* statement must return an *int*; otherwise your program will not compile. Here is an example:

```
int addValues(int lhs, int rhs)
{
    // ...
    return lhs + rhs;
}
```

The *return* statement should be at the end of your method because it causes the method to finish. Any statements after the *return* statement will not be executed (though the compiler will warn you about this problem if you put statements after the *return* statement).

If you don't want your method to return information (its return type is *void*), you can use a variation of the *return* statement to cause an immediate exit from the method. You write the keyword *return*, immediately followed by a semicolon. For example:

```
void showResult(int answer)
{
    ⋮
    if (...)
        return;
    ⋮
}
```

3

Methods and Scope

If your method does not return anything, you can also omit the *return* statement because the method will finish automatically when execution arrives at the closing curly brace at the end of the method. Although this practice is common, it is not always considered good style. Methods that return a value must contain a *return* statement.

In the following exercise, you will examine another version of the MathsOperators application from Chapter 2. This version has been improved by the careful use of some small methods.

▶ **Tip**   There is no minimum size for a method. If a method helps to avoid repetition and makes your program easier to understand, the method is useful regardless of how small it is.

Examine method definitions

1   Start Visual Studio .NET.

2   On the File menu, point to Open, and then click Project. The Open Project dialog box opens.

3   In the \Microsoft Press\Visual C# Step by Step\Chapter 3\Methods folder in your My Documents folder, open the Methods project. The Methods project opens in the programming environment.

4   On the Debug menu, click Start. Visual Studio .NET builds and runs the application.

5   Practice using the application for a while, and then click Quit. You return to the Visual Studio .NET programming environment.

6   In the Code pane, click the Form1.cs tab. (Right-click on the form and choose View Code if the Form1.cs tab isn't visible. If the form isn't visible, right-click Form1.cs in the Solution Explorer and choose View Code.) The Code View of Form1.cs opens in the Code pane.

7   In the Code pane, locate the *addValues* method. Your Code pane now looks like this:

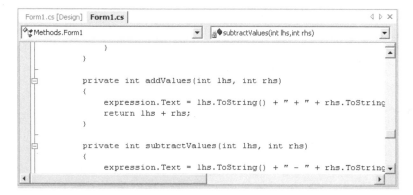

The *addValues* method contains two statements. The first statement assigns to the *expression.Text* property the string created by concatenating three strings. The second statement adds the values of the *lhs* and *rhs int* variables together using the + operator and returns the result of this addition. Notice that adding two *int* values together creates another *int* value and that the return type of *addValues* is *int*.

8   In the Code pane, locate the *showResult* method.

The *showResult* method contains one statement that assigns to the *result.Text* property a string representation of the *answer* parameter.

Calling Methods

Methods exist to be called! You call a method by name to ask it to perform its task. If the method requires information (as specified by its parameters), you must supply the information as requested. If the method returns information (as specified by its return type), you should arrange to catch this information somehow.

Specifying the Method Call Syntax

The syntax of a C# method call is as follows:

```
methodName ( argumentList )
```

- The *methodName* must exactly match the name of the method you're calling. Remember, C# is a case-sensitive language.

- The *argumentList* supplies the optional information that the method accepts. You must supply an argument for each parameter, and the value of each argument must be compatible with the type of its corresponding parameter. If the method you're calling has two or more parameters, you must separate the arguments with commas.

▶ **Important**   You must write the parentheses in every method call, even when calling a method with no arguments.

Here is the *addValues* method:

```
int addValues(int lhs, int rhs)
{
    // ...
}
```

The *addValues* method has two *int* parameters, so you must call it with two comma-separated *int* arguments:

```
addValues(39, 3)      // okay
```

If you try to call *addValues* in some other way, you will probably not succeed:

```
addValues           // compile time error, no parentheses
addValues()         // compile time error, not enough arguments
addValues(39)       // compile time error, not enough arguments
addValues("39", "3") // compile time error, wrong types
```

The *addValues* method returns an *int* value. This *int* value can be used wherever an *int* value can be used. Consider this example:

```
result = addValues(39, 3);     // on right hand side of an assignment
showResult(addValues(39, 3)); // as argument to another method call
```

The following exercise continues using the MathsOperators application that was introduced in Chapter 2. This time you will examine some method calls.

Examine method calls

1   In the \Microsoft Press\Visual C# Step by Step\Chapter 3\Methods folder in your My Documents folder, open the Methods project. (This project is already open in Visual Studio .NET if you're continuing from the previous exercise.)

2   In the Solution Explorer, right-click the Form1.cs entry, and then click View Code.

3   Locate the *calculate_Click* method. Look at the fourth statement of this method. It is as follows:

```
showResult(addValues(lhs, rhs));
```

4   In the Code pane, find the *showResult* method. The only statement of this method is this:

```
result.Text = answer.ToString();
```

Notice that the *ToString* method call uses parentheses even though there are no arguments.

▶   **Tip**   You can call methods belonging to other objects by prefixing the method with the name of the object. In the previous example, the expression *answer.ToString()* calls the method named *ToString* belonging to the object called *answer*.

Understanding Scope

You have seen that you can create a variable inside a method. The variable is created at the statement that defines it, and other statements in the *same method* that come afterwards can use the variable. In other words, a variable can be used only in certain places after it has been created. Once the method has finished, the variable disappears completely.

If an identifier can be used at a particular location in a program, the identifier is said to be *in scope* at that location. To put it another way, the scope of an identifier is simply the region of the program in which that identifier is usable. Scope applies to methods as well as variables. The scope of an identifier is linked to the location of the declaration that introduces the identifier into the program, as you'll now learn.

Creating Local Scope with a Method

The left and right curly braces that form the body of a method create a scope. Any variables you declare inside the body of a method are scoped to that method. These variables are called *local variables* because they are local to the method in which they are declared; they are not in scope in any other method. This arrangement means that you cannot use local variables to share information between methods. Consider this example:

```
class Example
{
    void method()
    {
        int variable;
        ⋮
    }
    void anotherMethod()
    {
        variable = 42; // compile time error
        ⋮
    }
}
```

Creating Class Scope with a Class

The left and right curly braces that form the body of a class also create a scope. Any "variables" you declare inside the body of a class (but not inside a method) are scoped to that class. As we saw in Chapter 2, the proper C# name for these variables is *fields*. In contrast to local variables, you can use fields to share information between methods. Here is an example:

```
class Example
{
    void method()
    {
        field = 42; // ok
        ⋮
    }
    void anotherMethod()
```

```
    {
        field = 42; // ok
        ⋮
    }
    int field;
}
```

▶ **Note** In a method, you must declare a variable before you can use it. Fields
are a little different. A method can use a field before the field is defined—the
compiler sorts out the details for you!

Overloading Identifiers

If two identifiers have the same name and are declared in the same scope, you
say that they are *overloaded*, that they overload each other. Most of the time an
overloaded identifier is a bug that gets trapped as a compile-time error. For
example, if you declare two local variables with the same name in the same
method, you'll get a compile-time error. Similarly, if you declare two fields with
the same name in the same class or two identical methods in the same class,
you'll also get a compile-time error. This fact must seem hardly worth mention-
ing given that everything so far has turned out to be a compile-time error. Well,
there is a way that you can overload an identifier, and that way is both useful
and important.

You are allowed to overload a method, but only when the two methods have
different parameters; that is, they have the same name but a different number
of parameters, or the types of the parameters differ. This capability is allowed
so that, when you call a method, you supply comma-separated arguments and
the number and type of the arguments is used to select one of the overloaded
methods.

The *WriteLine* method of the *Console* class is a good example of overloading. If
you want to write a *string* to the console, you pass a *string* argument to *Write-
Line*, and *WriteLine(string s)* is automatically called. If you want to write an
int to the console, you pass an *int* argument to *WriteLine* and *WriteLine(int i)* is
automatically called. Once again, the compiler sorts out the details for you.

At compile time, the compiler looks at the types of the arguments you are passing in and then calls the version of the named method that has a matching set of
parameters. Here is an example:

```
static void Main()
{
    Console.WriteLine("The answer is ");
    Console.WriteLine(42);
}
```

Whereas you can overload the parameters of a method, you can't overload the return type of a method. In other words, you can't declare two methods with the same name that differ only in their return type. (The compiler is clever, but not that clever.)

▶ **Tip** C++ and Visual Basic programmers should notice that C# does not support default arguments. However, you can mimic default arguments using overloaded methods.

Writing and Calling Methods

In the following exercises, you'll use the C# Method Wizard to help you write some methods that calculate how much a consultant would charge for a given number of consultancy days at a fixed daily rate. Next, you'll run these methods in a console application to get a feel for the program. Finally, you'll use the Visual Studio .NET debugger to step in and out of the method calls as they run.

Write a method using the C# Method Wizard

1 On the File menu, point to Open, and then click Project. The Open Project dialog box opens.

2 In the \Microsoft Press\Visual C# Step by Step\Chapter 3\DailyRate folder in your My Documents folder, open the DailyRate project. The DailyRate project opens.

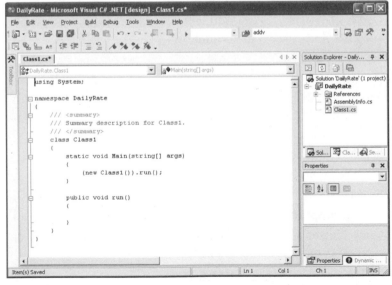

3 On the View menu, click Class View. The Class View window appears.

4 In the Class View window, click the + sign to the left of DailyRate. The *DailyRate* namespace appears.

5 In the Class View window, click the + sign to the left of { } DailyRate. The *Class1* class appears.

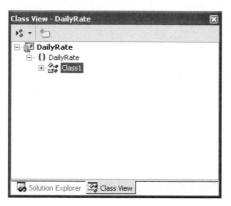

6 In the Class View window, right-click Class1. A menu appears.

7 On the menu, point to Add, and then click Add Method. The C# Method Wizard opens.

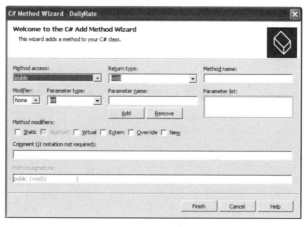

8 Select *double* from the Return Type list.

9 Type **readDouble** in the Method Name box.

10 Select *string* from the Parameter Type list.

11 Type **prompt** in the Parameter Name box, and then click Add.

12 Click Finish. The C# Method Wizard closes and the following method declaration appears in the Code pane:

```
public double readDouble(string prompt)
{
    return 0;
}
```

13 Delete the return statement and enter the following statements inside the *readDouble* method:

```
Console.Write(prompt);
string line = Console.ReadLine();
return double.Parse(line);
```

14 On the Build menu, click Build Solution.

15 Verify that the *readDouble* method you have created compiles without error.

Write the remaining methods

1 Use the C# Method Wizard to create another method using the following settings:

Control name	Setting
Return type	*int*
Method name	*readInt*
Parameter type	*string*
Parameter name	*prompt*

2 Click Finish. The C# Method Wizard closes and the following method declaration appears in the Code pane:

```
public int readInt(string prompt)
{
    return 0;
}
```

3 Delete the return statement. Type the following statements inside the *readInt* method:

```
Console.Write(prompt);
string line = Console.ReadLine();
return int.Parse(line);
```

4 On the Build menu, click Build Solution.

5 As before, verify that the *readInt* method you have declared compiles without error.

6 Use the C# Method Wizard to create another method using the following settings. (You will need to click Add after creating each parameter.)

Control name	Setting
Return type	*double*
Method name	*calculateFee*
Parameter type	*double*
Parameter name	*dailyRate*
Parameter type	*int*
Parameter name	*noOfDays*

7   Click Finish. The C# Method Wizard closes and the following method declaration appears in the Code pane:

```
public double calculateFee(double dailyRate, int noOfDays)
{
    return 0;
}
```

8   Change the return statement to calculate the fee, as shown here:

```
return dailyRate * noOfDays;
```

9   On the Build menu, click Build Solution.

10   Verify that the *calculateFee* method you have declared compiles without error.

11   Use the C# Method Wizard to create another method using the following settings:

Control name	Setting
Return type	*void*
Method name	*writeFee*
Parameter type	*double*
Parameter name	*fee*

12   Click Finish. The C# Method Wizard closes and the following method declaration appears in the Code pane:

```
public void writeFee(double fee)
{

}
```

13   Type the following statements inside the *writeFee* method:

```
Console.WriteLine("The consultant's fee is: {0}", fee * 1.1);
```

14   On the Build menu, click Build Solution.

15   Verify that the *writeFee* method you have declared compiles without error.

> ▶ **Tip**   If you feel sufficiently comfortable with the syntax, you can also write methods by typing them directly in the Code pane; you do not always have to use the C# Method Wizard.

Call the methods and run the program

1   In the Code pane, locate the *run* method.

2   Type the following statements inside the *run* method:

```
double dailyRate = readDouble("Enter your daily rate: ");
int noOfDays = readInt("Enter the number of days: ");
writeFee(calculateFee(dailyRate, noOfDays));
```

3   On the Debug menu, click Start Without Debugging. Visual Studio .NET builds the program and then runs it. A console window appears.

4   At the Enter Your Daily Rate prompt, type **525** and then press Enter.

5   At the Enter The Number Of Days prompt, type **17** and then press Enter. The program writes the following message to the console window:

```
The consultant's fee is: 9817.5
Press any key to continue
```

6   Press any key to return control to the Visual Studio .NET programming environment.

In the final exercise, you'll use the Visual Studio .NET debugger to run your program in slow motion. You'll see when each method is called (this action is referred to as *stepping into* the method) and then see each return statement transfer control back to the caller (also known as *stepping out* of the method).

While you are stepping in and out of methods, you'll use the tools on the Debug toolbar. The Debug toolbar should appear automatically when you debug a program. If the toolbar does not appear, you can display it by pointing to Toolbars on the View menu and then clicking Debug.

Step through the methods using the Visual Studio .NET debugger

1   In the Code pane, find the *run* method.

2   Move the mouse pointer to the first statement in the *run* method. The first statement in the *run* method is as follows:

```
double dailyRate = readDouble("Enter your daily rate: ");
```

Right-click anywhere on this line.

3

Methods and Scope

3   On the pop-up menu, click Run To Cursor. The program runs to the statement underneath the cursor.

A yellow arrow in the left margin of the Code pane indicates which is the current statement. The current statement is also highlighted with a yellow background.

4   On the View menu, point to Toolbars, and then click Debug (if it is not already selected). The Debug toolbar opens.

The Debug toolbar might appear docked with the other toolbars. If you cannot see the toolbar, try deselecting it using the Toolbars command on the View menu, and notice which buttons disappear. Then display the toolbar again.

▶   **Tip**   To make the Debug toolbar appear in its own window, click the handle on the left edge of the toolbar and drag it over the Code pane.

5   On the Debug toolbar, click Step Into. The yellow cursor jumps to the first statement of the *readDouble* method.

6   On the Debug toolbar, click Step Out. The program displays the Enter Your Daily Rate prompt in a console window.

7   Type **525** in the console window, and then press Enter. Control returns to the Visual Studio .NET programming environment. (You might need to click on the Visual Studio .NET window to bring it to the foreground.) The yellow cursor has stepped out of the *readDouble* method and is now back at the first statement of the *run* method.

8   On the Debug toolbar, click Step Into. The yellow cursor moves to the second statement in the *run* method:

```
int noOfDays = readInt("Enter the number of days: ");
```

9   On the Debug toolbar, click Step Into. The yellow cursor jumps into the first statement of the *readInt* method.

10 On the Debug toolbar, click Step Out. The program displays the Enter The Number Of Days prompt in the console window.

11 Type **17** and then press Enter. Control returns to the Visual Studio .NET programming environment. The yellow cursor has stepped out of the *readInt* method and is now back at the second statement of the *run* method.

12 On the Debug toolbar, click Step Into. The yellow cursor moves to the third statement of the *run* method:

```
writeFee(calculateFee(dailyRate, noOfDays));
```

13 On the Debug toolbar, click Step Into. The yellow cursor jumps into the first statement of the *calculateFee* method.

14 On the Debug toolbar, click Step Out. The yellow cursor jumps back to the third statement of the *run* method.

15 On the Debug toolbar, click Step Into. The yellow cursor jumps into the first statement of the *writeFee* method.

16 On the Debug toolbar, click Step Out. The yellow cursor jumps to the closing curly brace at the end of the *run* method. In the console window, the program displays the consultant's fee, as shown in the following illustration.

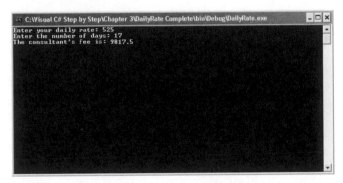

17 On the Debug toolbar, click Stop Debugging

18 On the Debug toolbar, click Close.

Congratulations! You've successfully written and called methods and used the Visual Studio .NET debugger to step in and out of methods as they run.

▶ **Tip** When debugging an application, you can press F11 instead of clicking the Step Into button on the Debug toolbar.

If you want to continue to the next chapter

■ Keep Visual Studio .NET running and turn to Chapter 4.

If you want to exit Visual Studio .NET now

■ On the File menu, click Exit. If you see a Save dialog box, click Yes.

Methods and Scope

Chapter 3 Quick Reference

To	Do this	Button
Declare a method	Write the method inside a class. For example: ```\nint addValues(int lhs, int rhs)\n{\n ⋮\n}\n```	
Return a value from inside a method	Write a *return* statement inside the method. For example: ```\nreturn lhs + rhs;\n```	
Return from a method before the end of the method	Write a *return* statement inside the method. For example: ```\nreturn;\n```	
Call a method	Write the name of the method, together with any arguments between parentheses. For example: ```\naddValues(39, 3);\n```	
Use the C# Method Wizard to help you write a method	In Class View, right-click the name of the class. On the pop-up menu, point to Add, and then click Add Method.	
Display the Debug toolbar	On the View menu, point to Toolbars, and then click Debug.	
Step into a method	On the Debug toolbar, click Step Into. Or On the Debug menu, click Step Into.	
Step out of a method	On the Debug toolbar, click Step Out. Or On the Debug menu, click Step Out.	

Chapter

4

Using Decision Statements

In this chapter, you will learn how to:

■ Use Boolean operators to create expressions whose outcome is either true or false.

■ Write *if* statements to perform decision-making based on the result of a Boolean expression.

■ Write switch statements to perform more complex decision-making.

In Chapter 3, you learned how to group related statements into methods; you also learned how to use arguments and parameters to pass information to a method and how to use *return* statements to pass information out of a method. Useful though these methods might be, they have a shortcoming: they always do the same thing. Many programs need to solve large and complex problems. To manage this complexity, you need to be able to write methods that selectively perform different actions at different times, depending on the circumstances. In this chapter, you'll see how to do this.

Declaring *bool* Variables

In the world of programming (unlike in the real world), everything is black or white, right or wrong, true or false. For example, if you create an integer variable called x, assign the value 99 to x, and then ask, "Does x contain the value 99?" the answer definitely will be true. If you ask, "Is x less than 10?" the answer definitely will be false. These are examples of *Boolean expressions*. A Boolean expression always evaluates to true or false.

Microsoft Visual C# has a primitive data type called *bool* that you use to declare variables whose values are either true or false. You can assign a value to a *bool* variable using the keywords *true* and *false*. For example, the following three statements declare a *bool* variable called *areYouReady*, assign *true* to the variable, and then write it to the console:

```
bool areYouReady;
areYouReady = true;
Console.WriteLine(areYouReady); // writes True
```

Using Boolean Operators

A *Boolean operator* is an operator whose outcome is either true or false. C# has several very useful Boolean operators. The simplest Boolean operator is the NOT operator, which uses the exclamation point symbol (!). You apply the ! operator to a single Boolean value, and the value returns the opposite of that value. In other words, *!false* is true and *!true* is false.

▶ **Note**   Operators that work on a single operand are called *unary operators*, and operators that work on two operands are called *binary operators*.

Understanding Equality and Relational Operators

Two much more commonly used Boolean operators are the *equality* and *inequality* operators. You use these binary operators to find out whether a value is the same as another value of the same type. Closely related to these two operators are the relational operators. You use the *relational* operators to find out whether a value is less than or greater than another value of the same type. The symbols that C# uses for the equality and relational operators are shown in the following table:

Operator	Meaning	Example	Outcome if age is 42
==	Equal to	age == 100	false
!=	Not equal to	age != 0	true
<	Less than	age < 21	false
<=	Less than or equal to	age <= 18	false
>	Greater than	age > 16	true
>=	Greater than or equal to	age >= 30	true

▶ **Note**   Don't confuse the equality operator, ==, with the assignment operator, =. Code such as x==y compares x to y, and has the value *true* if the values are the same. Code such as x=y assigns the value of y to x.

Understanding Logical Operators

C# also provides two other Boolean operators: the logical AND operator, which uses the && symbol, and the logical OR operator, which uses the || symbol. The purpose of these operators is to combine Boolean expressions together into bigger expressions. These binary operators are similar to the equality and relational operators in that their outcome is either true or false, but differ in that the values they operate on must themselves be either true or false.

The outcome of the && operator is true if and only if both of the Boolean expressions it operates on are true. Use the && operator to determine whether a combination of Boolean expressions is true. For example, the following statement assigns the value *true* to *validPercentage* if and only if the value of *percent* is greater than or equal to zero and the value of *percent* is less than or equal to 100:

```
bool validPercentage;
validPercentage = (percent >= 0) && (percent <= 100);
```

> ▶ **Note**   A common beginner's error is to try to combine the two tests by naming the percent variable only once, like this:
>
> percent >= 0 && <= 100 // error, this statement will not compile.

The outcome of the || operator is true if either of the Boolean expressions it operates on are true. You use the || operator to determine whether any one of a combination of Boolean expressions is true. For example, the following statement assigns the value *true* to *invalidPercentage* if the value of *percent* is less than zero, or the value of *percent* is greater than 100:

```
bool invalidPercentage;
invalidPercentage = (percent < 0) || (percent > 100);
```

Short Circuiting

The && and || operators both exhibit a feature called *short circuiting*. Sometimes the result of the && and || operators can be determined solely from their left-side Boolean expression. In these cases, the && and || operators will bypass the evaluation of their right-side Boolean expressions. Here are some examples:

```
(percent >= 0) && (percent <= 100)
```

In this expression, if the value of *percent* is less than zero, the Boolean expression on the left side of && evaluates to false. This value means that the result of the entire expression must be false regardless of the remaining expression; therefore, the Boolean expression on the right side of && is not evaluated.

```
(percent < 0) || (percent > 100)
```

In this expression, if the value of *percent* is less than zero, the Boolean expression on the left side of || evaluates to true. This value means that the result of the entire expression must be true; therefore, the Boolean expression on the right side of || is not evaluated.

Summarizing Operator Precedence and Associativity

The following table summarizes the precedence and associativity of all the operators you have learned so far. Operators in the same category have the same precedence. Operators in a higher category take precedence over operators in a lower category.

Category	Operators	Description	Associativity
Primary	( )	Precedence override	Left
Unary	!	NOT	Left
Multiplicative	*	Multiply	Left
	/	Divide	
	%	Division remainder	
Additive	+	Addition	Left
	−	Subtraction	
Relational	<	Less than	Left
	<=	Less than or equal	
	>	Greater than	
	>=	Greater than or equal	
Equality	==	Equal to	Left
	!=	Not equal to	
Boolean	&&	Logical AND	Left
	||	Logical OR	
Assignment	=		Right

Executing *if* Statements

You use an *if* statement when you want to execute one or more statements when the result of a Boolean expression is true. You can also use an optional *else* clause when you want to execute one or more statements when the result of the Boolean expression is false.

Understanding *if* Statement Syntax

The syntax of an *if* statement is as follows (*if* and *else* are keywords):

```
if ( booleanExpression )
    statement-1
else
    statement-2
```

If *booleanExpression* evaluates to true, then *statement-1* runs; otherwise, the *booleanExpression* is false and *statement-2* runs. The *else* keyword and the following *statement-2* are optional. If there is no *else* clause, nothing happens when the *booleanExpression* is false.

For example, here's an *if* statement that increments the seconds hand of a stopwatch (minutes are ignored for now):

```
int seconds;
:
if (seconds == 59)
    seconds = 0;
else
    seconds = seconds + 1;
```

Boolean Expressions Only Please!

The expression in an *if* statement must be enclosed in parentheses. Additionally, the expression must be a Boolean expression. Some other languages (notably C and C++) allow you to write an integer expression and silently convert the integer value to true (nonzero) or false (zero). C# never does this silent conversion.

Also, if you're writing an *if* statement and you accidentally write an assignment instead of an equality test, the C# compiler will recognize your mistake, for example:

```
int seconds;
:
if (seconds = 59)  // compile-time error
:
if (seconds == 59) // ok
```

Finally, you can use a Boolean variable as the expression, as in this example:

```
bool inWord;
:
if (inWord == true) // ok, but non-idiomatic
:
if (inWord)         // better
```

Using Blocks to Group Statements

Sometimes you'll want to run two or more statements when a Boolean expression is true. You could group the statements inside a new method and then call the new method, but a simpler solution is to group the statements inside a *block*. A block is simply a sequence of statements grouped between a left and a right brace. In the following example, two assignment statements are grouped inside a block and the whole block runs if the value of *seconds* is equal to 59:

```
int seconds;
int minutes;
⋮
if (seconds == 59)
{
    seconds = 0;
    minutes = minutes + 1;
}
else
    seconds = seconds + 1;
```

▶ **Important**   If you omit the braces, the C# compiler will associate only the first statement (`seconds = 0`) with the *if* statement. The subsequent statement (`minutes = minutes + 1`) would always run regardless of the *if* statement, if the program compiled. However, you would not be able to run the program because the compiler would discover the *else* keyword, not know what to do with it, give up, and report a syntax error.

Cascading *if* Statements

You can nest *if* statements inside other *if* statements. In this way, you can chain together a sequence of Boolean expressions, which are tested one after the other until one of them evaluates to true. In the following example, if the value of *day* is 0, the first test evaluates to true and *dayName* is assigned *Sunday*. If the value of *day* is not 0, the first test fails and control passes to the *else* clause, which will run the second *if* statement and compare the value of *day* with 1. The second *if* statement is reached only if the first test is false. Similarly, the third *if* statement is reached only if the first and second tests are false.

```
if (day == 0)
    dayName = "Sunday";
else if (day == 1)
    dayName = "Monday";
else if (day == 2)
    dayName = "Tuesday";
else if (day == 3)
    dayName = "Wednesday";
else if (day == 4)
```

```
    dayName = "Thursday";
else if (day == 5)
    dayName = "Friday";
else if (day == 6)
    dayName = "Saturday";
else
    dayName = "unknown";
```

In the following exercise, you'll write a method that uses a cascading *if* statement to compare two dates.

Write *if* statements

1 Start Microsoft Visual Studio .NET.

2 On the File menu, point to Open, and then click Project. The Open Project dialog box opens.

3 Open the Selection project, located in the \Microsoft Press\Visual C# Step by Step\Chapter 4\Selection folder in your My Documents folder. The Selection project opens in the programming environment.

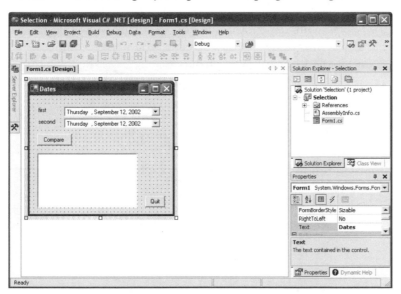

4 On the Debug menu, click Start Without Debugging.

▶ **Tip** The keyboard shortcut for Start Without Debugging is Ctrl+F5.

Visual Studio .NET builds and runs the application. There are two *DateTimePicker* controls on the form called *first* and *second*. Both are currently set to today's date.

5   Click Compare. The following text appears in the text box:

```
first == second : False
first != second : True
first <  second : False
first <= second : False
first >  second : True
first >= second : True
```

The Boolean expression `first == second` should be true because both first and second are set to today's date. In fact, only the less than and greater than or equal to operators seem to be correct!

6   Click Quit. You return to the Visual Studio .NET programming environment.

7   Scroll through the Code pane, and locate the *dateCompare* method. The *dateCompare* method should look like this:

```
private int dateCompare(DateTime lhs, DateTime rhs)
{
    // TO DO
    return 42;
}
```

You need to implement this method to correctly compare two dates. For the application to work correctly, you need to implement *dateCompare* with the following behavior:

```
if lhs < rhs, then return any int value less than zero
if lhs == rhs, then return zero
if lhs > rhs, then return any int value greater than zero
```

8   Remove the // TODO comment and the *return* statement from the *dateCompare* method.

9   Type the following statements in the body of the *dateCompare* method:

```
int result;
if (lhs.Year < rhs.Year)
    result = -1;
else if (lhs.Year > rhs.Year)
    result = +1;
else if (lhs.Month < rhs.Month)
    result = -1;
else if (lhs.Month > rhs.Month)
    result = +1;
else if (lhs.Day < rhs.Day)
    result = -1;
else if (lhs.Day > rhs.Day)
    result = +1;
else
    result = 0;
return result;
```

Notice that if `lhs.Year < rhs.Year` is false, and `lhs.Year >` `rhs.Year` is false, then `lhs.Year == rhs.Year` must be true, and the program flow correctly moves on to compare the *Month* property of *lhs* and *rhs*. Similarly, if `lhs.Month < rhs.Month` is false and `lhs.Month > rhs.Month` is false, then `lhs.Month == rhs.Month` must be true, and the program flow again correctly moves on to compare the *Day* property of *lhs* and *rhs*. Lastly, if `lhs.Day < rhs.Day` is false, and `lhs.Day > rhs.Day` is false, then `lhs.Day == rhs.Day` must be true and, because the *Month* and *Year* properties must also be true, the two dates must be the same.

10 On the Debug menu, click Start Without Debugging. The application is rebuilt and restarted. Once again, the two *DateTimePicker* controls, *first* and *second*, are set to today's date.

11 Click Compare. The following text appears in the text box:

```
first == second : True
first != second : False
first <  second : False
first <= second : True
first >  second : False
first >= second : True
```

These are the correct answers.

12 Move the second *DateTimePicker* control onto tomorrow's date.

13 Click Compare. The following text appears in the text box:

```
first == second : False
first != second : True
first <  second : True
first <= second : True
first >  second : False
first >= second : False
```

These are the correct answers.

14 Click Quit. You return to the Visual Studio .NET programming environment.

Using *switch* Statements

When you write a cascading *if* statement, you sometimes find that all the *if* statements look very similar; they all evaluate an identical expression. The only difference is that each *if* compares the result of the expression with a different value, for example:

```
if (day == 0)
    dayName = "Sunday";
else if (day == 1)
    dayName = "Monday";
else if (day == 2)
    dayName = "Tuesday";
else if (day == 3)
    ⋮
else
    dayName = "Unknown";
```

In these situations, you can often rewrite the cascading *if* statements as a *switch* statement to make your program more efficient and more readable. It's also sometimes possible to rewrite a cascading *if* statement using arrays. Arrays are covered in Chapter 10.

Understanding *switch* Statement Syntax

The syntax of a *switch* statement is as follows (*switch*, *case*, and *default* are keywords):

```
switch ( controllingExpression )
{
case constantExpression :
    statements
    break;
case constantExpression :
    statements
    break;
⋮
default :
    statements
    break;
}
```

The *controllingExpression* is evaluated once and the statements underneath the case whose *constantExpression* value is equal to the result of the *controllingExpression* run as far as the *break* statement. The *switch* statement then finishes and the program continues at the first statement after the closing brace of the *switch* statement.

If none of the *constantExpression* values are equal to the value of the *controllingExpression*, the *statements* underneath the optional *default :* run.

▶ **Note**   An error does not result if the value of the controlling expression does not match any of the case labels and there's no default label. Program execution will continue with the first statement after the closing brace of the *switch* statement.

For example, you can rewrite the previous cascading *if* statement as the following *switch* statement:

```
switch (day)
{
case 0 :
    dayName = "Sunday";
    break;
case 1 :
    dayName = "Monday";
    break;
case 2 :
    dayName = "Tuesday";
    break;
:
default :
    dayName = "Unknown";
    break;
}
```

Following the *switch* Statement Rules

The *switch* statements are very useful but, unfortunately, you can't always use them when you might like to. Your *switch* statements must adhere to the following rules:

- You can use *switch* only on primitive data types (such as *int*) and *string*. If you need to use *switch* on any other types, you'll have to use an *if* statement.

- Your case labels must be constant expressions, such as 42 or "42". If you need to calculate your case label values at run time, you'll have to use an *if* statement.

- Your case labels must be unique expressions. In other words, you're not allowed to write two case labels with the same value.

- You must repeat the case label syntax for every individual value if you want to run the same statements for more than one value. There is no shortcut for grouping a sequence of case label values. You must provide a label for each case. Here is an example:

```
switch (trumps)
{
case Hearts :
case Diamonds:
    color = "Red";
    break;
case Clubs :
case Spades :
```

```
        color = "Black";
        break;
}
```

No Fall-Through

C and C++ programmers should note that the *break* statement is mandatory for every case in a *switch* statement that contains executable code (even the default case). This requirement is a good thing; one of the most expensive computer bugs ever was eventually tracked down to an unintentional fall-through caused by a missing *break* statement in a C program. In C and C++, if you omit the *break* statement, execution falls through to the next case and continues executing those statements.

In C#, fall-through is always a compile-time error. The last statement of a case section that contains executable code is not allowed to fall through to the next case. The *break* statement is the most common way to stop fall-through, but you can also use a *return* statement or a *throw* statement.

If you really want to, you can mimic fall-through in C# by using a *goto* statement to go to the following case or default label. This usage is not recommended though, and this book will not show you how to do it!

In the following exercise, you will complete a program that reads the characters of a string and maps each character to its XML representation. For example, the "<" character has a special meaning in XML (it's used to form elements) and must be translated into "<". You will write a *switch* statement that tests the value of the character and traps the special XML characters as case labels.

Write *switch* statements

1   Start Visual Studio .NET.

2   On the File menu, point to Open, and then click Project. The Open Project dialog box opens.

3   Open the switchStatement project, located in the \Microsoft Press\Visual C# Step by Step\Chapter 4\switchStatement folder in your My Documents folder. The switchStatement project opens in the programming environment.

4   On the Debug menu, click Start Without Debugging. Visual Studio .NET builds and runs the application. There are two text boxes separated by a Copy button.

5 Type the following statement into the upper text box:

```
inRange = (lo <= number) && (number <= hi);
```

6 Click Copy. The statement is copied, character-by-character, into the lower text box.

7 Click Close. You return to the Visual Studio .NET programming environment.

8 Scroll through the Code pane, and locate the copyOne method. The copyOne method copies one character from the upper text box to the lower text box. At the moment, copyOne contains a switch statement with a single default section.

In the following few steps, you will modify this switch statement to convert characters that are significant in XML to their XML mapping. For example, the "<" character will be converted to the string "<".

9 Add the following statements to the *switch* statement:

```
case '<' :
    target.Text += "&lt;";
    break;
case '>' :
    target.Text += "&gt;";
    break;
case '&' :
    target.Text += "&amp;";
    break;
    case '\"' :
        target.Text +=   "&#34;";
        break;
    case '\'' :
        target.Text += "&#39;";
    break;
```

10 On the Debug menu, click Start Without Debugging. Visual Studio .NET builds and runs the application.

11 Type the following statement into the upper text box:

```
inRange = (lo <= number) && (number <= hi);
```

12 Click Copy. The statement is copied into the lower text box.

This time, each character undergoes the XML mapping implemented in the *switch* statement.

13 Click Close. You return to the Visual Studio .NET programming environment.

If you want to continue to the next chapter

■ Keep Visual Studio .NET open, and turn to Chapter 5.

If you want to exit Visual Studio .NET now

■ On the File menu, click Exit. If you see a Save dialog box, click Yes.

Chapter 4 Quick Reference

To	Do this	Example
See if two values are equivalent	Use the == or != operators	`answer == 42`
Compare the size of two values	Use the <, <=, >, >= operators	`Age >= 21`
Declare a Boolean	Use the *bool* keyword as the type of the variable	`bool inRange;`

Create a Boolean expression that is true only if two other conditions are true	Use the && operator	`inRange =`
		`   (lo <= number)`
		`   && (number <= hi);`

Create a Boolean expression that is true if either of two other conditions is true	Use the ‖ operator	`outOfRange =`
		`   (number < lo)`
		`   || (hi < number);`

Run a statement if a condition is true	Use an *if* statement	`if (inRange)` `   process();`

Run more than one statement if a condition is true	Use a block	`if (seconds == 59)`
		`{`
		`   seconds = 0;`
		`   minutes = minutes + 1;`
		`}`

Associate different statements with different values of a controlling expression	Use a *switch* statement	`switch (current)`
		`{`
		`case '<' :`
		`   ⋮`
		`   break;`
		`default :`
		`   ⋮`
		`   break;`
		`}`

Using Iteration Statements

In this chapter, you will learn how to:

- Use the compound assignment operators for updating the value of a variable.

- Increment and decrement the value of a variable by one unit using the ++ and — operators.

- Write *while*, *for*, and *do* statements to repeatedly run one or more statements.

- Step through a do method and watch as the values of the variables change.

In Chapter 4, you learned how to use the *if* and *switch* constructs to selectively run statements. In this chapter, you'll see how to use a variety of iteration (or looping) statements to repeatedly run one or more statements. When you write iteration statements, you usually need to update the value of a variable to control the number of iterations performed. You'll learn about some special assignment operators that you should use to update the value of a variable.

Using Compound Assignment Operators

You've already seen how to create new values using arithmetic operators. For example, the following statement uses the + operator to create a value that is 42 greater than the variable *answer*. The new value is then written to the console:

```
Console.WriteLine(answer + 42);
```

You've also seen how to use assignment statements to change the value held in a variable. The following statement uses the assignment operator to change the value of *answer* to 42:

```
answer = 42;
```

If you want to add 42 to the value of a variable, you can combine the assignment operator and the addition operator. For example, the following statement adds 42 to *answer*. In other words, after this statement runs, the value of *answer* is 42 more than it was before:

```
answer = answer + 42;
```

Although this statement works, you'll probably never see an experienced programmer write this. Adding a value to a variable is so common that Microsoft Visual C# lets you do it by using the compound assignment operator +=. To add 42 to *answer*, an experienced programmer would write the following statement:

```
answer += 42;
```

The proper name for the += operator is the *compound addition* operator. You can use this shortcut to combine any arithmetic operator with the assignment operator, as the following table shows:

Don't write this	Write this
variable = variable * number;	variable *= number;
variable = variable / number;	variable /= number;
variable = variable % number;	variable %= number;
variable = variable + number;	variable += number;
variable = variable - number;	variable -= number;

▶ **Tip**   The *=, /=, %=, +=, and −= operators share the same precedence and right associativity as the simple assignment operator.

The += operator also works on strings. It appends one string to the end of another. For example, the following code will display "Hello John" on the console:

```
string name = "John";
string greeting = "Hello ";
greeting += name;
Console.WriteLine(greeting);
```

You cannot use any of the other compound assignment operators on strings.

▶ **Note**   Use the ++ and −− operators when incrementing or decrementing a variable by 1 in preference to using a compound assignment operator. For example, replace

```
count += 1;
```

with

```
count++;
```

Writing *while* Statements

You use a *while* statement to repeatedly run a statement while a Boolean expression remains true. The syntax of a *while* statement is:

```
while ( booleanExpression )
    statement
```

The Boolean expression is evaluated and, if it's true, the statement runs and the Boolean expression is evaluated again. If the expression is still true, the statement is repeated and the expression evaluated again. This process continues until the Boolean expression evaluates to false when the *while* statement exits. A *while* statement shares many syntactic similarities with an *if* statement (in fact the syntax is identical except for the keyword):

- The Boolean expression must be a Boolean expression.

▶ **Note**   C and C++ programmers should remember that there are no silent (or automatic) conversions from integers to Boolean expressions in C#.

- The Boolean expression must be written inside parentheses.
- If the Boolean expression evaluates to false when first evaluated, the statement will not run.
- If you want to combine two or more statements under the control of a *while* statement, you must group those statements in a block using braces.

Here's a *while* statement that writes the values 0 through 9 to the console:

```
int i = 0;
while (i != 10)
{
    Console.WriteLine(i);
    i++;
}
```

All *while* statements should terminate at some point. A common beginner's mistake is forgetting to include a statement to eventually cause the Boolean expression to evaluate to false and terminate the loop. In the example, the *i*++ statement performs this role.

▶ **Note**   Another very common beginner's mistake is thinking that the Boolean expression is a termination condition. It's a continuation condition; while the condition is true, carry on.

Writing *for* Statements

Most *while* statements have the following general structure:

```
initialization
while (booleanExpression)
{
    statement
    updateControlVariable
}
```

A *for* statement allows you to write a more formal version of this kind of *while* statement by combining the initialization, the Boolean expression, and the update (all the loop's "housekeeping"). You'll find the *for* statement useful because it makes it much harder to forget any one of the three parts. The syntax of a *for* statement is this:

```
for (initialization; booleanExpression; updateControlVariable)
    statement
```

The initialization occurs once at the start of the loop. If the Boolean expression evaluates to true, the statement runs. The control variable update occurs and the Boolean expression is re-evaluated. If the condition is still true, the statement is executed again, the control variable is updated, the Boolean expression is evaluated again, and so on. By now, you might have spotted a trend. Basically, the *for* statement keeps repeating until the Boolean expression is false.

Notice that the initialization occurs only once, that the statement always executes before the update occurs, and that the update occurs before the Boolean expression evaluates.

You can omit any of the three parts of a *for* statement. If you omit the Boolean expression, it defaults to true. The following *for* statement will run forever:

```
for (int i = 0; ;i++)
{
    Console.WriteLine("somebody stop me!");
}
```

If you omit the initialization and update parts, you have a strangely spelled *while* loop.

```
int i = 0;
for (; i != 10; )
{
    Console.WriteLine(i);
    i++;
}
```

> ▶ **Tip**   The *initialization*, *booleanExpression*, and *updateControlVariable* parts of a
> *for* statement must always be separated by semicolons.

Here's the running example that writes the values 0 through 9 to the console,
this time using a *for* statement:

```
for (int i = 0; i != 10; i++)
{
    Console.WriteLine(i);
}
```

> ▶ **Tip**   It's considered good style to use an explicit statement block for the body
> of *if*, *while*, and *for* statements even when the block contains only one state-
> ment. By writing the block, you make it easier to add statements to the block at
> a later date. Without the block, to add another statement, you'd have to remem-
> ber to add both the extra statement *and* the braces, and it's very easy to forget
> the braces.

Understanding *for* Statement Scope

You should have noticed that you can declare a variable in the initialization part
of a *for* statement. That variable is scoped to the body of the *for* statement and
disappears when the *for* statement finishes. This rule has two important consequences. First, you cannot use that variable after the *for* statement has ended
because it's no longer in scope. Here's an example:

```
for (int i = 0; i != 10; i++)
{
    ⋮
}
Console.WriteLine(i); // compile time error
```

Second, you can write two or more *for* statements next to each other that use
the same variable name because each variable is in a different scope. Here's an
example:

```
for (int i = 0; i != 10; i++)
    ⋮
for (int i = 0; i != 20; i += 2) // okay
    ⋮
```

Writing *do* Statements

The *while* statement and the *for* statement both test their Boolean expression at
the top of the loop. This means that if the expression is false on the very first
test, the body of the loop will not run, not even once. Sometimes you'll want to
write a statement where you know that the body of the loop will run at least

once. In these situations, what you need is a statement where the expression is evaluated at the bottom of the loop, after the body of the loop runs. This is the purpose of the *do* statement.

The syntax of a *do* statement is as follows (don't forget the final semicolon):

```
do
    statement
while (booleanExpression);
```

If you want the body of the *do* loop to contain two or more statements, you must group the statements in a block. Here's a version of the previous example that writes the values 0 through 9 to the console, this time using a *do* statement:

```
int i - 0;
do
{
    Console.WriteLine(i);
    i++;
}
while (i != 10);
```

In the following exercise, you will see an example of each of the iteration statements.

Display iteration statements

1   Start Microsoft Visual Studio .NET.

2   On the File menu, point to Open, and then click Project. The Open Project dialog box opens.

3   Open the Iteration project, located in the \Microsoft Press\Visual C# Step by Step\Chapter 5\Iteration folder in your My Documents folder. The Iteration project opens.

4   On the Debug menu, click Start Without Debugging. Visual Studio .NET builds and runs the application.

There are two text boxes and a group of four Keywords options.

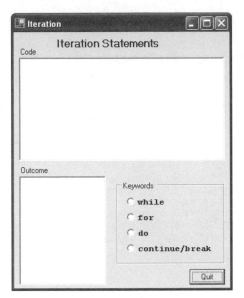

5   Under Keywords, select the While option. The following *while* state-
    ment appears in the Code text box.

    This statement is the *while* statement you saw previously that writes
    the values 0 through 9 to the console. The text that this code writes
    to the console is displayed in the Outcome text box.

```
int i = 0;
while (i != 10)
{
    Console.WriteLine("while " + i);
    i++;
}
```

6   Select the For option. The following *for* statement appears in the
    Code box. (Again, this is the *for* statement you saw previously that
    writes the values 0 through 9 to the console.)

    The text that this code writes to the console is displayed in the Out-
    come box.

```
for (int i = 0; i != 10; i++)
{
    Console.WriteLine("for " + i);
}
```

7   Select the Do option. The Code box displays a *do* statement that
    implements a loop to write the values 0 through 9 to the console.

8   Select the Continue/Break option. The Code box displays a *while*
    loop that uses a *break* and *continue* statement to write the values 0
    through 9 to the console.

9   Click Quit. You return to the Visual Studio .NET programming environment.

The *break* and *continue* Statements

In Chapter 4, you saw the *break* statement being used to jump out of a *switch* statement. You can also use a *break* statement to jump out of the body of an *iteration* statement. When you break out of a loop, there is no delay; it's immediate. Neither the update nor the continuation condition is re-run.

In contrast, the *continue* statement causes the program to immediately re-evaluate the Boolean expression and perform the next iteration of the loop. For example, here's the example that writes the values 0 through 9 to the console, this time using a *break* and a *continue* statement:

```
int i = 0;
while (true)
{
    Console.WriteLine(i);
    i++;
    if (i != 10)
        continue;
    else
        break;
}
```

This code is absolutely ghastly. Many programming guidelines recommend using *continue* cautiously or not at all because it is often associated with hard-to-understand code. The behavior of *continue* is also quite subtle. For example, if you run a *continue* statement from inside a *for* statement, the update part will run.

In the following exercise, you will write a *while* statement to read the contents of a source file one line at a time and write each line to a text box in a Microsoft Windows application.

Write a *while* statement

1   On the File menu, point to Open, and then click Project. The Open Project dialog box opens.

2   Open the whileStatement project, located in the \Microsoft Press\Visual C# Step by Step\Chapter 5\whileStatement folder in your My Documents folder. The whileStatement project opens.

3   On the Debug menu, click Start Without Debugging. Visual Studio
.NET builds and runs the Windows application.

4   Click Open File. The Open dialog box opens.

5   Navigate to the \Microsoft Press\Visual C# Step by Step\Chapter
5\whileStatement folder in your My Documents folder.

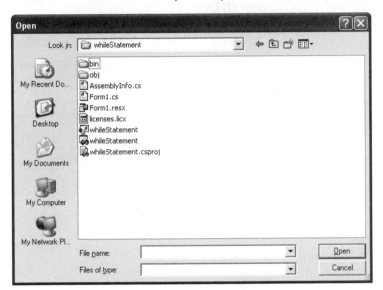

6   Select the Form1.cs file, and then click Open. The name of the source
file, Form1.cs, appears in the small text box, but the contents of
Form1.cs do not appear in the large text box.

This behavior occurs because the code that will read the contents of
the source file and display it in the large text box has not yet been
implemented. In the following few steps, you will add this functionality.

7   Click Close. You return to the Visual Studio .NET programming
environment.

8   In the Code pane, locate the *openFileDialog_FileOk* method. (If the
code is not displayed in the Code pane, right-click Form1.cs in the
Solution Explorer and click View Code.)

The body of the method is currently implemented as follows:

```
string fullPathname = openFileDialog.FileName;
FileInfo src = new FileInfo(fullPathname);
filename.Text = src.Name;
/* add while loop here */
```

The first statement declares a *string* variable called *fullPathname* and
initializes it to the *FileName* property of the *openFileDialog* field.

This statement initializes *fullPathname* to the full name (including the folder) of the source file selected in the Open dialog box.

The second statement declares a *FileInfo* variable called *src* and initializes it to an object that represents the file selected in the Open dialog box. (*FileInfo* is a class provided by the Microsoft .NET Framework that allows you to manipulate files.)

The third statement assigns the *Text* property of the *filename* control to the *Name* property of the *src* variable. The *Name* property of the *src* variable holds the name of the file selected in the Open dialog box without its folder. This assignment makes the name of the file appear in the filename component of the Windows form.

9   Replace the /* add while loop here */ comment with the following statements:

```
source.Text = "";
TextReader reader = src.OpenText();
string line;
while ((line = reader.ReadLine()) != null)
{
    source.Text += line + "\n";
}
reader.Close();
```

The first statement is:

```
source.Text = "";
```

This statement resets the *Text* property of the source text box.

The second statement is:

```
TextReader reader = src.OpenText();
```

This statement declares a *TextReader* variable called *reader*. (*TextReader* is another class provided by the .NET Framework that you can use for reading streams of characters from sources such as files.) It also initializes *reader* to a *TextReader* object returned from the *src.OpenText* method call. The *reader* variable can now be used to read the file associated with the *src* variable.

The third statement is:

```
string line;
```

This statement declares a *string* called *line*. This variable will hold each line of text as the reader reads it from the file.

The fourth statement is the *while* loop:

```
while ((line = reader.ReadLine()) != null)
{
    ⋮
}
```

The call to *reader.ReadLine* returns the next line from the file or a special value called *null* if there were no more lines to read. The result of this call is assigned to the *line* variable. The result of this assignment (which is *line*) is then compared to *null* using the != operator. If a string was successfully read from the file, *line* will not be *null*, the Boolean expression will be true, and the body of the *while* statement will be run. Notice that the parentheses are required to override precedence because = has a lower precedence than !=. The body of the *while* statement contains the single statement:

```
source.Text += line + "\n";
```

This statement appends the *line* to the *Text* property of *source* (the text box). The extra "\n" is a newline. This newline is required because the *ReadLine* method strips off any trailing newline characters and we want to put them back again. Remember, += is really the same as combining the = and the + operators, and both the = and the + operators can be used on strings to append one string to the end of another.

Eventually all the lines will have been read from the file and appended to the text box. At this point, the final *reader.ReadLine* call will return *null*, the != comparison to *null* will be false, and the *while* statement will terminate.

The final statement is:

```
reader.Close();
```

This statement closes the file the reader is reading from. Notice how this call to *Close* matches the *Open* in *src.OpenText()*. This is a classic *while* loop.

10 On the Debug menu, click Start Without Debugging. Visual Studio .NET builds and runs the application.

11 Click Open File. The Open dialog box opens.

12 Select the Form1.cs file and then click Open. This time the contents of the selected file are displayed in the text box.

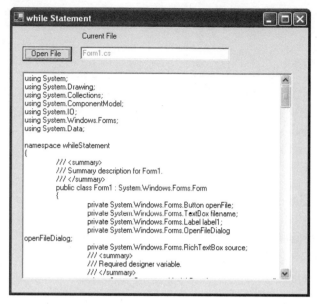

13 In the text box, locate the *openFileDialog_FileOk* method. This method contains the *while* statement you just added.

14 Click Close. You return to the Visual Studio .NET programming environment.

In the following exercise, you will write a *do* statement to convert a number to its string representation.

Write a *do* statement

1 On the File menu, point to Open, and then click Project. The Open Project dialog box opens.

2 Open the doStatement project, located in the \Microsoft Press\Visual C# Step by Step\Chapter 5\doStatement folder in your My Documents folder. The doStatement project opens.

3 On the Debug menu, click Start Without Debugging. Visual Studio .NET builds and runs the Windows application.

The application has two text boxes and the Show Steps button. You enter a positive number in the upper text box, and when you click the Show Steps button, the lower text box shows the steps used to create a string representation of this number.

4 Enter **2693** in the upper text box.

5 Click Show Steps. The lower text box displays the steps used to create a string representation of 2693:

6 Close the window to return to the Visual Studio .NET programming environment.

7 In the Code pane, locate the *showSteps_Click* method. (If the code is not displayed in the Code pane, right-click Form1.cs in the Solution Explorer and click View Code.)

This method contains the following statements:

```
int amount = System.Int32.Parse(number.Text);
steps.Text = "";
string current = "";
do
{
    int digitCode = '0' + amount % 10;
    char digit = Convert.ToChar(digitCode);
    current = digit + current;
    steps.Text += current + "\r\n";
    amount /= 10;
}
while (amount != 0);
```

The first statement of the method is this:

```
int amount = System.Int32.Parse(number.Text);
```

This statement converts the string entered into the *Text* property of the *number* text box into an *int* using the *Parse* method of *System.Int32*.

The second statement of the method is this:

```
steps.Text = "";
```

This statement resets the *Text* property of the *steps* text box.

The third statement of the method is this:

```
string current = "";
```

This statement declares a *string* variable called *current* and initializes it to the empty string.

The fourth statement of the method is the *do* statement:

```
do
{
    ⋮
}
while (amount != 0);
```

This statement will repeatedly run the body of the *do* statement while the continuation condition (amount != 0) remains true. Notice that the body must run at least once. This behavior is exactly what is required because even the number 0 has one digit.

The first statement inside the *do* loop is:

```
int digitCode = '0' + amount % 10;
```

This statement declares an *int* variable called *digitCode* and initializes it to the result of the following expression:

```
'0' + amount % 10
```

This expression requires a little explanation! The value of '0' is the character zero. In the character set used by Windows, this character equates to the integer value 48 (each character has its own unique character code which is an integer value). The value of amount % 10 is the remainder you get when you divide *amount* by 10. For example, if *amount* equals 2693, then 2693 % 10 is 3. (2693 divided by 10 is 269 with a remainder of 3.) Therefore, if *amount* equals 2693, then '0' + amount % 10 is the same as '0' + 3, which is 51. The + operator performs an implicit cast, converting '0' to the integer value 48 to allow this expression to be evaluated. It just so happens that the numeric characters are contiguous ('0' is 48, '1' is 49, '2' is 50, and so on), so 51 is the value of the character '3'.

The second statement inside the *do* loop is:

```
char digit = Convert.ToChar(digitCode);
```

This statement declares a *char* variable called *digit* and initializes it to the result of the *Convert.ToChar(digitCode)* method call. This method call returns the *char* with the integer character code value of the argument. In other words, the value of Convert.ToChar('0' + 3) is the value of '3'.

The third statement inside the *do* loop is:

```
current = digit + current;
```

This statement *prepends* the *char digit* just calculated to the *current* string. Notice that this statement cannot be replaced by current += digit; because that would *append* the digit.

The fourth statement inside the *do* loop is:

```
steps.Text += current + "\r\n";
```

This statement appends another step to the *Text* property of the Steps text box.

The final statement inside the *do* loop is:

```
amount /= 10;
```

This statement is the same as amount = amount / 10;. If the value of *amount* is 2693, the value of *amount* after this statement runs is 269. Notice that each iteration through the *do* statement removes the last digit from *amount* and prepends that digit to the *current* string.

In the final exercise, you will use the Visual Studio .NET debugger to step through the previous *do* statement as it runs.

Step through a *do* statement

1   In the Code pane, find the *showSteps_Click* method.

2   Move the cursor to any position in the first statement of the *showSteps_Click* method. The first statement in the *showSteps_Click* method is as follows:

```
int amount = System.Int32.Parse(number.Text);
```

3   Right-click anywhere in this first statement and click Run To Cursor. Visual Studio .NET builds and runs the application.

4   Enter **2693** in the upper text box.

5   Click Show Steps. You return to the Visual Studio .NET programming environment.

A yellow arrow on the left margin of the Code pane indicates the current statement.

6   On the View menu, point to Toolbars, and then click Debug (if it is not already selected). The Debug toolbar opens.

7   On the Debug toolbar, click the Breakpoints drop-down arrow. The following menu appears:

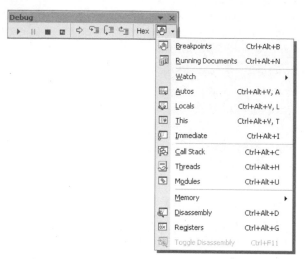

8   On the menu, click Locals. The Locals window appears. This window displays the name, type, and value of the local variables of the current method. This window displays the *amount* local variable and that the value of *amount* is currently zero:

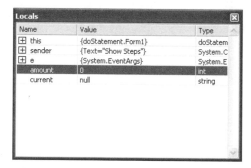

9   On the Debug toolbar, click the Step Into button. The debugger runs the current statement:

```
int amount = System.Int32.Parse(number.Text);
```

The value of *amount* in the Locals window changes to 2693 and the yellow arrow moves to the next statement.

10   On the Debug toolbar, click the Step Into button. The debugger runs the current statement:

```
steps.Text = "";
```

This statement does not affect the Locals window because steps is a field and not a local variable. The yellow arrow moves to the next statement.

11 On the Debug toolbar, click the Step Into button. The debugger runs the current statement:

```
string current = "";
```

The yellow arrow moves to the first statement inside the *do* loop. The *do* loop contains two local variables of its own, *digitCode* and *digit*. Notice that these local variables have appeared in the Locals window and that value of *digitCode* is zero.

12 On the Debug toolbar, click the Step Into button. The debugger runs the current statement:

```
int digitCode = '0' + amount % 10;
```

The value of *digitCode* in the Locals window changes to 51. This is because the value of '0' is 48 and the value of amount % 10 is 3 (the value of *amount* is 2693). The yellow arrow moves to the next statement inside the *do* loop.

13 On the Debug toolbar, click the Step Into button. The debugger runs the current statement:

```
char digit = Convert.ToChar(digitCode);
```

The value of *digit* changes to '3' in the Locals window. The locals window shows *char* values using both the underlying numeric value (in this case 51) and also the character representation ('3'). The yellow arrow moves to the next statement inside the *do* loop. Note that in the Locals window, the value of *current* is "".

14 On the Debug toolbar, click the Step Into button. The debugger runs the current statement:

```
current = current + digit;
```

The value of *current* changes to "3" in the Locals window. The yellow arrow moves to the next statement inside the *do* loop.

15 On the Debug toolbar, click the Step Into button. The debugger runs the current statement:

```
steps.Text += current + "\r\n";
```

In the Locals window, the value of *amount* is 2693. The yellow arrow moves to the next statement inside the *do* loop.

16 On the Debug toolbar, click the Step Into button. The debugger runs the current statement:

```
amount /= 10;
```

The value of *amount* changes to 269 in the Locals window. The yellow arrow moves to the next statement in the *do* loop, which is the part that tests the continuation condition. Notice that the *digitCode* and *digit* variables have disappeared from the Locals window. This is because these two variables are declared inside the *do* loop and, therefore, scoped to the *do* loop. They are no longer in scope. The continuation condition is as follows:

```
while (amount != 0);
```

The value of *amount* is 269, and 269 != 0 is true, so the *do* loop should iterate again.

17 Click the Step Into button on the Debug toolbar. The debugger runs the current statement:

```
while (amount != 0);
```

As predicted, this continuation condition is true, so the yellow arrow has jumped to re-run the first statement inside the *do* loop. The *digit-Code* and *digit* variables are now back in scope and have reappeared in the Locals window.

18 On the Debug toolbar, click the Step Into button 17 more times and watch the values of the local variables change in the Locals window.

In the Locals window, the value of *amount* is now zero and the value of *current* is "2693". The yellow arrow is on the continuation condition of the *do* loop:

```
while (amount != 0);
```

The value of *amount* is now 0, and 0 != 0 is false, so the *do* loop should terminate.

19 On the Debug toolbar, click the Step Into button. The debugger runs the current statement:

```
while (amount != 0);
```

As predicted, this expression is now false, the *do* loop terminates, and the yellow arrow moves to the right brace that ends the *showSteps_Click* method.

20 On the Debug toolbar, click the Step Into button. The application window opens, displaying the four steps used to create a string representation of 2693: "3", "93", "693", and "2693".

21 Click Close. You return to the Visual Studio .NET programming environment.

Congratulations! You have successfully written meaningful *while* and *do* statements and used the Visual Studio .NET debugger to step through the *do* statement.

If you want to continue to the next chapter

■ Keep Visual Studio .NET running and turn to Chapter 6.

If you want to exit Visual Studio .NET now

■ On the File menu, click Exit. If you see a Save dialog box, click Yes.

Chapter 5 Quick Reference

To	Do this
Add an amount to a variable	Use the compound addition operator. For example: ```variable += amount;```
Subtract an amount from a variable	Use the compound subtraction operator. For example: ```variable -= amount;```
Increment a variable by one	Use the increment operator. For example: ```variable++;```
Decrement a variable by one	Use the decrement operator. For example: ```variable--;```

Run one or more statements while a continuation condition is true	Use a *while* statement. For example:
	
	```Int I = 0;```
	```while (I != 10)```
	```{```
	``` Console.WriteLine(i);```
	``` i++;```
	```}```
	
	Alternatively, use a *for* statement. For example:
	
	```for (int i = 0; i != 10; i++)```
	```{```
	``` Console.WriteLine(i);```
	```}```

Run one or more statements one or more times	Use a *do* statement. For example:
	
	```Int I = 0;```
	```do```
	```{```
	``` Console.WriteLine(i);```
	``` i++;```
	```}```
	```while (I != 10);```

Managing Errors and Exceptions

In this chapter, you will learn how to:

■ Use the *try*, *catch*, and *finally* statements to handle exceptions.

■ Control integer overflow using the *checked* and *unchecked* keywords.

■ Raise exceptions from your own methods using the *throw* keyword.

■ Trap exceptions in the Microsoft Visual Studio .NET debugger.

In Chapters 2 through 5, you've learned almost all the core Microsoft Visual C# statements you need to know to read and write methods; declare variables; use operators to create values; write *if* and *switch* statements to selectively run code; and write *while*, *for*, and *do* statements to repeatedly run code. However, the chapters you've completed so far haven't considered the possibility that sometimes things go wrong. They can, and they will. In this final chapter of Part 1, you'll learn how C# throws exceptions to signal that an error has occurred and how to use the *try*, *catch*, and *finally* statements to catch and handle the errors that these exceptions represent. By the end of this chapter, you'll have a solid foundation in C#, which you will use in Part 2.

Coping with Errors

It's a fact of life that bad things sometimes happen. Tires get punctured, batteries run down, and screwdrivers are never where you left them. This observation is just as true in programming as it is in life. Unfortunately, one common way of coping with this problem is to arrange for each method to set a special global variable when the method fails. Then, after each call to a method, you check the global variable to see whether the method failed. This solution is very poor because of the following reasons:

- The main program logic becomes intertwined with alternating code to check and handle the errors. The program quickly becomes hard to understand.

- The error checking and handling code is typically very repetitive and can easily double the size of the program. A large program is harder to understand than a small program simply because it's larger. Duplicate code is always a warning sign.

- The error codes, such as –1 , are not inherently meaningful. What does –1 mean? Integer error codes don't describe the errors they represent. They're very programmatic. Once again, the program becomes harder to understand and maintain.

- All the methods typically have to agree to set the global variable to a value that is not used by any other method. In effect, every method becomes tightly linked to every other method. Programs become a maintenance nightmare.

- It's just too easy to ignore the return value and assume the method will work. Many programmers don't like to read documentation, or perhaps the method isn't documented.

For these reasons, C# and most object-oriented languages don't handle errors in this way. It's just too painful. They use *exceptions* instead. If you want to write robust C# programs, you need to know about exceptions.

▶ **Important**   The Microsoft .NET Framework classes use exceptions to report errors. If you want to program in C# (or indeed in any language that supports the .NET common language runtime), you have to know about exceptions. Exceptions are the object-oriented solution to error handling.

Trying Code and Catching Exceptions

The core idea in exception handling is to separate the code that implements the main flow of the program from the error handling code. When these two parts are separated, they both immediately become easier to understand because they're no longer intertwined. To write exception-aware programs, you need to do two things.

First, write your code inside a *try* block (*try* is a keyword). You *try* to complete all the statements inside the *try* block, and if none of the statements generates an exception, they all run, one after the other, to completion.

Second, you write one or more *catch* handlers (*catch* is a keyword) immediately after the *try* block. If any one of the statements inside the *try* block generates an exception, the normal left-to-right, top-to-bottom flow of the program halts, and control transfers directly to an appropriate *catch* handler. (Make sure there is one.) Here's an example:

```
try
{
    int lhs = System.Int32.Parse(lhsOperand.Text);
    int rhs = System.Int32.Parse(rhsOperand.Text);
    int answer = doCalculation(lhs, rhs);
    result.Text = answer.ToString();
}
catch (System.FormatException caught)
{
    // Handle the exception
    ⋮
}
```

The *System.Int32.Parse* method attempts to convert its string argument into an integer. For example, "99" is converted into 99. What should *System.Int32.Parse* return when passed a string in the wrong format, such as "Tommy Trewblew"? The answer is that there is no correct answer. Whatever value it returns (–1 , for example) to indicate that the format is not valid would be indistinguishable from a genuine non-error reason for returning that value (from converting "–1 " for example). So *System.Int32.Parse* doesn't return at all. Instead, it generates *FormatException* to represent the parse failure. The application then "jumps" directly to the *catch* handler that catches *FormatException* objects, which, in this case, is the one directly underneath the *try* block.

▶ **Note** If a statement in a *try* block generates an exception, it does not return. The remaining statements inside the *try* block are not run. In effect, the program is now in reverse gear. If it can't find a *catch* handler in the current method, the current method terminates and returns to the calling method. Next, the program looks here for a *catch* handler. If it finds one, it runs it. If not, this method also terminates, returning to its calling method, and so on. The program continues backing up in this way until it finds an appropriate *catch* handler or drops out of *Main* when the common language runtime catches the exception and starts asking you questions about which debugger you want to use.

Using Multiple *catch* Handlers

Of course, different errors throw different kinds of exceptions to represent different kinds of failure. For example, suppose you use a method called *doCalculation* that can throw a *DivideByZeroException*. To cope with this, you could write multiple *catch* handlers, one after the other, like this:

```
try
{
    int lhs = System.Int32.Parse(lhsOperand.Text);
    int rhs = System.Int32.Parse(rhsOperand.Text);
    int answer = doCalculation(lhs, rhs);
    result.Text = answer.ToString();
}
catch (System.FormatException caught)
{
    //...
}
catch (System.DivideByZeroException caught)
{
    //...
}
```

The really great thing about this *try/catch* arrangement (apart from the separation already mentioned) is that the common language runtime directs the program to the correct *catch* handler for the exception based on its type. You don't have to explicitly connect the exception to the *catch* handler—it's done automatically.

Writing a General *catch* Handler

But it gets even better. If you don't want to write a specific *catch* handler for each different kind of exception (which could be very tedious because there are many different kinds of exceptions), you can write one *catch* handler that will catch every exception (even exceptions you weren't aware of!). Consider this example:

```
try
{
    int lhs = System.Int32.Parse(lhsOperand.Text);
    int rhs = System.Int32.Parse(rhsOperand.Text);
    int answer = doCalculation(lhs, rhs);
    result.Text = answer.ToString();
}
catch (System.Exception caught) // this is the general catch handler
{
    //...
}
```

> ▶ **Tip**   An alternative syntax for the general *catch* handler is *catch { ... }*. In this
> case, you do not need to specify the type of the exception.

Here is one other thing you ought to know about *catch* handlers: more than one handler could match your exception. In this case, the first one found that matches your exception is used and the others are ignored. You can use this to your advantage. You can place specialist *catch* handlers above a general *catch* handler after a *try* block. If none of the specialist *catch* handlers matches the exception, the general *catch* handler will. Don't put the general *catch* handler first, though! Enough talk—it's time for you to try it for yourself.

Write a *try/catch* statement

1 Start Visual Studio .NET.

2 Open the MathsOperators project, located in the \Microsoft Press\Visual C# Step By Step\Chapter 6\MathsOperators folder in your My Documents folder. You first saw this program in Chapter 2. It was used to demonstrate the different arithmetic operators.

The MathsOperators project opens. Before running this application you will first reset the Exception settings of Visual Studio so that the debugger does not automatically start when an exception is thrown. In later exercises in this chapter, you will change these settings back and use the debugger.

3 On the Debug menu, click Exceptions. The Exceptions dialog box opens.

4 In the Exceptions list, select the Common Language Runtime Exceptions category.

5 Under When The Exception Is Thrown, select Continue.

6 Under If The Exception Is Not Handled, select Continue.

7 Click OK. The Exceptions dialog box closes.

8 On the Debug menu, click Start.

▶ **Tip**   The shortcut key for Start is F5.

Visual Studio .NET builds and runs the Windows application. The Exceptions Form appears.

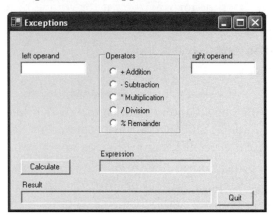

You are now going to deliberately enter some text that is not valid in the Left Operand text box. This operation will demonstrate the lack of robustness in the current version of the program.

9   Enter **John** in the Left Operand text box, and then click Calculate. The application shuts down and you return to the Visual Studio .NET programming environment. The error in the text you entered in the Left Operand text box has caused the application to fail.

Read the diagnostic messages in the Output window. (If the Output window is not visible, point to Other Windows on the View menu, and click Output.) You will see a number of messages about various DLLs being loaded by the runtime. Below these, you will see these messages:

```
An unhandled exception of type 'System.FormatException'
 occurred in mscorlib.dll

Additional information: Input string was not in a correct format.

Unhandled Exception: System.FormatException: Input string was
 not in a correct format.
   at System.Number.ParseInt32(String s, NumberStyles style,
     NumberFormatInfo info)
   ⋮
   at Methods.Form1.calculate_Click(Object sender, EventArgs e) in
     C:\Visual C# Step By Step\Chapter 6\MathsOperators\Form1.cs:line
 257
   ⋮
```

From this text, you can ascertain that the exception was thrown by the call to *System.Int32.Parse* inside the *calculate_Click* method.

10 Add a *try* block around the four statements inside the *calculate_Click* method exactly as follows:

```
try
{
    int lhs = System.Int32.Parse(lhsOperand.Text);
    int rhs = System.Int32.Parse(rhsOperand.Text);
    int answer = doCalculation(lhs, rhs);
    result.Text = answer.ToString();
}
```

Add a *catch* block after this new *try* block, exactly as follows:

```
catch (System.FormatException caught)
{
    result.Text = caught.Message;
}
```

This *catch* handler catches the *FormatException* thrown by *System.Int32.Parse*, and then writes its *Message* property to the *Text* property of the *result* text box at the bottom of the form.

11 On the Debug menu, click Start. Visual Studio .NET rebuilds and runs the application. You will now enter the same values that previously caused the application to fail.

12 Type **John** in the Left Operand text box, and then click Calculate. The *catch* handler successfully catches the *FormatException*, and the message "Input string was not in a correct format." is written to the Result text box. The application is now a little more robust.

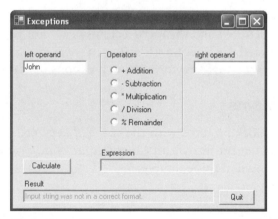

13 Click Quit. You return to the Visual Studio .NET programming environment.

Using Checked and Unchecked Integer Arithmetic

In Chapter 2, you learned how to use binary arithmetic operators such as +
and * on the primitive data types such as *int* and *double*. You also saw that
the primitive data types have a fixed size. For example, a C# *int* is exactly 32
bits. Because *int* has a fixed size, you know exactly what the integer range is:
it is -2^{32} to $2^{32}-1$.

> ▶ **Tip**   If you want to determine the minimum or maximum value of *int* in code,
> you can use the *System.Int32.MinValue* or *System.Int32.MaxValue* fields.

The fixed size of the *int* type creates a problem: what happens if you write an
int expression whose answer is either too large or too small to fit inside *int*? For
example, what is the value of *System.Int32.MaxValue + 1*? It can't be larger
than *System.Int32.MaxValue* because, if it were, the *System.Int32.MaxValue*
would not be the maximum value of *int*. The answer is that, by default, integer
arithmetic is not checked and silently overflows. In other words, you get the
wrong answer. (In fact, *System.Int32.MaxValue + 1* wraps to the largest negative value.)

In many cases, the possibility of integer overflow is acceptable because you'll
know (or think you know) that your *int* values won't reach their limits. However, you can use the *checked* and *unchecked* keywords to selectively turn on
and off integer arithmetic overflow checking. When integer arithmetic is
checked, any overflow is detected and the incorrect answer is not returned—
because no answer is returned. Instead, an *OverflowException* is thrown. You
can use the *checked* and *unchecked* keywords on expressions or statements.

Writing *checked* Statements

A *checked statement* is a block prefixed with the *checked* keyword. All integer
arithmetic in a checked statement throws an *OverflowException* rather than
silently overflowing, as shown in this example:

```
int number = System.Int32.MaxValue;
checked
{
    int willThrow = number++;
    Console.WriteLine("this won't be reached");
}
```

> ▶ **Important**   Only integer arithmetic directly inside the *checked* block is
> checked. For example, if one of the checked statements is a method call, the
> checking does not encapsulate the method call.

You can also use the *unchecked* keyword to create an *unchecked* block statement. All integer arithmetic in an *unchecked* block is not checked. For example:

```
int number = System.Int32.MaxValue;
unchecked
{
    int wontThrow = number++;
    Console.WriteLine("this will be reached");
}
```

▶ **Important** You cannot use the *checked* and *unchecked* keywords to control floating point (non-integer) arithmetic. The *checked* and *unchecked* keywords control only integer arithmetic. Floating point arithmetic never throws exceptions—not even when you divide by 0.0.

Writing Checked Expressions

You can also use the *checked* and *unchecked* keywords to control overflow checking on integer expressions by prefixing just the individual parenthesized expression with the *checked* or *unchecked* keyword, as shown in this example:

```
int wontThrow = unchecked(System.Int32.MaxValue + 1);
int willThrow = checked(System.Int32.MaxValue + 1);
```

The compound operators, such as += and − = , and the increment (++) and decrement (−−) operators are arithmetic operators and can be controlled using the *checked* and *unchecked* keywords. Remember, x += y; is the same as x = x + y;.

▶ **Tip** You can also control the overflow checking of whole source files from the command line. The */checked+* option turns on overflow checking as the default so that only unchecked statements and expressions are unchecked.

Use checked expressions

1 On the Debug menu, click Exceptions. The Exceptions dialog box opens.

2 Select Common Language Runtime Exceptions.

3 Under When The Exception Is Thrown, select Continue (if it is not already selected).

4 Under If The Exception Is Not Handled, select Break Into The Debugger and then click OK.

5 On the Debug menu, click Start. Visual Studio .NET builds and runs the Windows application. You will now attempt to multiply two very large values.

6

Errors and Exceptions

6 Type **9876543** in the Left Operand text box, type **9876543** in the Right Operand text box, select the Multiplication option under Operators, and then click Calculate. The value –1 195595903 appears in the Result text box on the form. This is a negative value, which cannot possibly be correct. This value is the result of a multiplication operation that silently overflowed the 32-bit limit of the *int* type.

7 Click Quit. You return to the Visual Studio .NET programming environment.

8 In the Code window, locate the *multiplyValues* method:

```
private int multiplyValues(int lhs, int rhs)
{
    expression.Text = lhs.ToString() + " * " + rhs.ToString();
    return lhs * rhs;
}
```

This is the multiplication operation that is silently overflowing.

9 Edit the *return* statement so that the return value is checked. The *multiplyValues* method should look exactly as follows:

```
private int multiplyValues(int lhs, int rhs)
{
    expression.Text = lhs.ToString() + " * " + rhs.ToString();
    return checked(lhs * rhs);
}
```

The multiplication is now checked and will throw an *OverflowException* rather than silently returning the wrong answer. The question now is whether the program contains a *catch* handler to catch this new type of exception. It would be a lengthy task to find the answer by reading the entire program. Fortunately, there is a better way. You can set the Exception options in Visual Studio .NET so that an unhandled exception automatically triggers the debugger.

10 On the Debug menu, click Start. Visual Studio .NET builds and runs the Windows application. You will now repeat the same arithmetic operation to force an overflow.

11 Type **9876543** in the Left Operand text box, type **9876543** in the Right Operand text box, select the Multiplication option under Operators, and then click Calculate. You return to the Visual Studio .NET programming environment and the following message box appears. This message tells you that a statement in the code has thrown an unhandled *OverflowException*.

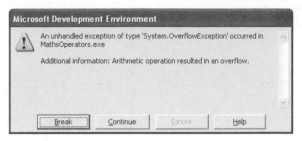

12 Click Break. The message box closes. You are now viewing the Code window in debug mode. The yellow arrow denoting the current debug line is to the left of the return statement in the *multiplyValues* method:

```
return checked(lhs * rhs);
```

This is the statement causing the overflow, which now results in an *OverflowException* because the multiplication is checked. The next step is to catch this exception.

▶ **Tip**   Move the cursor over the variable *rhs* in this statement. A tip will appear telling you that the current value of *rhs* is 9876543.

13 On the Debug menu, click Stop Debugging. If the Debug window is open, you can also click the Stop Debugging button.

14 In the Code window, locate the *calculate_Click* method.

15 Add the following *catch* handler immediately after the existing *catch* handler in the *calculate_Click* method:

```
catch (System.OverflowException caught)
{
    result.Text = caught.Message;
}
```

16 On the Debug menu, click Start. Visual Studio .NET builds and runs the Windows application. Once again, enter the same large values that cause an *OverflowException* to occur. The Exception settings have not changed, but the program now handles the *OverflowException* so the debugger should not automatically start.

17 Type **9876543** in the Left Operand text box, type **9876543** in the Right Operand text box, select the Multiplication option under Operators, and then click Calculate. The second *catch* handler successfully catches the *OverflowException* and the debugger does not start. A diagnostic message is written to the Result text box.

Errors and Exceptions

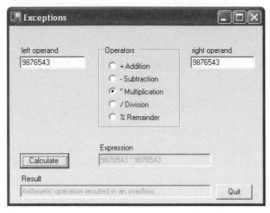

18 Click Quit. You return to the Visual Studio .NET programming environment.

Throwing Exceptions

Suppose you are implementing a method called *monthName* that accepts a single *int* argument and returns the name of the corresponding month. For example, *monthName(1)* will return "January." The question is: what should the method return when the integer argument is less than 1 or greater than 12? What is the name of month −16 or month 1356? It's an unanswerable question! There is no universally agreed to string that means, "I'm not the name of a month." The best answer is that the method shouldn't return anything at all; it should throw an exception. The .NET Framework class libraries contain lots of exception classes specifically designed for throwing exceptions. Most of the time, you will find that one of these classes will describe your exceptional condition and you can use it. (If not, you can easily create your own exception class, but you need to know a bit more before you can do that.) In this case, the existing .NET Framework *System.ArgumentOutOfRangeException* class is just right:

```
public static string monthName(int month)
{
    switch (month)
    {
        case 1 :
            return "January";
        case 2 :
            return "February";
        :
        case 12 :
            return "December";
        default :
```

```
        throw new System.ArgumentOutOfRangeException("Bad month");
    }
}
```

The following statement is an example of a *throw* statement:

```
throw new System.ArgumentOutOfRangeException("Bad month");
```

A *throw* statement has two parts. The first part is the *throw* keyword. You use the *throw* keyword to throw the exception object. The *throw* keyword is well-named. The second part is the object you're throwing. This object might be an object you've already created or an expression that creates a new object. This example uses an expression that creates a new object. The following expression is the part that creates an *ArgumentOutOfRange* object (which lives in the System namespace) containing the message "Bad month":

```
new System.ArgumentOutOfRangeException("Bad month")
```

This is an example of a *constructor method*. Constructors are covered in detail in Chapter 7.

Throw your own exception

1 On the Debug menu, click Start. Visual Studio .NET builds and runs the Windows application.

2 Click Calculate without selecting an operator option.

3 Type **24** in the Left Operand text box, type **24** in the Right Operand text box, and then click Calculate. The value zero appears in the Result text box.

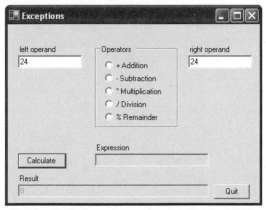

The fact that you have not selected an operator option is not immediately obvious. It would be better to write a diagnostic message in the Result text box.

4 Click Quit. You return to the Visual Studio .NET programming environment.

5 In the Code window, locate the *doCalculation* method. The *doCalculation* method should be exactly as follows:

```
private int doCalculation(int lhs, int rhs)
{
    int result = 0;
    if (addition.Checked)
        result = addValues(lhs, rhs);
    else if (subtraction.Checked)
        result = subtractValues(lhs, rhs);
    else if (multiplication.Checked)
        result = multiplyValues(lhs, rhs);
    else if (division.Checked)
        result = divideValues(lhs, rhs);
    else if (remainder.Checked)
        result = remainderValues(lhs, rhs);
    return result;
}
```

The addition, subtraction, multiplication, division, and remainder variables are the fields that implement the operator option on the form. Each one has a *Checked* Boolean property that holds the value true if the option is selected. (This cascading *if* statement cannot be replaced by a *switch* statement because each *if* statement tests a different condition.) If none of the options are selected, none of the *if* statements will be true and the method will return a result that is initialized to zero. You could try to solve the problem by adding one more *else* statement to the *if-else* cascade, to write a message to the Result text box, as follows:

```
if (addition.Checked)
    result = addValues(lhs, rhs);
    ⋮
else if (remainder.Checked)
    result = remainderValues(lhs, rhs);
else
    result.Text = "no operator selected";
```

However, this solution is not a good idea. With this code, you would have two methods in the program that write diagnostic messages to the Result text box—*calculate_Click* and *doCalculation*. It is better to separate the detection and signaling of an error from the catching and handling of that error. (Another reason this code wouldn't work is because *result* is also the name of a local variable.) Instead, add one more *else* statement to the *if-else* cascade and throw an *Invalid-OperationException* exactly as follows:

```
if (addition.Checked)
    result = addValues(lhs, rhs);
```

```
    ⋮
else if (remainder.Checked)
    result = remainderValues(lhs, rhs);
else
    throw new InvalidOperationException("no operator selected");
```

You will now change the Exception settings so that, when this exception is thrown, the debugger will start, regardless of whether the exception is handled.

6   On the Debug menu, click Exceptions. The Exceptions dialog box opens.

7   Select Common Language Runtime Exceptions from the list.

8   Under When The Exception Is Thrown, select Break Into The Debugger.

9   Under If The Exception Is Not Handled, select Continue.

10   Click OK. The Exceptions dialog box closes. Now when you don't select an operator, the final *else* statement will throw an exception and the debugger will automatically start.

11   On the Debug menu, click Start. Visual Studio .NET builds and runs the Windows application.

You will now run the application again and click Calculate without selecting an arithmetic operator option. This will cause an *InvalidOperationException*, which will start the debugger.

12   Type **24** in the Left Operand text box, type **24** in the Right Operand text box, and then click Calculate. You return to the Visual Studio .NET programming environment and the following message box appears. This message tells you that an *InvalidOperationException* has been thrown.

13   Click Break. The message box closes. You are now viewing the Code pane in debug mode. The yellow arrow is positioned on the last statement of the *doCalculation* method, which is called from the *calculate_Click* method.

14   On the Debug menu, click Stop Debugging.

> ▶ **Tip**   If the Debug window is open, you can also click the Stop Debugging button. Alternatively, you can use the shortcut key Shift+F11.

Now that you have written a *throw* statement and verified that it throws an exception, you will write a *catch* handler to catch this exception.

Catch your own exception

1   In the Code window, locate the *calculate_Click* method.

2   Add the following catch handler immediately below the existing two catch handlers in the *calculate_Click* method:

```
catch (System.InvalidOperationException caught)
{
    result.Text = caught.Message;
}
```

This code will catch the *InvalidOperationException* that is thrown when no operator option is selected. First, you will reset the Exception settings so that, when the exception is thrown, it does not automatically start the debugger.

3   On the Debug menu, click Exceptions. The Exceptions dialog box appears.

4   Under When The Exception Is Thrown, select Continue.

5   Under If The Exception Is Not Handled, select Continue.

6   Click OK. The Exceptions dialog box closes.

7   On the Debug menu, click Start. Visual Studio .NET builds and runs the Windows application.

You will now *not* select an operator option to see the *catch* handler you have just written catch the *InvalidOperationException*, display the diagnostic message in the Result text box, and not fail.

8   Type **24** in the Left Operand text box, type **24** in the Right Operand text box, and then click Calculate.

9   Click Quit.

The application is now a lot more robust than it was.

However, several exceptions could still arise that would not be caught and might cause the application to fail. For example, if you attempt to divide by zero, an unhandled *DivideByZeroException* will be thrown. A poor way to solve this would be to write an ever larger number of *catch* handlers inside the *calculate_Click* method, all containing exactly the same statement. A better solution is to replace all the *catch* handlers with a single, general *catch* handler.

10 In the Code window, locate the *calculate_Click* method.

11 Replace all three of the *catch* handlers with the following single *catch* handler:

```
catch (System.Exception caught)
{
    result.Text = caught.Message;
}
```

This *catch* handler will catch all exceptions, whatever their specific type.

12 On the Debug menu, click Start. Visual Studio .NET builds and runs the Windows application.

You will now attempt some calculations known to cause exceptions and confirm that they are all caught by the general *catch* handler.

13 Type **24** in the Left Operand text box, type **24** in the Right Operand text box, and then click Calculate. Confirm that the diagnostic message "No Operator Selected" appears in the Result text box.

14 Type **John** in the Left Operand text box, and then click Calculate. Confirm that the diagnostic message "Input String Was Not In A Correct Format" appears in the Result text box.

15 Type **24** in the Left Operand text box, type **0** in the Right Operand text box, select the Divide option under Operators, and then click Calculate. Confirm that the diagnostic message "Attempted To Divide By Zero" appears in the Result text box.

16 Click Quit.

Writing a *finally* Block

One of the hardest things to remember about exceptions is that, when they're thrown, they cause the program to "jump," which means you can't guarantee that a statement will always run when the previous statement finishes. The previous code statement might not finish. It might not return at all. It might throw an exception. Look at the following example. It's very easy to assume the call to *reader.Close* will always occur. After all, it's right there in the code.

```
TextReader reader = src.OpenText();
string line;
while ((line = reader.ReadLine()) != null)
{
    source.Text += line + "\n";
}
reader.Close();
```

Most of the time, it's not a problem if one particular statement is not run. But sometimes it is a problem. Sometimes the statement releases a resource that was acquired in a previous statement. This example is just such a case. If the call to *src.OpenText* succeeds, then it acquires a resource (a file handle) and you must make sure that you call *reader.Close* to release the resource. If you don't, sooner or later (probably sooner) you'll run out of file handles.

This acquire-and-release pairing also happens in real life. For example, suppose you rent a video from a video rental store. If you don't return the video, the video store probably won't let you rent another one next time. Or perhaps the store lets you continue to rent even though you don't return any of the videos. In this case, you will eventually have a house full of videos, the store will be empty, and you will have some hefty rental charges to pay. The moral of the story is that it is always a good idea to return resources when your application has finished with them.

The way to ensure a statement is always run, whether or not an exception has been thrown, is to write that statement inside a *finally* block (*finally* is a keyword). You can only write a *finally* block immediately after a *try* block or immediately after the last *catch* handler after a *try* block. As long as the program enters the *try* block associated with a *finally* block, the *finally* block will always be run. So the solution to the *reader.Close* problem is as follows:

```
TextReader reader = null;
try
{
    reader = src.OpenText();
    string line;
    while ((line = reader.ReadLine()) != null)
    {
        source.Text += line + "\n";
    }
}
finally
{
    if (reader != null)
    {
        reader.Close();
    }
}
```

You'll see another way to solve this problem in Chapter 13.

If you want to continue to the next chapter

■ Keep Visual Studio .NET running and turn to Chapter 7.

If you want to exit Visual Studio .NET now

■ On the File menu, click Exit. If you see a Save dialog box, click Yes.

Chapter 6 Quick Reference

To	Do this

Throw an exception	Use a *throw* statement. For example:
	
	``
	throw new FormatException(source);
	``

Catch a specific exception	Write a *catch* handler that catches the specific exception class. For example:
	
	``
	try
	{
	    ⋮
	}
	catch (FormatException caught)
	{
	    ⋮
	}
	``

Catch all exceptions in a single *catch* handler	Write a *catch* handler that catches the Exception class. For example:
	
	``
	try
	{
	    ⋮
	}
	catch (Exception caught)
	{
	    ⋮
	}
	``

Ensure that some code will always be run, even if an exception is thrown	Write that code inside a *finally* block. For example:
	
	``
	Try
	{
	    ⋮
	}
	finally
	{
	    // always run
	}
	``

Use the Visual Studio .NET debugger to monitor exceptions as a program runs	On the Debug menu, click Exceptions. In the Exceptions dialog box, select the Break Into The Debugger options.

Understanding the C# Language

Chapter

7

Creating and Managing Classes and Objects

In this chapter, you will learn how to:

■ Group related methods and data in a class.

■ Control the accessibility of a class's members by using the *public* and *private* keywords.

■ Create objects by using the *new* keyword and a constructor.

■ Write and call your own constructors.

■ Use the static keyword to create methods and data that can be shared by all instances of the same class.

In Part 1, you learned how to declare variables, use operators to create values, call methods, and write all the statements you need when implementing a method. You now know enough to progress to the next important stage of combining methods and data into your own classes. The Microsoft .NET Framework contains thousands of classes, but you'll still write many classes yourself. The chapters in Part 2 provide you with all you need to know to create your own classes.

What Is Classification?

The root word of classification is class. When you form a class, you systematically arrange information into something meaningful. This arranging is an act of classification and is something that everyone does—not just programmers. For example, all cars share common *behaviors* (they can be steered, stopped, accelerated, and so on) and common *attributes* (they have a steering wheel, an engine, and so on). You use the word *car* to mean all the objects that share these common behaviors and attributes. As long as everyone agrees on what a word means, it all works well; you can express complex but precise ideas in a concise form.

Without classification, it's hard to imagine how people could think or communicate at all; classification is a fundamental skill that all people possess. It's one of the things that makes us people. Given that classification is so deeply ingrained into the way we think and communicate, it makes sense to try to write programs by classifying the different concepts inherent in a problem and its solution, and then modeling these classes in a programming language. This is exactly what modern object-oriented programming languages, such as Microsoft Visual C#, allow you to do; they allow you to define classes that combine behavior (methods) and attributes (data).

What Is Encapsulation?

Encapsulation is another of those long words that consultants use. The root word of encapsulation is capsule; encapsulation means putting things into a capsule. There are two important uses of encapsulation:

- To combine methods and data inside a class; in other words, to support classification.
- To control the accessibility of the methods and data; in other words, to control the use of the class.

The *class* is the programming construct that provides the syntax and semantics to support these two fundamental uses. Here is a C# class called *Circle* that contains one method (to calculate the circle's area) and one piece of data (the circle's radius):

```
class Circle
{
    double Area()
    {
        return 3.141592 * radius * radius;
    }
    double radius;
}
```

The keyword *class* is followed by the name of the concept you are classifying, which is followed by an opening and closing brace that form the body of the class (in the same way as the opening and closing brace of a method form the body of the method). The body of a class contains methods (such as *Area*) and variables (such as *radius*). You've already seen how to declare variables in Chapter 2 and how to write methods in Chapter 3; in fact, there's almost no new syntax here.

▶ **Note**   The proper name for a variable declared in the scope of a class is a *field*.

Controlling Accessibility

Unfortunately, the *Circle* class is currently of no practical use because we have not yet considered the second key aspect of encapsulation: accessibility. After you have encapsulated your methods and data inside a class, the class forms a boundary. Anything between the braces is on the inside, whereas anything before the opening brace or after the closing brace is on the outside. You can use the *public* and *private* keywords to control whether the methods and fields are accessible from the outside:

- A method or field is said to be *private* if it is accessible only from the inside of the class. To declare that a method or field is *private*, you write the keyword *private* before its declaration.

- A method or field is said to be *public* if it is accessible from both the inside and the outside of the class. To declare that a method or field is *public*, you write the keyword *public* before its declaration.

Here is the *Circle* class again. This time *Area* is declared as a *public* method and *radius* is declared as a *private* field:

```
class Circle
{
    public double Area()
    {
        return 3.141592 * radius * radius;
    }
    private double radius;
}
```

▶ **Note**   C++ programmers should note that there is no colon after the *public* or *private* keywords. You must repeat the keyword on every declaration.

If you don't declare a method or field as *public* or *private*, it defaults to *private*. This is why the first *Circle* class was of no practical use; it had no *public* members.

Note that *radius* is declared as a *private* field; it is not accessible from outside the class. However, *radius* is accessible from inside the *Circle* class. This is why the *Area* method can (and does) access the *radius* field; *Area* is inside the *Circle* class, so the body of *Area* has access to *radius*.

▶ **Important** Don't declare two *public* class members whose names differ only in case. If you do, your class will not conform to the Common Language Specification (CLS), which is important for language interoperability. However, it's perfectly okay to declare two class members whose names differ only in case when only one of the members is *public*.

Abstract Data Types

You make use of abstractions every minute of the day. You're so good at abstracting that, unless you think about it, you're not even aware you do it. When you drive a car, you turn the wheel with your hands and press the pedals with your feet but, unless you are a mechanic, you are probably not aware of exactly what is going on under the hood to make the car go in the direction or at the speed that you want. The pedals and wheel form an "interface" that lets you provide enough information to the electronics and other engine parts in the car to let it know what you want to do, and the car does it.

Abstract data types are just like this. C# lets you create classes that contain *private* fields containing *private* data and *private* methods performing *private* calculations. You cannot access these fields or methods from outside the class. However, to be useful, the class must provide some form of "interface" for communicating. This interface is a set of *public* methods that applications can call. These methods define the functionality of the call to those applications. The *public* methods can use other *private* methods and access the *private* data to do their work, but the user does not care about this as long as the methods do what they say they will do. Because the *mechanisms* used by the *public* methods are private, or hidden, the developer implementing the class has complete freedom to perform computations or access data in whatever way he or she sees fit. What is more, a later version of the class can completely change these internal details (for example, the class might use some super new algorithm that is 100 times faster than the original), but as long as the public "interface" does not change (the same set of *public* methods are available), all existing applications that reference this class will still work.

Working with Constructors and the *new* Keyword

A *constructor* is a method of a class used to create a new instance of the class. To see why constructors are required, let's compare the ways in which variables of primitive types and class types are declared and initialized.

You can use the name of your class to declare a variable. The syntax is exactly the same as when you declare a variable of a primitive type (such as *int*); the name of the type on the left is followed by the name of the variable and a semicolon:

```
int i;
Circle c;
```

As you'll recall, you can use the value of a variable only after you've made sure that the variable definitely has a value (the definite assignment rule):

```
int i;
Console.WriteLine(i); // error: use of unassigned local variable
```

Quite reasonably, this rule holds for all variables, whatever their type:

```
Circle c;
Console.WriteLine(c); // error: use of unassigned local variable
```

Of course, it's easy to ensure that *i* definitely has a value: you just assign it a literal value, such as 42:

- You can initialize *i* to a value as you declare it:

  ```
  int i = 42;
  Console.WriteLine(i);
  ```

- You can assign *i* to a value after you declare it:

  ```
  int i;
  i = 42;
  Console.WriteLine(i);
  ```

But now there is a problem: you can't ensure that a variable of type *Circle* named *c* is definitely assigned by using this solution because *c* is a *Circle* and there is no literal syntax to assign a *Circle* value directly. Only the primitive types have literal values. What you have to do is use the *new* keyword and call *Circle*'s constructor:

```
new Circle()
```

This is what you write to create a *Circle* object in much the same way as 42 is what you write to create an *int* value.

▶ **Note**   An instance of a class is called an *object*, whereas an instance of a primitive type (such as *int*) is called a *value*. The distinction is important, as you'll see in Chapter 8.

The result is as follows:

■ You can initialize *c* to an object as you declare it:

```
Circle c = new Circle();
Console.WriteLine(c);
```

■ You can assign an object to *c* after you declare it:

```
Circle c;
c = new Circle();
Console.WriteLine(c);
```

A constructor is a special method whose name is always the same as the name of its class. The purpose of a constructor is to initialize the fields of a newly created object. If you don't write a constructor for your class, the compiler writes one for you. In other words, the original *Circle* class, which appeared to contain only one method and one field, actually contained an invisible constructor as well. It's as if the class were written like this:

```
class Circle
{
    public Circle()
    {
        radius = 0.0;
    }
    public double Area()
    {
        return 3.141592 * radius * radius;
    }
    private double radius;
}
```

The compiler-generated constructor is *public*, has no return type (not even *void*), takes no arguments, sets any numeric fields to 0, sets any Boolean fields to *false*, and sets any reference fields to *null* (reference types are covered in Chapter 8). The lack of a return type on a constructor might seem strange. However, the name of a class is the name of a type, so you can think of the constructor as specifying the name of a method *and* the return type.

After *c* is initialized or assigned an object, you can call its *Area* method by using the familiar dot notation:

```
c.Area()
```

This is the only way you can call *Area*. The *Area* method is declared inside the *Circle* class, and that means that *Area* must be called on *Circle*. This syntax is how the body of the *Area* method is able to refer to its fields; the fields implicitly refer to the fields of the *Circle* object that the *Area* method is called on.

Overloading Constructors

You're almost home but not quite. You can now declare a *Circle* variable, set it to a newly created *Circle* object, and then call its *Area* method:

```
Circle c = new Circle();
Console.WriteLine(c.Area());
```

However, there is still one last problem: the area of all *Circle* objects will always be 0. The default constructor sets the radius to 0 and it stays at 0 (it's *private*, remember). Therefore, *Area* will always return 0 because 0 multiplied by anything is 0. One way to solve this problem is to realize that a constructor is just a special kind of method and it—like all methods—can be overloaded. In other words, you can write your own constructor with the value of *radius* as a parameter. Because all constructors have the same name as their class and never have a return type, the *Circle* class now looks like this:

```
class Circle
{
    public Circle(double initialRadius)
    {
        radius = initialRadius;
    }
    public double Area()
    {
        return 3.141593 * radius * radius;
    }
    private double radius;
}
```

If you write your own constructor for a class, the compiler does not generate the default constructor. If you've written your own constructor that accepts one or more parameters and you also want a default constructor, you'll have to write the default constructor yourself.

▶ **Tip** When you write your own class constructor, remember that the fields you don't initialize are still implicitly initialized to 0, *false*, or *null*. This often means you don't have to explicitly initialize all the fields.

In the following exercise, you will be working with a simple console application where you will declare a class with two *public* constructors and two *private* fields. You will create instances of the class by using the *new* keyword and calling the constructors.

Write constructors and create objects

1   Start Microsoft Visual Studio .NET.

2   Open the Classes project, located in the \Microsoft Press\Visual C# Step by Step\Chapter 7\Classes folder in your My Documents folder. The Classes project opens.

3   In the Code pane of the Code And Text Editor window, locate the *Main* method of the *Application* class within the Point.cs file.

The *Main* method is where the program starts running. The *Main* method contains just one statement: a call to *Entrance* that is wrapped in a *try* block and followed by a *catch* handler. This *try/ catch* block allows you to write, in the *Entrance* method, the code that would normally go inside *Main*, knowing that no exceptions will drop off *Main*.

4   In the Code pane, locate the *Point* class.

The *Point* class is currently empty. Because you have not written a constructor, the compiler will write one for you. You can call this compiler-generated constructor, which you will do now.

5   In the Code pane, locate the *Entrance* method of the *Application* class. Edit the body of the *Entrance* method to contain the following statement:

```
Point origin = new Point();
```

6   On the Build menu, click Build Solution.

The code builds without error. This proves that the compiler has written the default constructor for the *Point* class.

7   In the Code pane, locate the *Point* class. Edit the *Point* class to contain a *public* constructor that accepts two *int* arguments. The body of this constructor will call *Console.WriteLine* to display the values of the arguments to the console. The *Point* class should look exactly like this:

```
class Point
{
    public Point(int x, int y)
    {
        Console.WriteLine("x:{0}, y:{1}", x, y);
    }
}
```

8 On the Build menu, click Build Solution. There is an error:

```
No overload for method 'Point' takes '0' arguments
```

The call to the default constructor in *Entrance* no longer works because there is no longer a default constructor. Because you have written a constructor for the *Point* class, the compiler has not automatically generated the default constructor. You will now fix this by writing your own default constructor.

9 In the Code pane, locate the *Point* class. Edit the *Point* class to contain a *public* default constructor.

The body of this constructor will call *Console.WriteLine* to write the string "default constructor called" to the console. The *Point* class should now look exactly like this:

```
class Point
{
    public Point()
    {
        Console.WriteLine("default constructor called");
    }
    public Point(int x, int y)
    {
        Console.WriteLine("x:{0}, y:{1}", x, y);
    }
}
```

10 In the Code pane, locate the *Entrance* method of the *Application* class. Edit the body of the *Entrance* method so that it also contains a statement that declares a variable called *bottomRight* of type *Point* and initializes it to a new *Point* object.

The *Point* object is created by calling the *Point* constructor that accepts the two *int* arguments 600 and 800. The *Entrance* method should now look exactly like this:

```
static void Entrance()
{
    Point origin = new Point();
    Point bottomRight = new Point(600, 800);
}
```

11 On the Debug menu, click Start Without Debugging.

The code now builds without errors and runs. The following messages are written to the console (the last message is written by Visual Studio .NET):

```
default constructor called
x:600, y:800
Press any key to continue
```

12 Press any key. The console window closes, and you return to the Visual Studio .NET programming environment. You will now add two *int* fields to the *Point* class and modify the constructors to initialize these fields.

13 Edit the *Point* class to contain two *private* instance fields called *x* and *y* of type *int*.

Because the fields are *private*, their names should start with lowercase letters. The *Point* class should now look exactly like this:

```
class Point
{
    public Point()
    {
        Console.WriteLine("default constructor called");
    }
    public Point(int x, int y)
    {
        Console.WriteLine("x:{0}, y:{1}", x, y);
    }
    private int x, y;
}
```

14 Edit the default *Point* constructor to initialize *x* and *y* to 0.

The *Point* class should now look exactly like this:

```
class Point
{
    public Point()
    {
        x = 0;
        y = 0;
    }
    public Point(int x, int y)
    {
        Console.WriteLine("x:{0}, y:{1}", x, y);
    }
    private int x, y;
}
```

▶ **Tip**   Because the *x* and *y* fields will default to 0 anyway, you could choose to omit the initialization of *x* and *y* to 0 if you wanted (of course, you will still have to declare the empty default *Point* constructor). One disadvantage of letting fields default to 0, *false*, or *null* is that it's unclear to anyone reading the code whether those fields have simply been forgotten.

15 Edit the second *Point* constructor to initialize the *x* and *y* fields to the values of the *x* and *y* parameters.

There is a potential trap when you do this. If you don't change the names of the parameters or fields, the second constructor will look exactly as follows:

```
class Point
{
    ⋮
    public Point(int x, int y)
    {
        x = x;
        y = y;
    }
    private int x, y;
}
```

If you think about it, you'll realize that there is no way these assignments can possibly work as you want them to work. When you write x = x;, the *x* on the left side will be resolved in exactly the same way as the *x* on the right side. As you'd expect, both uses of *x* resolve to the same thing—either both to the parameter called *x* or both to the field called *x*. So which is it? If your use of *x* resolves to the parameter called *x*, the field called *x* will not be initialized. Instead, the parameter will be assigned to itself (rather pointless but not a compile-time error). On the other hand, if your use of *x* resolves to the field called *x*, you'll be attempting to retrieve the value of an unassigned field (which is a compile-time error). In fact, the use of *x* resolves to the parameter and you get a warning telling you that the *private* field called *x* is never used in the constructor. One way to fix this is to change the name of the parameter and avoid the name clash, which you will do now.

16 Change the names of the parameters of the second constructor to *initialX* and *initialY*, and then edit the body of the constructor accordingly.

The second constructor will look exactly as follows:

```
class Point
{
    ⋮
    public Point(int initialX, int initialY)
    {
        x = initialX;
        y = initialY;
    }
    private int x, y;
}
```

17 On the Build menu, click Build Solution. Confirm that the code compiles without errors or warnings.

Naming and Accessibility

There's a .NET Framework recommendation that relates directly to the accessibility of class members:

- Identifiers that are *public* should start with a capital letter. For example, *Area* starts with A (not a) because it's *public*. This system is known as the *PascalCase* naming scheme (it was first used in the Pascal language).

- Identifiers that are not *public* (which include local variables) should start with a lowercase letter. For example, *radius* starts with r (not R) because it's *private*. This system is known as the *camelCase* naming scheme.

There's only one exception to this rule: class names should start with a capital letter and constructors must match the name of their class exactly; therefore, a *private* constructor must start with a capital letter.

In the following exercise, you will write a *Point* instance method called *DistanceTo* that calculates the distance between two points.

Write and call instance methods

1 Edit the *Point* class so that it contains a *public* instance method called *DistanceTo* that accepts a single *Point* argument called *other* and returns a *double*.

The *DistanceTo* method should look like this:

```
class Point
{
    ⋮
    public double DistanceTo(Point other)
    {
    }
    private int x, y;
}
```

2 Edit the body of the *DistanceTo* instance method to calculate and return the distance between the *Point* object being used to make the call and the *Point* object passed as a parameter. To do this task, you will need to calculate the difference between the *x* coordinates and the *y* coordinates.

3   Declare a local *int* variable called *xDiff*, and initialize it to the difference between *x* and *other.x*.

4   Declare a local *int* variable called *yDiff*, and initialize it to the difference between *y* and *other.y*.

The *DistanceTo* method should now look like this:

```
class Point
{
    ⋮
    public double DistanceTo(Point other)
    {
        int xDiff = x - other.x;
        int yDiff = y - other.y;
    }
    private int x, y;
}
```

To calculate the distance, you now need to work out the square root of the sum of the square of *xDiff* and the square of *yDiff*. The simplest way to do this task is to use the static *Sqrt* method of the *Math* class. The *DistanceTo* method should now look like this:

```
class Point
{
    ⋮
    public double DistanceTo(Point other)
    {
        int xDiff = x - other.x;
        int yDiff = y - other.y;
        return Math.Sqrt(xDiff * xDiff + yDiff * yDiff);
    }
    private int x, y;
}
```

You will now write a statement that calls the *DistanceTo* method.

5   Locate the *Entrance* method of the *Application* class. After the statements that declare and initialize the *origin* and *bottomRight Point* variables, declare a variable called *distance* of type *double*. Initialize this *double* variable to the result that you get when you call the *DistanceTo* method on the *origin* object and when you pass the *bottomRight* object to it as an argument.

The *Entrance* method should now look like this:

Classes and Objects

7

```
static void Entrance()
{
    Point origin = new Point();
    Point bottomRight = new Point(600, 800);
    double distance = origin.DistanceTo(bottomRight);
}
```

6   Add a fourth statement to the *Entrance* method that writes the value of the distance to the console by using the *Console.WriteLine* method.

The *Entrance* method should now look like this:

```
static void Entrance()
{
    Point origin = new Point();
    Point bottomRight = new Point(600, 800);
    double distance = origin.DistanceTo(bottomRight);
    Console.WriteLine("Distance is :{0}", distance);
}
```

7   On the Debug menu, click Start Without Debugging. The code builds and runs.

8   Confirm that the value of 1000 is written to the console window.

9   Edit the call to the *DistanceTo* method to call it on the *bottomRight* object and to pass *origin* as the argument.

The *Entrance* method should now look like this:

```
static void Entrance()
{
    Point origin = new Point();
    Point bottomRight = new Point(600, 800);
    double distance = bottomRight.DistanceTo(origin);
    Console.WriteLine("Distance is :{0}", distance);
}
```

10   On the Debug menu, click Start Without Debugging. The code builds and runs.

11   Confirm that the value of 1000 is still written to the console window.

12   Press any key. The console window closes and you return to the Visual Studio .NET programming environment.

Understanding *static* Methods and Data

The .NET Framework includes a class called *Math* that contains many useful mathematical functions such as *Sin*, *Cos*, and *Sqrt*. These methods are not implemented as instance methods (an *instance method* is a method that is called on an object and can access the object's instance fields). To learn why they're not instance methods, it's best to consider what would happen if they were. Suppose the *Sqrt* method of the *Math* class were an instance method. (Again, just to be clear, in the real *Math* class, it's not.)

```
class Math
{
    public double Sqrt(double d) { ... }
       ⋮
}
```

If *Sqrt* were an instance method of *Math*, you'd have to create a *Math* object to call *Sqrt* on:

```
Math m = new Math();
double d = m.Sqrt(42.24);
```

This would be cumbersome. The *Math* object would play no part in the calculation of the square root. The fact is that *Sqrt* is a genuine procedural function. That is, all the input data that it needs is provided in the parameter list, and the single result is returned to the caller using the method's return value. Classes are not really needed here, and forcing *Sqrt* into an object-oriented straitjacket is just not a good idea. But what can you do? In C#, all methods must be declared inside a class. Fortunately, there is an answer: you can prefix the declaration of a method with the *static* keyword. You call a *static* method by using the name of the class and not the name of an instance. No instance is required. This is how the methods of the real *Math* class are declared:

```
class Math
{
    public static double Sqrt(double d) { ... }
       ⋮
}
```

And here's an example of how to call the real *Sqrt*:

```
double d = Math.Sqrt(42.24);
```

Isn't this much easier? A *static* method is not called on an object and, therefore, does not have access to the instance fields. Remember, an instance method can access the fields of the object that called it. However, a *static* method is not called on an object; it is called on the class. There are no instance fields because there is no object.

Creating a Shared Field

You can also use the *static* keyword to create a single field that is shared between all objects rather than existing in each object. Just prefix the field declaration with the keyword *static*.

▶ **Tip**   Methods that are *static* methods are called by using the name of the class and are also called *class* methods. Methods declared without the *static* keyword are called on objects and are also called *instance* methods. Similarly, non-*static* fields are also called instance fields (or sometimes instance variables). However, *static* fields tend not to be called *class* fields; they're just called *static* fields (or sometimes *static* variables).

Creating a *static* Field with the *const* Keyword

You can also declare that a field is *static* and that its value will never change by prefixing the field with the *const* keyword. A *const* field does not use the *static* keyword in its declaration but is nevertheless *static*. However, for reasons that are beyond the scope of this book to describe, you can declare a field as *const* only when the field is an *enum*, a primitive type, or a string. For example, here's how the real *Math* class declares *PI* as a *const* field (it declares *PI* to many more decimal places than shown here):

```
class Math
{
    public static double Sqrt(double d) { ... }
    public const double PI = 3.141593;
}
```

▶ **Note**   It was indicated earlier in this chapter that making your fields publicly accessible was a bad idea because this strategy breaks encapsulation. The one exception to this rule is when the field is constant.

Here's the *Circle* class from earlier in this chapter reworked to use *Math.PI*:

```
class Circle
{
    public Circle(double initialRadius)
    {
        radius = initialRadius;
    }
    public double Area()
    {
        return Math.PI * radius * radius;
    }
    private double radius;
}
```

In the final exercise, you will add a *private static* field to the *Point* class and initialize the field to 0. You will increment this count in both constructors. Finally, you will write a *public static* method to return the value of this *private static* field. This field will enable you to find out how many *Point* objects have been created.

Write *static* members and call *static* methods

1   In the Code pane, locate the *Point* class.

2   Add a *private static* field called *objectCount* of type *int* to the *Point* class. Initialize it to 0 as you declare it.

The *Point* class should now look like this:

```
class Point
{
    ⋮
    private int x, y;
    private static int objectCount = 0;
}
```

▶   **Note**   You can write the keywords *private* and *static* in any order. The preferred order is *private* first, *static* second.

3   Add a statement to both *Point* constructors to increment *object-Count*.

Each time an object is created, its constructor will be called. The only way you can create an object is through a constructor. As long as you increment the *objectCount* in each constructor (including the default constructor), *objectCount* will hold the number of objects created so far. This strategy works only because *objectCount* is a shared *static* field. If *objectCount* were an instance field, each object would have its own personal *objectCount* field, which would be set to one. The *Point* class should now look like this:

```
class Point
{
    public Point()
    {
        x = 0;
        y = 0;
        objectCount++;
    }
    public Point(int initialX, int initialY)
    {
        x = initialX;
        y = initialY;
        objectCount++;
    }
    ⋮
    private int x, y;
    private static int objectCount = 0;
}
```

The question now is this: how can users of the *Point* class find out how many *Point* objects have been created? At the moment, the *objectCount* field is *private* and not available outside the class. A poor solution would be to make the *objectCount* field publicly accessible. This strategy would break the encapsulation of the class; you would then have no guarantee that its value was correct because anyone could increment or decrement the field. A much better idea is to provide a *public static* method that returns the value of the *objectCount* field. This is what you will do now.

4   Add a *public static* method to the *Point* class called *ObjectCount* that returns an *int* and accepts no parameters. Implement this method to return the value of the *objectCount* field.

The *Point* class should now look like this:

```
class Point
{
    public static int ObjectCount()
    {
        return objectCount;
    }
    ⋮
    private static int objectCount;
}
```

If the *ObjectCount* method were an instance method, you could call it only on an object, and to create the object would itself increment the *objectCount static* field. Notice that the *ObjectCount* method is *public* and starts with a capital O, whereas the *objectCount* field is *private* and starts with a lowercase o.

5   Locate the *Entrance* method of the *Application* class.

6   Add a statement to the *Entrance* method to write the value returned from the *ObjectCount* method of the *Point* class to the console.

The *Entrance* method should look exactly like this:

```
static void Entrance()
{
    Point origin = new Point();
    Point bottomRight = new Point(600, 800);
    double distance = origin.distanceTo(bottomRight);
    Console.WriteLine("Distance is :{0}", distance);
    Console.WriteLine("No of Point objects :{0}",
        Point.ObjectCount());
}
```

The *ObjectCount* method is called by using *Point*, the name of the class, and not the name of a *Point* variable (such as *origin* or *bottom-*

Right). Because two *Point* objects have been created by the time *ObjectCount* is called, the method should return a value of 2.

7   On the Debug menu, click Start Without Debugging. The code builds and runs.

8   Confirm that the value of 2 is written to the console window.

Congratulations. You have successfully created a class with both instance and *public* class methods and called both of these types of methods. You have also implemented these methods by using *private* instance and *static* fields.

If you want to continue to the next chapter

■   Keep Visual Studio .NET running, and turn to Chapter 8.

If you want to exit Visual Studio .NET now

■   On the File menu, click Exit. If you see a Save dialog box, click Yes.

Chapter 7 Quick Reference

To	Do this
Declare a class	Write the keyword *class*, followed by the name of the class, followed by an opening and closing brace. The methods and fields of the class are declared between the opening and closing brace. For example: ```class Point\n{\n ⋮\n}```
Declare a constructor	Write a method whose name is the same as the name of the class and that has no return type (not even *void*). For example: ```class Point\n{\n public Point(int x, int y)\n {\n ⋮\n }\n}```
Call a constructor	Write the keyword *new*, followed by a call to the constructor. For example: ```Point origin = new Point(0, 0);```

To	Do this
| Declare a class method | Write the keyword *static* before the declaration of the method. For example:<br><br>```csharp
class Point
{
    public static int ObjectCount()
    {
        ⋮
    }
}
``` |
| Call a class method | Write the name of the class, followed by a dot, followed by the name of the method. For example:<br><br>```csharp
int pointsCreatedSoFar =
    Point.ObjectCount();
``` |
| Declare a *static* field | Write the keyword *static* before the declaration of the field. For example:<br><br>```csharp
class Point
{
    ⋮
    private static int objectCount;
}
``` |
| Declare a *const* field | Write the keyword *const* before the declaration of the field. For example:<br><br>```csharp
class Math
{
    ⋮
    public const double PI = ...;
}
``` |
| Access a *static* field | Write the name of the class, followed by a dot, followed by the name of the *static* field. If the access is taking place inside a method of the class, you can just use the name of the *static* field. For example:<br><br>```csharp
double area = Math.PI * radius *
    radius;
``` |
```

Understanding Values and References

In this chapter, you will learn how to:

■ Copy a value type variable.

■ Copy a reference type variable.

■ Use the *ref* and *out* keywords to gain access to the arguments of method parameters.

■ Box a value by initializing or assigning a variable of type *object* to the value.

■ Unbox a value by casting the object reference that refers to the boxed value.

In Chapter 7, you learned how to declare your own classes and create instances of your class (that is, to create objects) by calling a class constructor in combination with the *new* keyword. In this chapter, you will learn about the very different characteristics of primitive types (such as *int*) and class types (such as *Circle*).

Copying *int* Variables and Classes

The primitive types such as *int* are called value types. This is because an *int* variable holds an integer value (such as 42). However, class types, such as *Circle* (covered in Chapter 7), are not value types; they're reference types. A *Circle* variable does not hold a "Circle value"; what it holds is a reference to a *Circle* object. In other words, value types hold values and reference types hold references. Because of the different ways that they hold data, value types are sometimes called *direct* types, and reference types are sometimes called *indirect* types. You need to fully understand the difference between value types and reference types.

The effect of declaring *i* as an *int* is that *i* becomes the name of a variable that holds an integer value. If you declare *copyi* as another *int*, it also becomes the name of a variable that holds an integer value. If you choose to initialize or assign *copyi* to *i*, *copyi* will hold the same value as *i*. However, the fact that *copyi* and *i* happen to hold the same value does not alter the fact that there are two copies of the value 42: one inside *i* and the other inside *copyi*. Let's see this in code:

```
int i = 42;

int copyi = i;
```

The effect of declaring *c* as a *Circle* (the name of a class) is very different. When you declare *c* as a *Circle*, *c* becomes the name of a variable that refers to a *Circle* object. If you declare *refc* as another *Circle*, it becomes the name of a variable that can also refer to a *Circle* object. If you choose to initialize or assign *refc* to *c*, *refc* will refer to the same *Circle* object that *c* does; there is only one *Circle* object, and *refc* and *c* both refer to it. Let's see this in code:

```
Circle c = new Circle(42);

Circle refc = c;
```

And now let's see both examples in a diagram.

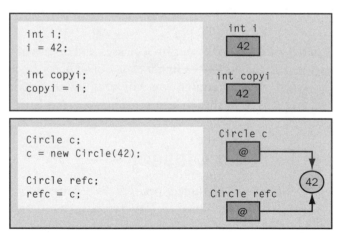

This difference is very important. In particular, it means that the behavior of method parameters depends on whether they are value types or reference types. You'll explore this difference in the following exercise where you will be working with a simple console application.

Use value parameters and reference parameters

1 Start Microsoft Visual Studio .NET.

2 Open the Parameters project, located in the \Microsoft Press\Visual C# Step by Step\Chapter 8\Parameters folder in your My Documents folder. The Parameters project opens.

3 Open the Pass.cs source file in the Code pane of the Code And Text Editor window, and then locate the *Pass* class. Add a *public static* method called *Value* to the *Pass* class.

   This method will accept a single *int* parameter (a value type) called *param* and will have a return type of *void*. The body of *Value* will assign 42 to *param*. The *Pass* class should look exactly like this:

```
namespace Parameters
{
    class Pass
    {
        public static void Value(int param)
        {
            param = 42;
        }
    }
}
```

4 Open the Main.cs source file in the Code pane, and then locate the *Entrance* method of the *Application* class. The *Main* method is where the program starts running.

   The *Main* method contains only one statement: a call to *Entrance*, which is wrapped in a *try* block and followed by a *catch* handler.

5 Add four statements to the *Entrance* method.

   The first will declare a local *int* variable called *i* and initialize it to 0. The second statement will write the value of *i* to the console. The third statement will call *Pass.Value*, passing *i* as an argument. The fourth statement will again write the value of *i* to the console. The calls to *Console.WriteLine* before and after the call to *Pass.Value* allow you to see whether *Pass.Value* modifies the value of *i*. The *Entrance* method should look exactly like this:

```
static void Entrance()
{
    int i = 0;
    Console.WriteLine(i);
    Pass.Value(i);
    Console.WriteLine(i);
}
```

6   On the Debug menu, click Start Without Debugging.

▶   **Tip**   The shortcut key for Start Without Debugging is Ctrl+F5.

The program builds and runs.

7   Confirm that the value of 0 is written to the console window twice.

The assignment inside *Pass.Value* was assigned to a copy of the argument and the original argument *i* is completely unaffected. You will now see what happens when you pass an *int* parameter that is wrapped inside a class.

8   Open the WrappedInt.cs source file in the Code pane, and then locate the *WrappedInt* class. Add a *public* instance field called *Number* of type *int* to the *WrappedInt* class.

The *WrappedInt* class should look exactly like this:

```
namespace Parameters
{
    class WrappedInt
    {
        public int Number;
    }
}
```

9   Open the Pass.cs source file in the Code pane, and then locate the *Pass* class. Add a *public* static method called *Reference* to the *Pass* class.

This method will accept a single *WrappedInt* parameter called *param* and have a return type of *void*. The body of *Reference* will assign 42 to *param.Number*. The *Pass* class should look exactly like this:

```
namespace Parameters
{
    class Pass
    {
        public static void Value(int param)
        {
            param = 42;
        }
        public static void Reference(WrappedInt param)
        {
            param.Number = 42;
        }
    }
}
```

10   Open the Main.cs source file in the Code pane, and then locate the *Entrance* method of the *Application* class.

11 Add four more statements to the *Entrance* method.

The first statement will declare a local *WrappedInt* variable called *wi* and will initialize it to a new *WrappedInt* object by calling the default constructor. The second statement will write the value of *wi.Number* to the console. The third statement will call the *Pass.Reference* method, passing *wi* as an argument. The fourth statement will again write the value of *wi.Number* to the console. As before, the calls to *Console.WriteLine* allow you to see whether *Pass.Reference* modifies the value of *wi.Number*. The *Entrance* method should look exactly like this:

```
static void Entrance()
{
    int i = 0;
    Console.WriteLine(i);
    Pass.Value(i);
    Console.WriteLine(i);

    WrappedInt wi = new WrappedInt();
    Console.WriteLine(wi.Number);
    Pass.Reference(wi);
    Console.WriteLine(wi.Number);
}
```

12 On the Debug menu, click Start Without Debugging. The program builds and runs.

As before, the first two values written to the console window are 0 and 0, before and after the call to *Pass.Value*.

13 For the next two values, which correspond to value in *wi* before and after *Pass.Reference*, confirm that the value of 0 and then the value of 42 are written to the console window.

The value of *wi.Number* is initialized to 0 by the compiler-generated default constructor. The *wi* variable contains a reference to the newly created *WrappedInt* object (which contains an *int*). The *wi* variable is then passed as an argument to the *Pass.Reference* method. Because *WrappedInt* is a class, *wi* and *param* now both refer to the same *WrappedInt* object.

Using *ref* and *out* Parameters

In the previous exercise, you saw that when you pass an argument to a method, the parameter is initialized as a copy of the argument. This arrangement means it's impossible for any change to the parameter to affect the actual argument. For example:

```
static void Value(int param)
{
    param++;
}
static void Main()
{
    int arg = 42;
    Value(arg);
    Console.WriteLine(arg); // writes 42 not 43
}
```

The guarantee that the argument cannot be affected holds even if the parameter is a reference type. Of course, as you've seen, if the parameter is a reference type, the parameter and the argument will both refer to the same object. It is possible to modify the object that the argument refers to through the parameter, but it's not possible to modify the argument itself (for example, to set it to refer to a completely new object). Most of the time, this guarantee is very useful and it makes the program much easier to understand. However, occasionally you might want to write a method that needs to modify the actual argument. C# provides the *ref* and *out* keywords to allow you to do this.

Creating *ref* Parameters

If you prefix a parameter with the *ref* keyword, the parameter becomes an alias for the actual argument rather than a copy of the argument. This alias system means that anything you do to the parameter, you do automatically to the argument because the parameter is an alias for the argument. When you pass an argument to a *ref* parameter, you must also prefix the argument with the *ref* keyword. This system provides a useful visual indication that the argument might change. Here's the previous example again, this time using the *ref* keyword:

```
static void Value(ref int param) // using ref
{
    param++;
}
static void Main()
{
    int arg = 42;
    Value(ref arg);           // using ref
    Console.WriteLine(arg); // writes 43
}
```

The standard definite assignment rule—you must assign a value to a variable before you can use it—still applies to *ref* arguments. For example, in the following example, *arg* is not initialized and the example does not compile. This failure is because *param++* inside *Value* is really *arg++*, and *arg++* is allowed only if *arg* is definitely assigned:

```
static void Value(ref int param)
{
    param++;
}
static void Main()
{
    int arg;                    // not initialized
    Value(ref arg);
    Console.WriteLine(arg);
}
```

Creating *out* Parameters

The *out* keyword is very similar to the *ref* keyword. You can prefix a parameter with the *out* keyword and this again means that the parameter becomes an alias for the argument. This also means that anything you do to the parameter, you also do automatically to the argument because the parameter is an alias for the argument. When you pass an argument to an *out* parameter, you must also prefix the argument with the *out* keyword. The difference between a *ref* parameter and an *out* parameter is that a method doesn't have to assign a value to a *ref* parameter but it has to assign a value to an *out* parameter. In other words, the following example does not compile because *Value* does not assign a value to *param*:

```
static void Value(out int param)
{
}
```

However, the following example does compile because *Value* assigns a value to *param*:

```
static void Value(out int param)
{
    param = 42;
}
```

Because an *out* parameter must be assigned a value, you're allowed to bind it to an argument that isn't definitely assigned. When the method call has finished, the argument is considered definitely assigned and its value can be read. For example:

```
static void Value(out int param)
{
    param = 42;
}
```

```
static void Main()
{
    int arg;                    // not initialized
    Value(out arg);
    Console.WriteLine(arg); // writes 42
}
```

Use *ref* parameters

1   Open the Parameters project, located in the \Microsoft Press\Visual C# Step by Step\Chapter 8\Parameters folder in your My Documents folder.

2   Open the Pass.cs source file in the Code pane, and then locate the *Value* method in the *Pass* class.

3   Edit the *Value* method to accept its *int* argument as a *ref* parameter. The *Value* method should look exactly like this:

```
class Pass
{
    public static void Value(ref int param)
    {
        param = 42;
    }
    ⋮
}
```

4   Open the Main.cs source file in the Code pane, and locate the *Entrance* method of the *Application* class. Edit the third statement of this method so that the *Pass.Value* method call passes its argument by *ref*.

The *Entrance* method should look exactly like this:

```
class Application
{
    static void Entrance()
    {
        int i = 0;
        Console.WriteLine(i);
        Pass.Value(ref i);
        Console.WriteLine(i);
        ⋮
    }
}
```

On the Debug menu, click Start Without Debugging. The program builds and runs.

This time, the first two values written to the console window are 0 and then 42. This result shows that the call to the *Pass.Value* method has modified the argument *i*.

▶ **Note**   You can use the *ref* and *out* modifiers on reference type parameters as well as value type parameters. The effect is exactly the same. The parameter becomes an alias for the argument. If you reassigned the parameter to a newly constructed object, you would actually be reassigning the argument to the newly constructed object.

What Are the Stack and the Heap?

Computer memory is conceptually divided into a number of separate chunks. Two of the chunks of memory are called *the stack* and *the heap*. The stack and the heap serve very different purposes:

- When you call a method, memory is required for its parameters and for its local variables. The memory for parameters and local variables is always acquired from the stack. When the method finishes (either because it returns or it throws an exception), the memory acquired for the parameters and local variables is automatically released back to the stack.

- When you create an object (an instance of a class) using the *new* keyword and a constructor call, memory is required to construct the object. The memory for objects is always acquired from the heap. When the method finishes (either because it returns or throws an exception), the memory acquired for objects is not automatically released back to the heap.

Using the Stack and the Heap

Now let's go through what happens when the following *Method* is called:

```
void Method(int param)
{
    Circle c;
    c = new Circle(param);
    ⋮
}
```

Suppose the value to be passed into *param* is the value 42. A small chunk of memory (just enough for an *int*) is allocated from the stack. This is how *param* comes into existence. The value inside this small chunk of stack memory is initialized to a bit pattern that represents the *int* value 42. This is how *param* is initialized.

Another chunk of memory (just enough for a *Circle*) is allocated from the heap. This is what the *new* keyword does.

▶ **Note**   Heap memory is not infinite. If heap memory is exhausted, *new* will throw an *OutOfMemoryException* and the following steps will not occur.

The *Circle* constructor runs to convert this raw heap memory into a *Circle* object. The constructor might also have parameters and local variables. If so, these are dealt with in exactly the same way: by acquiring memory from the stack. If the call to the constructor succeeds, a *Circle* object has been successfully created.

Another small chunk of memory (just enough for a reference) is allocated from the stack. This is how *c* comes into existence. The value inside this small chunk of stack memory is initialized to a value that refers to the particular part of the heap memory where the *Circle* exists. This is how *c* is initialized.

▶ **Note**   The *Circle* constructor could also throw an exception. If it does, the memory allocated to the *Circle* object will be reclaimed and the value returned by the constructor will be a null reference.

Then the function call ends. The parameters and local variables go out of scope. The memory acquired for *c* is automatically released back to the stack. The memory acquired for *param* is also automatically released back to the stack. However, the memory acquired for the newly constructed *Circle* object is not released back to the stack.

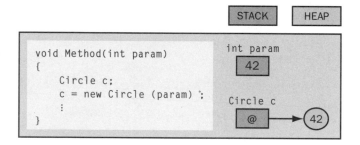

What Is *System.Object*?

One of the most important reference types is the *Object* class in the *System* namespace of the Microsoft .NET Framework:

```
namespace System
{
    class Object
    {
        ⋮
    }
}
```

It's such an important class that the *object* keyword is in fact just an alias for *System.Object*. In your code, you can write object or you can write *System.Object*; they mean exactly the same thing.

> ▶ **Tip** Use the keyword *object* in preference to *System.Object*. It's more direct and it's also consistent with using other keywords that have longer synonyms, as you'll discover in Chapter 9. If your program contains a `using System;` directive, you could also just write *Object* with a capital O (without the *System.* prefix), but it's best to be consistent. Use the simpler keyword object.

All classes implicitly inherit from the *System.Object* class. You don't need to declare that your class derives from *System.Object* (although you can if you want). The fact that your class is a class means that it automatically derives from *System.Object*. In other words, if you write this:

```
class Circle
{
    ⋮
}
```

It's exactly the same as if you'd written this:

```
class Circle : System.Object
{
    ⋮
}
```

Inheritance (deriving classes from base classes) is covered in detail in Chapter 12. For now, all you need to know is that the consequence of all classes implicitly deriving from *System.Object* is that a variable of type *object* can refer to an instance of any class. In the following example, the variables *c* and *o* both refer to the same *Circle* object. The fact that the type of *c* is *Circle* and the type of *o* is *object* (the alias for *System.Object*) in effect provides two different "views" of the same object:

```
Circle c;
c = new Circle(42);

object o;
o = c;
```

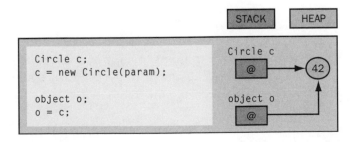

Boxing

As you have just seen, variables of type *object* can refer to any object of any reference type. That is, they can refer to any instance of a class. However, variables of type *object* can also refer to any value of any type. For example, the following two statements initialize the variable *i* (of type *int*, a value type) to 42 and then initialize the variable *o* (of type *object*, a reference type) to *i*:

```
int i = 42;
object o = i;
```

The effect of this second initialization is subtle. The reference inside the variable *o* does not refer to the variable *i*. You have to remember that *i* is a value type and it exists in the stack. If the reference inside *o* referred to *i*, the reference would be referring to the stack. Because this would seriously compromise the robustness of the program (and create a potential security flaw), it is not allowed. Instead, an exact copy of the value inside *i* is made on the heap and the reference inside *o* refers to the copy. This automatic copying is called *boxing*. Here's an illustration to show what happens.

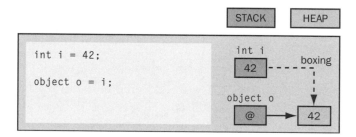

▶   **Important**   Be careful with boxing. Remember, if you modify the original value of a variable, you are not modifying the value that now exists on the heap, because it's just a copy.

Because of boxing, a variable of type *object* can refer to either of two things. First, the variable can refer to any instance of a reference type (to any object). Second, it can refer to a copy of any value type (to any value) through boxing. In other words, a variable of type *object* can refer to absolutely anything, no matter what its type.

Unboxing

Because a variable of type *object* can refer to a boxed copy of a value, it's only reasonable to allow you to get at that boxed value through the variable. You might expect to be able to access the boxed *int* value that a variable *o* refers to by using `int i = o;`. However, if you try this syntax, you'll get a compile time error, as in this example:

```
object o = 42; // okay
int i = o;     // compile time error
```

If you think about it, it's pretty sensible that you can't use the `int i = o;` syntax. After all, as you know now, *o* could be referencing absolutely anything. However, there is a way to get the value of the boxed copy. You use what is known as a *cast*, an operation that converts one type to another. You prefix the *object* variable with the name of the type between parentheses, as in this example:

```
object o = 42;  // boxes
int i = (int)o; // compiles okay
```

The effect of this cast is subtle. The compiler notices that you've specified the type *int* in the cast. Next, the compiler checks exactly what it is that *o* actually refers to. It could be absolutely anything. Just because your cast says *o* refers to an *int*, that doesn't mean it actually does. If *o* really does refer to a boxed *int* and everything matches, the cast succeeds and the compiler extracts the value from the boxed *int*. (In this example, the boxed value is then used to initialize *i*.) This is called *unboxing*, and, in this example, it happened successfully. Here's an example of successful unboxing.

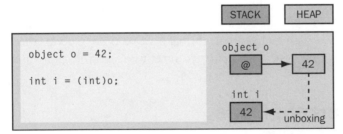

However, if *o* does not refer to a boxed *int*, there is a type mismatch, causing the cast to fail and not return. Instead, the compiler throws an *InvalidCastException*. Here's an example of an unboxing cast that fails:

```
Circle c = new Circle(42);
object o = c;          // doesn't box because Circle is a class
int i = (int)o;        // compiles okay, but throws at runtime
```

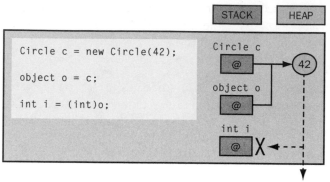

throw InvalidCastException

> ▶ **Note**   The type you specify in the unboxing cast must exactly match the type
> actually in the box. For example, if the box holds a copy of an *int* and you try to
> unbox it into a *long*, you will get an *InvalidCastException*. The fact that there is
> a built-in implicit conversion from an *int* to a *long* is irrelevant. The match
> must be exact.

Congratulations. You have learned some important differences between value types that hold their value directly on the stack and reference types that refer indirectly to their objects on the heap. You have also learned how to use the *ref* and *out* keywords on method parameters to gain access to the arguments. You have seen how assigning a variable of the *System.Object* class to a value (such as 42) causes the variable to refer to a boxed copy of the value made on the heap. You have seen how assigning a variable of a value type to a variable of the *System.Object* class causes the boxed copy to refer to a variable of a value type (such as *int*).

Pointers and Unsafe Code

Now it's time for a history lesson. This section is purely for your information and is aimed at developers who are familiar with C or C++. If you are new to programming, feel free to skip this section!

If you have already developed in languages such as C or C++, much of the preceding discussion concerning object references might be familiar. Although neither C nor C++ have explicit reference types, both languages have a construct that provides similar functionality—pointers.

A *pointer* is a variable that holds the address of, or a reference to, an item in memory. A special syntax is used to identify a variable as a pointer. For example, the following statement declares the variable *pi* as a pointer to an integer:

```
int *pi;
```

Although the variable *pi* is declared as a pointer, it does not actually point anywhere until you initialize it. For example, to use *pi* to point to the integer variable *i*, you can use the following statements and the & operator, which returns the address of a variable:

```
int i = 99;
⋮
pi = &i;
```

You can access and modify the value held in the variable *i* through the pointer variable *pi* like this:

```
*pi = 100;
```

This code will, of course, update the variable *i* to have the value 100, because *pi* points to the same memory location as the variable i.

One of the main problems that developers learning C and C++ have is understanding the syntax used by pointers. The * operator has at least two meanings (besides also being the arithmetic multiplication operator), and there is often great confusion about when to use & as opposed to *. The other issue with pointers is that it is very easy to point to somewhere invalid, or forget to point somewhere at all, and then try and reference the data pointed to. The result will either be garbage or a failed program with an error because the operating system will detect an attempt to access an illegal address in memory.

Reference variables were added to C# to avoid all these problems. If you really want to, you can continue to use pointers in C#, but you must mark the code as *unsafe*. The *unsafe* keyword can be used to mark a block of code, or an entire method, as shown here:

```
public static void Main(string [] args)
{
    int x = 99, y = 100;
    unsafe
    {
        swap (&x, &y);
    }
    Console.WriteLine("x is now {0}, y is now {1}", x, y);
}

public static unsafe void swap(int *a, int *b)
{
    int temp;
    temp = *a;
    *a = *b;
    *b = temp;
}
```

When you compile programs containing unsafe code, you must specify the /*unsafe* option.

Unsafe code also has a bearing on how memory is managed, and objects created in unsafe code are said to be unmanaged. We will discuss this issue in more detail in Chapter 13.

If you want to continue to the next chapter

■   Keep Visual Studio .NET running and turn to Chapter 9.

If you want to exit Visual Studio .NET now

■   On the File menu, click Exit. If you see a Save dialog box, click Yes.

Chapter 8 Quick Reference

To	Do this

Copy a value type variable	Simply make the copy. Because the variable is a value type, you will have two copies of the same value. For example:
	
	``csharp
	int i = 42;
	int copyi = i;
	``

Copy a reference type variable	Simply make the copy. Because the variable is a reference type, you will have two references referring to the same object. For example:
	
	``csharp
	Circle c = new Circle(42);
	Circle refc = c;
	``

Pass an argument to a *ref* parameter	Prefix the argument with the *ref* keyword. This will make the parameter an alias for the actual argument rather than a copy of the argument. For example:
	
	``csharp
	static void Main()
	{
	    int arg = 42;
	    Value(ref arg);
	    Console.WriteLine(arg);
	}
	``

To	Do this
| Pass an argument to an *out* parameter | Prefix the argument with the *out* keyword. This will make the parameter an alias for the actual argument rather than a copy of the argument. For example:<br><br>```csharp
static void Main()
{
    int arg = 42;
    Value(out arg);
    Console.WriteLine(arg);
}
``` |
| Box a value | Initialize or assign a variable of type object to the value. For example:<br><br>```csharp
object o = 42;
``` |
| Unbox a value | Cast the object reference that refers to the boxed value to the type of the value. For example:<br><br>```csharp
int i = (int)o;
``` |
```

Creating Value Types with Enumerations and Structs

In Chapter 8, you learned about the two fundamental kinds of types that exist in Microsoft Visual C#: value types and reference types. A variable of a value type holds its value directly on the stack, whereas a variable of a reference type holds a reference that refers to an object on the heap. In Chapter 7, you learned how to write your own classes, thus creating your own reference types. In this chapter, you'll learn how to write your own value types. You can create your own value types in two ways: by writing enumerations and by writing structs.

Working with Enumerations

Suppose you want to represent the seasons of the year in a program. You could use the integers 0, 1, 2, and 3 to represent spring, summer, fall, and winter, respectively. This system would work but it's not very intuitive and fails to represent the problem. If you used the integer value 0 in code, it wouldn't be obvious that a particular 0 (and not some other 0) represented spring. It also wouldn't be a very robust solution. For example, nothing would stop you from using any integer value rather than just 0, 1, 2, and 3. C# offers a better solution. You can use the *enum* keyword to create an enumeration type (sometimes called an *enum type*) whose values are limited to a set of symbolic names.

Declaring an Enumeration Type

Here's how to declare an enumeration type, called *Season*, whose literal values are limited to the symbolic names *Spring*, *Summer*, *Fall*, and *Winter*:

```
enum Season { Spring, Summer, Fall, Winter }
```

The symbolic names must appear between a pair of braces in a comma-separated list. These names enumerate the values of a new type called *Season* that is an enumeration type.

Choosing Enumeration Literal Values

Each enumeration has a set of values associated with each element. By default, the numbering starts at 0 for the first element and goes up in steps of 1. You can associate a specific integer constant (such as 1) with an enumeration literal (such as *Spring*), as in the following example:

```
enum Season { Spring = 1, Summer, Fall, Winter }
```

▶ **Important** The integer value that you initialize an enumeration literal with must be a compile-time constant value (such as 1). That is, it must be a constant whose value does not depend on any run-time behavior (such as a method call).

If you don't explicitly give an enumeration literal a constant integer value, the compiler gives it a value that is one more than the value of the previous enumeration literal, except for the very first enumeration literal, to which the compiler gives a value of 0. In the previous version of *Season*, the underlying values of *Spring*, *Summer*, *Fall*, and *Winter* are 1, 2, 3, and 4. In the following version of *Season*, *Spring*, *Summer*, *Fall*, and *Winter* have values of 0, 1, 2, and 3:

```
enum Season { Spring, Summer, Fall, Winter }
```

You are allowed to give more than one enumeration literal the same underlying value. For example, in the United Kingdom, fall is called autumn, which you could code as follows:

```
enum Season { Spring, Summer, Fall, Autumn = Fall, Winter }
```

Choosing an Enumeration's Underlying Type

When you declare an enumeration type, the enumeration literals are given values of type *int*. In other words, the underlying type defaults to an *int*. You can also choose to base your enumeration type on a different underlying integer type. For example, to declare that *Season*'s underlying type as a *short* rather than an *int*, you can write this:

```
enum Season : short { Spring, Summer, Fall, Winter }
```

You can base an enumeration on any of the eight integer types: *byte*, *sbyte*, *short*, *ushort*, *int*, *uint*, *long*, or *ulong*. The values of all the enumeration literals must fit inside the range of the chosen base type. For example, the following will generate a compile-time error because *byte.MaxValue + 1* is outside the range of a byte:

```
enum Season : byte { Spring, Summer, Fall, Winter = byte.MaxValue + 1}
```

Now that you know how to create an enumeration type, the next step is to use it.

Using an Enumeration

Once you have declared your enumeration type, you can use the name of the enumeration as the name of a type in exactly the same way as any other type. If *Season* is the name of your enumeration type, you can create variables of type *Season*, fields of type *Season*, and parameters of type *Season*, as shown in this example:

```
enum Season { Spring, Summer, Fall, Winter }

class Example
{
    public void Method(Season parameter)
    {
        Season localVariable;
        ⋮
    }
    private Season field;
}
```

An enumeration type is a value type. This means that enumeration variables hold their values directly and live on the stack (as discussed in Chapter 8). This is not really surprising when you remember that the underlying type of an enumeration is always an integral type. The definite assignment rule applies to enumeration variables just as it applies to all other variables:

```
Season colorful;
Console.WriteLine(colorful); // compile time error
```

Before you can use the value of an enumeration variable, it must be definitely assigned a value, for example:

```
Season colorful = Season.Fall;
string name = colorful.ToString();
Console.WriteLine(name);     // writes out 'Fall'
Console.WriteLine(colorful); // writes out 'Fall'
```

There are a few of points of interest in this example:

- You have to write *Season.Fall* rather than *Fall*. All enumeration literal names are scoped inside their enumeration type. This is very useful as it allows different enumeration types to coincidentally contain literals with the same name.

- You can convert an enumeration variable into a string that contains the name of its enumeration literal value. To do this, you call the *ToString* method on the enumeration variable. In many languages other than C#, you'd have to write this conversion yourself.

- When you write out an enumeration variable, the compiler automatically writes out the name of the literal whose value matches the value of the variable.

It's also possible to retrieve the underlying integer value of an enumeration variable. To do this, you must cast it to its underlying type. Casting a type is another way of saying that you will be converting the data from one type to another. For example, the following code fragment will write out the value 2 and not the word *Fall*:

```
enum Season { Spring, Summer, Fall, Winter }
 ⋮
Season colorful = Season.Fall;
Console.WriteLine((int)colorful); // writes out '2'
```

All the standard operators that you can use on integral variables can also be used on enumeration variables (except the bitwise and shift operators, which are covered in Chapter 15). For example, you can compare two enumeration variables of the same type for equality by using the == operator.

▶ **Note**   All enumeration types automatically inherit some useful enumeration-related methods from the *System.Enum* class.

In the following exercise, you will work with a console application and declare and use an enumeration class that represents the months of the year.

Create and use an enumeration type

1   Start Microsoft Visual Studio .NET.

2   Open the StructsAndEnums project, located in the \Microsoft Press\Visual C# Step by Step\Chapter 9\StructsAndEnums folder in your My Documents folder. The StructsAndEnums project opens.

3   In the Code pane, open the Month.cs source file. The source contains an empty namespace called *StructsAndEnums*.

4   In the Code pane, add an enumeration type called *Month* inside the *StructsAndEnums* namespace.

The 12 enumeration literals for *Month* are January through December. The *Month* enumeration should look exactly like this:

```
namespace StructsAndEnums
{
    enum Month
    {
        January, February, March, April,
        May, June, July, August,
        September, October, November, December
    }
}
```

5   In the Code pane, open the Main.cs source file, and then locate the *Entrance* method.

As in previous exercises, the *Main* method calls the *Entrance* method and traps any exceptions that occur.

6   In the Code pane, add a statement to the *Entrance* method that declares a variable called *first* of type *Month* and initializes it to *Month.January*. Add another statement that writes the value of the first variable to the console.

The *Entrance* method should look exactly like this:

```
namespace StructsAndEnums
{
    ⋮
    static void Entrance()
    {
        Month first = Month.January;
        Console.WriteLine(first);
    }
    ⋮
}
```

7   On the Debug menu, click Start Without Debugging. Visual Studio .NET builds and runs the program.

8   Confirm that the word January is written to the console.

9   Press any key. The console window closes and you return to the Visual Studio .NET programming environment.

Working with Struct Types

There is one more way to create your own value types in C#. You can use the *struct* keyword. A struct (short for *structure*) can have its own fields, methods, and constructors just like a class (and unlike an enumeration), but it is a value type and not a reference type.

Declaring Struct Types

To declare your own struct value type, you use the *struct* keyword followed by the name of the type, followed by the body of the struct between an opening and closing brace. For example, here is a struct called *Time* that contains three *public int* fields called *hours*, *minutes*, and *seconds*:

```
struct Time
{
    public int hours, minutes, seconds;
}
```

However, making the fields of a struct *public* is a violation of encapsulation and in most cases is not advisable. There is no way to ensure the values of *public* fields are valid. For example, anyone could set the value of *minutes* or *seconds* to greater than 60. A better idea is to make the fields *private* and provide your struct with constructors and methods, as shown in this example:

```
struct Time
{
    public Time(int hh, int mm, int ss)
    {
        hours = hh % 24;
        minutes = mm % 60;
        seconds = ss % 60;
    }
    public int Hours()
    {
        return hours;
    }
    ⋮
    private int hours, minutes, seconds;
}
```

Understanding Struct and Class Differences

A struct and a class are syntactically very similar but there are a few important differences. Let's look at each of these differences.

You can't declare a default constructor (a constructor with no parameters) for a struct. For instance, the following example would compile if *Time* were a class, but because *Time* is a struct it fails to compile:

```
struct Time
{
    public Time() { ... } // compile time error
    ⋮
}
```

You can't declare your own default constructor in a struct because the compiler *always* writes one. In a class, the compiler will write the default constructor only if you don't write a constructor yourself. In a struct, the compiler will always write the default constructor, even if you write one or more other constructors yourself.

▶ **Note**   The compiler always generates a default constructor for a struct, and this default constructor always sets the fields to 0, *false*, or *null*—just like for a class. Therefore, you should make sure that a struct value created by the default constructor behaves logically and makes sense with these default values.

If you don't initialize a field in a class constructor, the compiler will automatically initialize it for you to 0, *false*, or *null*. However, if you don't initialize a field in a struct constructor, the compiler won't initialize it for you. This means you must explicitly initialize all the fields in all the struct constructors or you'll get a compile-time error. For instance, the following example would compile if *Time* were a class and would silently initialize *seconds* to 0, but because *Time* is a struct, it fails to compile.

```
struct Time
{
    public Time(int hh, int mm)
    {
        hours = hh;
        minutes = mm;
    }   // compile time error: seconds not initialized
    ⋮
    private int hours, minutes, seconds;
}
```

In a class, you can initialize instance fields at their point of declaration. In a struct, you cannot. For instance, the following example would compile if *Time* were a class, but because *Time* is a struct, it causes a compile-time error (reinforcing the rule that every struct must initialize all its fields in all its constructors):

```
struct Time
{
    ⋮
    private int hours = 0; // compile time error
    private int minutes;
    private int seconds;
}
```

These differences are summarized in the following table.

Question	Struct	Class
Is this a value type or a reference type?	A struct is a value type.	A class is a reference type.
Do instances live on the stack or the heap?	struct instances are called values and live on the stack.	Class instances are called objects and live on the heap.
Can you declare a default constructor?	No	Yes
If you declare your own constructor, will the compiler still write the default constructor?	Yes	No
If you don't initialize a field in your own constructor, will the compiler automatically initialize it for you?	No	Yes
Are you allowed to initialize instance fields at their point of declaration?	No	Yes

There are other differences between classes and structs concerning inheritance. For example, a class can inherit from a base class but a struct cannot. These differences will be covered in Chapter 12. Now that you know how to declare structs, the next step is to use them to create values.

Declaring Struct Variables

After you have declared your struct type, you can use the name of the struct as the name of a type in exactly the same way as any other type. If *Time* is the name of your struct type, you can create variables of type *Time*, fields of type *Time*, and parameters of type *Time*, as shown in this example:

```
struct Time
{
    ⋮
    private int hours, minutes, seconds;
}

class Example
{
    public void Method(Time parameter)
    {
        Time localVariable;
        ⋮
    }
    private Time field;
}
```

A struct type is a value type. This means that struct variables hold their values directly and live on the stack (as discussed in Chapter 8). For example, our *Time* struct contains three *int* fields called *hours*, *minutes*, and *seconds*. When you declare a local variable of type *Time* called *now*, you're really declaring three local *int* variables called *now.hours*, *now.minutes*, and *now.seconds*, all on the stack:

```
Time now;
```

There are no objects and no heap memory is involved, as illustrated in the following diagram.

> ▶ **Note**   Use structs for implementing simple concepts whose main feature is their value. For example, an *int* is a value type because its main feature is its value. If you have two *int* variables that contain the same value (such as 42), one is as good as the other. When you copy a value type variable, you get two copies of the value. In contrast, when you copy a reference type variable, you get two references to the same object. In summary, use structs for lightweight concepts where it makes sense to copy the value, and use classes for more heavyweight concepts where it doesn't make sense to copy the value.

Understanding Struct Definite Assignment

The definite assignment rules for a struct variable are the natural consequence of the combination of the definite assignment rules for all of its fields. When you declare a struct variable, the fields inside the variable are not initialized and their values cannot be read until they have been definitely assigned (just as if they had been declared as individual local variables). For instance, the following example will not compile because it attempts to read the value of *now.hours* before it has been definitely assigned (ignoring the private access for a moment):

```
Time now;
Console.WriteLine(now.hours); // now.hours not assigned
```

If you assign a definite value to a struct field, the field can then be read but the other fields remain uninitialized. For example (again ignoring the private access for a moment):

```
Time now;
now.hours = 11;
Console.WriteLine(now.hours);    // compiles okay
Console.WriteLine(now.minutes);  // now.minutes not assigned
```

Calling Struct Constructors

The easiest way to initialize all the fields in a struct variable is to call the struct's default constructor. As explained previously in this chapter, the default constructor for a struct always exists and always initializes all the struct fields to 0, *false*, or *null*. For instance, the following example is guaranteed to initialize all the *int* fields of *now* to 0 and so compiles (again ignoring the private access for a moment):

```
Time now = new Time();
Console.WriteLine(now.hours);    // compiles okay, writes out 0
Console.WriteLine(now.minutes);  // compiles okay, writes out 0
Console.WriteLine(now.seconds);  // compiles okay, writes out 0
```

The following illustration shows the effect of this example.

▶ **Important**   When you call a constructor, you must always precede it with the *new* keyword. This does not change the fact that a struct value lives on the stack. The *new* keyword behaves differently in different contexts: For a class, it allocates memory from the heap, whereas for a struct, it allocates memory from the stack.

If you've written your own struct constructor, you can also use that to initialize a struct variable. As explained previously in this chapter, a struct constructor must always explicitly initialize all its fields. For example:

```
struct Time
{
    public Time(int hh, int mm)
    {
        hours = hh;
        minutes = mm;
        seconds = 0;
```

```
    }
      ⋮
    private int hours, minutes, seconds;
}
```

The following example initializes *now* by calling this user-defined constructor (again we're ignoring the private access):

```
Time now = new Time(12, 30);
Console.WriteLine(now.hours);   // compiles okay, writes out 12
Console.WriteLine(now.minutes); // compiles okay, writes out 30
Console.WriteLine(now.seconds); // compiles okay, writes out 0
```

The following illustration shows the effect of this example.

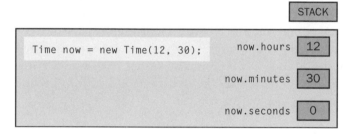

Copying Struct Variables

You're allowed to initialize or assign one struct variable to another struct variable, but only if the struct variable on the right side is definitely assigned (that is, if all its fields are definitely assigned). For instance, the following example compiles because *now* is definitely assigned:

```
Time now = new Time(12, 30);
Time copy = now;
```

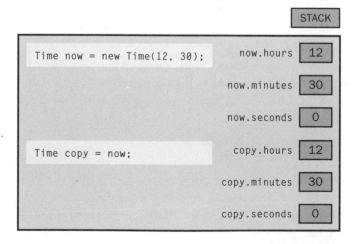

The following example fails to compile because *now* is not definitely assigned:

```
Time now;
Time copy = now; // compile time error: now unassigned
```

▶ **Important**   When you copy a struct variable, each field on the left side is copied directly from its corresponding field on the right side. This copying is done as a fast single-block copy that never throws an exception. C++ programmers should note that this copy behavior cannot be changed.

Understanding Keyword-Type Equivalences

You now know the three ways to create values. You can use a primitive type such as *int*, you can use enumeration types such as *Season*, or you can use struct types such as *Time*. At least that's the way it appears on the surface. In fact, it's time to come clean and reveal the true picture. There are only two ways to create values in C#. You can use enumerations, or you can use structs. This is because the primitive types such as *int* are really structs in disguise. For example, the *int* keyword is really an alias for the struct type called *Int32* that lives in the *System* namespace. In other words, you can write this:

```
int number = 42;
```

Or you can write this:

```
System.Int32 number = 42;
```

As far as the compiler is concerned, these lines of code are exactly the same. The *int* keyword and *System.Int32* are completely interchangeable. And if a using System; directive is in scope, the *int* keyword and *Int32* are also completely interchangeable. This means that there are a total of four ways to initialize an *int* variable to 0:

```
int firstWay = new System.Int32();
int secondWay = new Int32(); // assuming a using System; directive
int thirdWay = new int();
int fourthWay = 0;
```

This equivalence also means that where *System.Int32* contains a static field or method (such as *Parse*), you can access that field or method by using the *int* keyword or by using *System.Int32*. For example, the following two statements are equivalent:

```
int hour = System.Int32.Parse(Console.ReadLine());
int hour = int.Parse(Console.ReadLine());
```

This keyword-type equivalence shouldn't come as too much of a surprise when you remember that the *object* keyword is an alias for the *System.Object* class (as mentioned in Chapter 8). Here's a table of all the primitive types and their equivalent struct or class.

Keyword	Type equivalent	Class or struct
bool	*System.Boolean*	struct
byte	*System.Byte*	struct
decimal	*System.Decimal*	struct
double	*System.Double*	struct
float	*System.Single*	struct
int	*System.Int32*	struct
long	*System.Int64*	struct
object	*System.Object*	class
sbyte	*System.SByte*	struct
short	*System.Int16*	struct
string	*System.String*	class
uint	*System.UInt32*	struct
ulong	*System.UInt64*	struct
ushort	*System.UInt16*	struct

▶ **Tip**   When you declare your own struct type, the compiler does not automatically implement any operators for it. By default, you cannot use operators such as == and != on your own struct type variables. However, you can declare operators for your own struct types. The syntax for doing this is covered in Chapter 17.

It's time to put this knowledge into practice. In the following exercise, you will create and use a struct type to represent a date.

Create and use a struct type

1   Open the StructsAndEnums project, located in the \Microsoft Press\Visual C# Step by Step\Chapter 9\StructsAndEnums folder in your My Documents folder.

2   In the Code pane, open the Date.cs source file.

3   In the Code pane, add a struct called *Date* inside the *StructsAndEnums* namespace.

This struct will contain three private fields: one called *year* of type *int*, one called *month* of type *Month* (as declared in the previous exercise), and one called *day* of type *int*. The *Date* struct should look exactly as follows:

```
namespace StructsAndEnums
{
    struct Date
    {
        private int year;
```

Enumerations and Structs

9

```
            private Month month;
            private int day;
    }
}
```

Now consider the default constructor for *Date* that the compiler will write. This constructor will set the *year* to 0, the *month* to 0 (the value of January), and the *day* to 0. The *year* value of 0 is not valid (there was no year 0), and the *day* value of 0 is also not valid (each month starts on day 1). One way to fix this problem is to translate the *year* and *day* values. You will implement the *Date* struct so that when the *year* field holds the value *Y*, this value represents the year *Y* + 1900, and when the *day* field holds a value of *D*, this value represents the day *D* + 1. This will mean that the default constructor will set the three fields to values that represent the *Date*: 1 January 1900.

4   In the Code pane, add a *public* constructor to the *Date* struct.

This constructor takes three parameters: an *int* called *ccyy* for the *year*, a *Month* called *mm* for the *month*, and an *int* called *dd* for the *day*. Use these three parameters to initialize the corresponding fields. A *year* field of *Y* represents the year *Y* + 1900, so you will need to initialize the *year* field to the value *ccyy* −1900. A *day* field of *D* represents the day *D* + 1, so you will need to initialize the *day* field to the value *dd* −1. The *Date* struct should now look like this:

```
namespace StructsAndEnums
{
    struct Date
    {
        public Date(int ccyy, Month mm, int dd)
        {
            year = ccyy - 1900;
            month = mm;
            day = dd - 1;
        }
        private int year;
        private Month month;
        private int day;
    }
}
```

5   In the Code pane, add a *public* method called *Write* to the *Date* struct.

This method takes no arguments and returns nothing. It writes the date to the console. Remember, the value of the *year* field represents *year* + 1900, and the value of the *day* field represents *day* + 1. The *Write* method should look as follows:

```
namespace StructsAndEnums
{
    struct Date
    {
        ⋮
        public void Write()
        {
            Console.Write(month);
            Console.Write(" ");
            Console.Write(day + 1);
            Console.Write(" ");
            Console.Write(year + 1900);
        }
        ⋮
    }
}
```

6 In the Code pane, open the Main.cs source file, and then locate the *Entrance* method.

7 In the Code pane, add a statement to *Entrance* that declares a local variable called *defaultDate* and initializes it to a *Date* value constructed by using the *defaultDate* constructor. Add another statement to *Entrance* to write *defaultDate* to the console by calling its *Write* method. Add another statement to *Entrance* to write a new line to the console by calling *Console.WriteLine*.

The *Entrance* method should now look exactly like this:

```
namespace StructsAndEnums
{
    class Application
    {
        static void Entrance()
        {
            ⋮
            Date defaultDate = new Date();
            defaultDate.Write();
            Console.WriteLine();
        }
    }
    ⋮
}
```

8 On the Debug menu, click Start Without Debugging. Visual Studio .NET builds and runs the program.

9 Confirm that January followed by January 1 1900 is written to the console.

10 Press any key to return to the Visual Studio .NET programming environment.

11 In the Code pane, return to the *Entrance* method.

12 In the Code pane, add three more statements to the *Entrance* method.

The first statement will declare a local variable called *halloween* and initialize it to October 31 2003. The second statement will write *halloween* to the console by calling its *Write* method. The third statement will write a new line to the console. The *Entrance* method should now look exactly like this:

```
namespace StructsAndEnums
{
    class Application
    {
        static void Entrance()
        {
            ⋮
            Date halloween = new Date(2003, Month.October, 31);
            halloween.Write();
            Console.WriteLine();
        }
    }
}
```

13 On the Debug menu, click Start Without Debugging. Visual Studio .NET builds and runs the program.

14 Confirm that October 31 2003 is written to the console after the previous information.

Congratulations. You have successfully used the *enum* and *struct* keywords to declare your own value types and then used these types in code.

If you want to continue to the next chapter

■ Keep Visual Studio .NET running and turn to Chapter 10.

If you want to exit Visual Studio .NET now

■ On the File menu, click Exit. If you see a Save dialog box, click Yes.

Chapter 9 Quick Reference

To	Do this
Declare an enumeration type	Write the keyword *enum*, followed by the name of the type, followed by a pair of braces containing a comma-separated list of the enumeration literal names. For example: `enum Suit { Clubs, Diamonds, Hearts, Spades }`
Declare an enumeration variable	Write the name of the enumeration type on the left followed by the name of the variable, followed by a semicolon. For example: `Suit trumps;`

Initialize or assign an enumeration variable to a value	Always write the name of the enumeration literal name in combination with the name of the enumeration type it belongs to. For example:
	
	`trumps = Hearts; // compile time error`
	`trumps = Suit.Hearts; // okay`

Declare a struct type	Write the keyword *struct*, followed by the name of the struct type, followed by the body of the struct (the constructors, methods, and fields). For example:
	
	`struct Time`
	`{`
	`    public Time(int hh, int mm, int ss) { ... }`
	`    ⋮`
	`    private int hours, minutes, seconds;`
	`}`

Declare a struct variable	Write the name of the struct type, followed by the name of the variable, followed by a semicolon. For example: `Time now;`

Initialize or assign a struct variable to a value	Initialize or assign the variable to a struct value created by calling a struct constructor. For example:
	
	`Time lunch = new Time(12, 30, 0);`
	`lunch = new Time(12, 30, 0);`

Chapter

10

Using Arrays and Collections

In this chapter, you will learn how to:

- Declare, initialize, copy, and use array variables.

- Declare, initialize, copy, and use variables of various collection types.

What Is an Array?

An *array* is a sequence of elements. All the elements in an array have the same type (unlike the fields in a struct or class, which can have different types). The elements of an array live in a contiguous block of memory and are accessed using integer indexes (unlike fields in a struct or class, which are accessed by name). An array is particularly useful when a program must handle an ordered group of similar items, in which case it is a more flexible and powerful alternative to creating many individual variables.

Declaring Array Variables

You use the standard *type name* pattern to declare an array. You declare an array type on the left by writing the name of the element type followed by a pair of square brackets. The square brackets signify that the variable is an array. For example, to declare an array of *int* variables called *pins*, you would write this:

```
int[] pins;
```

Microsoft Visual Basic programmers should note that you use square brackets and not parentheses. C and C++ programmers should note that the size of the array is not part of the declaration. Java programmers should note that you must place the square brackets *before* the variable name.

Creating Array Instances

Arrays are reference types, not value types. This means that an array variable *refers* to an array instance on the heap (just as a class variable refers to an object on the heap) and does not hold its array elements directly on the stack (as a struct does). (To review values and references and the differences between the stack and the heap, see Chapter 8.) Therefore, when you declare an array variable, you do not declare its size. You need the size of an array only when you are creating an array instance.

▶ **Important**   When you declare an array variable, you do not create an array instance. Likewise, when you declare a class variable, you do not create a class instance. Arrays and classes are reference types.

To create an array instance, you write the *new* keyword followed by the name of the element type, followed by the size of the array you're creating between square brackets. For example, to create a new array of four integers, you write this:

```
new int[4]
```

Of course, unless you use the result of this array creation expression, the newly created array instance will be lost. The following example is more useful:

```
int[] pins = new int[4]; // Personal Identification Numbers
```

Here's a diagram illustrating this statement.

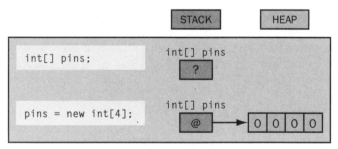

The size of an array instance can be calculated at run time. It does not need to be a compile-time constant, as shown in this example:

```
int size = int.Parse(Console.ReadLine());
int[] pins = new int[size];
```

You're allowed to create an array whose size is 0. This might sound bizarre, but it's useful in situations where the size of the array is determined dynamically and could be 0. An array of size 0 is not *null*.

▶ **Note** It's also possible to create multidimensional arrays. For example, to create a two-dimensional array, you create an array that requires two integer
indexes. Multidimensional arrays are beyond the scope of this book, but here's
a sample:

```
int[,] table = new int[4,6];
```

Initializing Array Variables

When you create an array instance, all the elements of the array instance are initialized to a default value depending on their type:

■ Built-in numeric types (such as *int*) are initialized to 0. Enumerations
are also initialized to 0 (even if none of their literal values is 0).

■ *bool* elements are initialized to *false*.

■ Reference type elements are initialized to *null*.

The compiler applies this rule recursively when initializing an array of structs. If
each struct contains an *int* field, a *bool* field, and a reference type field, then
each *int* field is initialized to 0, each *bool* field is initialized to *false*, and each
reference type field is initialized to *null*. It's as if the default struct constructor
automatically initializes each struct element.

You can initialize the elements of an array to specific values. You write a
comma-separated list of the specific values between a pair of curly brackets. For
example, to initialize *pins* to an array of 4 *int* variables whose values are 9, 3, 7,
and 2, you would write this:

```
int[] pins = new int[4]{ 9, 3, 7, 2 };
```

The values between the curly brackets do not have to be constants. They can be
values calculated at run time by calling methods, as shown in this example:

```
Random r = new Random();
int[] pins = new int[4]
{
    r.Next() % 10,
    r.Next() % 10,
    r.Next() % 10,
    r.Next() % 10
};
```

The number of values between the curly brackets must exactly match the size of
the array instance being created:

```
int[] pins = new int[3]{ 9, 3, 7, 2 }; // compile time error
int[] pins = new int[4]{ 9, 3, 7 };    // compile time error
int[] pins = new int[4]{ 9, 3, 7, 2 }; // okay
```

When you're initializing an array variable, you can use this syntax shorthand: write just the comma-separated values between curly brackets. For example, instead of writing this:

```
int[] pins = new int[4]{ 9, 3, 7, 2 };
```

You can write this:

```
int[] pins = { 9, 3, 7, 2 };
```

However, this shortcut only works for initializing the array. If you are assigning an already-declared array variable, the shorthand isn't allowed:

```
int[] pins = { 9, 3, 7, 2 };           // okay
    pins = { 9, 3, 7, 2 };             // compile time error
    pins = new int[4]{ 9, 3, 7, 2 };   // okay
```

You can initialize each struct in an array of structs by calling the struct constructor, as shown in this example:

```
Time[] schedule = new Time[2]{ new Time(12,30), new Time(5,30) };
```

Accessing Individual Array Elements

To access an individual array element, you write the name of the array variable followed by the integer index of the element you're accessing between square brackets. Array indexing is zero-based. The initial element of an array lives at index zero and not index one. An index of one accesses the second element. This means that to access the third element of the array referred to by *pins*, you would write this:

```
pins[2]
```

You can use this expression in a read or a write context. For example:

```
pins[2] = 6;                // write context
Console.WriteLine(pins[2]); // read context
```

All array element access is bounds-checked. If you use an integer index that is less than 0 or greater than or equal to the length of the array, the compiler will throw an *IndexOutOfRangeException*, as in this example:

```
try
{
    int[] pins = { 9, 3, 7, 2 };
    Console.WriteLine(pins[4]); // oops, the 4th element is at index 3
}
catch (IndexOutOfRangeException caught)
{
    ⋮
}
```

Iterating Through an Array

You can iterate through all the elements of an array using a *for* statement. The following sample code writes the array element values to the console:

```
int[] pins = { 9, 3, 7, 2 };
for (int index = 0; index != pins.Length; index++)
{
    int pin = pins[index];
    Console.WriteLine(pin);
}
```

Termination Condition

Some programmers prefer to use the != operator instead of the <= operator in the termination condition because that index represents an invariance (meaning something that's always true). In this case, index represents the number of digits written to the console. At the start of the iteration, the value of index is 0, which means that no digits have been written to the console. At the end of the iteration, index should still identify the number of digits that have been written to the console. If you use a != operator, without even looking at the body of the iteration, you know exactly what the value of index will be when the iteration ends—it will be *pins.Length* (because if it wasn't, the iteration would still be going). On the other hand, if you use a <= operator, you can conclude only that, at the end of the iteration, the value of index will be greater than or equal to *pins.Length*.

There are a lot of ways you can get this iteration wrong. You might accidentally start at index one instead of index zero, in which case you'd miss the initial element. You might accidentally use the <= operator in your termination condition, in which case you have an off-by-one error causing an *IndexOutOfRangeException*. You might forget to increment the index, in which case the *for* statement would never exit. Fortunately, a better way bypasses all these potential problems: You can use a *foreach* statement to iterate through the elements of an array. For example, here's the previous *for* statement rewritten as an equivalent *foreach* statement:

```
int[] pins = { 9, 3, 7, 2 };
foreach (int pin in pins)
{
    Console.WriteLine(pin);
}
```

The *foreach* statement declares an iteration variable (in the example, *int pin*) that automatically acquires the value of each element in the array. This construct is much more declarative; it expresses the intention of the code much more directly and all of the *for* loop scaffolding drops away. The *foreach* statement is the preferred way to iterate through an array. However, in a few cases, you'll find you have to revert to a *for* statement.

- A *foreach* statement always iterates through the whole array. If you want only to iterate through a known portion of an array (for example, the first half), or to bypass certain elements (for example, every third element), it's easier to use a *for* statement.

- A *foreach* statement always iterates from index zero though index *Length* −1. If you want to iterate backwards, it's easier to use a *for* statement.

- If the body of the loop needs to know the index of the element rather than just the value of the element, you'll have to use a *for* statement.

- If you need to modify the elements of the array, you'll have to use a *for* statement. This is because the iteration variable of the *foreach* statement is a read-only variable.

Copying Arrays

Arrays are reference types. An array variable contains a reference to an array instance. This means that when you copy an array variable, you end up with two references that refer to the same array instance, for example:

```
int[] pins = { 9, 3, 7, 2 };
int[] alias = pins; // alias and pins refer to the same array instance
```

If you want to make a copy of the array instance that an array variable refers to, you have to do two things. First, you need to create a new array instance of the same type and the same length as the array you are copying, as in this example:

```
int[] pins = { 9, 3, 7, 2 };
int[] copy = new int[4];
```

This works, but if you change the length of the original array, you must remember to also change the size of the copy. It's better to determine the length of an array by using its *Length* property, as shown in this example:

```
int[] pins = { 9, 3, 7, 2 };
int[] copy = new int[pins.Length];
```

▶ **Note** A *property* is a method that's disguised as a field. Properties are discussed in Chapter 14. For now, just note carefully that *Length* does not have any parentheses; it looks and behaves like a field.

The values inside *copy* are now all initialized to their default value of 0. The second thing you need to do is set the values inside the new array to the same values as in the original array. You could do this by using a *for* statement, as shown in this example:

```
int[] pins = { 9, 3, 7, 2 };
int[] copy = new int[pins.Length];
for (int i = 0; i != copy.Length; i++)
{
    copy[i] = pins[i];
}
```

You'll also see a few alternative ways to copy an array in the following section. No matter how you decide to copy an array, it's very important to realize that an array copy is a *shallow* copy and not a *deep* copy. To illustrate this principle, consider the effect of creating and copying an array whose element type is, itself, a reference type. The following example creates an array of four triangles:

```
Triangle[] triangles = new Triangle[4];
```

If *Triangle* is a class, the rules of array instance initialization state that each element is initialized to *null* (remember what we learned in the earlier section). In other words, a diagram of the previous statement looks like this.

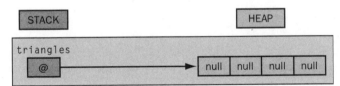

Suppose you then fill the *triangles* array with four new *Triangle* objects, like this:

```
Triangle[] triangles = new Triangle[4];
for (int i = 0; i != triangles.Length; i++)
{
    triangles[i] = new Triangle();
}
```

A diagram of this example looks like this.

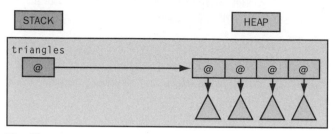

Finally, suppose you now make a copy of the *triangles* array, like this:

```
Triangle[] copy = new Triangle[triangles.Length];
for (int i = 0: i != copy.Length; i++)
{
    copy[i] = triangles[i];
}
```

A diagram of this example looks like this.

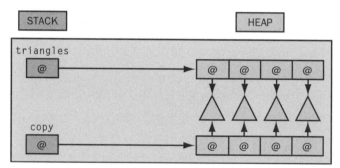

This all makes sense when you think about it carefully. An array of objects is really an array of references to objects. The references inside each array element live in contiguous memory, but the objects that these references refer to almost certainly do not. When you copy an array of references, you get two arrays whose corresponding references refer to the same objects.

Using the *System.Array* Class

In Chapter 9, you learned that the keyword *int* is, in fact, just an alias for the *System.Int32* struct. This is why *int* types are value types; all structs are value types. Knowing this helped to make sense of statements that call a method on an integer literal, for example:

```
string rep = 42.ToString();
```

It shouldn't come as too much of a shock to learn that all array types (such as *int[]*, *double[]*, and *object[]*) inherit from the *System.Array* class. This is why all array types are reference types, and all classes are reference types. The *System.Array* class provides the *Length* property for all arrays. In other words, there is no difference between the following two statements:

```
int[] pips = new int[4]{ 9, 3, 7, 2 };
Array pips = new int[4]{ 9, 3, 7, 2 };
```

However, you'll rarely see the *Array* class in code. Its main purpose is to bring all array types into the common language runtime (CLR). Also, the useful initialization shortcut doesn't work when initializing an array variable:

```
int[] pips = { 9, 3, 7, 2 }; // okay
Array pips = { 9, 7, 3, 2 }; // compile time error
```

However, the *Array* class does automatically provide some useful methods that you can use on your array variables. For example, rather than writing a *for* statement to copy the elements in one array to another array, you can use the *System.Array* instance method called *CopyTo*, which copies the contents of one array into another array given a specified starting index:

```
int[] pins = { 9, 3, 7, 2 };
int[] copy = new int[pins.Length];
pins.CopyTo(copy, 0);
```

Another way to copy the values is to use the *System.Array* static method called *Copy*. As with *CopyTo*, the target array must be initialized before the *Copy* call is made:

```
int[] pins = { 9, 3, 7, 2 };
int[] copy = new int[pins.Length];
Array.Copy(pins, copy, copy.Length);
```

Yet another alternative is to use the *System.Array* instance method called *Clone*, which can be used to create an entire array and copy it in one action:

```
int[] pins = { 9, 3, 7, 2 };
int[] copy = (int[])pins.Clone();
```

What Are Collection Classes?

Arrays are only one way to collect elements of the same type. The Microsoft .NET Framework has a namespace called *System.Collections* that contains several classes whose job is also to collect elements together. These classes provide ready-made solutions for situations when you need to collect elements in specialized ways.

All *collection classes* accept, hold, and return their elements as objects. That is, the element type of a collection class is always *object* (*System.Object*). To understand the implications of this, it is helpful to contrast an array of *int* variables (*int* is a value type) with an array of objects (*object* is a reference type). Because *int* is a value type, an array of *int* variables holds its *int* values directly, as shown in the following diagram.

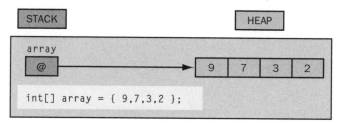

Now consider the effect when the array is an array of objects. You can still add integer values to this array (in fact, you can add values of any type to it). When you add an integer value, it is automatically boxed and the array element (an object reference) refers to the boxed copy of the integer value (for a reminder on boxing, refer to Chapter 8). This is illustrated in the following diagram.

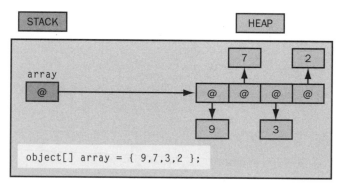

Remember that the element type of a collection class is always *object*. This means that when you insert a value into a collection, it is always boxed, and when you remove a value from a collection, you must unbox it by using a cast. The following sections provide a very quick overview of four of the most useful *Collection* classes. Refer to the .NET Framework documentation for more details on each class.

ArrayList

ArrayList is a helpful class for shuffling elements around in an array. You might have noticed that there are occasions when an array can be too restrictive:

- If you want to resize an array, you have to create a new array, copy the elements (leaving out some if the new array is smaller), and then update the array references.

- If you want to remove an element from an array, you have to make a copy of the element and then shuffle all the trailing elements up by one place. Even this doesn't quite work because you end up with two copies of the last element.

- If you want to insert an element into an array, you have to shuffle elements down by one place to make a free slot. Even this doesn't quite work because you lose the last element.

Here's how you can overcome the restrictions of the *ArrayList* class:

- You can remove an element from an *ArrayList* by using its *Remove* method. The *ArrayList* automatically takes care of all the element shuffling.

- You can add an element to the end of an *ArrayList* by using its *Add* method. You supply only the element to be added. The *ArrayList* knows its own length and will resize itself if necessary.

- You can insert an element into the middle of an *ArrayList* by using its *Insert* method. Again, the *ArrayList* will resize itself if necessary.

Here's an example that shows how you could use *ArrayList* to write the numbers 10 through 1 to the console window:

```
using System;
using System.Collections;
⋮
ArrayList numbers = new ArrayList();
⋮
// fill the ArrayList
foreach (int number in new int[12]{10,9,8,7,7,6,5,10,4,3,2,1})
{
    numbers.Add(number);
}
⋮
// remove first element whose value is 7 (the 4th element, index 3)
numbers.Remove(7);
// remove the element that's now the 7th element, index 6 (10)
numbers.RemoveAt(6);
⋮
// iterate remaining 10 elements using a for statement
for (int i = 0; i != numbers.Count; i++)
{
    int number = (int)numbers[i];
    Console.WriteLine(number);
```

```
}
  :
// iterate remaining 10 using a foreach statement
foreach (int number in numbers)
{
    Console.WriteLine(number);
}
```

The output for this program is:

```
10
9
8
7
6
5
4
3
2
1
10
9
8
7
6
5
4
3
2
1
```

You always use the *Count* property to find out how many elements are inside a collection. Yes, this is different from arrays: arrays use the *Length* property, and collection classes use the *Count* property.

You are in complete control of where the elements live within an *ArrayList*. You can choose the exact index where an element is located.

Queue

The *Queue* class implements the classic first-in first-out (FIFO) collection. An element joins the queue at the back (Enqueue) and leaves the queue at the front (Dequeue). As with an *ArrayList*, you are in complete control of where the elements live within a *Queue*.

Here's an example of a queue and its operations:

```
using System;
using System.Collections;
  :
```

```
Queue numbers = new Queue();
  ⋮
// fill the queue
foreach (int number in new int[4]{9, 3, 7, 2})
{
    numbers.Enqueue(number);
    Console.WriteLine(number + " has joined the queue");
}
  ⋮
// iterate through the queue
foreach (int number in numbers)
{
    Console.WriteLine(number);
}
  ⋮
// empty the queue
while (numbers.Count != 0)
{
    int number = (int)numbers.Dequeue();
    Console.WriteLine(number + " has left the queue");
}
```

The output from this program is:

```
9 has joined the queue
3 has joined the queue
7 has joined the queue
2 has joined the queue
9
3
7
2
9 has left the queue
3 has left the queue
7 has left the queue
2 has left the queue
```

▶ **Tip**   A useful naming convention is to name your array and collection variables
using plurals, such as *names* (where each element is a name), *people* (where
each element is a person), or *surfaces* (where each element is a surface).

Stack

The *Stack* class implements the classic last-in first-out (LIFO) collection. An element joins the stack at the top (Push) and leaves the stack at the top (Pop). To
visualize this, think of a stack of dishes: new dishes are added to the top and
dishes are removed from the top, making the first dish to be placed onto the

stack the last one to be removed. Once again, you are in complete control of where the elements live within a *Stack*. Here's an example:

```
using System;
using System.Collections;
⋮
Stack numbers = new Stack();
⋮
// fill the stack
foreach (int number in new int[4]{9, 3, 7, 2})
{
    numbers.Push(number);
    Console.WriteLine(number + " has been pushed on the stack");
}
⋮
// iterate through the stack
foreach (int number in numbers)
{
    Console.WriteLine(number);
}
⋮
// empty the stack
while (numbers.Count != 0)
{
    int number = (int)numbers.Pop();
    Console.WriteLine(number + " has been popped off the stack");
}
```

The output from this program is:

```
9 has been pushed on the stack
3 has been pushed on the stack
7 has been pushed on the stack
2 has been pushed on the stack
2
7
3
9
2 has been popped off the stack
7 has been popped off the stack
3 has been popped off the stack
9 has been popped off the stack
```

SortedList

The array and *ArrayList* types provide a way to map an integer index to an element. You provide an integer index inside square brackets (for example, [4]), and you get back the element at index 4 (which is the fifth element). However, sometimes you might want to provide a mapping where the type you map from is not an *int* but rather some other type, such as *string*, *double*, or *Time*. In other languages, this is often called an *associative array*. The *SortedList* class provides this functionality by internally maintaining two object arrays, one for the *keys* you're mapping from and one for the *values* you're mapping to. The keys array is always sorted (it is called a *SortedList*, after all). This means that the elements held inside the keys array must be comparable. (If they're not, you'll get an exception.)

When you insert a key/value pair into a *SortedList*, the key is inserted into the keys array at the correct index to keep the keys array sorted. The value is then inserted into the values array at the same index. This means you can insert key/value pairs into a *SortedList* in any order you like; they will always be held in a sorted order based on the value of the keys. There are some important consequences of this design:

- In contrast to the other collection classes, you are not in control of where the elements live within a *SortedList*.

- A *SortedList* cannot contain duplicate keys. If you call the *Add* method to add a key that is already present in the keys array, you'll get an exception. However, if you use the square bracket notation to add a key/value pair (see the following example), then you don't get an exception.

- When you use a *foreach* statement to iterate through a *SortedList*, you get back a *DictionaryEntry*. This is because there are two arrays inside a *SortedList*. The *DictionaryEntry* class provides access to the elements in both arrays through the *Key* property and the *Value* property.

Here is an example of these consequences:

```
using System;
using System.Collections;
  ⋮
SortedList map = new SortedList();
  ⋮
// fill the SortedList
string[] keys = { "these", "are", "the", "keys" };
for (int i = 0; i != keys.Length; i++)
{
    string key = keys[i];
    int value = i;
    map[key] = value; // this adds key and value to map
}
  ⋮
// iterate using a foreach statement
foreach (DictionaryEntry element in map)
```

```
{
    string key = (string)element.Key;
    int value = (int)element.Value;
    Console.WriteLine("Key: {0}, Value: {1}", key, value);
}
```

The output from this program is:

```
Key: are, Value: 1
Key: keys, Value: 3
Key: the, Value: 2
Key: these, Value: 0
```

▶ **Note** If you're a C++ programmer, you will recognize that the *ArrayList* class is similar to *std::vector<>* and the *SortedList* class is similar to *std::map<>*.

Comparing Arrays and Collections

Here's a summary of the important differences between arrays and collections:

- An array declares the type of the element it holds, whereas a collection class doesn't. This is because the collection classes store their elements as objects.

- An array instance has a fixed size and cannot grow or shrink. A collection class can dynamically resize itself as required.

- An array is a read/write data structure; there is no way to create a read-only array. However, it is possible to use the collection classes in a read-only fashion through the *ReadOnly* method. (Any attempt to write to them then causes a run-time exception.)

Using Collection Classes to Play Cards

The following exercise presents a Microsoft Windows application that simulates dealing a pack of cards to four players. The pack of cards is implemented as an *ArrayList*. You might think that a pack should be implemented as an array. After all, there are always 52 cards in a pack. This is true, but it overlooks the fact that much of the time, the cards will not be in the pack because they will have been dealt in the game. If you use an array, you'll have to record how many slots in the array actually hold a *PlayingCard*. You will study the code and then write two methods: one to shuffle a pack of cards and one to return the cards in a hand to the pack.

Deal the cards

1 Start Microsoft Visual Studio .NET.

2 Open the Aggregates project, located in the \Microsoft Press\Visual C# Step by Step\Chapter 10\Aggregates folder in your My Documents folder. The Aggregates project opens.

3 On the Debug menu, click Start Without Debugging. Visual Studio .NET builds and runs the program. The Windows form displays the cards in the hands of the four players (North, South, East, and West). There are also two buttons: one to deal the cards and one to return the cards to the pack.

4 Click Deal on the Windows form. The 52 cards in the pack are dealt to the four hands, 13 cards per hand.

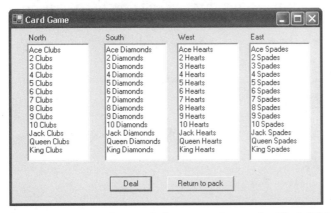

As you can see, the cards have not been shuffled. This is because the *Shuffle* method has not yet been implemented.

5 Click Return To Pack. Nothing happens because the method to return the cards to the pack has also not yet been written.

6 Click Deal. This time the cards in each of the hands disappear because before dealing the cards, each hand is reset. Because there are no cards in the pack (the method has not been written yet), there is nothing to deal.

7 Close the form. You return to the Visual Studio .NET programming environment.

Now that you know what the problems are, you will fix them.

Shuffle the pack

1   Open the Pack.cs source file in the Code pane of the Code and Text Editor window.

The *Pack* class contains a private *ArrayList* field called *cards*. The Pack.cs source file contains a using System.Collections; directive. Notice also that the *Pack* class has a constructor that creates and adds the 52 *PlayingCards* to the *ArrayList*.

2   Locate the *Shuffle* method of the *Pack* class. The method is not currently implemented.

There are a number of ways to simulate shuffling a pack of cards. Perhaps the simplest is to choose each card in sequence and swap it with another card selected at random. The .NET Framework contains a class called *Random* that you will now use to generate random integer numbers. If you did not need to shuffle the pack and just needed to deal the top card, a *Stack* would have been a good choice for the collection of cards.

3   Declare a local variable of type *Random* called *random* and initialize it to a newly created *Random* object using the default *Random* constructor.

The *Shuffle* method should now look exactly like this:

```
public void Shuffle()
{
    Random random = new Random();
}
```

4   Add a *for* statement that iterates an *int i* from 0 up to the number of elements inside the cards *ArrayList*.

The *Shuffle* method should now look exactly like this:

```
public void Shuffle()
{
    Random random = new Random();
    for (int i = 0; i != cards.Count; i++)
    {
    }
}
```

The next step is to choose a random index between 0 and *cards.Count*. You will then swap the card at index *i* with the card at this random index. You can generate a positive random integer by calling the *Random.Next* instance method. The value of this positive random integer will almost certainly be greater than *cards.Count*.

You must then convert this value into the range 0 to *cards.Count* −1 inclusive. The easiest way to do this is to use the % operator to find the remainder when dividing by *cards.Count*.

5   Inside the *for* statement, declare a local variable called *too* and initialize it to a random number between 0 and *cards.Count*.

The *Shuffle* method should now look exactly like this:

```
public void Shuffle()
{
    Random random = new Random();
    for (int i = 0; i != cards.Count; i++)
    {
        int too = random.Next() % cards.Count;
    }
}
```

The final step is to swap the card at index *i* with the card at index *too*. To do this, you must use a temporary local variable. Remember that the elements inside a collection class (such as *ArrayList*) are of type *System.Object* (*object*).

6   Add three statements to swap the card at index *i* with the card at index *too*.

The *Shuffle* method should now look exactly like this:

```
public void Shuffle()
{
    Random random = new Random();
    for (int i = 0; i != cards.Count; i++)
    {
        int too = random.Next() % cards.Count;
        object temp = cards[i];
        cards[i] = cards[too];
        cards[too] = temp;
    }
}
```

Notice that you have to use a *for* statement here. A *foreach* statement would not work because you need write access to each element as you swap it.

7   On the Debug menu, click Start Without Debugging. Visual Studio .NET builds and runs the program.

8   Click Deal. This time the pack is shuffled before dealing. (Your screen will differ slightly each time, because the card order is now random).

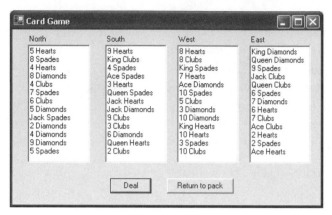

9   Close the form. You return to the Visual Studio .NET programming environment.

The final step is to add the code to return the cards to the pack.

Return the cards to the pack

1   In the Code pane, Open the Hand.cs source file. The *Hand* class also contains an *ArrayList* called *cards*.

The idea is that at any one time, each card is either in the pack or in a hand.

2   Locate the *ReturnCardsTo* method in the *Hand* class. (This class is located in the Hand.cs file.)

The *Pack* class has a method called *Accept* that takes a single parameter of type *PlayingCard*. You need to create a loop that goes through the cards in the hand and passes them back to the pack.

3   Complete the *ReturnCardsTo* method as follows:

```
public void ReturnCardsTo(Pack pack)
{
    foreach (PlayingCard card in cards)
    {
        pack.Accept(card);
    }
    cards.Clear();
}
```

A *foreach* statement is convenient here because you do not need write access to the element and you do not need to know the index of the element. It is important to call *cards.Clear* after returning the cards to the pack so that the cards aren't in both the pack and the hand.

4   On the Debug menu, click Start Without Debugging. Visual Studio .NET builds and runs the program.

5   Click Deal. The shuffled cards are dealt to the four hands as before.

6   Click Return To Pack. The hands are cleared. The cards are now back in the pack.

7   Click Deal. The shuffled cards are once again dealt to the four hands.

8   Close the form. You return to the Visual Studio .NET programming environment.

If you want to continue to the next chapter

■   Keep Visual Studio .NET running and turn to Chapter 11.

If you want to exit Visual Studio .NET now

■   On the File menu, click Exit. If you see a Save dialog box, click Yes.

Chapter 10 Quick Reference

To	Do this
Declare an array variable	Write the name of the element type, followed by square brackets, followed by the name of the variable, followed by a semicolon. For example: `bool[] flags;`
Create an instance of an array	Write the keyword *new*, followed by the name of the element type, followed by the size of the array between square brackets. For example: `bool[] flags = new bool[10];`

Initialize the elements of an array instance to specific values	Write the specific values in a comma-separated list between a pair of curly brackets. For example:
	
	`bool[] flags = { true, false,`
	`    true, false };`

Find the number of elements in an array	Use the *Length* property. For example: `int noOfElements = flags.Length;`
Access a single array element	Write the name of the array variable, followed by the integer index of the element between square brackets. Remember, array indexing starts at zero, not one. For example: `bool initialElement = flags[0];`

To	Do this
Iterate through the elements of an array/collection	Use a *for* statement or a *foreach* statement. For example:

```
bool[] flags = { true, false,
    true, false };
for (int i = 0;
    i != flags.Length; i++)
{
    Console.WriteLine(flags[i]);}
foreach (bool flag in flags)
{
    Console.WriteLine(flag);
}
```

To	Do this
Use a *Stack*	using System.Collections;

```
⋮
Stack p = new Stack();
p.Push("World");
p.Push("Hello ");
Console.Write(p.Pop());
Console.WriteLine(p.Pop());
```

To	Do this
Find the number of elements in a collection	Use the *Count* property. For example:

```
int noOfElements = flags.Count;
```

Understanding Parameter Arrays

In this chapter, you will learn how to:

- Write a method that can accept any number of arguments by using the *params* keyword.

- Write a method that can accept any number of arguments of any type by using the *params* keyword in combination with the object type.

- Process command-line arguments in the *Main* method.

Creating Overloaded Methods

Overloading is the technical term for declaring two or more methods with the same name in the same scope. Being able to overload a method is very useful in cases where you want to perform the same action on arguments of different types. The classic example of overloading in Microsoft Visual C# is *Console.WriteLine*. The *WriteLine* method is overloaded numerous times so that you can pass any primitive type argument:

```
class Console
{
    public static void WriteLine(int parameter)
    ⋮
    public static void WriteLine(double parameter)
    ⋮
    public static void WriteLine(decimal parameter)
    ⋮
}
```

As useful as overloading is, it doesn't cover every case. In particular, overloading doesn't easily handle a situation where it's not the type of parameters that vary, but the number of them. For example, what if you want to write many values to the console? Do you have to repeat the call to *Console.WriteLine* for each and every value? That would quickly get tedious. Or what if you wanted to find the minimum of two values, or three, four, five, or more? How many overloads of *Min* do you provide? And doesn't the massive duplication of all these overloaded *Min* methods worry you? It should. Code duplication should always worry you. Fortunately, there is a way to write one method that takes a variable number of arguments (a so-called *variadic method*): You can use a parameter array (a parameter declared with a *params* keyword). Before seeing how *params* arrays help to solve this problem, it helps to first understand the uses and shortcomings of plain arrays.

Using Array Arguments

One way you could find the minimum of a variable number of values would be to use an array. For example, to find the smallest value of a number of *int* values, you could write a static method called *Min* that had a single parameter that was an array of *int* values:

```
class Util
{
    public static int Min(int[] array)
    {
        if (array == null || array.Length == 0)
        {
            throw new ArgumentException("Util.Min");
        }
        int currentMin = array[0];
        foreach (int i in array)
        {
            if (i < currentMin)
            {
                currentMin = i;
            }
        }
        return currentMin;
    }
}
```

To use the *Min* method to find the minimum of two *int* values, you would write this:

```
int[] array = new int[2];
array[0] = first;
array[1] = second;
int min = Util.Min(array);
```

To use the *Min* method to find the minimum of three *int* values, you would write this:

```
int[] array = new int[3];
array[0] = first;
array[1] = second;
array[2] = third;
int min = Util.Min(array);
```

This solution is generic and thus avoids the need for a large number of overloads, but it does so at a high price: It increases the amount of code that has to be written. All we have really done is move the duplication; we haven't gotten rid of it. Fortunately, there is a way to get the best of both solutions by avoiding duplication altogether—you get the compiler to write some of the code for you by using the *params* keyword to declare a *params* array.

Declaring *params* Arrays

You use the *params* keyword as an array parameter modifier. For example, here's *Min* again, this time with its array parameter declared as a *params* array:

```
class Util
{
    public static int Min(params int[] array)
    {
        // exactly as before
    }
}
```

The effect of the *params* keyword on the *Min* method is that it allows you to call it by using any number of integer arguments. For example, to find the minimum of two integer values, you would write this:

```
int min = Util.Min(first, second);
```

And the compiler translates this call into the following code:

```
int[] array = new int[2];
array[0] = first;
array[1] = second;
int min = Util.Min(array);
```

To find the minimum of three integer values, you would write this:

```
int min = Util.Min(first, second, third);
```

And the compiler translates this call into the following code:

```
int[] array = new int[3];
array[0] = first;
array[1] = second;
array[2] = third;
int min = Util.Min(array);
```

In other words, both calls to *Min* (one call with two arguments and another with three arguments) resolve to the *Min* method with the *params* keyword. And as you can probably guess, you can call this *Min* method with any number of *int* arguments. The compiler just counts the number of *int* arguments, creates an *int* array of that size, fills the array with the arguments, and then calls the method by passing the single array parameter.

▶ **Note**   C and C++ programmers might recognize *params* as a type-safe equivalent of the *varargs* macros from the header file stdarg.h.

There are several points worth noting about *params* arrays:

■ You can use the *params* keyword only on single-dimension arrays, as in this example:

```
// compile-time error
public static int Min(params int[,] table)
    ⋮
```

■ You can't overload based solely on the *params* keyword. The *params* keyword does not form part of a method's signature, as shown in this example:

```
// compile-time error: duplicate declaration
public static int Min(int[] array)
    ⋮
public static int Min(params int[] array)
    ⋮
```

■ You're not allowed *ref* or *out params* arrays, as shown in this example:

```
// compile-time errors
public static int Min(ref params int[] array)
    ⋮
public static int Min(out params int[] array)
    ⋮
```

- A *params* array must be the last parameter. (This means you can have only one *params* array per method.) Consider this example:

```
// compile-time error
public static int Min(params int[] array, int i)
  ⋮
```

- Type conversion rules apply to the arguments.

- The compiler detects and rejects any potentially ambiguous overloads. For example, the following two *Min* methods are ambiguous; it's not clear which one should be called if you pass two *int* arguments:

```
// compile-time error
public static int Min(params int[] array)
  ⋮
public static int Min(int, params int[] array)
  ⋮
```

- A non-*params* method always takes priority over a params method. This means if you want to, you can still overload for the common cases. For example:

```
public static int Min(int lhs, int rhs)
  ⋮
public static int Min(params int[] array)
  ⋮
```

Adding the non-*params* array method might be a useful optimization technique because the compiler won't have to create and populate so many arrays.

Type Conversions

C# allows you to convert data of one type into data of another type if it makes sense to do so. C# supports implicit conversions and explicit conversions. *Implicit conversions* occur automatically, and you have probably been using them without even being aware of it. For example, consider the following statement:

```
float myFloat = 99;
```

The constant 99 is actually an integer. The compiler generates code that converts it to a floating-point value before assigning it to *myFloat*. Implicit conversions occur where data is widened. *Widening* means that the domain of the value being converted to is bigger than the domain of the original value, so there is no danger of losing any information. In the previous example, all integers can be converted to floating-point values safely and without any loss of data.

An explicit conversion requires a cast and is usually used where data is "narrowed." In these cases, the domain of the value being converted to is a subset of the domain of the original value, and there is a chance that information could be lost:

```
float myFloat = 99.9F;
int myInt = (int)myFloat;
```

In this example, not all floating-point values have an equivalent integer value, and converting from a float to an *int* will truncate the data. For this reason, you must use a cast to acknowledge this fact—you are telling the compiler that you know that some data could disappear but you are willing to take the risk.

Conversions and conversion operators are covered in more detail in Chapter 17. You can also find more information in the Microsoft Visual Studio .NET documentation.

Using *params object[ ]*

A *params int* array is very useful because it allows any number of *int* arguments in a method call. However, what if not only the number of arguments vary but also the argument types? C# has a way to solve this problem, too. The technique is based on the fact that *System.Object* (*object*) is the root of all classes. Let's take the explanation one step at a time. Consider the following two statements. The first assigns a *string* object (*string* is a reference type) to an object reference, and the second assigns an *int* value (*int* is a value type) to an object reference:

```
object r0 = "42";
object r1 = 42;
```

Both of these statements compile. The first statement compiles because *object* is an implicit base class of the string class. The second statement compiles because C# automatically boxes; a copy of 42 is placed on the heap and the object reference refers to this boxed copy. Because every single type in C# is either a reference type (in which case it has *object* as an implicit base class) or a value type (in which case it can be boxed), an object reference can refer to anything. Absolutely anything. From these two statements, it's a small step to the following code.

```
object[] r = new object[2];
r[0] = "42";
r[1] = 42;
```

This code should look familiar. This is exactly the kind of code that we can get the compiler to write for us by using a params array. You can use a *params* object array to declare a method that accepts any number of arguments of any type. Look at this example:

```
class Black
{
    public static void Hole(params object [] array)
    ⋮
}
```

I've called this method *Black.Hole*, not because it swallows every argument but because no argument can escape from it:

- You can pass it no arguments at all, in which case the compiler will pass an object array whose length is 0:

  ```
  Black.Hole();
  // converted into
  Black.Hole(new object[0]);
  ```

  ▶ **Tip** It's safe to iterate through a zero-length array using a *foreach* statement.

- You can call it by passing *null* as the argument. An array is a reference type, so you're allowed to initialize an array with *null*:

  ```
  Black.Hole(null);
  ```

- You can pass it an actual array. In other words, you can manually create the array normally created by the compiler:

  ```
  object[] array = new object[2];
  array[0] = "42";
  array[1] = 42;
  Black.Hole(array);
  ```

- You can pass it any other arguments and these arguments will automatically be wrapped inside an object array:

  ```
  Black.Hole("42", 42);
  //converted into
  Black.Hole(new object[]{"42", 42});
  ```

Console.WriteLine

The *Console* class contains many overloads for the *WriteLine* method. One of these overloads looks like this:

```
public static void WriteLine(string format, params object[] array);
```

Here's an example of a call to this method:

```
Console.WriteLine("Key:{0}, Value:{1}", key, value);
```

The compiler resolves this call into the following:

```
Console.WriteLine("Key:{0}, Value:{1}", new object[2]{key, value});
```

Note that the {0} placeholders aren't needed to determine how many arguments have been passed to the *params* array. The params array itself tells *WriteLine* that information. (If you pass too few arguments, you'll get a *FormatException*.) The {0} placeholders simply say where you want the argument to appear and which argument it is. You don't even have to write the placeholders in sequential order; {1} can come before {0} if you want (although this usage is not recommended). Look at this example:

```
Console.WriteLine("Key:{1}, Value:{0}", value, key);
```

Using *params* Arrays

In the following exercise, you will work with a console application and write a *static* method called *Util.Min* whose purpose is to find and return the minimum of a variable number of *int* arguments passed to it. You will do this by writing *Util.Min* with a params *int[]* parameter. You will implement two precondition checks on the *params* parameter to ensure the *Util.Min* method is completely robust. Finally you will call the *Util.Min* method with a variety of different arguments to confirm its universally callable nature.

Write a *params* array method

1   Start Visual Studio .NET.

2   Open the ParamsArrays project, located in the \Microsoft Press\Visual C# Step by Step\Chapter 11\ ParamsArrays folder in your My Documents folder. The ParamsArrays project opens.

3   Open the Util.cs source file in the Code pane of the Code And Text Editor window. The Util.cs file contains an empty class called *Util* in the *ParamsArrays* namespace.

4 In the Code pane, add a public static method called *Min* to the *Util* class. The *Util.Min* method returns an *int* and accepts a *params* array of *int* values.

Util.Min should look like this:

```
class Util
{
    public static int Min(params int[] array)
    {
    }
}
```

The first step in implementing *Util.Min* is to check the *array* parameter. It could be *null* and it could also be an array of zero length. In both of these cases, the best option is to throw an exception.

5 In the Code pane, add a statement to *Util.Min* that throws an *ArgumentException* if *array* is *null*. *Util.Min* should now look like this:

```
class Util
{
    public static int Min(params int[] array)
    {
        if (array == null)
        {
            throw new ArgumentException("Util.Min: null array");
        }
    }
}
```

6 In the Code pane, add a statement to *Util.Min* that throws an *ArgumentException* if the length of *array* is 0.

Util.Min should now look like this:

```
class Util
{
    public static int Min(params int[] array)
    {
        if (array == null)
        {
            throw new ArgumentException("Util.Min: null array");
        }
        if (array.Length == 0)
        {
            throw new ArgumentException("Util.Min: empty array");
        }
    }
}
```

If the length of *array* is not 0, then it must be one or more because an array cannot hold a negative number of elements. The next step is to find the smallest *int* element inside the array. Because you do not need to know the index of the smallest element, you can use a *foreach* statement for this step. You will also need a local variable to hold the smallest current value.

7   In the Code pane, add a *foreach* statement to *Util.Min* to find the smallest *int* element in the array and return it from *Util.Min* with a return statement.

Util.Min should now look like this:

```
class Util
{
    public static int Min(params int[] array)
    {
        :

        int currentMin = array[0];
        foreach (int i in array)
        {
            if (i < currentMin)
            {
                currentMin = i;
            }
        }
        return currentMin;
    }
}
```

This works, but the *if* statement inside the *foreach* statement is a little clumsy and not as direct as it could be. In the following few steps, you will refactor this part of the code.

8   In the Code pane, add another public static method called *Min* to the *Util* class. This method will return an *int* and accept two *int* parameters. Implement this *Util.Min* with a single return statement that uses the ternary operator and the less than operator.

The new *Util.Min* should look like this:

```
class Util
{
    public static int Min(int lhs, int rhs)
    {
        return lhs < rhs ? lhs : rhs;
    }
    :
}
```

9 In the Code pane, replace the *if* statement inside the *foreach* statement in the original *Util.Min* method with a call to the new *Util.Min* method.

The original *Util.Min* should look like this:

```
class Util
{
    ⋮
    public static int Min(params int[] array)
    {
        if (array == null)
        {
            throw new ArgumentException("Util.Min: null array");
        }
        if (array.Length == 0)
        {
            throw new ArgumentException("Util.Min: empty array");
        }
        int currentMin = array[0];
        foreach (int i in array)
        {
            currentMin = Min(currentMin, i);
        }
        return currentMin;
    }
}
```

10 On the Build menu, click Build Solution. Confirm that there are no errors in your code.

Call a *params* array method

1 In the Code pane, open the Program.cs source file.

2 In the Code pane, locate the *Entrance* method in the *Program* class.

3 In the Code pane, add the following statement to the *Entrance* method:

```
Console.WriteLine(Util.Min(null));
```

4 On the Debug menu, click Start Without Debugging or use the shortcut key Ctrl+F5. The program builds and runs, writing the following message to the console:

```
Exception: Util.Min: null array
```

This confirms that a *params* parameter can be *null*, so the first precondition check inside *Util.Min* is indeed necessary.

5   In the Code pane, change the call to *Console.WriteLine* in *Entrance* to the following statement:

```
Console.WriteLine(Util.Min());
```

6   On the Debug menu, click Start Without Debugging or use the short-cut key Ctrl+F5. The program builds and runs, writing the following message to the console:

```
Exception: Util.Min: empty array
```

This confirms that calling a *params* method with no arguments results in a zero length array and is not *null*, so the second precondition check inside *Util.Min* is also necessary.

7   Change the call to *Console.WriteLine* in *Entrance* to the following:

```
Console.WriteLine(Util.Min(10,9,8,7,6,5,4,3,2,1));
```

8   On the Debug menu, click Start Without Debugging or use the short-cut key Ctrl+F5.

9   The program builds, runs, and writes 1 to the console.

Using the *Main* Method

The *Main* method forms the entry point of an application. When the operating system runs an executable program, it starts the execution at the *Main* method.

▶   **Tip**   If your program contains two or more classes that contain static methods called *Main*, you can choose which one will be the executable's entry point by using the */main* option from the csc command-line compiler. This capability is useful because many programmers write a *Main* for each class whose purpose is to act as a test case for that class.

Several varieties of *Main* are permitted:

■   If you want to, you can return an *int* value from *Main* to indicate success or failure:

```
class Game
{
    static int Main()
    ⋮
}
```

■   If you don't want to return anything from *Main*, that's allowed, too:

```
class Game
{
    static void Main()
    ⋮
}
```

■ If you want to call *Main* with some command-line arguments, you're allowed to declare that *Main* accepts an array of strings:

```
class Game
{
    static void Main(string[] args)
    ⋮
}
```

Suppose this last version of *Main* is the entry point for an executable program called Game.exe. You could then call Game.exe from the command line and pass information to it. For example, you might program *Main* so that it allows the names of the players to be passed as command line parameters, like this:

```
c:\>Game.exe Peter Jill Paul Sue
```

In this case, the operating system would automatically pass Peter, Jill, Paul, and Sue into *Main* as four strings inside the array parameter. In other words, it would be as if the operating system had written this:

```
string[] array = { "Peter", "Jill", "Paul", "Sue" };
Game.Main(array)
```

You could pass any number of command-line arguments, though whatever you pass gets put into the array. This capability could be very useful; many games can have a variable number of players. You might imagine that this capability to accept any number of arguments would mean that *Main*'s array should be declared as a *params* array, like this:

```
static void Main(params string[] args)
⋮
```

This would probably be a mistake. The point is that you don't call *Main* from the inside; the operating system calls *Main* from outside. Unless you plan to call *Main* from inside the program (which would be a strange thing to do), the *params* keyword is not required.

▶ **Note**   C and C++ programmers should note that the name of the executable program itself is not passed as argument zero.

If you want to continue to the next chapter

■ Keep Visual Studio .NET running and turn to Chapter 12.

If you want to exit Visual Studio .NET now

■ On the File menu, click Exit. If you see a Save dialog box, click Yes.

Parameter Arrays

11

Chapter 11 Quick Reference

To	Do this
Write a method that accepts any number of arguments of a given type	Write a method whose parameter is a *params* array of the given type. For example, a method that accepts any number of *bool* arguments would be:

```
someType Method(
    params bool[] flags)
{
    ⋮
}
```

To	Do this
Write a method that accepts any number of arguments of any type	Write a method whose parameter is a *params* array of an object. For example:

```
someType Method(
    params object[] many)
{
    ⋮
}
```

To	Do this
Accept command-line arguments in *Main*	Write *Main* to accept an array of strings. (The *params* keyword is not necessary in this case.)

```
For example:
static void Main(
    string[] args)
{
    ⋮
}
```

Working with Inheritance

In this chapter, you will learn how to:

■ Create a derived class that inherits from a base class.

■ Call a base class constructor from the derived class constructor.

■ Control method hiding/overriding by using the *new*, *virtual*, and *override* keywords.

■ Limit accessibility within an inheritance hierarchy by using the *protected* keyword.

■ Create an interface containing only the names of methods.

■ Implement an interface in a struct or class by writing the bodies of the methods.

■ Capture implementation commonality in an abstract class.

■ Declare that a class cannot be derived by using the *sealed* keyword.

■ Write a class that implements multiple interfaces.

■ Implement interface methods by using the explicit interface implementation technique.

What Is Inheritance?

There is generally a lot of confusion among programmers as to what inheritance is. Part of this trouble stems from the fact that the word "inheritance" itself is overloaded with meanings. If someone bequeaths something to you in a will, you are said to inherit it. Similarly, we say that you inherit half of your genes from your mother and half of your genes from your father. Both of these uses of the word inheritance have absolutely nothing to do with inheritance in programming.

Inheritance in programming is all about classification; it's a relationship between classes. For example, when you were at school, you probably learned about mammals and that a horse is a mammal. In Microsoft Visual C#, you could model this by creating two classes, one called *mammal* and one called *horse*, and declare that *horse* inherits from *mammal*. The inheritance would model that there is a relationship and would capture the fact that *all* horses are mammals.

▶ **Important**   Inheritance is a class relationship rather than an object relationship. By declaring that the relationship exists at the class level, you ensure that the relationship always holds for all objects of the class.

Understanding Core Syntax

This section covers the essential inheritance-related syntax that you need to know to create classes that inherit from other classes. You will learn what this syntax means when you see it in code or in documentation.

Base Classes and Derived Classes

The syntax for declaring that a class inherits from another class is as follows:

```
class DerivedClass : BaseClass
{
    ⋮
}
```

The derived class inherits from the base class. This means that the derived class is a base class. A class is allowed to derive from, at most, one class. In other words, a class is not allowed to derive from two or more classes.

▶ **Tip**   C++ programmers should note that you do not and cannot explicitly specify whether the inheritance is public, private, or protected. C# inheritance is always implicitly public. Java programmers should note that there is no *extends* keyword.

The *System.Object* class is the root class for all classes. In other words, all classes implicitly derive from the *System.Object* class. Suppose you declare a class like this:

```
class Token
{
    public Token(string name)
    {
        ⋮
    }
    ⋮
}
```

The compiler silently rewrites the code to the following (which you can write explicitly if you really want to, but it's best not to):

```
class Token : System.Object
{
    public Token(string name)
    {
        ⋮
    }
    ⋮
}
```

Calling Base Class Constructors

A derived class constructor must call its base class constructor. You always use the *base* keyword to call the base class constructor. There is no ambiguity in using the *base* keyword because a class can have at most one base class. Here's an example:

```
class IdentifierToken : Token
{
    public IdentifierToken(string name)
        : base(name) // calls Token(name)
    {
        ⋮
    }
    ⋮
}
```

If you don't explicitly call a base class constructor in a derived class constructor, the compiler will attempt to silently insert a call to the base class's default constructor. The full story of the previous example is that the compiler will rewrite this:

```
class Token
{
    public Token(string name)
    {
        ⋮
    }
    ⋮
}
```

The rewritten code becomes this:

```
class Token : System.Object
{
    public Token(string name)
        : base()
    {
        ⋮
```

```
        }
        ⋮
    }
```

This works because *System.Object* does have a public default constructor. However, not all classes have a public default constructor, in which case forgetting to call the base class constructor will result in a compile-time error. For example:

```
class IdentifierToken : Token
{
    public IdentifierToken(string name)
    // error, base class Token does not have
    // a public default constructor
    {
        ⋮
    }
    ⋮
}
```

new Methods

If a base class and a derived class happen to declare two methods with the same signature (the method signature is the name of the method and the number and types of its parameters), the two methods are nonetheless completely unrelated. For example, if you compile the following example, the compiler will generate a warning message telling you that *IdentifierToken.Name* hides *Token.Name*:

```
class Token
{
    ⋮
    public string Name() { ... }
}
class IdentifierToken : Token
{
    ⋮
    public string Name() { ... }
}
```

The warning is reminding you that, because the two methods share the same signature and they are unrelated, the definition of *Name* in *IdentifierToken* hides the *Name* method in *Token*. Most of the time, such a coincidence is at best a source of confusion, and you should consider renaming them to avoid clashes. However, if you're sure that you want the two methods to have the same signature, you can silence the warning by using the *new* keyword as follows:

```
class Token
{
    ⋮
```

```
    public string Name() { ... }
}
class IdentifierToken : Token
{
    ⋮
    new public string Name() { ... }
}
```

Using the *new* keyword like this does not change the fact that the two methods are still completely unrelated and that hiding still occurs. It just turns the warning off. In effect, the *new* keyword says, "I'm a professional programmer, and I know what I'm doing."

To fully understand what hiding means, consider the following example and think about which of the two *Name* methods will be called:

```
static void Method(Token t)
{
    Console.WriteLine(t.Name());
}
static void Main()
{
    IdentifierToken variable = new IdentifierToken("variable");
    Method(variable);
}
```

In this example, *Main* declares a variable of type *IdentifierToken* and initializes it to an object of type *IdentifierToken*. The variable is then passed as an argument to *Method*. Importantly, *Method* declares its parameter to be of type *Token*, not of type *IdentifierToken*. This is allowed because an *IdentifierToken* is a *Token* and can therefore substitute as a *Token*. The body of *Method* then calls *Name* on the parameter. As human beings, we can look at this code and know that in this particular case the parameter, although typed as a *Token*, actually refers to an object of type *IdentifierToken*. You might therefore expect the call to *Name* to resolve to the *IdentifierToken.Name*. But it doesn't; it resolves to *Token.Name*. This occurs because the two *Name* methods are completely unrelated and effectively hide each other. This is probably not the behavior you want. Fortunately, there is a way to make the call work the way you'd expect.

virtual Methods

To make the call work the way you'd expect, you have to use polymorphism. *Polymorphism* literally means "many forms." In programming, polymorphism means being able to implement the same method more than once. Using polymorphism, you can connect the previously unrelated base and derived class *Name* methods and declare that they are two implementations of the same method. You have to explicitly use the *virtual* keyword to turn on polymorphism for a given method. For example:

```
class Token
{
    ⋮
    public virtual string Name() { ... }
}
```

The *virtual* keyword says that this is the first implementation of a method called *Name*. In contrast, without the *virtual* keyword (as it was previously), it is the only implementation of a method called *Name*.

By default a C# method is not virtual. (This is the same as in C++ but a major difference from Java where, by default, a method is virtual.)

override Methods

If a base class declares that a method is virtual, a derived class can use the *override* keyword to declare another implementation of that method. For example:

```
class IdentifierToken : Token
{
    ⋮
    public override string Name() { ... }
}
```

There are some important rules you must follow when declaring polymorphic methods using the *virtual* and *override* keywords:

- You're not allowed to declare a private method with the *virtual* or *override* keyword. If you try, you'll get a compile-time error. Private really is private.

- The two methods must be identical. That is, they must have the same name, the same parameter types, and the same return type. (C# does not support return type co-variance.)

- The two methods must have the same access. For example, if one of the two methods is public, the other must also be public. (C++ programmers should take note. In C++, the methods can have different accessibility.)

- You can override only a virtual method. If the base class method is not virtual and you try to override it, you'll get a compile-time error. This is sensible; it should be up to the base class to decide whether its methods can be overridden.

- If the derived class does not declare the method by using the *override* keyword, it does not override the base class method. In other words, it becomes an implementation of a completely different method that happens to have the same name. As before, this will cause a compile-time hiding warning, which you can silence by using the *new* keyword as previously described.

■ An *override* method is implicitly virtual and can itself be overridden in a further derived class. However, you are not allowed to explicitly declare that an *override* method is virtual by using the *virtual* keyword. The idea is that each method has no qualifiers if it's a plain non-polymorphic, non-hiding method; otherwise it has just one qualifier (this rule almost always holds).

Now that the base class method is declared as virtual and the derived class method is declared to override it, we can revisit our previous example:

```
static void Method(Token t)
{
    Console.WriteLine(t.Name());
}
static void Main()
{
    IdentifierToken variable = new IdentifierToken("variable");
    Method(variable);
}
```

This time, when the compiler compiles the call to *Name* made on the parameter *t* (which is declared as a *Token*), it notices that *Token.Name* is virtual. Because of this, it does not directly call *Token.Name* (as it did before). It calls the "most derived" implementation of *Token.Name* that exists in the actual object that *t* refers to. In this particular case, *t* refers to an object of type *IdentifierToken*, which is a class that does override *Token.Name*; the call to *t.Name* resolves to *IdentifierToken.Name* as expected.

protected Access

The *public* and *private* access keywords create two extremes of accessibility: public members of a class are accessible to everyone whereas private members of a class are accessible to no one (except the class itself, of course). These two extremes are sufficient when considering classes in isolation. However, as all experienced object-oriented programmers know, isolated classes cannot solve complex problems. The secret of solving complex and large problems is learning how to connect classes together, learning how to move from programming in the small through to programming in the large. Inheritance is one very powerful way of connecting classes, and there is clearly a very special and close relationship between a derived class and its base class (but not vice versa). The *protected* keyword is a reflection of the special derived-to-base relationship that inheritance creates:

■ A derived class can access a protected base class member. In other words, inside the derived class, a protected base class member is effectively public.

■ If the class is not a derived class, it can't access a protected class member. In other words, inside a class that is not a derived class, a protected class member is effectively private.

C# gives programmers complete freedom to declare both methods and fields as protected. However, most object-oriented guidelines recommend keeping your fields strictly private. Public fields violate encapsulation because all users of the class have direct, unrestricted access to the fields. Protected fields maintain encapsulation for users of a class, for whom the protected fields are inaccessible. However, protected fields still allow encapsulation to be violated by classes that inherit from the class.

▶ **Note**   You can access a protected base class member not only in a derived class, but in classes derived from the derived class as well. A protected base class member retains its protected accessibility in a derived class and is accessible to further derived classes.

Creating Interfaces

Inheriting from a class is a powerful mechanism, but the real power of inheritance comes from inheriting from an interface. Interfaces are the real reason that inheritance exists. Interfaces are important. An interface allows you to completely separate the name of a method from the implementation of a method. Up to now that hasn't been possible (a virtual method must have a body). The separation that an interface affords is tremendously powerful.

Interfaces allow you to truly separate the "what" from the "how." The interface tells you only what the name of the method is. Exactly how the method is implemented is not a concern of the interface. The interface represents how you want an object to be *used* rather than how it happens to be implemented at a particular moment in time. This corresponds very closely with how we work as human beings. You use lots of devices every day with no conscious thought as to how they work. For example, the way telephones work is irrelevant to you because you're only using them, you're not making them. It's enough to know what their function is and how to get them to perform that function. It's enough to know the interface. As a user you don't know how the telephones work and you don't care how they work. Why should you? You just want to use them.

Syntax

To declare an interface, you use the *interface* keyword instead of the *class* or *struct* keyword. Inside the interface, you declare methods exactly as in a class or a struct except that you never specify an access modifier (no public, private, or protected access), and you replace the method body with a semicolon. For example:

```
interface IToken
{
    string Name();
}
```

> ▶ **Tip**   The Microsoft .NET Framework documentation recommends that you prefix the name of your interfaces with a capital I. This convention is the last vestige of Hungarian Notation in C#.

Restrictions

The essential idea to remember is that an interface never contains any implementation. The following restrictions are natural consequences of this:

- You cannot create instances of an interface. If you were allowed to create an instance of an interface, what would it mean to call one of its methods which, by definition, would only be named and not implemented?
- You're not allowed any fields in an interface. A field is an implementation of an object attribute. Fields are not allowed in an interface, not even static ones.
- You're not allowed any constructors in an interface. A constructor contains the statements used to initialize a newly created object instance, and you're not allowed to create an instance of an interface.
- You're not allowed a destructor in an interface. A destructor contains the statements used to destroy an object instance, but to destroy an object, you have to first create it, which you can't do because this is an interface.
- You cannot write an access modifier. All methods in an interface are implicitly public. An interface represents usage.
- You cannot nest any types (enums, structs, classes, interfaces, or delegates) inside an interface.
- You're not allowed to inherit an interface from a struct or a class. Structs and classes contain implementation; if an interface were allowed to inherit from either, it would be inheriting some implementation.

Implementing an Interface

To implement an interface, you declare a class (or a struct) that inherits from the interface and implements all the interface methods. For example:

```
class Token : IToken
{
    ⋮
    public string Name()
    {
        ⋮
    }
}
```

When you implement an interface, you must ensure that each method matches its corresponding interface method exactly:

- The method must be explicitly declared as being public because the interface method is implicitly public.
- The return types must match exactly.
- The method names must match exactly.
- The parameters (if there are any) must match exactly (including *ref* and *out* keyword modifiers, although not the *params* keyword modifier).

If there is any difference, the compilation will fail because the interface method will not have been implemented. By default, a method that implements an interface method is not virtual (exactly as before). If you need to override the implementation of a class method in a further derived class, you must declare that the class method is virtual (again, exactly as before). For example:

```
class Token : IToken
{
    ⋮
    public virtual string Name()
    {
        ⋮
    }
}
class IdentifierToken : Token
{
    ⋮
    public override string Name()
    {
        ⋮
    }
}
```

This behavior fits exactly with the idea that the *virtual* keyword declares the first implementation of a method (and there can be more in further derived classes), whereas a non-virtual method declares the *only* implementation of a method.

A class can extend another class and implement an interface. In this case, C# does not distinguish between the base class and the base interface by using keywords as, for example, Java does. Instead, C# uses a positional notation. The base class is named first, followed by a comma, followed by the base interface. For example:

```
interface IToken
{
    :
}
class DefaultTokenImpl
{
    :
}
class IdentifierToken : DefaultTokenImpl , IToken
{
    :
}
```

Abstract Classes

You almost always find that many classes or structs implement a given interface. For example, the *IToken* interface could be implemented by five classes, one for each type of token in a C# source file: *IdentifierToken*, *KeywordToken*, *LiteralToken*, *OperatorToken*, and *PunctuatorToken*. (You might also have classes for comments and whitespace.) In these situations, it's quite common for parts of the derived classes to share common implementations. For example, the duplication in these two classes is obvious:

```
class IdentifierToken : IToken
{
    public IdentifierToken(string name)
    {
        this.name = name;
    }
    public virtual string Name()
    {
        return name;
    }
    :
    private string name;
```

12

Inheritance

```
}
class StringLiteralToken : IToken
{
    public StringLiteralToken(string name)
    {
        this.name = name;
    }
    public virtual string Name()
    {
        return name;
    }
    ⋮
    private string name;
}
```

Duplication in code is a warning sign. You should refactor the code to avoid the duplication. However, there is a right way and a wrong way to do this. The wrong way is to push all the commonality up into the interface. This is wrong because it would mean you'd have to change the interface to a class (because an interface can't contain any implementation). Interfaces exist for good reasons. Leave the interface alone. The right way to avoid the duplication is to refactor it into a new class, whose purpose is specifically to hold the common implementation. For example:

```
class DefaultTokenImpl
{
    public DefaultTokenImpl(string name)
    {
        this.name = name;
    }
    public string Name()
    {
        return name;
    }
    private string name;
}
class IdentifierToken : DefaultTokenImpl, IToken
{
    public IdentifierToken(string name)
        : base(name)
    {
    }
    ⋮
}
class StringLiteralToken : DefaultTokenImpl, IToken
{
    public StringLiteralToken(string name)
```

```
        : base(name)
    {
    }
    :
}
```

This is a good solution but there is one thing that is still not quite right: You can now create instances of the *DefaultTokenImpl* class. This arrangement doesn't really make sense. The *DefaultTokenImpl* class exists to provide a common default implementation. Its sole purpose is to be inherited from (or not to be inherited from—each derived class can choose). The *DefaultTokenImpl* class is abstract, in the same sense that an interface is abstract. You automatically can't create instances of an interface, but to declare that you're not allowed to create instances of a class, you must explicitly declare that the class is abstract by using the *abstract* keyword. For example:

```
abstract class DefaultTokenImpl
{
    public DefaultTokenImpl(string name)
    {
        this.name = name;
    }
    public string Name()
    {
        return name;
    }
    private string name;
}
```

Notice that the new class *DefaultTokenImpl* does not implement the *IToken* interface. It could, but it doesn't really fit with its purpose. An abstract class is all about common implementation whereas an interface is all about usage. It's usually best to keep these two aspects separate and to let the non-abstract classes (such as *StringLiteralToken*) determine how to implement their interfaces:

- They can inherit from *DefaultTokenImpl* and *IToken*, in which case *DefaultTokenImpl.Name* becomes the implementation of *IToken.Name*. Notice that this means *DefaultTokenImpl.Name* must be public. You could make the constructor for *DefaultTokenImpl* protected, but the *Name* method must remain public if it is to qualify as an implementation of *IToken.Name* in a derived class.

- They can decide not to inherit from *DefaultTokenImpl*, in which case they'll have to implement *IToken.Name* themselves. A class might decide not to inherit for a number of reasons (one of which is the simple fact that a class can have at most one base class).

Sealed Classes

Using inheritance wisely is not easy. This is not really surprising; if you write an interface or an abstract class, you are knowingly writing something that will be inherited from in the future. The trouble is that predicting the future is a difficult business. It takes skill, effort, and knowledge of the problem you are trying to solve to craft a flexible, easy-to-use hierarchy of interfaces, abstract classes, and classes. To put it another way, unless you consciously design a class with the intention of using it as a base class, it's extremely unlikely that it will function very well as a base class. Fortunately, C# allows you to use the *sealed* keyword to prevent a class from being used as a base class. For example:

```
sealed class LiteralToken : DefaultTokenImpl, IToken
{
    ⋮
}
```

If any class declares *LiteralToken* as a base class, it will generate a compile-time error. A sealed class cannot declare a virtual method. The sole purpose of the *virtual* keyword is to declare that this is the *first* implementation of a method that you intend to override in a derived class, but a sealed class cannot be derived from. Note also that a struct is implicitly sealed. You can never derive from a struct.

Sealed Methods

You can also use the *sealed* keyword to declare that an individual method is sealed. This means that a derived class cannot then override the sealed method. You can only seal an override method. You can think of the interface, *virtual*, *override*, and *sealed* keywords as follows:

- An interface introduces the *name* of a method.
- A virtual method is the *first implementation* of a method.
- An override method is *another implementation* of a method.
- A sealed method is the *last implementation* of a method.

Extending an Inheritance Hierarchy

In the following exercise, you will familiarize yourself with a small hierarchy of interfaces and classes that together implement a very simple framework.

▶ **Tip** A framework differs from a library in that a library only be used can directly, in one specific way, whereas a framework can be used indirectly in many different ways by creating many different classes that all derive from carefully crafted interfaces to the framework.

The framework is a Microsoft Windows application that simulates reading a C# source file and classifying its contents into tokens (for example, identifiers, keywords, operators, and so on). In the second exercise, you will create a class that derives from the key framework interface and whose implementation displays the tokens of the source file in a rich text box in color syntax.

Familiarize yourself with the inheritance hierarchy

1 Start Microsoft Visual Studio .NET.

2 Open the CSharp project, located in the \Microsoft Press\Visual C# Step by Step\Chapter 12\CSharp folder in your My Documents folder. The CSharp project opens.

3 Open the SourceFile.cs source file in the Code pane. The *SourceFile* class contains a private array field called *tokens*:

```
private IVisitableToken[] tokens =
{
    new KeywordToken("using"),
    new WhitespaceToken(" "),
    new IdentifierToken("System"),
    new PunctuatorToken(";"),
        ⋮
};
```

This array contains a sequence of objects that all implement the *IVisitableToken* interface. Together, these tokens simulate the tokens of a simple "hello, world" source file. A complete version of this project would parse a named source file and construct these tokens dynamically. The *SourceFile* class also contains a public method called *Accept*. The *Accept* method has a single parameter of type *ITokenVisitor*. The body of the *Accept* method iterates through the tokens, calling their *Accept* methods:

```
public void Accept(ITokenVisitor visitor)
{
    foreach (IVisitableToken token in tokens)
    {
        token.Accept(visitor);
    }
}
```

In this way, the visitor parameter visits each token in sequence.

4 Open the IVisitableToken.cs source file in the Code pane. The *IVisitableToken* interface inherits from two other interfaces, the *IVisitable* interface and the *IToken* interface:

```
interface IVisitableToken : IVisitable, IToken
{
}
```

5 Open the IVisitable.cs source file in the Code pane. The *IVisitable* interface declares a single *Accept* method:

```
interface IVisitable
{
    void Accept(ITokenVisitor visitor);
}
```

Each object in the array of tokens inside the *SourceFile* class is held through the *IVisitableToken* interface. The *IVisitableToken* interface inherits the *Accept* method. This means that each token must implement the *Accept* method.

6 Open the SourceFile.cs source file in the Code pane and locate the *IdentifierToken* class.

The *IdentifierToken* class inherits from the *DefaultTokenImpl* abstract class and the *IVisitableToken* interface. It implements the *Accept* method as follows:

```
void IVisitable.Accept(ITokenVisitor visitor)
{
    visitor.VisitIdentifier(ToString());
}
```

The other token classes follow a similar pattern.

7 Open the ITokenVisitor.cs source file in the Code pane.

The *ITokenVisitor* interface contains one method for each type of token. The net result of this hierarchy of interfaces, abstract classes, and classes is that you can create a class that implements the *ITokenVisitor* interface, create an instance of this class, and pass this instance as the parameter to the *Accept* method of a *SourceFile*. For example:

```
class MyVisitor : ITokenVisitor
{
    public void VisitIdentifier(string token)
    {
        ⋮
    }
    public void VisitKeyword(string token)
    {
        ⋮
    }
    ⋮
    static void Main()
    {
        SourceFile source = new SourceFile();
        MyVisitor visitor = new MyVisitor();
        source.Accept(visitor);
    }
}
```

12

Inheritance

This will result in each token in the source file calling the matching method in the visitor object. You could create a number of different visitor classes to perform numerous different tasks as each token is visited. For example:

- A displaying visitor that displays the source file in a rich text box.
- A printing visitor that converts tabs to spaces and aligns braces correctly.
- A spelling visitor that checks the spelling of each identifier.
- A guideline visitor that checks that the public identifiers start with a capital letter and that interfaces start with a capital I.
- A complexity visitor that monitors the depth of the brace nesting in the code.
- A counting visitor that counts the number of lines in each method, the number of members in each class, and the number of lines in each source file.

In the following exercise, you will create a *ColorSyntaxVisitor* that displays the source file in a rich text box in color syntax (for example, keywords in blue).

Write a *ColorSyntaxVisitor* class

1   In the Solution Explorer, double-click Form1.cs to display the Color Syntax form in the Designer View window.

This form contains an Open button for opening the file to be tokenized, and a rich text box for displaying the tokens.

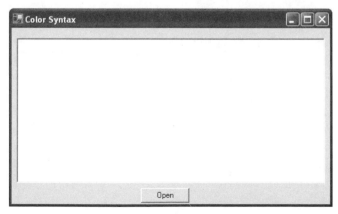

2   Open the Form1.cs source file in the Code pane, and then locate the two private fields called *codeText* and *Open* as shown on the following page.

```
private System.Windows.Forms.RichTextBox codeText;
private System.Windows.Forms.Button Open;
```

These are the two fields that implement the rich text box and the button you have just seen.

3   In the Code pane, locate the *Form1.Open_Click* method.

This is the method that is called when the Open button is clicked. You must implement this method so that it displays the tokens in the rich text box. Change the *Open_Click* method so that it looks exactly like this:

```
private void Open_Click(object sender, System.EventArgs e)
{
    SourceFile source = new SourceFile();
    ColorSyntaxVisitor visitor = new ColorSyntaxVisitor(codeText);
    source.Accept(visitor);
}
```

4   Open the ColorSyntaxVisitor.cs source file in the Code pane.

The *ColorSyntaxVisitor* class has been partially implemented. It inherits from the *ITokenVisitor* interface and already has two fields and a constructor to initialize the reference to the target rich text box. Your task is to implement the methods inherited from the *ITokenVisitor* interface, and then write the tokens to the target rich text box.

5   In the Code pane, implement a *Write* method in the *ColorSyntaxVisitor* class exactly as follows:

```
private void Write(string token, Color color)
{
    target.AppendText(token);
    target.Select(index, index + token.Length);
    index += token.Length;
    target.SelectionColor = color;
}
```

This code appends each token to the rich text box in the specified color. Each method will call this *Write* method.

6   In the Code pane, implement the remaining methods of the *ColorSyntaxVisitor* class. Use *Color.Blue* for keywords, *Color.Green* for *StringLiterals*, and *Color.Black* for all other methods:

```
void ITokenVisitor.VisitComment(string token)
{
    Write(token, Color.Black);
}

void ITokenVisitor.VisitIdentifier(string token)
{
    Write(token, Color.Black);
}
```

```
void ITokenVisitor.VisitKeyword(string token)
{
    Write(token, Color.Blue);
}

void ITokenVisitor.VisitOperator(string token)
{
    Write(token, Color.Black);
}

void ITokenVisitor.VisitPunctuator(string token)
{
    Write(token, Color.Black);
}

void ITokenVisitor.VisitStringLiteral(string token)
{
    Write(token, Color.Green);
}

void ITokenVisitor.VisitWhitespace(string token)
{
    Write(token, Color.Black);
}
```

7 On the Build menu, click Build Solution. Correct any errors, and then rebuild if necessary.

8 On the Debug menu, click Start Without Debugging. The Color Syntax form appears.

9 On the form, click Open. The dummy code is displayed in the rich text box, with keywords in blue and string literals in green.

10 Close the form. You return to Visual Studio .NET.

Working with Multiple Interfaces

A class can have at most one base class but is allowed an unlimited number of interfaces. A class must still implement all the methods it inherits from all its interfaces. An abstract class and a sealed class both follow the same inheritance rules as a class. An interface is not allowed to inherit from any kind of class (that would introduce implementation into the interface), but an interface is allowed to inherit from as many interfaces as it likes (this inheritance will never introduce any implementation).

Syntax

If an interface, struct, or class inherits from more than one interface, the interfaces are written in a comma-separated list. If a class also has a base class, the interfaces are listed *after* the base class. For example:

```
class IdentifierToken : DefaultTokenImpl, IToken, IVisitable
{
    ⋮
}
```

Explicit Interface Implementation

There is a second way that a struct or class can implement an interface method. In this alternative, the method name is explicitly qualified with the name of the interface and there is no accessibility modifier. For example, suppose the *IVisitable* interface looks like this:

```
interface IVisitable
{
    void Accept(IVisitor visitor);
}
```

You can implement the *IVisitable* interface like this:

```
class IdentifierToken : DefaultTokenImpl, IToken, IVisitable
{
    ⋮
    void IVisitable.Accept(IVisitor visitor)
    {
        ⋮
    }
}
```

This is called an *Explicit Interface Implementation* (EII). The EII method is effectively private to the implementing struct or class. For example:

```
IdentifierToken token = new IdentifierToken("token");
token.Accept(visitor); // compile-time error: not accessible
```

However, the method can be called through the explicitly named interface using a cast. For example:

```
IdentifierToken token = new IdentifierToken("token");
((IVisitable)token).Accept(visitor); // okay
```

Thus, the EII method is neither completely private nor completely public, which explains the absence of an access qualifier. EII methods are useful for at least two reasons.

First, EII methods create an even stronger separation between an interface that declares how to use an object (a usage type) and a class that declares how an object is created and implemented (a creation class). Because EII methods are effectively private to the class, the only way they can be called is by viewing the object through its usage interface.

Second, EII methods can solve a potential problem when a method name clashes across multiple interfaces. For example, suppose the *IToken* and the *IVisitable* interfaces both contain a method called *ToString*:

```
interface IToken
{
    ⋮
    string ToString();
}
interface IVisitable
{
    ⋮
    string ToString();
}
```

Whether you like it or not, the following class declares one implementation of *ToString*, which is the implementation of both these methods:

```
class IdentifierToken : IToken, IVisitable
{
    ⋮
    public string ToString()
    {
        ⋮
    }
}
```

EII provides a way to create different implementations of *ToString*, one for each interface method. For example:

```
class IdentifierToken : IToken, IVisitable
{
```

```
     ⋮
string IToken.ToString()
{
    ⋮
}
string IVisitable.ToString()
{
    ⋮
}
}
```

Note that an EII method is not virtual (and cannot be made virtual) and cannot be overridden in a further derived class.

Summarizing Keyword Combinations

The following table summarizes the various valid (yes) and invalid (no) keyword combinations.

Keyword	Interface	Abstract class	Class	Sealed class	struct
abstract	no	yes	no	no	no
new	yes[a]	yes	yes	yes	no[b]
override	no	yes	yes	yes	no[c]
private	no	yes	yes	yes	yes
protected	no	yes	yes	yes	no[d]
public	no	yes	yes	yes	yes
sealed	no	yes	yes	yes	no
virtual	no	yes	yes	no	no

a. An interface can extend another interface and introduce a new method with the same signature.

b. A struct implicitly derives from *System.Object*, which contains methods that the struct can hide.

c. A struct implicitly derives from *System.Object,* which contains virtual methods.

d. A struct is implicitly sealed and cannot be derived from.

If you want to continue to the next chapter

■   Keep Visual Studio .NET running and turn to Chapter 13.

If you want to exit Visual Studio .NET now

■   On the File menu, click Exit. If you see a Save dialog box, click Yes.

Chapter 12 Quick Reference

To	Do this
Create a derived class from a base class	Declare the new class name followed by a colon and the name of the base class. For example: ```\nclass Derived : Base\n{\n ⋮\n}\n```
Call a base class constructor	Supply a constructor parameter list before the body of the derived class constructor. For example: ```\nclass Derived : Base\n{\n ⋮\n public Derived(int x) : Base(x)\n {\n ⋮\n }\n ⋮\n}\n```
Declare a virtual method	Use the *virtual* keyword when declaring the method. For example: ```\nclass Animal\n{\npublic virtual string Talk()\n{\n ⋮\n}\n```
Declare an interface	Use the *interface* keyword. For example: ```\ninterface IDemo\n{\nstring Name();\n string Description();\n}\n```

12

Inheritance

To	Do this
Implement an interface	Declare a class using the same syntax as for inheritance, and then implement all the member functions of the interface. For example:

```
class Test : IDemo
{
    public string IDemo.Name()
    {
        ⋮
    }
    public string IDemo.Description()
    {
        ⋮
    }
}
```

Using Garbage Collection and Resource Management

In this chapter, you will learn how to:

■ Write code that runs when an object is finalized by using a destructor.

■ Manage system resources by using garbage collection.

■ Release a resource at a known point in time by writing your own disposal method.

■ Release a resource at a known point in time in an exception-safe manner by writing a *try/finally* statement.

■ Release a resource at a known point in time in an exception-safe manner by writing a using statement.

Garbage Collection

One of the great strengths of the Microsoft Visual C# language is that it makes a fundamental distinction between values and objects. Values and objects are different.

Comparing Values and Objects

The distinction between values and objects was covered in detail in Chapter 8. Here's a brief recap:

■ A value is an instance of a value type (an enumeration or a struct), whereas an object is an instance of a reference type (an array, a class, or a delegate):

```
int i = 42;                // i is a value
TextBox box = new TextBox(); // box refers to an object
```

- The lifetime of a value is tied to the scope in which it is declared, whereas the lifetime of an object is *not* tied to the scope in which it is created, as demonstrated by the following code:

```
{
    int i = 42;
    TextBox message = new TextBox();
} // i ends its life here,
    // but the object referred to by TextBox lives on
```

- Values typically have very short lifetimes whereas objects typically have long lifetimes.

The Life and Times of an Object

You create an object like this:

```
new TextBox();
```

From your point of view, this operation is atomic, but underneath, object creation is really a two-phase process. First, you have to allocate some raw memory from the heap. You do this using the *new* keyword. You have no control over this phase of an object's creation. Second, you have to convert the raw memory into an object; you have to initialize the object. You do this by using a constructor. In contrast to allocation, you do have control over this phase of an object's creation.

▶ **Note**   C++ programmers should note that in C#, you cannot overload *new* to control allocation.

It's common to create an object when initializing a reference variable. For example:

```
TextBox message = new TextBox();
```

You can then use the object that the reference refers to by using the dot operator. For example:

```
message.Text = "People of Earth, your attention please";
```

Object death is also a two-phase process. The two phases exactly mirror the two phases of creation. First, you have to convert the object back into raw memory. You do this by writing a *destructor*. The destructor is the opposite of the constructor. Second, the raw memory has to be given back to the heap; the binary bits that the object lived in have to be deallocated. Once again, you have no control over this phase. The process of returning memory back to the heap is known as *garbage collection*.

Writing Destructors

The syntax for writing a destructor is a tilde (~) followed by the name of the class. For example, here's a simple class that counts the number of live instances by incrementing a static count in the constructor and decrementing the static count in the destructor:

```
class Tally
{
    public Tally()
    {
        instanceCount++;
    }
    ~Tally()
    {
        instanceCount--;
    }
    public static int InstanceCount()
    {
        return instanceCount;
    }
    :
    private static int instanceCount = 0;
}
```

There are some very important destructor restrictions:

- You cannot declare a destructor in a struct. A struct is a value type.

  ```
  struct Tally
  {
      ~Tally() { ... } // compile-time error
  }
  ```

- You cannot declare an access modifier (such as public) for a destructor. This is because you never call the destructor yourself (the garbage collector does, as you'll see shortly).

  ```
  public ~Tally() { ... } // compile-time error
  ```

- You never declare a destructor with parameters. Again, this is because you never call the destructor yourself.

  ```
  ~Tally(int parameter) { ... } // compile-time error
  ```

  The compiler automatically translates a destructor into an override of the *Object.Finalize* method. In other words, the compiler translates the following destructor:

  ```
  class Tally
  {
      ~Tally() { ... }
  }
  ```

Here is the translation:

```
class Tally
{
    protected override void Finalize()
    {
        try { ... }
        finally { base.Finalize(); }
    }
}
```

The compiler-generated *Finalize* method contains the destructor body inside a *try* block, followed by a *finally* block that calls the base class *Finalize*. This ensures that a destructor always calls its base class destructor (just like in C++).

▶ **Tip** If you look at a destructor using the Microsoft Intermediate Language Disassembler (ILDasm.exe), you can see the converted *Finalize* method and its extra *try/finally* code.

It's important to realize that only the compiler can make this translation. You can't override *Finalize* yourself and you can't call *Finalize* yourself. In other words, *Finalize* really is just another name for the destructor.

Why Use the Garbage Collector?

The fundamental thing to remember about destructors is that you can never call them. The reason for this is that, in C#, you can never destroy an object yourself. There just isn't any syntax to do it. There are good reasons why the designers of C# decided to forbid you from explicitly writing code to destroy objects. If it was *your* responsibility to destroy objects, sooner or later:

- You'd forget to destroy the object. This would mean that the object's destructor (if it had one) would not be run and its memory would not be deallocated back to the heap. You'd quite easily run out of memory.

- You'd try to destroy an active object. Remember, objects are held by reference. If a class held a reference to a destroyed object, it would be a dangling reference. The dangling reference would end up referring either to unused memory or to a completely different object. Either way, the outcome of using such a dangling reference would be undefined. All bets would be off.

- You'd try and destroy the same object more than once.

These problems are unacceptable in a language like C#, which places robustness and security high on its list of design goals. Instead, the garbage collector is responsible for destroying objects for you. Only the garbage collector can destroy objects. The garbage collector guarantees the following:

- Each object is destroyed regardless of whether your application has explicitly destroyed all the objects it created. For example, when a program ends, all the current objects will be destroyed.

- Each object is destroyed only once.

- Each object is destroyed only when no other references refer to the object. This type of object is called an *unreachable* object.

These guarantees are tremendously useful and free you, the programmer, from tedious housekeeping chores that are easy to get wrong. They allow you to concentrate on the logic of the program itself and be more productive.

However, as with all design trade-offs, garbage collection comes at a price. You don't know the order in which objects will be destroyed. Objects are not necessarily destroyed in the reverse order of their creation (as they are in C++). You also don't know *when* the garbage collector will decide to destroy objects. An object is not destroyed at the moment that it becomes unreachable. Because destroying objects can be a time-consuming operation, the garbage collector destroys objects only when it is necessary (when the heap memory is exhausted) or when you explicitly ask it to (by calling the *System.GC.Collect* method). Clearly, this makes C# unsuitable for some time-critical applications.

How Does the Garbage Collector Run?

The garbage collector runs in its own thread and runs only when other threads are in a safe state (for example, when they are suspended). This is important because, as the garbage collector runs, it needs to move objects and update object references. The steps that the garbage collector takes when it runs are as follows:

1   It builds a graph of all reachable objects. It does this by repeatedly following reference fields inside objects. The garbage collector builds this graph very carefully and makes sure that circular references do not cause an infinite recursion. Any object *not* in this graph must be unreachable.

2   It checks to see whether any unreachable objects require finalization. In other words, it checks whether any of the unreachable objects has a destructor. Any unreachable object that requires finalization is placed in a special queue called the *freachable queue* (pronounced F-reachable).

3   The remaining unreachable objects (those that don't require finalization) are deallocated. The garbage collector performs this deallocation by moving the *reachable* objects down the heap, thus defragmenting the heap and freeing memory at the top of the heap. When the garbage collector moves a reachable object, it also updates any references to the object.

4   The garbage collector now allows other threads to resume.

5   The unreachable objects that require finalization (now in the freachable queue) are finalized in a separate thread.

Recommendations

Writing classes that contain destructors adds complexity to your code and to the garbage collection process and makes your program run more slowly. If your program does not contain any destructors, the garbage collector does not need to perform Steps 3 and 5 (in the previous section). Clearly, not doing something is faster than doing it. (There's no code faster than no code.) The first recommendation is, therefore, to try to avoid using destructors except when you really need them (for example, consider a *using* statement instead; this statement is covered in the following section).

You need to write a destructor very carefully. In particular, you need to be aware that, if your destructor calls other objects, those other objects might have *already* had their destructor called by the garbage collector. (Remember that the order of finalization is not guaranteed.) The second recommendation is therefore to ensure that each destructor reclaims one resource and nothing else. This recommendation can require splitting a class into two classes (one of which is the class dedicated to managing the resource).

Resource Management

Sometimes it's inadvisable to release a resource in a destructor; some resources are just too valuable and too scarce to lie around unreleased for arbitrary lengths of time. (Remember, you don't know when the garbage collector will call an object's destructor.) Scarce resources need to be released, and they need to be released as soon as possible. In these situations, your only option is to release the resource yourself. A *disposal* method is a method that disposes of a resource. If a class has a disposal method, you can call it explicitly and thus control when the resource is released.

The Disposal Method Pattern

An example of a class that contains a disposal method is the *TextReader* class from the *System.IO* namespace. *TextReader* contains a virtual method called *Close*. The *StreamReader* class (which reads characters from a stream) and the *StringReader* class (which reads characters from a string) both derive from *TextReader,* and both override the *Close* method. Here's an example that reads lines from a file using the *StreamReader* class:

```
TextReader reader = new StreamReader(filename);
string line;
```

```
while ((line = reader.ReadLine()) != null)
{
    Console.WriteLine(line);
}
reader.Close();
```

It's important to call *Close* when you have finished with *reader* to release the
file handle (and encoding) resources. However, there is a problem with this
example; it's not exception-safe. If the call to *ReadLine* (or *WriteLine*) throws
an exception, the call to *Close* will not happen; it will be bypassed.

Exception-Safe Disposal

One way to ensure that a disposal method is always called, regardless of
whether there is an exception, is to call the disposal method inside a *finally*
block. Here's the previous example using this technique:

```
TextReader reader = new StreamReader(filename);
try
{
    string line;
    while ((line = reader.ReadLine()) != null)
    {
        Console.WriteLine(line);
    }
}
finally
{
    reader.Close();
}
```

Using a *finally* block like this works, but it has several drawbacks that make it a
less than ideal solution:

- ■ It quickly gets unwieldy if you have to dispose of more than one
  resource (you end up with nested *try* and *finally* blocks).

- ■ In some cases, you might have to modify the code (for example, reorder the declaration of the resource reference, remember to initialize
  the reference to *null*, and remember to check that the reference isn't
  null in the *finally* block).

- ■ It fails to create an abstraction of the solution. This means the solution is hard to understand and must be repeated every time.

- ■ The reference to the resource remains in scope after the *finally* block.
  This means that you can accidentally use the resource after it has
  been released.

The *using* statement is designed to solve all these problems.

The *using* Statement

The syntax for a *using* statement is as follows:

```
using ( type variable = initialization ) embeddedStatement
```

Such a *using* statement is precisely equivalent to the following translation:

```
{
    type variable = initialization;
    try
    {
        embeddedStatement
    }
    finally
    {
        if (variable != null)
        {
            ((IDisposable)variable).Dispose();
        }
    }
}
```

▶ **Note**   Note the outer block scope. This arrangement means that the variable you declare in a *using* statement goes out of scope at the end of the embedded statement.

This equivalence means that the variable you declare in a *using* statement must be of a type that implements the *IDisposable* interface. The *IDisposable* interface lives in the *System* namespace and contains just one method called *Dispose*:

```
namespace System
{
    interface IDisposable
    {
        void Dispose();
    }
}
```

You can use a *using* statement as a clean, exception-safe, robust way to ensure that a resource is always automatically released. You just need to make sure that:

- The class containing the disposal method (for example, *Close* in *Text-Reader*) implements the *IDisposable* interface (as *TextReader* does).
- The class implements *Dispose* (as it must) to call the disposal method (for example, *TextReader.Dispose* calls *TextReader.Close*). For example:

```
abstract class TextReader : IDisposable
{
    ⋮
```

```
        public virtual void Dispose()
        {
            // calls Close
        }
        public virtual void Close()
        {
            ⋮
        }
    }
```

Here is the best way to make sure that your code always calls *Close* on a *TextReader*:

```
using (TextReader reader = new StreamReader(filename))
{
    string line;
    while ((line = reader.ReadLine()) != null)
    {
        Console.WriteLine(line);
    }
}
```

This solves all of the problems that existed in the manual *try/finally* solution. You now have a solution that does the following:

- Scales well if you need to dispose of multiple resources.
- Doesn't distort the logic of the program code.
- Nicely abstracts away the problem, thereby avoiding repetition.
- Is robust. You can't use the variable (the one declared inside the *using* statement, in this case, *reader*) after the *using* statement has ended because it's not in scope anymore—you'll get a compile-time error.

Adapting to *IDisposable*

It's instructive to consider how you could have used a *using* statement to ensure that your code always called *TextReader.Close* if the *TextReader* class didn't implement the *IDisposable* interface. You could do it like this:

```
struct AutoClosing : IDisposable
{
    public AutoClosing(TextReader target)
    {
        this.target = target;
    }
    public TextReader GetTextReader()
    {
        return target;
    }
    public void Dispose()
    {
```

```
        target.Close();
    }
    private readonly TextReader target;
}
```

Notice the following:

- *AutoClosing* does not extend the *TextReader* class. This avoids the need to replicate all the *TextReader* constructors inside the *Auto-Closing* struct. (The extension would also be invalid if *TextReader* were a sealed class.)

- *AutoClosing* is not designed to be a base class and does not extend a class. You want the memory deallocated as soon as it goes out of scope. It is best implemented as a struct rather than a class.

You can rewrite the *GetTextReader* accessor method as a read-only property. Properties are covered in Chapter 14.

You could then use this struct as follows:

```
using (AutoClosing safe = new AutoClosing(new StreamReader(filename)))
{
    TextReader reader = safe.GetTextReader();
    string line;
    while ((line = reader.ReadLine()) != null)
    {
        Console.WriteLine(line);
    }
}
```

Notice how the *reader* variable is still in the scope of the *using* statement.

> **Note** The compiler-generated translation of a *using* statement in which the variable is a struct is slightly more efficient than when the variable is a class. This is because the generated *finally* block can omit the *null* test. A struct is a value type, and value types can never be *null*.

Calling a Disposal Method from a Destructor

One of the drawbacks of the disposal method pattern is that it relies on you (the programmer) to call the disposal method, and programmers occasionally forget to do tasks like this. The trade-off in deciding whether to use destructors or disposal methods is this: A call to a destructor *will* happen but you just don't know when, whereas you know exactly when a call to a disposal method happens but you just can't be sure that it will actually happen because you might forget to call the method. However, it is possible to ensure that a disposal method is always called. The solution is to call the disposal method from a destructor. This acts as a useful "backup." You might forget to call the disposal method,

but at least you can be sure that it will be called, even if it's only when the program shuts down. An example of how to do this is:

```
class Example : IDisposable
{
    ⋮
    ~Example()
    {
        Dispose();
    }
    public virtual void Dispose()
    {
        if (!disposed)
        {
            try {
                // release scarce resource here
            }
            finally {
                disposed = true;
                GC.SuppressFinalize(this);
            }
        }
    }
    public void SomeBehavior()
    {
        checkIfDisposed();
        ⋮
    }
    ⋮
    private void checkIfDisposed()
    {
        if (disposed)
        {
            throw new ObjectDisposedException("Example");
        }
    }
    private Resource scarce;
    private bool disposed = false;
}
```

Notice the following:

■ The class implements *IDisposable*.

■ The *Dispose* method is public and can be called at any time.

■ The *Dispose* method can be safely called multiple times.

■ The destructor calls *Dispose*.

■ The *Dispose* method calls *GC.SuppressFinalize* to stop the garbage
   collector from needlessly calling the destructor. This is in fact optional;

it might turn out that calling *GC.SuppressFinalize* takes longer than letting the garbage collector call the destructor.

■   All the regular methods of the class check to see whether the object has already been disposed. If it has, they throw an exception.

Making Code Exception-Safe

In the following exercise, you will rewrite a small piece of code. The code opens a text file, reads its contents one line at a time, writes these lines to a rich text box on a Windows form, and then closes the text file. The problem is that the code is not exception-safe. If an exception arises as the file is read or as the lines are written to the rich text box, the call to close the text file will be bypassed. You will rewrite the code to use a *using* statement instead, thus ensuring that the code is exception-safe.

Write a *using* statement

1   Start Microsoft Visual Studio .NET.

2   Open the UsingStatement project, located in the \Microsoft Press\Visual C# Step by Step\Chapter 13\UsingStatement folder in your My Documents folder. The UsingStatement project opens.

3   On the Debug menu, click Start Without Debugging. The Windows form appears.

4   Click Open File on the form. The Open dialog box opens.

5   In the Open dialog box, navigate to the \Microsoft Press\Visual C# Step by Step\Chapter 13\UsingStatement folder in your My Documents folder and select the Form1.cs source file. This is the source file for the application itself.

6   Click Open. The contents of the file are loaded into the Windows form.

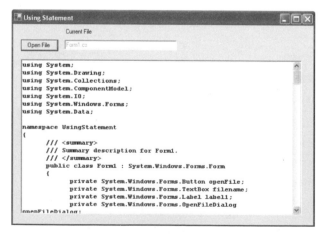

7   Close the form. You return to Visual Studio .NET.

8   Open the Form1.cs source file in the Code pane, and then locate the *openFileDialog_FileOk* method.

This method should look like this:

```
private void openFileDialog_FileOk(object sender,
    System.ComponentModel.CancelEventArgs e)
{
    string fullPathname = openFileDialog.FileName;
    FileInfo src = new FileInfo(fullPathname);
    filename.Text = src.Name;
    source.Text = "";
    TextReader reader = new StreamReader(fullPathname);
    string line;
    while ((line = reader.ReadLine()) != null)
    {
        source.Text += line + "\n";
    }
    reader.Close();
}
```

The filename, *openFileDialog*, and the source identifiers are three private fields of the *Form1* class. The problem with this code is that the final statement, the call to *reader.Close*, is not guaranteed to happen. If you are not used to handling exceptions, it can take quite a while to see the potential problem in this code.

9   Rewrite the *openFileDialog_FileOk* method exactly as follows:

```
private void openFileDialog_FileOk(object sender,
    System.ComponentModel.CancelEventArgs e)
{
    string fullPathname = openFileDialog.FileName;
    FileInfo src = new FileInfo(fullPathname);
    filename.Text = src.Name;
    source.Text = "";
    TextReader reader = new StreamReader(fullPathname);
    try
    {
        string line;
        while ((line = reader.ReadLine()) != null)
        {
            source.Text += line + "\n";
        }
    }
    finally
    {
        reader.Close();
    }
}
```

10 Rebuild and re-run the application to verify that it still works.

11 Rewrite the *openFileDialog_FileOk* method exactly as follows:

```
private void openFileDialog_FileOk(object sender,
    System.ComponentModel.CancelEventArgs e)
{
    string fullPathname = openFileDialog.FileName;
    FileInfo src = new FileInfo(fullPathname);
    filename.Text = src.Name;
    source.Text = "";
    using (TextReader reader = new StreamReader(fullPathname))
    {
        string line;
        while ((line = reader.ReadLine()) != null)
        {
            source.Text += line + "\n";
        }
    }
}
```

12 Rebuild and re-run the application to verify that it still works.

13 Confirm that the *reader* variable is in the scope of the *using* statement. To do this, try making a call to *reader.Close* after the *using* statement, like this:

```
private void openFileDialog_FileOk(object sender,
    System.ComponentModel.CancelEventArgs e)
{
    string fullPathname = openFileDialog.FileName;
    FileInfo src = new FileInfo(fullPathname);
    filename.Text = src.Name;
    source.Text = "";
    using (TextReader reader = new StreamReader(fullPathname))
    {
        string line;
        while ((line = reader.ReadLine()) != null)
        {
            source.Text += line + "\n";
        }
    }
    reader.Close();
}
```

You will find that this code does not compile. You will see an error message such as this:

```
The type or namespace name 'reader' could not be found (are you
 missing a using directive or an assembly reference?)
```

This error message appears because in the previous example, use of the variable *reader* is only permitted within the body of the *using* statement.

If you want to continue to the next chapter

■   Keep Visual Studio .NET running and turn to Chapter 14.

If you want to exit Visual Studio .NET now

■   On the File menu, click Exit. If you see a Save dialog box, click Yes.

Chapter 13 Quick Reference

To	Do this
Write a destructor	Write a method whose name is the same as the name of the class and is prefixed with a tilde (~). The method must not have an access modifier (such as public) and cannot have any parameters. For example: ```\nclass Example\n{\n ~Example()\n {\n ⋮\n }\n}\n```
Call a destructor	You can't call a destructor. Only the garbage collector can call a destructor.
Force garbage collection	Call *System.GC.Collect*
Release a resource at a known point in time	Write a disposal method (a method that disposes of a resource) and call it explicitly from the program. For example: ```\nclass TextReader\n{\n ⋮\n public virtual void Close()\n {\n ⋮\n }\n} class Example\n{\n void Use()\n {\n TextReader reader = ...;\n // use reader\n reader.Close();\n }\n}\n```

To	Do this
Release a resource at a known point in time in an exception-safe manner	Release the resource with a *using* statement. For example:

```
class TextReader : IDisposable
{
    ⋮
    public virtual void Dispose()
    {
        // calls Close
    }
    public virtual void Close()
    {
        ⋮
    }
}
class Example
{
    void Use()
    {
        using (TextReader
            reader = ...)
        {
            // use reader
        }
    }
}
```

Creating Components

Implementing Properties to Access Attributes

> **In this chapter, you will learn how to:**
>
> ■ Use properties to encapsulate logical fields.
>
> ■ Declare *get* accessors to control read access to properties.
>
> ■ Declare *set* accessors to control write access to properties.
>
> ■ Create interfaces that declare properties.
>
> ■ Implement properties in structs and classes that inherit from interfaces containing properties.
>
> ■ Implement an interface property using explicit interface implementation.

Comparing Fields and Methods

Consider the following small struct that represents a position on a screen as an *(X, Y)* coordinate. The problem with this struct is that it does not follow the golden rule of encapsulation; it does not keep its data private:

```
struct ScreenPosition
{
    public ScreenPosition(int x, int y)
    {
        X = rangeCheckedX(x);
        Y = rangeCheckedY(y);
    }
    public int X;
    public int Y;
```

```
        private static int rangeCheckedX(int x)
        {
            if (x < 0 || x > 600)
            {
                throw new ArgumentOutOfRangeException("X");
            }
            return x;
        }
        private static int rangeCheckedY(int y)
        {
            if (y < 0 || y > 800)
            {
                throw new ArgumentOutOfRangeException("Y");
            }
            return y;
        }
    }
```

Public data is a bad idea because its use cannot be checked and controlled. For example, the *ScreenPosition* constructor range checks its parameters, but no such range check can be done on the "raw" access to the public fields. Sooner or later (probably sooner), either *X* or *Y* will stray out of its range:

```
ScreenPosition topLeft = new ScreenPosition(65, 45);
⋮
int x = topLeft.X;
topLeft.Y = 810; // Oops
```

The common way to solve this problem is to make the fields private and add an accessor method and a modifier method to read and write the value of each private field respectively. The modifier methods can then range-check the new field values exactly because the constructor already checks the initial field values. For example, here's an accessor (*GetX*) and a modifier (*SetX*) for the *X* field. Notice how *SetX* checks its parameter value:

```
struct ScreenPosition
{
    ⋮
    public int GetX()
    {
        return x;
    }
    public void SetX(int newX)
    {
        x = rangeCheckedX(newX);
    }
    ⋮
    private static int rangeCheckedX(int x) { ... } // as before
```

```
        private static int rangeCheckedY(int y) { ... } // as before
        private int x, y;
}
```

The code now successfully enforces the range constraints, which is good. However, there is a price to pay for this valuable guarantee—*ScreenPosition* no longer has a natural field-like syntax; it now uses awkward method-based syntax instead. The following example increases the value of *X* by 10. To do so, it has to read the value of *X* using the *GetX* accessor method, and then write the value of *X* by using the *SetX* modifier method:

```
int x = topLeft.GetX();
topLeft.SetX(x + 10);
```

Compare this with the equivalent code if the *X* field were public:

```
topLeft.X += 10;
```

There is no doubt that, in this case, using fields is cleaner, shorter, and easier. Unfortunately, using fields breaks encapsulation. It would be nice to combine the best of both examples: to retain encapsulation while allowing a field-like syntax. This is exactly what properties allow you to do.

What Are Properties?

A *property* is a cross between a logical field and a physical method. You use a property in exactly the same way that you use a field. Hence, logically, a property looks like a field. However, the compiler automatically translates this field-like syntax into calls to special method-like accessors. The next code segment shows the *ScreenPosition* struct rewritten using properties. When reading this code, notice the following:

- Lowercase *x* and *y* are private fields.
- Uppercase *X* and *Y* are public field-like properties. *X* and *Y* are not methods. They do not have parentheses. They contain only a *get* accessor and a *set* accessor.

▶ **Note** The fields and properties follow the standard Microsoft Visual C# public/private naming convention.

```
struct ScreenPosition
{
    public ScreenPosition(int X, int Y)
    {
        x = rangeCheckedX(X);
        y = rangeCheckedY(Y);
    }
```

```
        public int X
        {
            get { return x; }
            set { x = rangeCheckedX(value); }
        }
        public int Y
        {
            get { return y; }
            set { y = rangeCheckedY(value); }
        }
        private static int rangeCheckedX(int x) { ... } // as before
        private static int rangeCheckedY(int y) { ... } // as before
        private int x, y;
    }
```

In this example, a private field directly implements each property. This is only one way to implement a property. All that is required is that a *get* accessor returns a value of the specified type. Such a value could easily be calculated (a deduced attribute), in which case there would be no need for a physical field.

When you use a property in an expression, you either use it in a read context (when you are not modifying its value) or in a write context (when you are modifying its value).

get Accessors

If you use a property in a read context, the compiler automatically translates your field-like code into a call to the *get* accessor of that property. For example, the compiler automatically translates this:

```
int x = topLeft.X;
```

Into this:

```
int x = topLeft.X { get { return x; } } // pseudocode
```

Which is really just this:

```
int x = topLeft.x;
```

set Accessors

Similarly, if you use a property in a write context, the compiler automatically translates your field-like code into a call to the *set* accessor of that property. For example, the compiler automatically translates this:

```
topLeft.X = 40;
```

Into this:

```
topLeft.X { set { x = rangeCheckedX(40); } } // pseudocode
```

Which is really just this:

```
topLeft.x = rangeCheckedX(40);
```

▶ **Note** When you use a property in a write context, the value you are assigning to the property (in this case, 40) becomes a hidden parameter called *value* inside the *set* accessor. The type of *value* is automatically the type of the property itself.

Read/Write Properties

It's also possible to use a property in a read/write context. In this case, both the *get* and the *set* accessor are used. For example, the compiler automatically translates this:

```
topLeft.X += 10;
```

Into this:

```
int temp = topLeft.X.get { return x; }
topLeft.X.set { x = rangeCheckedX(temp + 10); }
```

This works because, in this case, the property declares both a *get* and a *set* accessor.

Read-Only Properties

You're allowed to declare a property that contains only a *get* accessor. In this case, you can use the property only in a read context. For example, here's the *X* property of the *ScreenPosition* struct declared as a read-only property:

```
struct ScreenPosition
{
    ⋮
    public int X
    {
        get { return x; }
    }
}
```

The *X* property does not contain a *set* accessor; any attempt to use *X* in a write context will fail. For example:

```
topLeft.X = 40; // compile-time error
```

Write-Only Properties

Similarly, you're allowed to declare a property that contains only a *set* accessor. In this case, you can use the property only in a write context. For example, here's the *X* property of the *ScreenPosition* struct declared as a write-only property:

```
struct ScreenPosition
{
    ⋮
    public int X
    {
        set { x = rangeCheckedX(value); }
    }
}
```

The *X* property does not contain a *get* accessor; any attempt to use *X* in a read context will fail. For example:

```
Console.WriteLine(topLeft.X); // compile-time error
topLeft.X += 10;              // compile-time error
```

Understanding the Property Restrictions

Properties look, act, and feel like fields. However, they are not true fields, and certain restrictions apply to them:

- You can't initialize a property of a struct through a *set* accessor (whereas you can initialize a field with an assignment). For example:

  ```
  ScreenPosition location;
  location.X = 40; // compile-time error, location not assigned
  ```

- You can't use a property as a *ref* or *out* argument (whereas you can use a writeable field as a *ref* or *out* argument). For example:

  ```
  Method(ref topLeft.X); // compile-time error
  ```

- You can't declare multiple properties in a single declaration statement (whereas you can declare multiple fields in a single declaration statement). For example:

  ```
  public int X, Y { get { ... } set { ... } } // compile-time error
  ```

- You can't declare *const* or *readonly* properties. For example:

  ```
  const int X { get { ... } set { ... } } // compile-time error
  ```

Properties are not true fields, but they're not true methods either. Once again, certain restrictions apply to them.

- You can declare *only* a *get* or *set* accessor, or both, inside a property. Even if the *get* and the *set* accessor share common statements, you cannot refactor those statements before the *get* and *set* accessors:

```
public int X
{
    Console.WriteLine("common code"); // compile-time error
    get { ... }
    set { ... }
}
```

- You can't declare a property whose type is *void*. For example:

```
public void X { get { ... } set { ... } } // compile-time error
```

- You can't declare a property without a parameter. For example:

```
public /*nothing*/ X { get { ... } set { ... } }
// compile-time error
```

- You can't declare a property with two or more parameters:

```
public int,string X { get { ... } set { ... } }
// compile-time error
```

Using Static Properties

You can declare two kinds of fields in a class or struct: instance fields (one per object) and static fields (one per type). You can use properties to mimic instance fields and, not surprisingly, you can use static properties to mimic static fields. The syntax for a static property is exactly the same as for an instance property, except you prefix the property declaration with the keyword *static*. For example, here's the *ScreenPosition* struct again, this time with a static read-only property representing the dimensions of the screen:

```
struct ScreenPosition
{
    ⋮
    public static ScreenPosition Limits
    {
        get { return limits; }
    }
    ⋮
    private static int rangeCheckedX(int x)
    {
        if (x < 0 || x > limits.x)
        {
            throw new ArgumentOutOfRangeException("X");
        }
        return x;
    }
    private static int rangeCheckedY(int y)
    {
        if (y < 0 || y > limits.y)
        {
```

```
                throw new ArgumentOutOfRangeException("Y");
            }
            return y;
        }
        private static ScreenPosition vgaLimits =
            new ScreenPosition(600, 800);
        private static ScreenPosition limits = vgaLimits;
        private int x, y;
}
```

Structification

Properties are a powerful feature with a clean, field-like syntax. Used in the correct place, properties help to make code easier to understand and maintain. However, they are no substitute for careful object-oriented design that focuses on the behavior of objects rather than their properties. Accessing private fields through regular methods or through properties does not, by itself, make your code well designed. For example, a bank account holds a balance. You might therefore be tempted to create a *Balance* property on a *BankAccount* class, like this:

```
class BankAccount
{
    :
    public money Balance
    {
        get { ... }
        set { ... }
    }
    private money balance;
}
```

This would be a poor design. It fails to represent the common usage of withdrawing money from and depositing money into an account. (If you know of a bank that allows you to set your balance directly, please let us know.) When you're programming, try not to lose the expression of the problem in a mass of low-level syntax; try to express the problem you are solving in the solution:

```
class BankAccount
{
    :
    public money Balance { get { ... } }
    public void Deposit(money amount) { ... }
    public bool Withdraw(money amount) { ... }
    private money balance;
}
```

You access a static property by using the name of its enclosing struct or class. For example, the following statement uses *Limits* in a read context. The compiler translates it into a call to the *get* accessor of the static *Limits* property:

```
Console.WriteLine(ScreenPosition.Limits);
```

The following statement is translated into a call to the *get* accessor of the static *Limits* property (which returns a *ScreenPosition* instance), followed by a call to the *get* accessor of the *X* property on that instance:

```
Console.WriteLine(ScreenPosition.Limits.X);
```

Declaring Interface Properties

You can declare properties in an interface. To do this, you declare the *get* or *set* keyword, or both, but replace the body of the *get* or *set* accessor with a semicolon. For example:

```
interface IScreenPosition
{
    int X { get; set; }
    int Y { get; set; }
}
```

Any class or struct that implements this interface must implement the accessors. For example:

```
struct ScreenPosition : IScreenPosition
{
    ⋮
    public int X
    {
        get { return x; }
        set { x = rangeCheckedX(value); }
    }
    public int Y
    {
        get { return y; }
        set { y = rangeCheckedY(value); }
    }
    ⋮
    private int x, y;
}
```

If you implement the interface properties in a class, you can declare the property implementations as virtual, which allows further derived classes to override the implementations. For example:

```
class ScreenPosition : IScreenPosition
{
```

```
     ⋮
     public virtual int X
     {
         get { ... }
         set { ... }
     }
     public virtual int Y
     {
         get { ... }
         set { ... }
     }
     ⋮
     private int x, y;
}
```

▶ **Note**   The *virtual* keyword is not valid in structs because you can't derive from structs; structs are implicitly sealed.

You can also choose to implement a property by using the explicit interface implementation syntax covered in Chapter 12. An explicit implementation of a property is non-public and non-virtual (and cannot be overridden). For example:

```
struct ScreenPosition : IScreenPosition
{
    ⋮
    int IScreenPosition.X
    {
        get { return x; }
        set { x = rangeCheckedX(value); }
    }
    int IScreenPosition.Y
    {
        get { return y; }
        set { y = rangeCheckedY(value); }
    }
    ⋮
    private int x, y;
}
```

▶ **Tip**   You can declare interfaces as properties that are read-only (no *set* keyword) or write-only (no *get* keyword). You can even split the *get* and *set* accessors across different interfaces.

Using Properties in a Windows Application

In the following exercise, you will use some predefined properties of Microsoft Windows text boxes and Windows forms to create a simple application that continually displays the size of its main window.

Use properties

1   Start Microsoft Visual Studio .NET.

2   Open the Properties project, located in the \Microsoft Press\Visual C# Step by Step\Chapter 14\Properties folder in your My Documents folder. The Properties project opens.

3   On the Debug menu, click Start Without Debugging. The project builds and runs. A Windows form displays two empty text boxes labeled Width and Height. Your task is to ensure that these text boxes display the width and height of the application window.

4   Resize the form. The two text boxes remain empty. Your task is to ensure that the two text boxes always display the width and height of the application window, even when it is resized.

5   Close the form. You return to the Visual Studio .NET programming environment.

6   Open the Form1.cs source file in the Code pane, and then locate the declaration of the Width and Height text boxes.

These declarations are near the top of Form1.cs and look like this:

```
private System.Windows.Forms.TextBox width;
private System.Windows.Forms.TextBox height;
```

The *TextBox* class contains a public read/write string property called *Text* (it inherits this property from its base class: *TextBoxBase*):

```
abstract class TextBoxBase ...
{
    public override string Text
    {
        get { ... }
        set { ... }
    }
}
class TextBox : TextBoxBase
{
    ⋮
}
```

In the Form1.cs source file, locate the second *resize* method near the bottom of the source code. It is called by the *Form* constructor but is currently empty.

7   Add two statements to the *resize* method. The first statement assigns the string "232" to the *Text* property of the Width text box. The second statement assigns the string "96" to the *Text* property of the Height text box.

The *resize* method should look exactly like this:

```
private void resize()
{
    width.Text = "232";
    height.Text = "96";
}
```

8 On the Debug menu, click Start Without Debugging. The project builds and runs. The Windows form displays the two text boxes containing the values 232 and 96. The *set* accessor of the *TextBox.Text* property clearly does more than just hold a string. It also ensures that its string is displayed and so becomes visible.

The next step is to write the correct strings to the *TextBox.Text* properties so that the window always displays the correct values.

9 Close the form. You return to the Visual Studio .NET programming environment.

10 Scroll up the Form1.cs source file and locate the declaration of the *Form1* class. The *Form1* class derives from the *System.Windows.Forms.Form* class:

```
public class Form1 : System.Windows.Forms.Form
{
    ⋮
}
```

The *System.Windows.Forms.Form* class contains a public read/write *Size* property:

```
namespace System.Windows.Forms;
{
    class Form ...
    {
        ⋮
        public new Size Size
        {
            get { ... }
            set { ... }
        }
    }
}
```

The *Size* property returns an instance of a struct called *Size* that lives in the *System.Drawing* namespace. The *Size* struct contains two public read/write *int* properties, one called *Height* and one called *Width*:

```
namespace System.Drawing
{
    struct Size
    {
```

```
    public int Height
    {
        get { ... }
        set { ... }
    }
    public int Width
    {
        get { ... }
        set { ... }
    }
  }
}
```

Having these classes and structs together means that inside *Form1* methods (such as *resize*), you can write *Size.Width* to retrieve the current width of the form and *Size.Height* to retrieve the current height of the form.

11 Scroll down the Form1.cs source file and locate the second *resize* method.

12 Modify the two statements so that *Size.Width* is assigned to the *width.Text* property and *Size.Height* is assigned to the *height.Text* property. You will need to convert from an *int* to a string. The easiest way to do this is to use the *ToString* method.

Your *resize* method should now look exactly like this:

```
private void resize()
{
    int w = Size.Width;
    width.Text = w.ToString();
    int h = Size.Height;
    height.Text = h.ToString();
}
```

13 On the Debug menu, click Start Without Debugging. The project builds and runs.

14 Resize the Windows form. As you resize, the text boxes change to display the changing size (the *resize* method is being called whenever the *Resize* event occurs; events and delegates are explained in Chapter 16).

15 Close the form. You return to the Visual Studio .NET programming environment. Finally, you will display the size of the form as a form caption title.

16 Locate the second *resize* method in the Form1.cs source file.

17 Add two more statements to the *resize* method. The first statement will use the *string.Format* method to create a single string containing the width and height of the form. The second statement will write this string to the public read/write string *Text* property of the form. The *Text* property represents the title in the caption of the form.

Your *resize* method should now look exactly like this:

```
private void resize()
{
    int w = Size.Width;
    width.Text = w.ToString();
    int h = Size.Height;
    height.Text = h.ToString();
    string s = string.Format("({0},{1})", w, h);
    Text = s;
}
```

18 On the Debug menu, click Start Without Debugging. The project builds and runs. The caption now displays the size of the form and also changes as you resize the form.

19 Close the form. You return to the Visual Studio .NET programming environment.

If you want to continue to the next chapter

■ Keep Visual Studio .NET running and turn to Chapter 15.

If you want to exit Visual Studio.NET now

■ On the File menu, click Exit. If you see a Save dialog box, click Yes.

Chapter 14 Quick Reference

To	Do this

Declare a read/write property	Declare the type of the property, its name, a *get* accessor, and a *set* accessor. For example:
	
	``
	struct ScreenPosition
	{
	    ⋮
	    public int X
	    {
	        get { ... }
	        set { ... }
	    }
	    ⋮
	}
	``

To	Do this

Declare a read-only property	Declare a property with only a *get* accessor. For example:
	
	``
	struct ScreenPosition
	{
	    ⋮
	    public int X
	    {
	        get { ... }
	    }
	    ⋮
	}
	``

Declare a write-only property	Declare a property with only a *set* accessor. For example:
	
	``
	struct ScreenPosition
	{
	    ⋮
	    public int X
	    { set { ... }
	    }
	    ⋮
	}
	``

Declare a property in an interface	Declare a property with just the *get* or *set* keyword, or both. For example:
	
	``
	interface IScreenPosition
	{
	    int X { get; set; } // no body
	    int Y { get; set; } // no body
	}
	``

Implement an interface property	In the class or struct that implements the interface, declare the property and implement the accessors. For example:
	
	``
	struct ScreenPosition : IScreenPosition
	{
	    public int X
	    {
	        get { ... }
	        set { ... }
	    }
	    public int Y
	    {
	        get { ... }
	        set { ... }
	    }
	}
	``

14

Implementing Properties

To	Do this
Implement an interface property using explicit interface implementation	In the class or struct that implements the interface, do not declare the property access and explicitly name the interface. For example:

```
struct ScreenPosition : IScreenPosition
{
    int IScreenPosition.X
    {
        get { ... }
        set { ...}
    }
    int IScreenPosition.Y
    {
        get { ... }
        set { ... }
    }
}
```

Using Indexers

What Is an Indexer?

An *indexer* is a smart array in exactly the same way that a property is a smart field. In other words, the syntax that you use for an indexer is exactly the same as the syntax you use for an array. Let's work through an example. First, we'll describe a problem and see a weak solution that doesn't use indexers. Then we'll work through the same problem and see a strong solution that does use indexers. The problem concerns integers, or more precisely, the *int* type.

An Example That Doesn't Use Indexers

You normally use an *int* to hold an integer value. Internally an *int* stores its value as a sequence of 32 bits, where each bit can be either 0 or 1. Most of the time you don't care about this internal binary representation; you just use an *int* type as a bucket to hold an integer value. However, sometimes programmers use the *int* type for other purposes; some programs manipulate the individual bits within an *int*. In other words, occasionally a program might use an *int* because it holds 32 bits and not because it can represent an integer!

▶ **Note** Programmers sometimes do use *int* types to try to save memory. A single *int* holds 32 bits, each of which can be 1 or 0. Some programmers use 1 to indicate a value of true and 0 to indicate false, and then use an *int* as a set of Boolean values. In contrast, an array of 32 *bool* variables will take at least 32*8 bits of memory (eight times as much).

For example, the following expression uses the << and & bit manipulation operators to find out whether the bit at index 6 of the *int* called *bits* is set to 0 or to 1:

```
(bits & (1 << 6)) != 0
```

If the *bit* at index 6 happens to be 0, this expression will evaluate to *false*, whereas if the *bit* at index 6 happens to be 1, this expression will evaluate to *true*. This is a fairly complicated expression, but it's trivial in comparison to the following expression that sets the *bit* at index 6 to 0:

```
bits &= ~(1 << 6)
```

It's also trivial compared with this expression that sets the *bit* at index 6 to 1:

```
bits |= (1 << 6)
```

The trouble with these examples is that although they work, it's not clear why or how they work. They're complicated. The point is that it's not obvious what the purpose of these expressions is. The solution is a very low-level one. It fails to create an abstraction of the problem it solves.

The Bitwise and Shift Operators

You might have noticed some unfamiliar symbols in the expressions shown in these examples. In particular, ~, <<, |, and &. These are some of the bitwise and shift operators, and they are used to manipulate the individual bits held in the *int* and *long* data types.

The ~ operator performs a bitwise complement. It is a unary operator. For example, if you take the 8-bit value 11001100 (204 decimal) and apply the ~ operator to it, you obtain the result 00110011 (51 decimal).

The << operator performs a left-shift. It is a binary operator. The expression 204 << 2 returns the value 48 (in binary, 204 decimal is 11001100, and left-shifting it by two places yields 00110000, or 48 decimal). The far-left bits are discarded, and zeroes are introduced from the right. There is a corresponding right-shift operator >>.

The | operator performs a bitwise OR operation. It is a binary operator that returns a value containing a 1 in each position in which either of the operands has a 1. For example, the expression 204 | 24 has the value 220 (204 is 11001100, 24 is 00011000, and 220 is 11011100).

The & operator performs a bitwise AND operation. AND is similar to the bitwise OR operator, except that it returns a value containing a 1 in each position where both of the operands have a 1. So 204 & 20 is 8 (204 is 11001100, 24 is 00011000, and 8 is 00001000).

The ^ operator is another bitwise operator. It performs the bitwise XOR (exclusive or) of its two operands. The XOR operation returns a "1" in each bit where there is a "1" in one operand or the other, but not both. (Two "1"s yield a "0"—this is the "exclusive" bit of the operator.) So 204 ^ 24 is 212 (11001100 ^ 00011000 is 11010100).

The Same Example Using Indexers

Let's pull back from the previous low-level solution for a moment and stop to remind ourselves what the problem is. The problem is that we'd like to use an *int* not as an *int* but as an array of 32 bits. Therefore, the best way to solve this problem is to use an *int* as if it were an array of 32 bits! In other words, if *bits* is an *int*, what we'd like to be able to write to retrieve the *bit* at index 6 is:

```
bits[6]
```

To set the *bit* at index 6 to *true*, we'd like to be able to write:

```
bits[6] = true
```

To set the *bit* at index 6 to *false*, we'd like to be able to write:

```
bits[6] = false
```

Unfortunately, you can't use the square bracket notation on an *int*. You can use the square bracket notation only on an array or on a type that behaves like an array; that is, on a type that declares an indexer. So the solution to the problem is to create a new type that acts like, feels like, and is used like an array of *bool* variables. Let's call this new type *IntBits*. *IntBits* will contain an *int* value (initialized in its constructor), but the idea is that we'll use *IntBits* as an array of *bool* variables.

▶ **Note** Because *IntBits* is small and lightweight, it makes sense to create it as a struct rather than as a class.

```
struct IntBits
{
    public IntBits(int initialBitValue)
    {
        bits = initialBitValue;
    }
    // indexer declared here
    private int bits;
}
```

After the indexer has been declared, we can use a variable of type *IntBits* instead of an *int* and apply the square bracket notation as desired:

```
int adapted = 63;
IntBits bits = new IntBits(adapted);
bool peek = bits[6];    // retrieve bool at index 6
bits[0] = true;         // set the bit at index 0 to true
bits[31] = false;       // set the bit at index 31 to false
```

This syntax is certainly much easier to understand. It directly and succinctly captures the essence of the problem.

> ▶ **Tip**   The syntax that you use as part of a solution is an integral part of that solution. The syntax that you use should not be relegated to a last-minute detail. Syntax matters. Syntax is the interface to language.

All that remains is to declare the indexer so that the array-like notation works on the *IntBits* struct. Here it is:

```
struct IntBits
{
    ⋮
    public bool this [ int index ]
    {
        get { ... }
        set { ... }
    }
    ⋮
}
```

Notice the following:

- An indexer is not a method; there are no parentheses.
- The type of the indexer is *bool* (that is, *true* or *false*).
- The argument supplied between the square brackets is an *int* (for example, 6).

- All indexers use the *this* keyword in place of the method name.
- Indexers contain *get* and *set* accessors just like properties. The *get* and *set* accessors will contain the complicated bitwise expressions previously discussed.

get Accessors

If you read an indexer, the compiler automatically translates your array-like code into a call to the *get* accessor of that indexer. For example, consider the following example:

```
bool peek = bits[6];
```

This is automatically translated into a call to the *get* accessor for *bits* where index is 6, as demonstrated in the following example:

```
bool lowBit = bits.this[6] { get { ... } } // pseudocode
```

set Accessors

Similarly, if you write to an indexer, the compiler automatically translates your array-like code into a call to the *set* accessor of that indexer. For example, consider the following statement:

```
bits[6] = true;
```

It is automatically translated into a call to the *set* accessor for *bits* where the value of the index is 6:

```
bits.this[6] { set { ... } } // pseudocode
```

The value you are writing to the indexer (in this case, *true*) is automatically available inside the *set* accessor using the *value* keyword. The type of value is automatically the type of indexer itself (in this case, *bool*).

Read/Write Indexers

It's also possible to use an indexer in a combined read/write context. In this case, the *get* and the *set* accessors are used. For example, consider the following statement:

```
bits[6] ^= true;
```

It is automatically translated into this:

```
bits[6] = bits[6] ^ true;
```

This statement is the same as the following:

```
bool temp = bits[6] ^ true; // call to get accessor
bits[6] = temp;             // call to set accessor
```

This code works because in this case, the indexer declares both a *get* and a *set* accessor.

Read-Only Indexers

You're allowed to declare an indexer that contains only a *get* accessor. In this case, you can use the indexer only in a read context. For example, here's *IntBits* again, this time with a read-only indexer:

```
struct IntBits
{
    ⋮
    public bool this [ int index ]
    {
        get {
            return (bits & (1 << index)) != 0;
        }
    }
    ⋮
    private int bits;
}
```

The indexer does not contain a *set* accessor, so any attempt to use it in a write context will fail. For example:

```
bits[6] = false; // compile-time error
```

Write-Only Indexers

Similarly, you're allowed to declare an indexer that contains only a *set* accessor. In this case, you can use the indexer only in a write context. For example, here's *IntBits* again, this time with a write-only indexer:

```
struct IntBits
{
    ⋮
    public bool this [ int index ]
    {
        set {
            if (value)
                bits |=  (1 << index);
            else
                bits &= ~(1 << index);
        }
    }
    ⋮
    private int bits;
}
```

The indexer does not contain a *get* accessor, so any attempt to use it in a read context will fail. For example:

```
Console.WriteLine(bits[6]);    // compile-time error
bits[6] ^= false;              // compile-time error
```

Comparing Indexers and Methods

An indexer is like a *this* method that uses square brackets instead of parentheses. However, there are some important differences between indexers and methods:

- A method can have no parameters, whereas an indexer must have at least one parameter:

    ```
    public bool this [ ] { ... } // compile-time error
    ```

- An indexer must contain a *get* and/or a *set* accessor. Even if the *get* and *set* accessors share common code (such as bounds-checking the index), you cannot move the common code before or after the accessors:

    ```
    public bool this [ int index ]
    {
        boundsCheck(index); // compile-time error
        get { ... }
        set { ... }
    }
    ```

- A method can have a *void* return type, whereas an indexer can't:

    ```
    public void this [ int index ] { ... } // compile-time error
    ```

Comparing Indexers and Arrays

When you use an indexer, the syntax is deliberately very array-like. However, there are some important differences between indexers and arrays:

- Indexers can use non-integer subscripts, whereas arrays can use only integer subscripts:

    ```
    public int this [ string name ] { ... } // okay
    ```

- Indexers can be overloaded (just like methods), whereas arrays can't:

    ```
    public Name        this [ PhoneNumber number ] { ... }
    public PhoneNumber this [ Name name ] { ... }
    ```

- Indexers can't be used as *ref* or *out* parameters, whereas array elements can:

    ```
    IntBits bits;         // bits contains an indexer
    Method(ref bits[1]); // compile-time error
    ```

Comparing Indexers and Properties

Indexers and properties are similar in that both use *get* and *set* accessors. An indexer is like a property with multiple values. However, there are some important differences between indexers and properties. The most important is that you're allowed to declare *static* properties, but *static* indexers are illegal:

```
public static bool this [ int index ] { ... }
```

Interface Indexers

You can declare indexers in an interface. To do this, you declare the *get* and/or *set* keyword but replace the body of the *get* or *set* accessor with a semicolon. Any class or struct that implements the interface must implement the *indexer* accessors declared in the interface. For example:

```
interface IRawInt
{
    bool this [ int index ] { get; set; }
}

struct RawInt : IRawInt
{
    :
    public bool this [ int index ]
    {
        get { ... }
        set { ... }
    }
    :
}
```

If you implement the interface indexer in a class, you can declare the indexer implementations as virtual. This allows further derived classes to override the *get* and *set* accessors. For example:

```
class RawInt : IRawInt
{
    :
    public virtual bool this [ int index ]
    {
        get { ... }
        set { ... }
    }
    :
}
```

You can also choose to implement an indexer using the explicit interface implementation syntax covered in Chapter 12. An explicit implementation of an indexer is non-public and non-virtual (and so cannot be overridden). For example:

```
struct RawInt : IRawInt
{
    ⋮
    bool IRawInt.this [ int index ]
    {
        get { ... }
        set { ... }
    }
    ⋮
}
```

> ▶ **Tip**   You can also declare interface indexers that are read-only (meaning no *set* keyword) or write-only (meaning no *get* keyword). You can even split the *get* and *set* accessors across different interfaces.

Using Indexers in a Windows Application

In the following exercise, you will finish a simple phone book application. Your task will be to write two indexers in the *PhoneBook* class: one that accepts a *Name* parameter and returns a *PhoneNumber*, and another that accepts a *PhoneNumber* parameter and returns a *Name*. (The *Name* and *PhoneNumber* structs have already been written.) You will also need to call these indexers from the correct places in the program.

Familiarize yourself with the application

1   Start Microsoft Visual Studio .NET.

2   Open the Indexers project, located in the \Microsoft Press\Visual C# Step by Step\Chapter 15\Indexers folder in your My Documents folder. The Indexers project opens. It is a Microsoft Windows Forms application.

3   On the Debug menu, click Start Without Debugging. The project builds and runs. A Windows form displays two empty text boxes labeled Name and Phone Number. The form also contains three buttons: one to add a name/phone number pair; one to find a phone number when given a name; and one to find a name when given a phone number. Your task is to finish the application so that these buttons work.

4   Close the form.

5   Open the Name.cs source file in the Code pane. Familiarize yourself with the *Name* struct. Notice that it contains a read-only string property called *Text*. (The *Equals* and *GetHashCode* methods are required because you will be writing code to search through an array of *Name* values.)

6   Open the PhoneNumber.cs source file in the Code pane. Familiarize yourself with the *PhoneNumber* struct. (It is very similar to the *Name* struct.)

7   Open the PhoneBook.cs source file in the Code pane.

8   Notice that the *PhoneBook* class contains two private arrays: an array of *Name* values called *names*, and an array of *PhoneNumber* values called *phoneNumbers*. The *PhoneBook* class also contains an *Add* method, which is called when the Add button is clicked.

Write the indexers

1   In the PhoneBook.cs source file, add a *public* read-only *Name* indexer that accepts a single *PhoneNumber* parameter to the *PhoneBook* class and two arrays—one of *Name* objects, and the other containing *PhoneNumbers*.

The indexer and arrays should look like this:

```
sealed class PhoneBook
{
    ⋮
    public Name this [ PhoneNumber number ]
    {
        get { }
    }
    ⋮
    private Name[] names;
    private PhoneNumber[] numbers;
}
```

2   Implement the *get* accessor. To do this, you will need to call the static *IndexOf* method of the *Array* class. The first argument to *IndexOf* is the array to search through (*phoneNumbers*). The second argument to *IndexOf* is the element you are searching for. *IndexOf* returns the integer index of the element if it finds it, otherwise *IndexOf* will return −1. If *IndexOf* finds the phone number, it will return it, otherwise it will return an empty *Name* value. (Note that *Name* is a struct and will always have a default constructor that sets its *private* field to *null*.)

The indexer with its completed *get* accessor should look like this:

```
sealed class PhoneBook
{
    ⋮
    public Name this [ PhoneNumber number ]
    {
        get
        {
            int i = Array.IndexOf(phoneNumbers, number);
            return (i != -1) ? names[i] : new Name();
        }
    }
    ⋮
}
```

3 Add a second *public* read-only *PhoneNumber* indexer that accepts a single *Name* parameter to the *PhoneBook* class. This indexer is implemented in exactly the same way as the first one (again note that *PhoneNumber* is a struct and so always has a default constructor). The second indexer should look like this:

```
sealed class PhoneBook
{
    ⋮
    public PhoneNumber this [ Name name ]
    {
        get
        {
            int i = Array.IndexOf(names, name);
            return (i != -1) ? phoneNumbers[i] :
                new PhoneNumber();
        }
    }
    ⋮
}
```

Notice that because *Name* and *PhoneNumber* are structs, there is no need to check whether the parameters are *null* (since struct values can never be *null*). Notice also that these overloaded indexers co-exist because their signatures are different. If the *Name* and *Phone-Number* structs were replaced by strings (which they wrap), the over-loads would have the same signature and would not compile.

4 On the Build menu, click Build Solution.

5 Correct any syntax errors, and then rebuild.

Call the indexers

1   Open the Form1.cs source file in the Code pane, and then locate the *findPhone_Click* method.

This method is called when the first Search button is clicked. (This call is done by using events and delegates, which you will learn about in Chapter 16.) This method needs to read the *Text* string from the Name text box. If the *Text* string is not empty, it must then search by using an indexer for the phone number that corresponds to that name in the *PhoneBook* (notice that *Form1* contains a private *PhoneBook* field called *phoneBook*). You can then use the *Phone-Number* returned from the indexer to write to the *phoneNumber* text box.

2   Implement the *findPhone_Click* method now. It should look like this:

```
public class Form1 : System.Windows.Forms.Form
{
    ⋮
    private void findPhone_Click(object sender, System.EventArgs e)
    {
        string text = name.Text;
        if (text != "")
        {
            phoneNumber.Text = phoneBook[new Name(text)].Text;
        }
    }
    ⋮
    private PhoneBook phoneBook = new PhoneBook();
}
```

3   Locate the *findName_Click* method in the Form1.cs source file. It is below the *findPhone_Click* method.

The *findName_Click* method is called when the second search button is clicked. This method needs to read the *Text* string from the Phone Number text box. If the *Text* string is not empty, the method must then search by using an indexer for the name that corresponds to that phone number in the *PhoneBook*. You can then use the *Name* returned from the indexer to write to the Name text box. Implement this method now. It should look like this:

```
public class Form1 : System.Windows.Forms.Form
{
    ⋮
    private void findName_Click(object sender, System.EventArgs e)
    {
        string text = phoneNumber.Text;
```

```
            if (text != "")
            {
                name.Text = phoneBook[new PhoneNumber(text)].Text;
            }
        }
        ⋮
        private PhoneBook phoneBook = new PhoneBook();
    }
```

4 On the Build menu, click Build Solution.

5 Correct any syntax errors, and then rebuild.

Run the application

1 On the Debug menu, click Start Without Debugging. The project builds and runs.

2 Enter a name and phone number in the two text boxes, and then click the Add button. When you click the Add button, the *Add* method puts the entries into the phone book and clears the text boxes so that they are ready for a search.

3 Repeat Step 2 a few times so that the phone book contains a number of entries.

4 Enter a name you used in Step 2 into the Name text box, and then click the Search --> button. The phone number you added in Step 2 is retrieved from the phone book and is displayed in the Phone Number text box.

5 Delete the name from the Name text box, and then click the <-- Search button. The name is retrieved from the phone book and is displayed in the Name text box.

6 Enter a completely new name in the Name text box, and then click the Search --> button. This time the Phone Number text box is empty indicating that the name could not be found in the phone book.

7 Close the form.

If you want to continue to the next chapter

■ Keep Visual Studio .NET running and turn to Chapter 16.

If you want to exit Visual Studio .NET now

■ On the File menu, click Exit. If you see a Save dialog box, click Yes.

15

Using Indexers

Chapter 15 Quick Reference

To	Do this
Declare a read/write indexer	Declare the type of the indexer, followed by the keyword *this*, and followed by the indexer arguments between square brackets. The body of the indexer can contain a *get* and/or *set* accessor. For example:

```
struct RawInt
{
    ⋮
    public bool this [ int index ]
    {
        get { ... }
        set { ... }
    }
    ⋮
}
```

Declare a read-only indexer	Declare an indexer with only a *get* accessor. For example:

```
struct RawInt
{
    ⋮
    public bool this [ int index ]
    {
        get { ... }
    }
    ⋮
}
```

Declare a write-only indexer	Declare an indexer with only a *set* accessor. For example:

```
struct RawInt
{
    ⋮
    public bool this [ int index ]
    {
        set { ... }
    }
    ⋮
}
```

To	Do this
Declare an indexer in an interface	Declare an indexer with the *get* and/or *set* keywords. That is, replace the *get* and *set* accessors with semi-colons. For example:

```
interface IRawInt
{
    bool this [ int index ]  get; set; }
}
```

Implement an interface indexer	In the class or struct that implements the interface, declare the indexer and implement the accessors. For example:

```
struct RawInt : IRawInt
{
    ⋮
    public bool this [ int index ]
    {
        get { ... }
        set { ... }
    }
    ⋮
}
```

Implement an interface indexer using explicit interface implementation	In the class or struct that implements the interface, explicitly name the interface and do not declare the indexer access. For example:

```
struct RawInt : IRawInt
{
    ⋮
    bool IRawInt.this [ int index ]
    {
        get { ... }
        set { ... }
    }
    ⋮
}
```

Chapter

16

Delegates and Events

In this chapter, you will learn how to:

- Declare a delegate type to create an abstraction of a method signature.

- Create instances of delegates to create abstractions of specific methods.

- Call delegates using parentheses to call the underlying method.

- Declare an event field.

- Attach a delegate to an event by using the += operator.

- Detach a delegate from an event by using the —= operator.

- Raise an event.

Using Delegate Declarations and Instances

A *delegate* is a type that looks and behaves like a method. A delegate is an abstraction of a method. You can think of a delegate as a smart method in the same way that a property is a smart field and an indexer is a smart array. Delegates are very useful for creating callbacks and notification-style frameworks of collaborating classes. The best way to understand delegates is to see them in action, so let's work through an example. First, we'll describe a problem and see a solution that doesn't use a delegate. Then we'll work through the same problem and see a different solution that uses a delegate.

An Example That Doesn't Use a Delegate

Suppose that you need to write a program that performs a certain task every second. One way to implement this requirement is to implement the task in a method, and then create another class, named *Ticker*, that calls this method every second. Look at the following example:

```
class Ticker
{
    :
    public void Attach(Subscriber newSubscriber)
    {
        subscribers.Add(newSubscriber);
    }
    public void Detach(Subscriber exSubscriber)
    {
        subscribers.Remove(exSubscriber);
    }
    // Notify is called every second
    private void Notify()
    {
        foreach (Subscriber s in subscribers)
        {
            s.Tick();
        }
    }
    :
    private ArrayList subscribers = new ArrayList();
}
class Subscriber
{
    public void Tick()
    {
        :
    }
}
class ExampleUse
{
    static void Main()
    {
        Ticker pulsed = new Ticker();
        Subscriber worker = new Subscriber();
        pulsed.Attach(worker);
        :
    }
}
```

This solution certainly works, but it is a less than ideal. One problem is that the *Ticker* class is tightly coupled to the *Subscriber* class. In other words, only *Subscriber* instances can attach to a *Ticker*. If some other class has a method that you want a *Ticker* to call every second, you'll have to create a whole new *Ticker*-like class. To solve this problem, you could lift the *Tick* method into its own interface and associate the *Ticker* class with this interface.

```
interface Tickable
{
    void Tick();
}

class Ticker
{
    public void Attach(Tickable newSubscriber)
    {
        subscribers.Add(newSubscriber);
    }
    public void Detach(Tickable exSubscriber)
    {
        subscribers.Remove(exSubscriber);
    }
    // Notify is called every second
    private void Notify()
    {
        foreach (Tickable t in subscribers)
        {
            t.Tick();
        }
    }
    ⋮
    private ArrayList subscribers = new ArrayList();
}
```

This solution allows any class to implement the *Tickable* interface and thus subscribe to a *Ticker*, as shown in the following example:

```
class Clock : Tickable
{
    ⋮
    public void Tick()
    {
        ⋮
    }
    ⋮
}
class ExampleUse
{
    static void Main() // no change
    {
        Ticker pulsed = new Ticker();
        Clock wall = new Clock();
        pulsed.Attach(wall);
        ⋮
    }
}
```

The Same Example Using a Delegate

The interface-based design is a much better design but still has a few potential problems. The main problem is that it is a very intrusive and very public solution. Suppose you wanted to subscribe to many notification services, not just one. This is typically what you need to do when programming a graphical user interface (GUI). A typical GUI generates a large number of events to which you might need to subscribe. Another related problem is that the use of an interface means that the *Tick* method must be *public*. Any code, then, can call *Clock.Tick* at any time. It would be better if we could ensure that only the attached *Ticker* called *Clock.Tick*. Delegates allow you to solve these problems and create a safer, more robust, more encapsulated style of notification.

Declaring a Delegate

In our example, the *Tick* method of the *Tickable* interface returns *void* and expects no arguments:

```
interface Tickable
{
    void Tick();
}
```

We can declare a delegate that matches this method signature by using the *delegate* keyword. For example, here's the declaration of a delegate called *Tick* that is an abstraction of a method that returns *void* and expects no arguments:

```
delegate void Tick();
```

This declares a new type; *Tick* is the name of a type in just the same way that the name of an enum, a struct, or a class is also the name of a type. Accordingly, you can use *Tick* as a type name in a field declaration or a parameter declaration. For example, here's *Tick* being used as a method parameter type:

```
void Example(Tick param)
{
        ⋮
}
```

▶ **Note**   A delegate type is implicitly derived from the *System.Delegate* class. Delegate types contain methods, operators, and properties, and you can pass them as parameters to other methods if you want. Also, because the *System.Delegate* class is part of the Microsoft .NET Framework, you can use them in other languages—for example, you can create a delegate in Microsoft Visual C# and use it to call a method written in Microsoft Visual Basic .NET.

Calling a Delegate

The power and usefulness of delegates really becomes apparent when you consider what it is that you actually do with a delegate. For example, what can you do with *param* in the previous example? If *param* were an *int*, you would use its value and probably apply several operators to it, such as ==, !=, and <. However, *param* is not an *int*, it's a delegate. A delegate is an abstraction of a method (in just the same way that *int* is an abstraction of an integer value), so you use a delegate as you would a method; you call a delegate by using parentheses. For example:

```
void Example(Tick param)
{
    param();
}
```

> ▶ **Tip**   A delegate is a reference type and can be *null*. If *param* is *null* in this example, the compiler will raise a *NullReferenceException*.

When you call a delegate, you have to call it correctly, just as you do for any method. In this example, *param* has type *Tick*, and *Tick* is declared like this:

```
delegate void Tick();
```

This declaration tells you that when you call a *Tick* delegate (such as *param*), you can't pass any arguments (because there are no parameters between the parentheses) and that the call won't return anything (because the return type is *void*). For example:

```
void Fxample(Tick param)
{
    param(42);                 // compile-time error
    int hhg = param();         // compile-time error
    Console.WriteLine(param()); // compile-time error
}
```

You can declare a delegate with any signature you want. For example, here's another version of *Tick* that accepts three *int* arguments:

```
delegate void Tick(int hours, int minutes, int seconds);
```

> ▶ **Important**   You must supply a parameter name for each parameter when declaring a delegate type with parameters.

Here's an example of this version of the *Tick* delegate in use:

```
void Example(Tick method)
{
    method(12, 29, 59); // just before half past twelve
}
```

You can use a delegate to implement the *Ticker* class. Rather than connecting the class providing the notification (the "publisher") and the class receiving the notification (the "subscriber") by using an interface (which affects the entire receiving class), you connect them by using a delegate. For example:

```
delegate void Tick(int hours, int minutes, int seconds);
class Ticker
{
    ⋮
    public void Attach(Tick newSubscriber)
    {
        subscribers.Add(newSubscriber);
    }
    public void Detach(Tick exSubscriber)
    {
        subscribers.Remove(exSubscriber);
    }
    // Notify is called every second
    private void Notify(int hours, int minutes, int seconds)
    {
        foreach (Tick method in subscribers)
        {
            method(hours, minutes, seconds);
        }
    }
    ⋮
    private ArrayList subscribers = new ArrayList();
}
```

Creating a Delegate Instance

The final step that you need to perform is to create instances of the delegate type. An instance of a delegate is an abstraction of a method and is created by naming the method that it abstracts. For example, here's a class called *Clock* that contains the non-static method called *RefreshTime*:

```
class Clock
{
    ⋮
    public void RefreshTime(int hours, int minutes, int seconds)
    {
        ⋮
    }
    ⋮
}
```

And here's a reminder of the *Tick* delegate:

```
delegate void Tick(int hours, int minutes, int seconds);
```

The signature of *RefreshTime* exactly matches the signature of *Tick*. This means that you can create a *Tick* instance that is an abstraction of a call to *Refresh-Time* on a particular *Clock* object. For example:

```
Clock wall = new Clock();
⋮
Tick m = new Tick(wall.RefreshTime);
```

Notice in particular the following:

■ The syntax used to create a delegate instance matches the syntax used to create a class instance: the *new* keyword, followed by the name of the type (a constructor call—recall that *Tick* is the name of a type), followed by the arguments to the constructor between parentheses.

■ The delegate constructor argument is the name of a method only; there are no parentheses after *wall.RefreshTime* in the example. The *RefreshTime* method is not being called.

■ The signatures of *RefreshTime* and *Tick* must match exactly, including the return type.

■ *RefreshTime* is an instance method and not a static method, so you must create the delegate instance by naming the method (*Refresh-Time*) and the object on which to call that method (*wall*). You pass both these pieces of information together by joining them with the dot operator (this mimics the standard syntax).

Now that *m* has been initialized, you can write this:

```
m(12, 29, 59);
```

This statement resolves to the following (because this is what *m* is abstracting):

```
wall.RefreshTime(12, 29, 59);
```

And more to the point in our example, you can pass *m* as a parameter. This gives us all we need to complete the example using a delegate. Here's one way you could connect the *Ticker* class and the *Clock* class together. Notice that in this example, *Clock* does not implement any interfaces and that *RefreshTime* is a private method:

```
delegate void Tick(int hours, int minutes, int seconds);
⋮
class Clock
{
    ⋮
    public void Start()
    {
        ticking.Attach(new Tick(this.RefreshTime));
    }
}
```

```
    public void Stop()
    {
        ticking.Detach(new Tick(this.RefreshTime));
    }

    private void RefreshTime(int hours, int minutes, int seconds)
    {
        Console.WriteLine("{0}:{1}:{2}", hours, minutes, seconds);
    }

    private Ticker ticking = new Ticker();
}
```

Using Delegates

In the following exercise, you will create delegate objects to encapsulate a method that displays the time in a Microsoft Windows text box. You will attach these delegate objects to a *Ticker* class that calls all attached delegates every second. In this way, you will create a Windows application that displays the time in digital format.

Finish the digital clock application

1   Start Microsoft Visual Studio .NET.

2   Open the Delegates project, located in the \Microsoft Press\Visual C#
    Step by Step\Chapter 16\Delegates folder in your My Documents
    folder. The Delegates project opens.

Creating a Delegate from a Static Method

You can also create a delegate from a static method. In this case, you name the class and not the object when creating the delegate. For example, here's the *RefreshTime* method as a static method:

```
class Clock
{
    public static void RefreshTime(int hours, int minutes,
        int seconds)
    {
        ⋮
    }
}
```

Here's an example that creates a delegate instance that names this static method:

```
new Tick(Clock.RefreshTime);
```

3   On the Debug menu, click Start Without Debugging. The project builds and runs. A Windows form displays a digital clock. The clock displays the wrong time because some methods have not yet been implemented. Your task is to implement these methods.

4   Click Start, and then click Stop. Nothing happens. The *Start* and *Stop* methods have not been implemented.

5   Close the window to return to the Visual Studio .NET environment.

6   In the Code pane, open the Ticker.cs source file.

7   In the Code pane, locate the declaration of the *Tick* delegate. It is located near the top of the file and looks like this:

```
delegate void Tick(int hh, int mm, int ss)
```

Also, note the *Attach* and *Detach* methods that allow delegates to subscribe and unsubscribe:

```
class Ticker
{
    ⋮
    public void Attach(Tick newSubscriber) { ... }
    public void Detach(Tick exSubscriber)  { ... }
    ⋮
}
```

8   In the Code pane, open the Clock.cs source file. The *Clock* class contains a private *Ticker* field called *pulsed*:

```
class Clock
{
    ⋮
    private Ticker pulsed = new Ticker();
}
```

The *Clock* class also contains a private method called *RefreshTime* that displays in the private *time TextBox* field a time given as hours, minutes, and seconds:

```
private void RefreshTime(int hh, int mm, int ss )
{
    time.Text = string.Format("{0:D2}:{1:D2}:{2:D2}", hh, mm, ss);
}
    ⋮
private TextBox time;
```

9   The *Clock.Start* and *Clock.Stop* methods have empty bodies. This is why the program does not work as you might expect. Implement the *Clock.Start* method so that it creates a delegate for the *Clock.Refresh-Time* method and attaches this delegate to *pulsed* by using the *Ticker.Attach* method.

```
public void Start()
{
    pulsed.Attach(new Tick(this.RefreshTime));
}
```

10 Implement the *Clock.Stop* method so that it creates a delegate for the *Clock.RefreshTime* method and detaches this delegate from *pulsed* by using the *Ticker.Detach* method.

The *Start* and *Stop* methods should look like this:

```
public void Stop()
{
    pulsed.Detach(new Tick(this.RefreshTime));
}
```

11 On the Debug menu, click Start Without Debugging. The project builds and runs. The Windows form now displays the correct time and updates every second.

12 Click Stop. The display stops responding or "freezes." This is because the Stop button calls the *Clock.Stop* method, which now detaches the *RefreshTime* delegate from the *Ticker* field. In other words, *RefreshTime* is no longer being called every second.

13 Click Start. The display resumes processing and updates the time every second. This is because the Start button calls the *Clock.Start* method, which now attaches a *RefreshTime* delegate to the *Ticker* field. In other words, *ResfreshTime* is once again being called every second.

14 Close the form.

Enabling Notifications with Events

In the previous section, you saw how to declare a delegate type, call a delegate, and create delegate instances. However, you also had to write quite a lot of housekeeping code. You had to do the following:

■ Maintain a collection of delegates.

■ Allow a delegate to attach itself to this collection.

■ Allow a delegate to detach itself from this collection.

■ Iterate through the collection and call each attached delegate.

It would be tedious to repeat these chores every time you wanted to create a new kind of notification publisher. Fortunately, you don't have to. You can use the *event* keyword to do the work for you.

Declaring an Event

You declare an event in a way similar to declaring a field. The difference is that the type of event must be a delegate, and you must prefix the declaration with the *event* keyword. For example, here's the *Tick* delegate from the first section:

```
delegate void Tick(int hours, int minutes, int seconds);
```

And here's a declaration of an event called *tick* (of type *Tick*) inside the *Ticker* class:

```
class Ticker
{
    public event Tick tick;
    ⋮
}
```

An event maintains its own internal collection of attached delegates, so there is no need to manually maintain your own collection (such as the *ArrayList* used previously).

▶ **Tip**   An event automatically initializes itself; you never need to create an event instance using the *new* keyword as you do for other types.

Subscribing to an Event

Events come ready-made with a += operator. You can attach a delegate to an event by using its built-in += operator. The following example shows a *Clock* class that contains a *Ticker* field called *pulsed*. The *Ticker* class contains a public *tick* event of type *delegate Tick*. (See the previous section.) The *Clock.Start* method attaches a delegate (of type *Tick*) to *pulsed.tick* by using its += operator:

```
delegate void Tick(int hours, int minutes, int seconds);

class Ticker
{
    public event Tick tick;
    ⋮
}

class Clock
{
    ⋮
    public void Start()
    {
        pulsed.tick += new Tick(this.RefreshTime);
    }
    ⋮
```

```
private void RefreshTime(int hours, int minutes, int seconds)
{
    ⋮
}

private Ticker pulsed = new Ticker();
}
```

When the *pulsed.tick* event runs, it will call all the attached delegates, one of which is the delegate that abstracts the call to *RefreshTime*; thus *RefreshTime* will be called. There is no need to write an *Attach* method in the *Ticker* class.

Unsubscribing from an Event

Knowing that you use the += operator to attach a delegate to an event, you can probably guess that you use the −= operator to detach a delegate from an event. Calling the −= operator removes the delegate from the event's internal collection of attached delegates. For example, the following example shows the *Clock.Stop* method that detaches the *RefreshTime* delegate from *pulsed.tick*:

```
class Clock
{
    ⋮
    public void Stop()
    {
        pulsed.tick -= new Tick(this.RefreshTime);
    }
    private void RefreshTime(int hours, int minutes, int seconds)
    {
        ⋮
    }
    private Ticker pulsed = new Ticker();
}
```

▶ **Tip** The += and −= operators are based on the + and − operators. You can chain delegates together by using the + operator and unchain delegates by using the − operator. For example, adding two delegates together creates a new delegate that, when called, invokes both of the delegates that were added together.

Calling an Event

An event can be called, just like a delegate, by using parentheses. When you call an event, all the attached delegates are called in sequence. For example, here's the *Ticker* class with a private *Notify* method that calls the *tick* event:

```
delegate void Tick(int hours, int minutes, int seconds)

class Ticker
```

```
{
    public event Tick tick;
    ⋮
    private void Notify(int hours, int minutes, int seconds)
    {
        if (tick != null)
        {
            tick(hours, minutes, seconds);
        }
    }
    ⋮
}
```

There is no need to manually iterate through the delegates attached to the event; the call does this automatically.

> ▶ **Important**   The *null* check in the previous example is necessary because an event field is implicitly *null* and becomes non-*null* only when a delegate is attached to it by using the += operator. If you call a *null* event, you will get a *NullReferenceException*.

Events have a very useful built-in security feature. A public event (such as *tick*) can be called only from within a sibling method. For example, *tick* is an event inside the *Ticker* class, so only methods of the *Ticker* class can call the tick event:

```
class Example
{
    static void Main()
    {
        Ticker pulsed = new Ticker();
        pulsed.tick(12, 29, 59); // compile-time error :-)
    }
}
```

Understanding GUI Events

The .NET Framework GUI classes use events extensively. You'll see and use GUI events on many occasions in the second half of this book. In the following exercise, you'll run a Windows application that contains two buttons. These buttons are implemented by two fields of type *Button* (which is defined in the *System.Windows.Forms* namespace). The *Button* class derives from the *Control* class, inheriting a public event called *Click* of type *EventHandler*. Let's see this in code.

```
namespace System
{
    public delegate void EventHandler(object sender, EventArgs args);
```

```
        public class EventArgs
        {
            ⋮
        }
}
namespace System.Windows.Forms
{
    public class Control :
    {
        public event EventHandler Click;
        ⋮
    }
    public class Button : Control
    {
        ⋮
    }
}
```

The *Button* class automatically raises the *Click* event when you click the button on-screen. This arrangement makes it easy to create a delegate for a chosen method and attach that delegate to the required event. The following example shows a Windows form that contains a button called *okay*, a method called *okay_Click*, and the code to connect the *Click* event in the *okay* button to the *okay_Click* method:

```
class Example : System.Windows.Forms.Form
{
    private System.Windows.Forms.Button okay;
    ⋮
    public Example()
    {
        this.okay = new System.Windows.Forms.Button();
        this.okay.Click += new System.EventHandler(this.okay_Click);
        ⋮
    }

    private void okay_Click(object sender, System.EventsArgs args)
    {
        ⋮
    }
}
```

This is exactly the kind of code that the Visual Designer in Visual Studio .NET writes for you automatically.

The events that the GUI classes generate always follow the same pattern. The events are of a delegate type whose signature has a *void* return type and two arguments. The first argument is always the sender of the event and the second argument is always an *EventArgs* argument (or a class derived from *EventArgs*).

The sender argument allows you to reuse a single delegate for multiple events (for example, two or more buttons). The delegated method can compare the sender argument with the attached event sources and respond accordingly.

Using Events

In the following exercise, you will use events to simplify the program you completed in the first exercise. You will add an event field to the *Ticker* class and remove its *Attach* and *Detach* methods. You will then modify the *Clock.Start* and *Clock.Stop* methods to attach and detach the *RefreshTime* delegates using the events += and −= operators.

Rework the digital clock application

1   In the Code pane, open the Ticker.cs source file. This file contains the declaration of the *Tick* delegate type:

```
public delegate void Tick(int hh, int mm, int ss);
```

2   In the Code pane, locate the *Ticker* class in the Ticker.cs source file.

3   In the Code pane, add a public event called *tick* of type *Tick* to the *Ticker* class.

The *Ticker* class now looks like this:

```
class Ticker
{
    ⋮
    public event Tick tick;
    ⋮
}
```

4   In the Code pane, delete the *Attach* and *Detach* methods from the *Ticker* class.

The attach and detach functionality is automatically provided by the += and −= event operators.

5   In the Code pane, delete the declaration of the *subscribers* array from the *Ticker* class.

This array isn't needed because events automatically maintain their own internal collection.

6   In the Code pane, modify the *Ticker.Notify* method so that it calls the *tick* event instead of manually iterating through the *subscribers* array. Don't forget to check whether *tick* is *null* before calling the event.

The *Notify* method should look like this:

```
class Ticker
{
    public event Tick tick;
    ⋮
    private void Notify(int hours, int minutes, int seconds)
    {
        if (tick != null)
        {
            tick(hours, minutes, seconds);
        }
    }
    ⋮
}
```

7   In the Code pane, open the Clock.cs source file.

8   Change the *Clock.Start* method so that the delegate is attached to the *tick* event of the *pulsed* field using the += operator.

The *Clock.Start* method should look like this:

```
public void Start()
{
    pulsed.tick += new Tick(this.RefreshTime);
}
```

9   In the Code pane, change the *Clock.Stop* method so that the delegate is detached from the *tick* event of the *pulsed* field using the − = operator.

The *Clock.Stop* method should look like this:

```
public void Stop()
{
    pulsed.tick -= new Tick(this.RefreshTime);
}
```

10   On the Build menu, click Build Solution, and then correct any errors.

11   On the Debug menu, click Start Without Debugging. The project builds and runs. The digital clock form displays the correct time and updates the display every second.

12   Verify that the Stop and Start buttons still work, and then close the form.

If you want to continue to the next chapter

■   Keep Visual Studio .NET running and turn to Chapter 17.

If you want to exit Visual Studio .NET now

■   On the File menu, click Exit. If you see a Save dialog box, click Yes.

Chapter 16 Quick Reference

To	Do this
Declare a delegate type	Write the keyword *delegate*, followed by the return type, followed by the name of the delegate type, followed by the parameter types. For example:

```
delegate void Tick();
```

To	Do this
Call a delegate	Use the parentheses syntax exactly as if the delegate were a method. For example:

```
void Example(Tick m)
{
    m();
}
```

To	Do this
Create an instance of a delegate	Use the same syntax you use for a class or struct: write the keyword *new*, followed by the name of the type (the name of the delegate), followed by the argument between parentheses. The argument must be a method whose signature exactly matches the signature of the delegate. For example:

```
class Example
{
    private void Method() { ... }
    :
    private void Create()
    {
        Tick m = new Tick(this.Method);
        :
    }
}
```

To	Do this
Declare an event	Write the keyword *event*, followed by the name of the type (the type must be a delegate type), followed by the name of the event. For example:

```
delegate void TickHandler();

class Ticker
{
    public event TickHandler Tick;
}
```

To	Do this
Attach a delegate to an event	Create a delegate instance (of the same type as the event), and attach the delegate instance to the event by using the += operator. For example:

```
class Clock
{
    ⋮
    public void Start()
    {
        ticker.Tick += new TickHandler
            (this.RefreshTime);
    }
    private void RefreshTime()
    {
        ⋮
    }
    private Ticker ticker = new Ticker();
}
```

To	Do this
Detach a delegate from an event	Create a delegate instance (of the same type as the event), and detach the delegate instance from the event using the − = operator. For example:

```
class Clock
{
    ⋮
    public void Stop()
    {
        ticker.Tick -= new TickHandler
            (this.RefreshTime);
    }
    private void RefreshTime()
    {
        ⋮
    }
    private Ticker ticker = new Ticker();
}
```

To	Do this
Raise an event	Use parentheses exactly as if the event were a method. You must supply arguments to match the type of the event. Don't forget to check whether the event is *null*. For example:

```
class Ticker
{
    public event TickHandler Tick;
    ⋮
    private void Raise()
    {
        if (Tick != null)
        {
            Tick();
        }
    }
    ⋮
}
```

Operator Overloading

In this chapter, you will learn how to:

■ Declare and use binary operators for your own types.

■ Declare and use unary operators for your own types.

■ Write increment and decrement operators for structs and classes.

■ Implement some operators in special pairs.

■ Declare implicit conversion operators on your own types.

■ Declare explicit conversion operators on your own types.

Working with Operators

You use the standard operator symbols (such as + and –) to perform standard operations (such as addition and subtraction) on types (such as the *int* and the *double* types). The built-in numeric types come with their own predefined behaviors for each operator, but user-defined types don't. One of the decisions a programming language designer must make is whether to allow the programmer to implement operators for user-defined types. Some languages (for example, C++) allow this freedom, whereas other languages (such as Java) don't. Microsoft Visual C# allows user-defined types to implement their own custom behavior for operators, and this ability fits very well into the overall design of Visual C#, particularly with the ability to create user-defined value types.

Understanding Operators

Each operator symbol has a precedence. For example, the * operator has a higher precedence than the + operator. This means that alpha + beta * gamma is the same as alpha + (beta * gamma).

Each operator symbol also has an associativity to define whether the operator evaluates from left to right or from right to left. For example, the = operator is left-associative, so alpha = beta = gamma is the same as alpha = (beta = gamma).

A *unary* operator is an operator that has just one operand. For example, the increment operator (++) is a unary operator.

A *binary* operator is an operator that has two operands. For example, the multiplication operator (*) is a binary operator.

Implementing Operator Constraints

C# allows you to implement most of the existing operator symbols for your own types. However, when you do this, the operators you implement automatically fall into a well-defined framework with the following rules:

- You cannot change the precedence and associativity of a user-defined operator. The precedence and associativity are based on the operator symbol (for example, +) and not on the type (for example, *int*) on which the operator symbol is being used. Hence, alpha + beta * gamma is the same as alpha + (beta * gamma), which is true regardless of the type of alpha, beta, or gamma.

- You cannot change the multiplicity of an operator (the number of operands). For example, * is the symbol for multiplication, which is a binary operator. If you declare a * operator for your own type, it must be a binary operator.

- You cannot invent new operator symbols. For example, you can't create a new operator symbol (such as **) for raising one number to the power of another number. You'd have to create a method for that.

- You can't change the meaning of operators when applied to built-in types. For example, 1 + 2 has a predefined meaning and you're not allowed to override this meaning. If you could do this, things would be too complicated.

- There are some operator symbols that you can't overload. For example, you can't overload the dot operator (member access). Again, if you could do this, it would lead to unnecessary complexity.

▶ **Tip**   You can use indexers to simulate [ ] as an operator. Similarly, you can use properties to simulate = (assignment) as an operator, and you can use delegates to simulate a function call as an operator.

Overloaded Operators

To define your own operator behavior, you must overload a selected operator. You use method-like syntax with a return type and parameters, but the name of the method is the keyword *operator* together with the operator symbol you are declaring. For example, here's a user-defined struct called *Hour* that defines a binary + operator to add together two instances of *Hour*:

```
struct Hour
{
    public Hour(int initialValue)
    {
        value = initialValue;
    }
    public static Hour operator + (Hour lhs, Hour rhs)
    {
        return new Hour(lhs.value + rhs.value);
    }
    :
    private int value;
}
```

Notice the following:

- The operator is public. All operators *must* be public.
- The operator is static. All operators *must* be static. This means that operators are never polymorphic (so they cannot use the virtual, abstract, override, or sealed modifiers). This also means that a binary operator has two explicit arguments and a unary operator has one explicit argument (C++ programmers should note that operators never have a hidden *this* parameter).

▶ **Tip** When declaring highly stylized functionality (such as operators), it is useful to adopt a naming convention for the parameters. For example, you might use *lhs* and *rhs* (acronyms for left-hand side and right-hand side, respectively) for binary operators.

When you use the + operator on two expressions of type *Hour*, the C# compiler automatically converts your code into a call to the user-defined operator. In other words, the C# compiler converts this:

```
Hour Example(Hour a, Hour b)
{
    return a + b;
}
```

into this:

```
Hour Example(Hour a, Hour b)
{
    return Hour.operator+(a,b); // pseudocode
}
```

Note, however, that this syntax is not valid. You can use a binary operator only in its standard infix notation (with the symbol between the operands).

There is one final rule you must follow when declaring an operator: At least one of the parameters should always be of the containing type. In the previous *operator+* example for the *Hour* class, one of the parameters, *a* or *b*, should be an *Hour* object. In this example, both parameters are *Hour* objects. However, there could be times when you want to define additional implementations of *operator+* that add an integer (a number of hours) to an *Hour* object—the first parameter could be *Hour*, and the second parameter could be the integer. This rule makes it easy for the compiler to know where to look when trying to resolve an operator invocation, and it also ensures that you can't change the meaning of the built-in operators.

Creating Symmetric Operators

In the previous section, you saw how to declare a binary + operator to add together two instances of type *Hour*. The *Hour* struct has a constructor that creates an *Hour* from an *int*. This means that you can add together an *Hour* and an *int*—you just have to first use the *Hour* constructor to convert the *int* into an *Hour*. For example:

```
void Indirect(Hour a, int b)
{
    Hour sum = a + new Hour(b);
}
```

This is certainly valid code, but it is not as clear or as concise as adding together an *Hour* and an *int* directly, like this:

```
void Direct(Hour a, int b)
{
    Hour sum = a + b;
}
```

To make the expression (a + b) valid, you must declare what it means to add together an *Hour* (*a*, on the left) and an *int* (*b*, on the right). In other words, you must declare a binary + operator whose first parameter is an *Hour* and whose second parameter is an *int*:

```
struct Hour
{
    public Hour(int initialValue)
    {
        value = initialValue;
    }
    ⋮
    public static Hour operator+ (Hour lhs, Hour rhs)
    {
        return new Hour(lhs.value + rhs.value);
    }
    public static Hour operator+ (Hour lhs, int rhs)
    {
        return lhs + new Hour(rhs);
    }
    ⋮
    private int value;
}
```

It would be a mistake to provide many different versions of this operator, each with a different second parameter type. The point is that the *Hour* constructor takes a single *int* parameter; the extra *operator+* simply makes existing functionality easier to use.

This *operator+* declares how to add together an *Hour* as the left-hand operand and an *int* as the right-hand operator. It does not declare how to add together an *int* as the left-hand operand and an *Hour* as the right-hand operand:

```
Hour Direct(int a, Hour b)
{
    return a + b; // compile-time error
}
```

This is counter-intuitive. If you can write (a + b), you expect to also be able to write (b + a). Therefore you should provide a second overload of *operator+*:

```
struct Hour
{
    public Hour(int initialValue)
    {
        value = initialValue;
    }
    ⋮
    public static Hour operator+ (Hour lhs, int rhs)
    {
        return lhs + new Hour(rhs);
    }
    public static Hour operator+ (int lhs, Hour rhs)
    {
```

```
        return new Hour(lhs) + rhs;
    }
    :
    private int value;
}
```

▶ **Important**   You must provide the overload yourself. The compiler won't write it for you or silently swap the sequence of the two operands.

Operators and the Common Language Specification

Not all languages that execute use the common language runtime (CLR) support or understand operator overloading. For this reason, the Common Language Specification (CLS) requires that if you overload an operator, you should provide an alternative mechanism that supports the same functionality as the CLR. For example, suppose you implement *operator+* for the *Hour* struct:

```
public static Hour operator+ (Hour lhs, int rhs)
{
    :
}
```

You should also provide a method that achieves the same thing:

```
public static Hour Add(Hour lhs, int rhs)
{
    :
}
```

Understanding Compound Assignment

C# does not allow you to declare any user-defined assignment operators. However, a compound assignment operator (such as +=) is always evaluated in terms of its associated operator (such as +). In other words, this:

```
a += b;
```

Is automatically evaluated as this:

```
a = a + b;
```

And in general, a @= b (where @ represents any valid operator) is automatically evaluated as a = a @ b. If you have declared the appropriate simple operator, it is automatically called when you call its associated compound assignment operator. For example:

```
void Example(Hour a, int b)
{
    a += a; // same as a = a + a
    a += b; // same as a = a + b
}
```

The first compound assignment operator (a += a) is valid because *a* is of type *Hour* and the *Hour* type declares a binary *operator+* whose parameters are both *Hour*. Similarly, the second compound assignment operator (a += b) is valid because *a* is of type *Hour* and *b* is of type *int*. The *Hour* type also declares a binary *operator+* whose first parameter is an *Hour* and whose second parameter is an *int*. Note, however, that you cannot write b += a because that's the same as b = b + a. Although the addition is valid, the assignment is not valid because it is considered a change to the meaning of a built-in type.

Declaring Increment and Decrement Operators

C# also allows you to declare your own version of the increment (++) and decrement (−−) operators. The standard rules apply when declaring these operators; they must be public, they must be static, and they must be unary. For example, here is the increment operator for the *Hour* struct:

```
struct Hour
{
    ⋮
    public static Hour operator++ (Hour arg)
    {
        arg.value++;
        return arg;
    }
    ⋮
    private int value;
}
```

The increment and decrement operators are unique in that they can be used in prefix and postfix forms. C# cleverly uses the same single operator for both the prefix and postfix versions. The result of a postfix expression is the value of the operand before the expression takes place. In other words, the compiler effectively converts this:

```
Hour now = new Hour(9);
Hour postfix = now++;
```

Into this:

```
Hour now = new Hour(9);
Hour postfix = now;
now = Hour.operator++(now); // pseudocode
```

The result of a prefix expression is the return value of the operator. In other words, the C# compiler effectively converts this:

```
Hour now = new Hour(9);
Hour prefix = ++now;
```

Into this:

```
Hour now = new Hour(9);
now = Hour.operator++(now); // pseudocode
Hour prefix = now;
```

This equivalence means that the return type of the increment and decrement operators must be the same as the parameter type. Increment and decrement are the only operators that restrict the return type in this way. For example, the return type of a user-defined equality operator (==) is not constrained to be *bool*!

Using Operator Pairs

Some operators naturally come in pairs. For example, if you can compare two *Hour* values using the != operator, you would expect to be able to also compare two *Hour* values using the == operator. The C# compiler enforces this very reasonable expectation by insisting that if you declare *operator*== or *operator*!=, you must declare them both. This neither-or-both rule also applies to the < and > operators and the <= and >= operators. The C# compiler does not write any of these operator partners for you. You must write them all explicitly yourself, regardless of how obvious they might seem. Here are the == and != operators declared on the *Hour* struct:

```
struct Hour
{
    public Hour(int initialValue)
    {
        value = initialValue;
    }
    ⋮
    public static bool operator==(Hour lhs, Hour rhs)
    {
        return lhs.value == rhs.value;
    }
    public static bool operator!=(Hour lhs, Hour rhs)
    {
        return lhs.value != rhs.value;
    }
    ⋮
    private int value;
}
```

Implementing an Operator

In the following exercise, you will complete another Microsoft Windows digital clock application. This version of the code is similar to the exercise in Chapter 16. However, in this version, the *delegate* method does not receive the current *hour*, *minute*, and *second* values when the event is raised. Instead, the *delegate* method (which is called every second) keeps track of the time itself by updating three fields, one each for the *hour*, *minute*, and *second* values. The type of these three fields is *Hour*, *Minute*, and *Second*, respectively, and they are all structs. However, the application will not yet build because the *Minute* struct is not finished. In the first exercise, you will finish the *Minute* struct by implementing its missing addition operators.

Struct vs. Class

It is important to realize that the implementation of the increment operator in the *Hour* struct is correct only because *Hour* is a struct. If you change *Hour* into a class but leave the implementation of its increment operator unchanged, you will find that the postfix translation won't give the correct answer. If you remember that a class is a reference type and think through the compiler translations explained previously, you can see why this occurs. The correct implementation of the increment operator when *Hour* is a class is as follows:

```
class Hour
{
    public Hour(int initialValue)
    {
        value = initialValue;
    }
    :
    public static Hour operator++(Hour arg)
    {
        return new Hour(arg.value + 1);
    }
    :
    private int value;
}
```

It is recommended that you use operators only on value types.

Write the *operator+* overloads

1 Start Microsoft Visual Studio .NET.

2 Open the Operators project, located in the \Microsoft Press\Visual C# Step by Step\Chapter 17\Operators folder in your My Documents folder. The Operators project opens.

3 In the Code pane, open the Clock.cs source file and locate the declarations of the *hour*, *minute*, and *second* fields.

These fields hold the clock's current time:

```
class Clock
{
    ⋮
    private Hour hour;
    private Minute minute;
    private Second second;
}
```

4 In the Code pane, locate the *tock* method of the *Clock* class. A delegate for the *tock* method is called every second. You can see the code that sets up this delegation in the *Clock* constructor.

The *tock* method looks like this:

```
private void tock()
{
    second++;
    if (second == 0)
    {
        minute++;
        if (minute == 0)
        {
            hour++;
        }
    }
}
```

5 On the Build menu, click Build Solution. The project builds and displays the following error message in the Output pane:

```
Operator '==' cannot be applied to operands of type 'Operators.Minute
' and 'int'.
```

The problem is that the *tock* method contains the following *if* statement, but the appropriate *operator==* is not declared in the *Minute* struct:

```
if (minute == 0)
{
    hour++;
}
```

Your next task is to implement this operator for the *Minute* struct.

6 In the Code pane, open the Minute.cs file.

7 In the Code pane, implement a version of *operator==* that accepts a *Minute* as its left-hand operand and an *int* as its right-hand operand. Don't forget that the return type of this operator should be a *bool*. The completed operator should look exactly like this:

```
struct Minute
{
    ⋮
    public static bool operator==(Minute lhs, int rhs)
    {
        return lhs.value == rhs;
    }
    ⋮
    private int value;
}
```

8 On the Build menu, click Build Solution. The project builds and displays the following error message in the Output pane:

```
The operator 'Operators.Minute.operator ==(Operators.Minute, int)'
 requires a matching operator "!=" to also be defined.
```

There is a still an error. The problem is that you have declared a version of *operator==* but have not declared its required *operator!=* partner.

9 Implement a version of *operator!=* that accepts a *Minute* as its left-hand operand and an *int* as its right-hand operand.

The completed operator should look exactly like this:

```
struct Minute
{
    ⋮
    public static bool operator!=(Minute lhs, int rhs)
    {
        return lhs.value != rhs;
    }
    ⋮
    private int value;
}
```

10 On the Build menu, click Build Solution. The application builds without errors.

11 On the Debug menu, click Start Without Debugging. The application runs and displays a digital clock that updates itself every second.

12 Close the application. You return to the Visual Studio .NET programming environment.

Declaring Conversion Operators

A *conversion* is where a value of one type is converted to a value of another type. For example, the following method is declared with a single *double* parameter:

```
class Example
{
    public static void Method(double parameter)
    {
        ⋮
    }
}
```

You might reasonably expect that only values of type *double* could be used as arguments when calling *Method*, but this is not so. The C# compiler also allows *Method* to be called with an argument whose type is not *double*, but only as long as that value can be converted to a *double*.

Providing Built-In Conversions

The built-in types have built-in conversions. For example, an *int* can be implicitly converted to a *double*. An implicit conversion is sometimes called a widening conversion and requires no special syntax and never throws an exception:

```
Example.Method(42); // implicit int to double conversion
```

On the other hand, a *double* cannot be implicitly converted to an *int*:

```
Example.Method(42.0); // compile-time error
```

A *double* can be converted to an *int*, but the conversion requires an explicit notation (a cast):

```
Example.Method((int)42.0);
```

An explicit conversion is sometimes called a *narrowing conversion* and can throw an *OverflowException*. C# allows you to provide conversion operators for your own user-defined types to control whether they can be implicitly or explicitly converted to other types.

Declaring User-Defined Conversion Operators

The syntax for declaring a user-defined conversion operator is similar to an overloaded operator. A conversion operator must be public and must also be static. Here's a conversion operator that declares that an *Hour* can be implicitly converted into an *int*:

```
struct Hour
{
    :
    public static implicit operator int (Hour from)
    {
        return value;
    }
    private int value;
}
```

The type you are converting from is declared as the single parameter (in this case, *Hour*), and the type you are converting to is declared as the type name after the keyword *operator* (in this case, *int*). There is no conventional return type before the keyword *operator*. When declaring your own conversion operators, you must specify whether they are implicit conversion operators or explicit conversion operators. You do this by using the *implicit* and *explicit* keywords. For example, the *Hour* to *int* conversion operator mentioned previously is implicit, meaning that the C# compiler can use it implicitly (without a cast):

```
class Example
{
    public static void Method(int parameter) { ... }
    public static void Main()
    {
        Hour lunch = new Hour(12);
        Example.Method(lunch); // implicit Hour to int conversion
    }
}
```

If the conversion operator had been explicit, the previous example would not have compiled because an explicit conversion operator requires an explicit cast:

```
Example.Method((int)lunch); // explicit Hour to int conversion
```

▶ **Tip** If a conversion can throw an exception, it should be declared as an explicit conversion. You should consider making a conversion implicit only if it cannot possibly throw an exception.

Creating Symmetric Operators (Again)

Conversion operators provide you with an alternate way to resolve the problem of providing symmetric operators. For example, instead of providing three versions of *operator+* (*Hour + Hour*, *Hour + int*, and *int + Hour*) as before, you can provide a single version of *operator+* (that takes two *Hour* parameters) and an implicit *int* to *Hour* conversion:

```
struct Hour
{
    public Hour(int initialValue)
    {
        value = initialValue;
    }
    public static Hour operator+(Hour lhs, Hour rhs)
    {
        return new Hour(lhs.value + rhs.value);
    }
    public static implicit operator Hour (int from)
    {
        return new Hour (from);
    }
    ⋮
    private int value;
}
```

If you add an *Hour* and an *int* (in either order), the C# compiler automatically converts the *int* to an *Hour* and then calls *operator+* with two *Hour* arguments:

```
void Example(Hour a, int b)
{
    Hour eg1 = a + b; // b converted to an Hour
    Hour eg2 = b + a; // b converted to an Hour
}
```

Adding an Implicit Conversion Operator

In the following exercise, you will modify the digital clock application from the previous exercise. You will add an implicit conversion operator to the *Second* struct and remove the operators that it replaces.

Write the conversion operator

1   In the Code pane, open the Second.cs source file.

The *Second* struct currently contains three overloaded implementations of *operator==* and three overloaded implementations of *operator!=*. Each operator is overloaded for the types (*Second*, *Second*), (*Second*, *int*), and (*int*, *Second*).

2   In the Code pane, add an implicit conversion operator to the *Second* struct that converts from an *int* to a *Second*.

The conversion operator should look like this:

```
struct Second
{
    ⋮
```

```
        public static implicit operator Second (int arg)
        {
            return new Second(arg);
        }
        ⋮
}
```

3 On the Build menu, click Build Solution and correct any errors.

4 In the Code pane, delete the versions of *operator==* and *operator!=* that take one *Hour* and one *int* parameter. The following three oper-ators should be the only operators in the *Second* struct:

```
struct Second
{
    ⋮
    public static implicit operator Second (int arg)
    {
        return new Second(arg);
    }
    public static bool operator==(Second lhs, Second rhs)
    {
        return lhs.value == rhs.value;
    }
    public static bool operator!=(Second lhs, Second rhs)
    {
        return lhs.value != rhs.value;
    }
    ⋮
}
```

5 On the Build menu, click Build Solution and correct any errors.

The program still builds because the conversion operator and the remaining two operators together provide the same functionality as the deleted four operator overloads. The only difference is that using an implicit conversion operator is potentially a little slower than not using an implicit conversion operator.

6 On the Debug menu, click Start Without Debugging. The application runs.

7 Close the application. You return to the Visual Studio .NET pro-gramming environment.

If you want to continue to the next chapter

■ Keep Visual Studio .NET running and turn to Chapter 18.

If you want to exit Visual Studio .NET now

■ On the File menu, click Exit. If you see a Save dialog box, click Yes.

Chapter 17 Quick Reference

To	Do this
Declare an operator	Write the keywords *public* and *static*, followed by the return type, followed by the *operator* keyword, followed by the operator symbol being declared, followed by the correct number of parameters between parentheses. For example:

```
struct Hour
{
    ⋮
    public static bool operator==(Hour lhs,
        Hour rhs)s
    {
        ⋮
    }
    ⋮
}
```

To	Do this
Declare a conversion operator	Write the keywords *public* and *static*, followed by the keyword *implicit* or *explicit*, followed by the *operator* keyword, followed by the type being converted to, followed by the type being converted from as a single parameter between parentheses. For example:

```
struct Hour
{
    ⋮
    public static implicit operator Hour (int arg)
    {
        ⋮
    }
    ⋮
}
```

Working with Windows Applications

Introducing Windows Forms

In this chapter, you will learn how to:

- Create Microsoft Windows Forms applications.

- Use common Windows Forms controls such as labels, text boxes, and buttons.

- Change the properties of Windows Forms and controls at design time and programmatically at run time.

- Subscribe to and process events exposed by Windows Forms and controls.

Now that you have completed the exercises and examined the examples in the first three parts of this book, you should be well-versed in the Microsoft Visual C# language. You have learned how to write programs and create components by using C#, and you should understand many of the finer points of the language, such as the differences between value types and reference types. Because you now have the essential language skills, Part 4 will show you how to expand upon them and use C# to take advantage of the graphical user interface (GUI) libraries provided as part of the Microsoft .NET Framework. In particular, you will see how to use the objects in the *System.Windows.Forms* namespace to create Windows Forms applications.

In this chapter, you will learn how to build a basic Windows Forms application using many of the common components that are a feature of most GUI applications. You will see how to set the properties of Windows Forms and components by using the Visual Designer and the Properties window. You'll also learn how to change or examine the values of these properties dynamically by using C# code. Finally, you will learn how to intercept and handle many of the common events that Windows Forms and components expose.

Creating Your Application

As an example, you are going to create an application that allows a user to input and display details for members of the Middleshire Bell Ringers Association, an esteemed collection of the finest campanologists. Initially you will keep the application very simple, concentrating on laying out the form and making sure that it all works. In later chapters, you will provide menus and learn how to implement validation to make sure that the data that is entered makes sense. The following sample screen shows what the application will look like after you have completed it. (You can run the completed version by running BellRingers.exe, located in the \Microsoft Press\Visual C# Step by Step\Chapter 18\BellRingers Complete\bin\Release folder in your My Documents folder.)

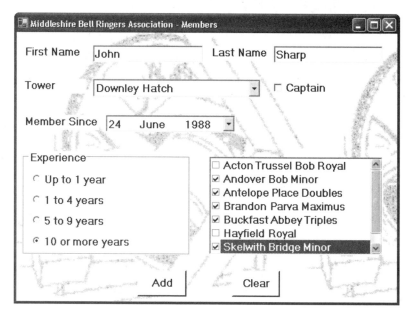

Creating a Windows Forms Application

In this exercise, you'll start building the Middleshire Bell Ringers Association application by creating a new project, laying out the form, and adding Windows Forms controls to the form. Because you have been using existing Windows Forms applications in Microsoft Visual Studio .NET in previous chapters, much of the first couple of exercises will be a review for you.

Create the MiddleShire Bell Ringers Association project

1   Start Visual Studio .NET.

2   On the File menu, point to New, and then click Project.

3   In the Project Types pane, select Visual C# Projects.

4   In the Templates pane, select Windows Application.

5   In the Name text box, type **BellRingers**.

6   In the Location list box, navigate to the Microsoft Press\Visual C# Step by Step\Chapter 18 folder in your My Documents folder.

7   Click OK. The new project is created and contains a blank form called *Form1*.

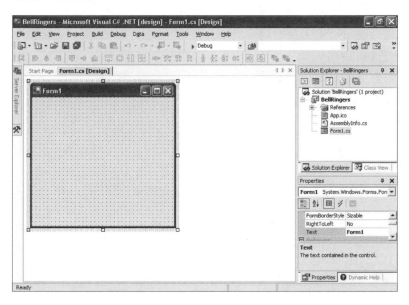

Set the properties of the form

1   Select the form in the Designer View window. In the Properties window, click the *(Name)* property, and then type **MemberForm** in the (Name) text box to change the name of the form. (If the Properties window is not displayed, click Properties Window on the View menu, or press F4.)

2   In the Properties window, click the *Text* property, and then type **Middleshire Bell Ringers Association – Members,** to change the title bar of the form.

3   In the Properties window, click the *BackgroundImage* property, and then click the Ellipses button in the adjacent text box. The Open dialog box opens.

4   In the Open dialog box, navigate to the \Microsoft Press\Visual C# Step by Step\Chapter 18 folder in your My Documents folder, select the Bell.gif file, and then click Open. The *BackgroundImage* property is now set to the bell image.

In the Properties window, click the *BackColor* property, and then click the down-arrow button in the adjacent text box. A dialog box opens.

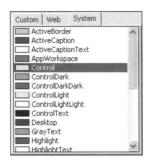

5   On the System tab of the dialog box, click Window. This sets the background color of all the controls that you drop onto the form to the same color as the window itself.

6   Select the *Font* property. This is a composite property that has many attributes. In the Properties window, click the plus sign (+) to expand the *Font* property and display the attributes. Set the *Size* attribute of the font to 12 and the *Bold* attribute to *True*.

▶   **Tip**   You can also change some composite properties, such as *Font*, by clicking the Ellipses button that appears when you select the property. When you click the Ellipses button, the standard Font dialog box opens and allows you to select the font and effects that you want.

7   Change the form's *Size* property, which is also a composite property. In the Properties window, click the plus sign (+) to expand the *Size* property and display the attributes. Set the *Width* attribute to *600* and the Height attribute to *450*.

The form should look like the image in the following illustration.

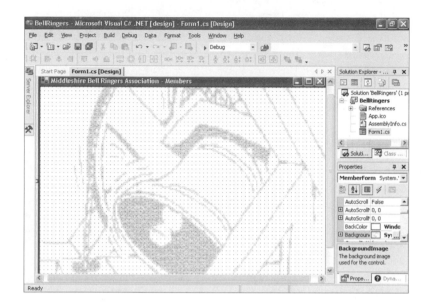

Compile the application

1 On the Build menu, click Build Solution. The project fails to build and the compiler displays the following error:

```
The type or namespace 'Form1' could not be found (are you missing
 a using directive or an assembly reference?)
```

This happens because you changed the form's name from *Form1* to *MemberForm*. The project contains code that tries to run *Form1* and, because it cannot find *Form1* anymore, you need to fix the problem.

2 Display the Form1.cs source code in the Code And Text Editor window.

3 Scroll down to find the *Main* method near the end of the file. It contains the following line of code:

```
Application.Run(new Form1());
```

This is how a Windows Forms application runs a form. Each form is actually a class that inherits from *System.Windows.Forms.Form*. (If you scroll to the top of the Form1.cs file, you see the definition of the *MemberForm* class—this is the form that you have been creating.) *Run* is a static method of the *Application* class that can load and run an instance of a form. The form was originally called *Form1*, but you changed the name of the class to *MemberForm*. The Visual Studio .NET integrated development environment (IDE) is not clever enough to search through your code and change all occurrences of *Form1* to *MemberForm* (even though it wrote the code in the first place!). You have to make the change yourself.

4   Modify the code in the *Main* method so that it reads as follows:

```
Application.Run(new MemberForm());
```

5   Build the application again. The build should be successful this time.

▶   **Note**   In most cases, when you change a property using the Property window, Visual Studio .NET automatically updates any code it has generated to match the new value. The name of a form is a special case where you have to make the change yourself.

What Are the Common Windows Forms Properties?

If you look closely at the Properties window when a form is selected, you can see that there are over fifty properties available. Some of them are fairly obvious, for example, the *Text* property that corresponds to the text displayed in the form's title bar. Some properties are useful under certain circumstances; for example, you can remove the Minimize, Maximize, and Close buttons, or remove the System menu from the title bar of a form by setting the *ControlBox* property to *False*—useful if you want to make sure users cannot close the form unless they execute some code that closes it explicitly. Other properties apply to very specific circumstances; for example, the *Opacity* property can be used to control the level of transparency of the form. The following table describes most of the common form properties that can be changed at design time. You should also be aware that there are additional properties not listed in the Properties window that you can use only programmatically at run time. For example, the *ActiveControl* property shows which control in the form currently has the focus.

Property	Description
(Name)	The name of the form. Two forms in the same project cannot have the same name.
BackColor	The default background color of any text and graphics in the form.
BackgroundImage	A bitmap, icon, or other graphic file to be used as a backdrop to the form. If the image is smaller than the form, it is tiled to fill the form.

Property	Description
Font	The default font used by the controls embedded on the form that display text. This is a compound property—you can set many attributes of the font including the font name, size, and whether the font appears italic, bold, or underlined.
ForeColor	The default foreground color of any text and graphics in the form.
FormBorderStyle	This controls the appearance and type of border of the form. The default setting is Sizable. Other options specify borders that are not resizable or do not have the various System menu buttons.
Icon	This specifies the icon that appears in the form's System menu and on the Windows taskbar. You can create your own icons by using Visual Studio .NET.
Location	This is another compound property that specifies the coordinates of the top left corner of the form with respect to its container, which might be another form or the screen.
MaximizeBox	This property specifies whether the Maximize command on the System menu and caption bar is enabled or disabled. By default, it is enabled.
MaximumSize	This specifies the maximum size of the form. The default value (0, 0) indicates that there is no maximum size and the user can resize the form to any size.
Menu	This property indicates which menu should appear on the menu bar of the form. The default value (none) specifies that the form has no menu of its own.
MinimizeBox	This property is similar to the *MaximizeBox* property. It specifies whether the Minimize command on the System menu and title bar is enabled or disabled. By default, it is enabled.
MinimumSize	This property specifies the minimum size of the form.
Size	This is the default size of the form when it is first displayed.
Text	This property contains the text that appears on the title bar of the form.
WindowState	This property determines the initial state of the form when it is first displayed. The default state (Normal) positions the form according to the *Location* and *Size* properties. The other options are Minimized and Maximized.

▶   **Tip**   You can view a summary of a property by selecting the property in the Properties window, right-clicking it, and then clicking Description. A pane displaying a description of any selected property appears at the bottom of the Properties window.

Changing Properties Programmatically

In addition to setting properties statically at design time, you can write code that changes properties dynamically at run time. For example, you can change the *Size* property of a form in your program to make it shrink or grow without the user dragging the border to resize it. In actual fact, if you look at the code behind the form, you will see that Visual Studio .NET generates code to change the properties of a form dynamically at run time according to the values you specify at design time. If you select Code on the View menu, you can see what Visual Studio does.

In the code for a form, you will notice that a form (which is simply a class that inherits from *System.Windows.Forms.Form*, as discussed previously) contains a few methods. In our example, these methods are *Main*, *Dispose*, and *Member-Form*. The *Main* method is the entry point to the application, and it creates and runs the form itself (you saw this previously as well). The *Dispose* method releases any resources held by the form. The *MemberForm* method is actually a constructor that, by default, calls the *InitializeComponent* method.

Where is the *InitializeComponent* method defined, though? If you look between the *Dispose* and the *Main* methods in the source code, you will see a contracted area of code marked as Windows Form Designer generated code, as shown in the following illustration.

```
BellRingers.MemberForm                    InitializeComponent()

            if( disposing )
            {
                if (components != null)
                {
                    components.Dispose();
                }
            }
            base.Dispose( disposing );
        }

        Windows Form Designer generated code

        /// <summary>
        /// The main entry point for the application.
        /// </summary>
        [STAThread]
        static void Main()
        {
            Application.Run(new MemberForm());
        }
    }
}
```

If you click the plus sign and expand this code, you will find the *InitializeComponent* method between #*region* and #*endregion* directives.

▶ **Tip**   The preprocessor directive *#region* lets you specify a block of code that can be expanded and contracted in the Visual Studio .NET programming environment. It has no effect whatsoever on the code itself. You can use this feature to add your own regions and break up your code into easy-to-read chunks.

The code in the *InitializeComponent* method, in addition to other tasks, sets the properties of the form to the values you specified in Design View—you will spot statements such as the following:

```
this.Name = "MemberForm";
this.Text = "Middleshire Bell Ringers Association - Members";
```

Also, if you change the values in the Properties window, Visual Studio .NET will keep the code in this method synchronized with your changes. In later exercises and chapters, you will write your own code to query and change the properties of forms and other controls.

▶ **Important**   You should not modify the code in the *InitializeComponent* method yourself. If you do, the changes you make will likely be lost the next time any property values are amended in Design View.

Adding Controls to the Form

So far you have created a form, set some of its properties, and examined the code that Visual Studio .NET generates. To make the form useful, you need to add controls and write some code of your own. The Windows Forms library contains a varied collection of controls. Some are fairly obvious—for example, *TextBox*, *ListBox*, *CheckBox*, and *ComboBox*—whereas other, more powerful controls (such as the *DateTimePicker*) might not be so familiar. In this chapter, you will use some of the common controls; the more exotic ones will be addressed in later chapters.

Using Windows Forms Controls

In the next exercise, you will add controls to the form that allow a user to enter member details. You will use a variety of different controls, each suited to a particular type of data input.

You will use *TextBox* controls for entering the first name and last name of the member. Each member belongs to a "tower" (a tower is where bells hang). The Middleshire district has several towers, but the list is static—new towers are not built very often and old towers tend not to fall down. The ideal control for handling this type of data is a *ComboBox*. The form also records whether the member is the tower "captain" (the captain is the person in charge of the tower who conducts the other ringers). A *CheckBox* is the best sort of control for this; it can either be selected (*True*) or cleared (*False*).

> ▶ **Tip**   *CheckBox* controls can actually have three states if the *ThreeState* property is set to *True*. The states are *True*, *False*, and *Indeterminate*. These states are useful if you are displaying information that has been retrieved from a relational database. Some columns in a table in a database allow *null* values, indicating that the value held is not defined or is unknown. If you want to display this data in a *CheckBox*, you can use the *Indeterminate* state to handle *null* values.

The application also gathers statistical information about when members joined the association and how much bell ringing experience they have (up to one year, between one and four years, between five and nine years, and ten or more years). A *DateTimePicker* control is very suitable for selecting and displaying dates, and a group of options, or radio buttons, is useful for indicating the member's experience—radio buttons provide a mutually exclusive set of values.

Finally, the application records the methods (tunes) the member can ring. Although a bell ringer only rings one bell at a time, a group of bell ringers under the direction of the tower captain can ring their bells in different sequences and generally play simple music. There are a variety of bell ringing methods, and they have names like Andover Bob Minor, Antelope Place Doubles, and Hayfield Royal. New methods are being written with alarming regularity, so the list of methods can vary over time. In a real-world application, you would store this list in a database. In this application, you will use a small selection of methods that you will hard-wire into the form. (You will see how to use databases in the next part of the book.) A good control for displaying this information and indicating whether a member can ring a method is the *CheckedListBox*.

When the user has entered the member's details, the Add button will validate and store the data. The user can click Clear to reset the controls on the form and cancel any data entered.

Add Windows Forms controls

1   Make sure that Form1 is displayed in the Designer View window. Using the Toolbox, verify that the Windows Forms category is selected, and then drag a *Label* control onto *MemberForm*. (If the Toolbox is not displayed, click Toolbox from the View menu.)

2   In the Properties window, click the *Location* property, and then type **10, 20** to set the *Location* property of the label.

3   From the Toolbox, drag a *TextBox* control onto *MemberForm*, next to the label. Do not worry about aligning the *TextBox* exactly

because you will set the *Location* property for this and the following controls later.

4   Add a second *Label* to the form. Place it next to the *TextBox* at location 300, 20.

5   Add another *TextBox* to *MemberForm* and position it next to the second *Label*.

6   From the Toolbox, drag a third *Label* onto the form. Place it directly under the first *Label*.

7   From the Toolbox, drag a *ComboBox* control onto the form. Place it on *MemberForm* under the first *TextBox* and next to the third *Label*.

8   From the Toolbox, drag a *CheckBox* control onto the form and place it under the second *TextBox*.

9   Add a fourth *Label* to *MemberForm* and place it under the third *Label*.

10   From the Toolbox, drag a *DateTimePicker* control and place it under the *ComboBox*.

11   From the Toolbox, drag a *GroupBox* control and place it under the fourth *Label* control.

12   From the Toolbox, drag the *RadioButton* control and place it inside the *GroupBox* control you just added. Notice that the *GroupBox* is selected when you drag the *RadioButton* into it.

13   Add three more *RadioButton* controls, vertically aligned with each other, to the *GroupBox*. You might need to make the *GroupBox* bigger to accommodate them.

14   From the Toolbox, drag a *CheckedListBox* control and place it under the second *Label* and to the right of the *GroupBox* control.

15   From the Toolbox, drag a *Button* control and place it near the bottom on the lower-left side of *MemberForm*.

16   Add another *Button* control to the bottom of the form, just to the right of the first.

Setting Control Properties

You now need to set the properties of the controls you just added to the form. To change the value of a control's property, click the control to select it, and then enter the correct value in the Properties window. You will start with the basic properties. The following table lists the properties and values you need to assign to each of the controls.

Control	Property	Value
label1	Text	First Name
	Location	10, 20
textBox1	(Name)	firstName
	Location	120, 20
	Size	170, 26
	Text	leave blank
label2	Text	Last Name
	Location	300, 20
textbox2	(Name)	lastName
	Location	400, 20
	Size	170, 26
	Text	leave blank
label3	Text	Tower
	Location	10, 72
comboBox1	(Name)	tower
	DropDownStyle	DropDownList (This setting forces users to pick one of the items in the list; users cannot type in a value of their own.)
	Location	120, 72
	Size	260, 28
checkBox1	(Name)	captain
	Location	400, 72
	Size	100, 26
	Text	Captain
	CheckAlign	MiddleLeft (When you click the drop-down arrow for this property, an interesting graphic containing a grid appears. Click the left square in the middle row.)
label4	Text	Member Since
	Location	10, 128
	Size	120, 23
DateTimePicker	(Name)	memberSince
	Location	140, 128
	Size	200, 26
groupBox1	(Name)	Experience

Control	Property	Value
	Location	10, 184
	Size	260, 160
	Text	Experience
radioButton1	*Name*	Novice
	Location	16, 32 (Note that this location is relative to the radio button's container, the *experience GroupBox*.)
	Size	220, 24
	Text	Up to 1 year
radioButton2	*(Name)*	Intermediate
	Location	16, 64
	Size	220, 24
	Text	1 to 4 years
radioButton3	*(Name)*	Experienced
	Location	16, 96
	Size	220, 24
	Text	5 to 9 years
radioButton4	*(Name)*	Accomplished
	Location	16, 128
	Size	220, 24
	Text	10 or more years
checkedListBox1	*(Name)*	Methods
	Location	300, 192
	Size	270, 160
	Sorted	True
button1	*(Name)*	Add
	Location	190, 368
	Size	75, 40
	Text	Add
button2	*(Name)*	Clear
	Location	335, 368
	Size	75, 40
	Text	Clear

Control Properties

Like forms, controls have many properties that you can set. Each different type of control has different properties. Also, like forms, you can set and query control properties dynamically in your own programs, and there are a number of properties that are available only at run time. If you want to learn more about the different properties available for each type of control, you can find a list of them in the .NET Framework SDK documentation supplied with Visual Studio .NET.

Changing Properties Dynamically

You have been using the Design View to set properties statically. When the form runs, it would be useful to reset the value of each control to an initial default value. To do this, you will need to write some code (at last). In the following exercises, you will create a *private* method called *Reset*. Later, you will call the *Reset* method when the form first starts and when the user clicks the Clear button.

Create the *Reset* method

1   On the View menu, click Class View.

2   In the Class View window, expand the BellRingers project, expand the { } BellRingers namespace, and then right-click the *MemberForm* class. A menu appears.

3   On the menu, point to Add, and then click Add Method. The C# Method Wizard opens.

4   Type **Reset** in the Method Name box, and then click Finish.

5   In the Code And Text Editor window, add the following lines of code to the *Reset* method:

```
firstName.Text = "";
lastName.Text = "";
```

These two statements ensure that the *firstName* and *lastName* text boxes are blank by assigning an empty string to their *Text* property.

Populating the *ComboBox*

If you recall, the Tower *ComboBox* will contain a list of all the bell towers in the Middleshire district. This information would usually be held in a database and you would write code to retrieve the list of towers and populate the *ComboBox*. A *ComboBox* has a property called *Items* that contains a collection of the data to be displayed. Because you have not been shown how to access a database yet, the application will use a hard-coded collection.

In the *Reset* method, after the code you have already written, add the following statements to clear the list (this is important because otherwise you would end up with many duplicate values in the list) and create four items in the *ComboBox*:

```
tower.Items.Clear();
tower.Items.Add("Great Shevington");
tower.Items.Add("Little Mudford");
tower.Items.Add("Upper Gumtree");
tower.Items.Add("Downley Hatch");
```

Setting the Current Date

You can also initialize the *memberSince DateTimePicker* control to the current date. The date can be set by using the *Value* property. You can obtain the current date by using the static property *Today* of the *DateTime* class. Add the following statement to the *Reset* method:

```
memberSince.Value = DateTime.Today;
```

Initializing the *CheckBox*

The *captain CheckBox* should default to *False*. To do this, you need to set the *Checked* property. Add the following statement to the *Reset* method:

```
captain.Checked = false;
```

Initializing the radio button group

The form contains four radio buttons that indicate the number of years of bell ringing experience the member has. A radio button is similar to a *CheckBox* in that it can contain a *True* or *False* value. However, the power of radio buttons increases when you put them together in a *GroupBox*. In this case, the radio buttons form a mutually exclusive collection—only one radio button in a group can be selected, and all the others will be cleared. By default, none of the buttons will be selected. You should rectify this by setting the *Checked* property of the *novice* radio button. Add the following statement to the *Reset* method:

```
novice.Checked = true;
```

Filling the *ListBox*

Like the Tower *ComboBox*, the *CheckedListBox* containing the list of bell ringing methods has a property called *Items* that contains a collection of values to be displayed. Also like the *ComboBox*, it is usually populated from a database.

However, as before, you will supply some hard-coded values for now. Complete the *Reset* method by adding the following code:

```
methods.Items.Clear();
methods.Items.Add("Andover Bob Minor");
methods.Items.Add("Antelope Place Doubles");
methods.Items.Add("Hayfield Royal");
methods.Items.Add("West Chiltington Doubles");
methods.Items.Add("Brandon Parva Maximus");
methods.Items.Add("Buckfast Abbey Triples");
methods.Items.Add("Skelwith Bridge Minor");
methods.Items.Add("Acton Trussel Bob Royal");
```

Calling the *Reset* method

You need to arrange for the *Reset* method to be called when the form is first displayed. A good place to do this is in the *MemberForm* constructor. In the Code And Text Editor window, scroll to the beginning of the *MemberForm* class and find the constructor (it is called *MemberForm*, just like the class). In the constructor, you should notice the following comment:

```
//
// TODO: Add any constructor code after InitializeComponent call
//
```

Insert a call to the *Reset* method after that comment:

```
this.Reset();
```

Compiling and testing the application

It is a good practice to name the file containing a form after the form itself.

1   In the Solution Explorer, right-click Form1.cs, click Rename, and then type **MemberForm.cs**.

2   On the Debug menu, click Start to verify that the project compiles and runs.

3   When the form runs, click the Tower *ComboBox*. You will see the list of bell towers, and you can select one of them.

4   Click the drop-down arrow on the right side of the Member Since date/time picker.

5   You will be presented with a calendar of dates. The default value will be the current date. You can click a date, and use the arrows to select a month.

6   Click each of the radio buttons in the Experience group. Notice that you cannot select more than one at a time.

7   In the Methods list box, click some of the methods and select the corresponding check box. You will have to click twice to select or clear a method.

8   Close the form and return to Visual Studio .NET.

Publishing Events in Windows Forms

If you are familiar with Microsoft Visual Basic, Microsoft Foundation Classes (MFC), or any of the other tools available for building GUI applications for Windows, you are aware that Windows uses an event-driven model to determine when to execute code. In Chapter 16, you saw how to publish your own events and subscribe to them. Windows Forms and controls have their own predefined events that you can subscribe to, and these events should be sufficient to handle most eventualities. If they do not, you can always use inheritance to create your own customized GUI components (inheritance will be covered in Chapter 23).

Processing Events in Windows Forms

Your task as a developer is to capture the events that you feel are relevant to your application and write the code that responds to these events. A familiar example is the *Button* control, which raises a "Somebody clicked the button" event when a user clicks it with the mouse or presses Enter when the button has the focus. If you want the button to do something, you write code that responds to this event. This is what you will do in the final exercise in this chapter.

Handle the *Click* event for the Clear button

1   In Design View (on the View menu, click Designer), select the Clear button on *MemberForm*.

    When the user clicks the Clear button, you want the form to be reset to its default values.

2   In the Properties window, click the Events button.

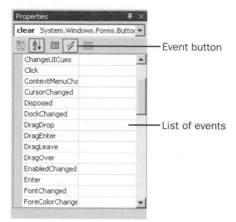

Event button

List of events

The list of properties is replaced with a list of events that you can intercept.

3   Select the *Click* event.

4   Type **clearClicked** in the text box and press Enter.

A new event method called *clearClicked* is created and displayed in the Code And Text Editor window. Notice that the event method conforms to the convention in that it takes two parameters: the sender (an *object*) and additional arguments (an *EventArgs*). The Windows Forms run time will populate these parameters with information about the source of the event and any additional information that might be useful when handling the event. You will not use these parameters in this exercise.

5   In the body of the *clearClicked* method, call the *Reset* method that you wrote previously.

The body of the method now should look exactly like this:

```
private void clearClicked(object sender, System.EventArgs e)
{
    this.Reset();
}
```

Handling the *Click* event for the Add button

The users will click the Add button when they have filled in all the data for a member and want to store the information. The *Click* event should validate the information entered to ensure it makes sense (for example, should you allow a tower captain to have less than one year of experience?) and, if it is okay, arrange for the data to be sent to a database or other persistent store. You will learn more about validation and storing data in later chapters. For now, the code for the *Click* event of the Add button will display a message box echoing the data input.

1   Return to Design View and select the Add button.

2   In the Properties window, make sure that you are displaying events rather than properties, type **addClick** in the *Click* event, and then press Enter. Another event method called *addClick* is created.

3   Add the following code to the *addClick* method:

```
string details;
details = "Member name " + firstName.Text + " " + lastName.Text +
    " from the tower at " + tower.Text;
MessageBox.Show(details, "Member Information");
```

This block of code creates a string variable called *details* that it fills with the name of the member and the tower that the member belongs to. Notice how the code accesses the *Text* property of the *TextBox* and *ComboBox* to read the current values of those controls. The *MessageBox* class contains static methods for displaying dialog boxes on the screen. The *Show* method used here will display the contents of the *details* string in the body of the message box and will put Member Information in the title bar. *Show* is an overloaded method, and there are other variants that allow you to specify icons and buttons to display in the message box, as well.

Handling the *Closing* event for the form

As an example of an event that can take a different set of parameters, you will also trap the *Closing* event for a form. The *Closing* event is raised when the user attempts to close the form but before the form actually closes. You can use this event to prompt the user to save any unsaved data or even ask the user whether she really wants to close the form—you can cancel the event in the event handler and prevent the form from closing.

1   Return to Design View and select the form (click anywhere on the background of the form rather than selecting a control).

2   In the Properties window, make sure that you are displaying events, type **memberFormClosing** in the *Closing* event, and then press Enter. An event method called *memberFormClosing* is created.

You should observe that the second parameter for this method has the type *CancelEventArgs*. The *CancelEventArgs* class has a Boolean property called *Cancel*. If you set *Cancel* to *true* in the event handler, the form will not close. If you set *Cancel* to *false* (the default value), the form will close when the event handler finishes.

3   Add the following statements to the *memberFormClosing* method:

```
DialogResult key = MessageBox.Show("Are you sure you want to quit",
                                   "Confirm",
                                   MessageBoxButtons.YesNo,
                                   MessageBoxIcon.Question);
e.Cancel = (key == DialogResult.No);
```

These statements display a message box asking the user to confirm whether to quit the application. The message box will contain Yes and No buttons and a question mark icon. When the user clicks either the Yes or No button, the message box will close and the button clicked will be returned as the value of the method (as a *DialogResult*—an enumeration specifying which button was clicked). If the user clicks No, the second line will set the *Cancel* property of the *CancelEventArgs* parameter (*e*) to *true*, preventing the form from closing.

Run the application

1   On the Debug menu, click Start to run the application.

2   Type in a first name and a last name, and then select a tower from the list. Click Add. In the message box that appears displaying the member data you entered, click OK.

Delegates for Windows Forms Events

When you use the Properties window to define an event method (see Chapter 16), Visual Studio .NET generates code that creates a delegate that references the method and subscribes to the event. If you look at the block of code that defines the Clear button in the *InitializeComponent* method, you will see the following statement:

```
//
// clear
//
   ⋮
this.clear.Click += new System.EventHandler(this.clearClicked);
```

The statement creates an *EventHandler* delegate pointing to the *clearClicked* method. It then adds the delegate to the *Click* event for the Clear button. As you create additional event methods, Visual Studio .NET will generate the required delegates and subscribe to the events for you.

3   Click Clear. The form will be reset to its default values.

4   Try to close the form. A dialog box appears asking if you really want to quit. If you click No, the form will continue running. If you click Yes, the form will close.

If you want to continue to the next chapter

■   Keep Visual Studio .NET running and turn to Chapter 19.

If you want to quit Visual Studio .NET for now

■   On the File menu, click Exit. If you see a Save dialog box, click Yes.

Chapter 18 Quick Reference

To	Do this
Create a Windows Forms project	Use the Windows Application template.
Change the properties of a form	Click the form in Design View. In the Properties window, select the property you want to change and enter the new value.
View the code behind a form	On the View menu, click Code.
Add controls to a form	Drag the control from the Toolbox to the form.
Change the properties of a control	While in Design View, click the control. In the Properties window, select the property you want to change and enter the new value.

Dynamically populate a *ComboBox* or a *ListBox*	Use the *Add* method of the Items property. For example:
	
	``
	tower.Items.Add(
	    "Sherston Parva");
	``
	
	You might need to clear the Items property first, depending on whether you want to retain the existing contents of the list. For example:
	
	``
	tower.Items.Clear();
	``

Initialize a *CheckBox* or radio button	Set the *Checked* property to *true* or *false*. For example:
	
	``
	novice.Checked = true;
	``

Handle an event for a control or form	Select the control or form in Design View. In the Properties window, click the Events button. Find the event you want to handle and type the name of an event method. Write the code that handles the event in the event method.

Working with Menus

In this chapter, you will learn how to:

- Create and edit menus for Windows Forms applications.

- Use the *MainMenu* control.

- Respond to menu events for performing processing when a user clicks a menu command.

- Manipulate menus programmatically and create dynamic menus.

- Create context-sensitive pop-up menus.

In Chapter 18, you saw how to create a simple Windows Forms application that used a selection of controls and events. Many professional Microsoft Windows applications also provide menus containing commands and options, giving the user the ability to perform various tasks related to the application. In this chapter, you will learn how to create menus and add them to forms by using the *MainMenu* control. You will see how to respond when the user clicks a command on a menu. You'll learn how to create pop-up menus whose contents vary according to the current context.

Menu Guidelines and Style

If you look at most Windows applications, you'll notice that some items on the menu bar tend to appear repeatedly in the same place, and the contents of these items are often predictable. For example, the File menu is typically the first item on the menu bar, and on this menu, you typically find commands for creating a new document, opening an existing document, saving the document, printing the document, and exiting the application. (The term *document* means the data that the application manipulates.) In Microsoft Excel, it would be a spreadsheet; in the Bell Ringers application that you created in Chapter 18, it could be a new member.

The order in which these commands appear tends to be the same across applications; for example, the Exit command is invariably the last command on the File menu. There might be other application-specific commands on the File menu as well. An application often has an Edit menu containing commands such as Cut, Paste, Clear, and Find. There are usually some further application-specific menus on the menu bar, but again, convention dictates that the final menu is the Help menu, containing access to help and "about" information, which contains copyright and licensing details for the application. Because most menus are predictable, Windows applications are easy to learn and use.

▶ **Tip**   Microsoft publishes a full set of guidelines for user interfaces, including menu design, on the Microsoft Web site at *http://msdn.microsoft.com/ui*.

Adding Menus and Processing Menu Events

Microsoft Visual Studio .NET lets you add menus and menu items to a form in two ways. You can use the Visual Studio .NET integrated development environment (IDE) and the menu editor to create a menu graphically. You can also write code that creates a *MainMenu* object (*MainMenu* is a class defined in the Windows Forms library), and then add *MenuItem* objects to it (*MenuItem* is another class in the Windows Forms library).

Laying out a menu is only half of the story. When a user clicks a command on a menu, the user expects something to happen! You activate the commands by trapping menu events and executing code in much the same way as you do for handling control events.

Creating a Menu

In the following exercise, you will use the graphical approach to create the menus for the Middleshire Bell Ringers Association application. We will cover how to manipulate and create menus programmatically later in this chapter.

Create the File menu

1   Start Visual Studio .NET.

2   Open the BellRingers project, located in the \Microsoft Press\Visual C# Step by Step\Chapter 19\BellRingers folder in your My Documents folder. This is the Middleshire Bell Ringers application. It should be the same as the version that you completed in Chapter 18.

3 Display *MemberForm* in the Design View window. (Click Member-Form.cs in the Solution Explorer, and then click Designer on the View menu). *MemberForm* appears.

4 In the Toolbox, drag a *MainMenu* control onto *MemberForm*.

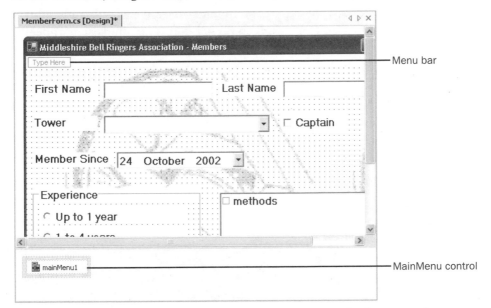

— Menu bar

— MainMenu control

The control, by default called *mainMenu1*, appears at the bottom of the form, and a menu bar containing the caption, Type Here, is added to the form.

5 Click the Type Here caption on the menu bar, type **&File**, and then press Enter. (If the menu bar disappears, click the *mainMenu1* control at the bottom of the form and the menu reappears.) As you type, a second Type Here caption appears to the right of the current item, and a third Type Here caption appears under the File menu item.

▶ **Note** The & character in front of a letter provides fast access to that menu item when the user presses the Alt key and the letter following the & (in this case, Alt+F). This is another common convention. When you click on the menu, the F at the start of File appears with an underscore. Do not use the same access key more than once on any menu because you will confuse the user (and probably the application).

6 Click the Type Here caption that appears under the File menu item, type **&New,** and then press Enter. Another Type Here caption appears under the New menu item.

7   Click the Type Here caption under the New menu item, type **&Open**, and then press Enter.

8   Click the Type Here caption under the Open menu item, type **&Save Member,** and then press Enter.

9   Click the Type Here caption under the Save Member menu item, type a minus sign (-), and then press Enter. The minus sign appears as a menu separator bar used to group related menu items together.

10   Click the Type Here caption under the separator bar, type **&Print**, and then press Enter.

11   Click the Type Here caption under the Print menu item, type a minus sign (-), and then press Enter. Another separator bar appears.

12   Click the Type Here caption under the second separator bar, type **E&xit,** and then press Enter.

Notice that the conventional access key for exit is "x." When you have finished, the menu should look like this:

Setting Menu Item Properties

In the following exercise, the task is to set the properties of the *MainMenu* control and the menu items. You will use the Properties window just as you did when you set the properties for the Windows form and controls.

Set the menu item properties

1   Click the *mainMenu1* control under the form. In the Properties window, change its name to *mainMenu*. (If the Properties window is not displayed, click Properties Window from the View menu.)

2   Right-click the File menu item on the menu bar of *MemberForm*. On the menu that appears, click Edit Names. The menu editor displays the names of the menu items as well as their text.

▶ **Tip** The menu editor also contains other useful commands such as Delete (to delete a menu item), Insert New (to insert a menu item at the current location on the menu), and Insert Separator (to add a separator bar at the current location on the menu). You can right-click any menu item to access these commands.

3 Click the *menuItem1* item on the menu bar, type **fileItem**, and press Enter. Change the names of the remaining menu items using the information in the following table.

Item	New name
[menuItem2]	*newItem*
[menuItem3]	*openItem*
[menuItem4]	*saveItem*
[menuItem6]	*printItem*
[menuItem8]	*exitItem*

4 When you have finished, right-click the *fileItem* menu and uncheck the Edit Names option.

The access keys for menu items (such as Alt+X for the Exit command) is available only when the menu is actually displayed. Commonly accessed menu items should also have shortcut keys that the user can press at any time to invoke the corresponding command. For example, the Save command can usually be executed by pressing Ctrl+S in many Windows applications. You can add a shortcut key to a menu item by using the Properties window.

5 Select the Save Member menu item in the File menu in *MemberForm*, and then click Shortcut in the Properties window. Select the CtrlS option from the drop-down list.

▶ **Note** Although the values for the shortcut keys have names like CtrlS and AltF4, when they are displayed on the menu, they appear like so: Ctrl+S and Alt+F4.

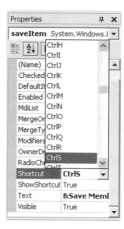

6 There is another property called *ShowShortcut* under the *Shortcut* property. This property determines whether the shortcut key is displayed on the menu when the application runs. Verify that this property is set to *True*.

7 Change the shortcut keys for the other menu items using the values in the following table. Make sure that the *ShowShortcut* property for each menu item remains set to *True*.

Item	Shortcut
newItem	*CtrlN*
openItem	*CtrlO*
printItem	*CtrlP*
exitItem	*AltF4*

Menu items can be enabled and disabled (they are unavailable or their text appears dimmed), depending on the current actions and context. For example, in the Middleshire Bell Ringers Association application, it would not make sense to allow the user to use the Print command if there is no data to print.

8 Click the *printItem* item on the File menu, and then click *Enabled* in the Properties window. Select the *False* option from the drop-down list. You will write some code later to update this property to *True* after data has displayed.

Test the menu

1 On the Debug menu, click Start (or press F5) to compile and run the application.

2 When the form appears, click the File menu. Your new menu appears.

Notice that the Print command is disabled. You can click any of the other commands (although they won't do anything yet).

3 Close the form. You can't use the Exit command on the File menu yet; use the System menu instead.

Other Menu Item Properties

Menu items have a small number of other properties. The following table describes the most common ones. If you want more information about the other properties, consult the online documentation supplied with Visual Studio .NET.

Property	Description
(Name)	This property is the name of the menu item.
Checked	Menu items can act like check boxes and cause a check mark to appear when they are clicked. Setting this property to *True* displays a check mark, and setting it to *False* hides the check mark.
DefaultItem	This property indicates whether the menu item is the default item on the menu. If you set this to *True*, when the user double-clicks the parent menu, the command corresponding to this item is executed. Default menu items appear bold when they are displayed.
Enabled	This property specifies whether the menu item is enabled or disabled. If a menu item is not enabled, it appears dimmed and the user will not be able to select it.
RadioCheck	This property operates in conjunction with the *Checked* property. If *RadioCheck* is *True*, the menu item appears with a "radio dot" rather than a check mark when it is selected.
Shortcut	This property specifies the shortcut key that a user can press to execute the corresponding menu command.
ShowShortcut	If this property is *True*, the shortcut key is displayed on the menu alongside the text of the menu item.

Property	Description
Text	This is the text that is displayed on the menu for the menu item. You can use the & character to specify an access key.
Visible	This property determines whether the item should be displayed on the menu. It is more common to use the *Enabled* property to show that a menu item is present but unavailable.

Menu Events

There are five different events that can occur when a user gains access to a menu item. Some are more useful than others. They are all described in the following table.

Event	Description
Click	This event occurs when the user clicks the menu item.
DrawItem	This event occurs when the item is being repainted. You will not use this event very often.
MeasureItem	This event occurs when the run time is determining the height of the menu item. You probably will not use this event very much.
Popup	This event occurs when the menu is about to be displayed. You can use it to dynamically adjust the properties of the menu item, depending on the current context and circumstances.
Select	This event occurs when the user has selected the menu item (by moving over it using the arrow keys, for example) but has not yet clicked it.

In the following exercise, you will learn more about menu events and how to process them. You will create *Click* events for the New and Exit menu items. When the user clicks the New command on the File menu, you want to remove the contents of *MemberForm* so that the user can start adding information about a new member. You can handle the Open, Save, and Print commands using the Windows common dialogs. These are covered in Chapter 22 and will not be addressed here.

Handle menu item events

1   In the *MemberForm*, click the File menu, and then click New.

2   In the Properties window, click the Events button. Select the *Click* event, type **newClick**, and then press Enter. A new event method is created and the source code displayed in the Code And Text Editor window.

3   In the body of the *newClick* event method, type the following statement:

```
this.Reset();
```

This calls the *Reset* method. If you remember in Chapter 18, the *Reset* method resets the controls on the form to their default values. (If you don't recall the *Reset* method, scroll the Code And Text Editor window to display the method and refresh your memory.)

You now need to enable the Print menu item to allow the user to print the current member's information. You can do this by setting the *Enabled* property of *printItem* to *true*.

4   After the call to the *Reset* method in the *newClick* event method, add the following statement:

```
printItem.Enabled = true;
```

Next, you need to create a *Click* event method for the Exit command. This method should cause the form to quit.

5   Return to the Design View displaying *MemberForm*, and then on the File menu, click Exit.

6   In the Properties window, verify that the events are displayed and select the *Click* event. Type **exitClick**, and press Enter. The *exitClick* event method is created and the source code displayed in the Code And Text Editor window.

7   In the body of the *exitClick* method, type the following statement:

```
this.Close();
```

The *Close* method of a form attempts to close the form. Notice the use of *attempts* in that sentence—a form might intercept the *Closing* event and prevent the form from closing. The Middleshire Bell Ringers Association application traps the *Closing* event and asks the user if he or she wants to quit. If the user says no, the form does not close and the application continues to run.

Test the menu events

1   On the Debug menu, click Start to compile and run the application.

2   Click the File menu. The Print command is disabled.

3   Click New. Click the File menu again. The Print command is now enabled.

4   Click Exit. The form tries to close. You are asked if you are sure you want to close the form. If you click No, the form remains open; if you click Yes, the form closes and the application finishes.

5   Click Yes to close the form.

Forms and Applications

The *Close* method of a form does not necessarily terminate an application. If there are other forms open, the application continues and exits only when the last form is closed.

You can force all the forms to close and the application to finish by using the *Application.Exit* method. This is a bit of a "sledge hammer" because, if any form has a *Closing* event, it is not executed and you run the risk of losing any unsaved data.

Pop-Up Menus

Most modern Windows applications make use of *pop-up* menus that appear when you right-click a form or control. These menus are usually context-sensitive and display commands that are applicable only to the control or form that currently has the focus. They are sometimes referred to as *context* menus.

Creating Pop-Up Menus

In the following exercises, you will create two pop-up menus. The first pop-up menu is attached to the *firstName* and *lastName* text box controls and allows the user to clear the controls. The second pop-up menu is attached to the form and contains commands for saving the currently displayed member's information and for clearing the form. To do this, you make use of an existing menu item as well as create a new one.

Create the *firstName* and *lastName* pop-up menus

1 In the Design View window displaying *MemberForm*, drag a *ContextMenu* control from the Toolbox and drop it on the form. (If the Toolbox isn't visible, click Toolbox from the View menu.) A *Context-Menu* object called *contextMenu1* appears at the bottom of the form.

> ▶ **Tip** You might find it useful to sort the items in the Toolbox by name to
> make them easier to find. To do this, right-click the Windows Forms tab in
> the Toolbox and click Sort Items Alphabetically.

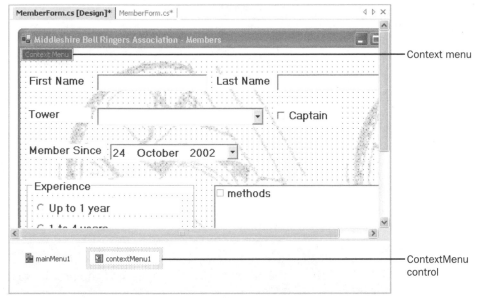

2 Select the *contextMenu1* control, type **textBoxMenu** in the *(Name)* text box in the Properties window, and then press Enter.

When you selected the pop-up menu (now called *textBoxMenu*), you might have noticed that the text "Context Menu" also appeared on the menu bar of *MemberForm*. The menu does not appear there when the form runs; it is just placed there by Visual Studio .NET to allow you to edit it and add menu items.

3 Click the Context Menu title text. The Type Here caption appears under it.

4 Click the Type Here caption, type **Clear Text**, and then press Enter.

5 Click the Clear Text caption, type **textBoxClearItem** in the *(Name)* text box in the Properties window, and then press Enter.

6 Click the *firstName* text box control (next to the First Name label). In the Properties window, change the *ContextMenu* property to *textBoxMenu*. The *ContextMenu* property determines which menu (if any) will be displayed when the user right-clicks the control.

7 Click the *lastName* text box control. In the Properties window, change the *ContextMenu* property to *textBoxMenu*. (Multiple controls are allowed to share the same pop-up menu.)

8 Right-click the *textBoxMenu* control at the bottom of the form, and then click Edit Menu. A menu appears beneath the Context Menu caption.

9 On the menu, click Clear Text.

10 In the Properties window, click the Events button, type **textBoxClearClick** in the *Click* event text box, and then press Enter. A new event method called *textBoxClearClick* is created and displayed in the Code And Text Editor.

11 Add the following statements to the *textBoxClearClick* event method:

```
if (textBoxMenu.SourceControl.Equals(firstName))
{
    firstName.Clear();
}
else
{
    lastName.Clear();
}
```

The *if* statement determines which of the two text boxes currently has the focus. If the *SourceControl* property of the pop-up menu refers to the *firstName* text box, the *firstName.Clear* method empties it. Otherwise, the *lastName.Clear* method is called.

12 On the Debug menu, click Start. The project compiles and runs.

13 When the form appears, type a name into the First Name and Last Name text boxes.

14 Right-click the First Name text box. The pop-up menu appears containing only the Clear Text command.

15 Click the Clear Text command. The First Name text box is cleared.

16 Type a name into the First Name text box, and then move to the Last Name text box. Right-click the Last Name text box to display the pop-up menu. Click the Clear Text command. This time, the Last Name text box is cleared (the first name information should still be there).

17 Right-click anywhere on the form. Because only the First Name and Last Name text boxes have pop-up menus, no pop-up menu appears.

18 Close the form.

To add a bit of variation and to show you how easy it is to create pop-up menus, in the following exercise you will create the *MemberForm* pop-up menu dynamically using code. The best place to put this code is in the constructor of the form.

Create the *MemberForm* context menu

1 Switch to the Code View of *MemberForm*. (On the View menu, click Code.)

2 Locate the constructor for *MemberForm*. This is actually the first method in the class after all the private data members have been defined. It is called *MemberForm*.

A menu contains an array of menu items. In this example, the pop-up menu for the form contains two menu items (Save Member and Clear).

3 In the constructor, after the call to the *Reset* method, add the following statement:

```
MenuItem[] formMenuItemList = new MenuItem[2];
```

This line of code creates an array big enough to hold two menu items.

4 The first item on the menu is a copy of the *saveItem* menu item you created earlier. Add it to the *formMenuItemList* array:

```
formMenuItemList[0] = saveItem.CloneMenu();
```

The *CloneMenu* method creates a copy of the menu item. You do this for two reasons. First, you might want to change the properties of this instance of the item without affecting the main menu of the form. Second, if you don't do this, the Save Member item disappears from the form's main menu. (Try it and you will see!)

5 The second item (Clear) does not yet exist, so you need to create it. However, in Chapter 18, you created a button (also called Clear) that did the same thing. You can take the event method of that button and recycle it for this menu item. Add the following statements:

```
MenuItem clearItem = new MenuItem("&Clear",
    new System.EventHandler(clearClicked));
formMenuItemList[1] = clearItem;
```

The first statement creates a new *MenuItem* called *clearItem*. The constructor specifies the text that appears and a delegate referring to the event method to be called when the *Click* event occurs. The second statement adds *clearItem* to the *formMenuItemList* array.

6 Add the following statement:

```
ContextMenu formMenu = new ContextMenu(formMenuItemList);
```

This creates a new *ContextMenu* containing the Save Member and Clear menu items.

7 Associate the pop-up menu with the form by adding the following statement:

```
this.ContextMenu = formMenu;
```

8 Compile and run the project. Enter some values. If you right-click anywhere on the form (apart from the First Name and Last Name text boxes), the pop-up menu appears. If you click Clear, the form resets back to its default values.

9 Close the form when you have finished.

If you want to continue to the next chapter

■ Keep Visual Studio .NET running and turn to Chapter 20.

If you want to quit Visual Studio .NET for now

■ On the File menu, click Exit. If you see a Save dialog box, click Yes.

Chapter 19 Quick Reference

To	Do this	Button
Create a menu for a form	Add a *MainMenu* control to the form.	MainMenu
Add menu items to a menu	Click the *MainMenu* control at the bottom of the form. Click the Type Here caption on the menu bar of the form and type the name of the menu item. To add additional items, replace the other Type Here captions that appear. You can add an access key to a menu item by prefixing the corresponding letter with a & character.	
Create a separator bar in a menu	Create a menu item by replacing the Type Here caption with a minus sign (-).	

To	Do this	Button
Add a shortcut key to a menu item	Select the menu item, and then set the *Shortcut* property to the required key combination in the Properties window.	
Enable or disable a menu item	At design time, set the *Enabled* property to *True* or *False* in the Properties window. At run time, assign the value *true* or *false* to the *Enabled* property of the menu item. For example: `    printItem.Enabled = true;`	
Perform an action when the user clicks a menu item	Select the menu item. In the Properties window, click Events. In the *Click* event, type the name of an event method. Add your code to the event method.	
Create a pop-up menu	Add a *ContextMenu* control to the form. Add items to the pop-up menu just as you add items to a main menu.	ContextMenu
Associate a pop-up menu with a form or control	Set the *ContextMenu* property of the form or control to refer to the pop-up menu itself.	

Determine the current context when handling an event for a pop-up menu item	Use the *SourceControl* property of the pop-up menu control. For example:
	
	`    if (textBoxMenu.SourceControl.`
	
	`        Equals(firstName))`
	
	`    {`
	
	`        ⋮`
	
	`    }`	

Create a pop-up menu dynamically	Create an array of menu items. Populate the array. Create the pop-up menu by using the array. Set the *ContextMenu* property of the form or control to refer to the pop-up menu.	

Performing Validation

In this chapter, you will learn how to:

■ Examine the information entered by a user to ensure that it does not violate any application or business rules.

■ Use the *CausesValidation* property and the validation events of forms and controls.

■ Perform validation effectively but unobtrusively.

■ Use the *ErrorProvider* control for reporting error messages.

In the previous two chapters, you saw how to create a Windows Forms application that uses a variety of controls for data entry. You created menus to make the application easier to use. You have learned how to trap events raised by menus, forms, and controls so that your application can actually do something besides just look pretty. While careful design of a form and the appropriate use of controls can help to make sure that the information entered by a user makes sense, there are often additional checks that you need to perform. In this chapter, you will learn how to validate the data entered by a user running an application to ensure that it matches any business rules specified by the application's requirements.

Validating Data

The concept of input validation is simple enough, but it is not always easy to implement, especially if validation involves cross-checking data the user has entered into two or more controls. The underlying business rule might be relatively straightforward, but all too often, the validation is performed at an inappropriate time making the form difficult (and often infuriating) to use.

The *CausesValidation* Property

Windows forms and controls have a Boolean property called *CausesValidation* that indicates whether the form or control raises validation events. If the property is set to *true* (which is the default) for a control, when that control receives the focus, the previous control (the one losing the focus) will be validated. If the validation fails, the focus will return to the previous control. It is important to realize that the *CausesValidation* property does not apply to the control itself but instead affects all the other controls on the form. If you are feeling a little confused by this statement, don't panic—you will see an example in a moment.

Validation Events

To validate data in a control, you can use two events: *Validating* and *Validated*. The *Validating* event occurs when focus leaves a control and attempts to switch to a control that has its *CausesValidation* property set to *true*. You can use the *Validating* event to examine the value of the control losing the focus. If you don't like what you see, you can set the *Cancel* property of the *CancelEventArgs* parameter that is passed to prevent the focus from changing. It would probably also help to report the reason why the validation failed.

The *Validated* event occurs after the *Validating* event (as long as it was not canceled) but before the control loses focus. You cannot cancel this event, so it is not as useful as the *Validating* event for checking the user's input.

▶ **Tip**   The *Validating* event fires only if you move to a control that has *CausesValidation* set to *true*. For this reason, it is unusual to have a form where some of the controls have this property set to *false* and others have it set to *true*—validation might occur depending on where the user clicks next. Don't do this unless you have a very good reason because it will confuse the user and could lead to inconsistent data.

An Example—Customer Maintenance

As an example, consider a simple scenario. You have been asked to build a Customer Maintenance application. Part of the application needs to record the essential details of a customer, including title, name, and gender. You decide to create a form like the one shown in the following illustration.

This is an example of a Multiple Document Interface (MDI) application that consists of a frame where other forms can be displayed. Don't worry too much about the details of MDI at the moment because it is covered in more detail later in this chapter.

Performing Validation with a Sledge Hammer

In the following exercises, you will examine the Customer Maintenance application and run it to see how easily you can get validation wrong.

Examine the program

1 Open the CustomerDetails project, located in the \Microsoft Press\Visual C# Step By Step\ Chapter 20\CustomerDetails folder in your My Documents folder.

2 In the Solution Explorer, double-click CustomerForm.cs to display the Customer Details form in Design View.

3 Click the Title list box on the form, and then click the *Items* property in the Properties window. It should appear as (Collection). Click the Ellipses button to display the strings in the collection.

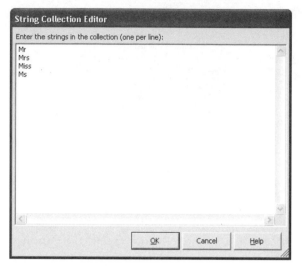

You can see from this collection that the list box contains four titles: Mr, Mrs, Miss, and Ms. Click Cancel to close the String Collection Editor window.

4   Examine the Gender group box and radio buttons. The group box contains two radio buttons called Male and Female.

The application enforces the business rule that the gender and the title must match. If the title is Mr, the gender must be male, and if the title is Mrs, Miss, or Ms, the gender must be female. Switch to the Code And Text Editor window displaying CustomerForm.cs and look at the *titleValidating* and *genderValidating* methods at the end of the file. These are implementations of the *Validating* event handler for the Title list box and the Gender group box. They both call the *checkTitleAndGender* method, and then set the *Cancel* property of the *CancelEventArgs* parameter to *true* if the *checkTitleAndGender* method returns *false*:

```
private void titleValidating(object sender,
    System.ComponentModel.CancelEventArgs e)
{
    if (!checkTitleAndGender())
    {
        e.Cancel = true;
    }
}

private void genderValidating(object sender,
    System.ComponentModel.CancelEventArgs e)
{
    if (!checkTitleAndGender())
```

```
        {
            e.Cancel = true;
        }
    }
```

5 Look at the *checkTitleAndGender* method situated immediately prior to these event methods:

```
// Cross check the gender and the title
// to make sure they correspond
private bool checkTitleAndGender()
{
    if (title.Text == "Mr")
    {
        // Check that gender is Male
        if (!male.Checked)
        {
            MessageBox.Show("If the title is Mr the gender must" +
                " be male", "Error",
                MessageBoxButtons.OK, MessageBoxIcon.Error);
            return false;
        }
    }
    else
    {
        // Check that the gender is Female
        if (!female.Checked)
        {
            MessageBox.Show("If the title is Mrs, Miss, or Ms " +
                "the gender must be female", "Error",
                MessageBoxButtons.OK, MessageBoxIcon.Error);
            return false;
        }
    }

    // Title and gender match
    return true;
}
```

This method performs a simple cross-check between the contents of the Title list box and the radio buttons in the Gender group box. If the title is Mr, the business rule states that the gender must be male, and the method checks to make sure that the Male radio button is selected. If this option is not selected, the method displays an error message and returns *false*. Likewise, if the title is one of the other values (Mrs, Miss, or Ms), the business rule states that the gender must be female, and the method looks at the Female radio button to make sure it is selected. Again, if this is not the case, a different error message is displayed and the method returns *false*. If the title and the gender match, the method returns *true*.

Now you'll run the application and see how it tries to validate the data.

Run the application

1   On the Debug menu, click Start to run the application. An empty Customer Maintenance frame appears.

This frame contains a menu and a toolbar. There are two buttons on the toolbar—the first opens a form for creating a new customer, and the second saves the customer information entered by the user.

2   Click the New Customer button. A form appears in the frame. The form allows you to enter the new customer's details. Notice that the default title is Mr and the default gender is Male.

3   Select Mrs from the Title list box and tab to or click the first Name text box. The *checkTitleAndGender* method generates and displays an error message because the title and the gender don't agree.

The next goal is to change the gender to female.

4   Click OK in the Error dialog box to close it, and then try to click the Female radio button in the group box. You will fail, as the *Causes-Validation* property of the group box makes the *Validating* event run again, causing the error message to be displayed once more.

5   Click OK in the Error dialog box. Set the title to Mr and click the Female radio button.

Remember that the *Validating* event fires just before the focus is passed to the Female radio button. When the *checkTitleAndGender* method is called, the title (Mr) and the gender (male) will agree. You are successfully able to set the gender to female.

6   Now that you have now set the gender to female, try to save the customer's details by clicking the Save Customer button on the toolbar. This action works without error and the text Customer Saved appears in the status bar at the bottom of the Customer Maintenance frame. Confused? Keep going.

7   Correct the (non-reported) error by trying to set the title to Mrs. The *Validating* event (this time for the Gender group box) runs, spots that the gender and title don't match, and then displays an error. You will not be able to escape until you set the Gender to Male again (but then you are back to square one).

8   Exit the application.

▶ **Tip** Use the *Validating* event to validate controls in isolation only; don't use it to check the contents of one control against another.

The validation strategy failed because the *Validating* event fires only when you move to another control on the same form (and not to a control in a toolbar or a menu bar, for example). Developers often put much effort into getting it all to work. The next sections explain how to get it to work by using the tools properly.

Being Unobtrusive

The issue with the Customer Maintenance application is that the validation is performed at the wrong time, is inconsistently applied, and interferes too much. The actual business logic is fine though. We need an alternative approach to handling the validation.

A better solution would be to check the user's input when the user saves the data. This way you can be sure that the user has finished entering all the data and that it is consistent. If there are any problems, an error message will appear and prevent the data from being saved until the data is corrected. In the following exercise, you will change the Customer Maintenance application to postpone validation until the customer information is saved.

Change the point where data is validated

1 Return to the *CustomerForm* Design View window. Select the Title list box.

2 In the Properties window, click the Events button. Scroll down to the *Validating* event, and then delete the *titleValidating* method. This unsubscribes the Title list box from the *Validating* event.

3 On the *CustomerForm*, select the Gender group box.

4 In the Properties window, click the Events button. Find the *Validating* event, and then delete the *genderValidating* method.

▶ **Important** Unsubscribing from an event in this way detaches the event method from the event itself and then deletes the event method. Be careful—if you pick the wrong event, you could lose code that you want. Also note that if you delete an event method in the Code And Text Editor window without unsubscribing from the event, your application will not compile.

You are going to call the *checkTitleAndGender* method from the MDI frame.

5   In the Code And Text Editor, locate the *checkTitleAndGender* method in CustomerForm.cs. Change the accessibility of the *checkTitleAndGender* method from *private* to *public*.

The method definition should look like this:

```
public bool checkTitleAndGender()
```

6   In the Solution Explorer, double-click the Frame.cs file to display the *Frame* form in the Design View window.

This is the MDI frame that runs the Customer Details form and contains the toolbar (and a menu that contains the same options).

7   Click the toolbar in the Frame form. In the Properties window, display the events and select the *ButtonClick* event. This should already be filled in with the event method called *toolButtonClick*.

8   Change to the Code And Text Editor window for the Frame form, and then locate the *toolButtonClick* method towards the bottom of the file.

This event method executes whenever the user clicks any of the buttons on the toolbar. The *ToolBarButtonClickEventArgs* parameter identifies which button the user clicked. You can see that the method fires whether the New Customer button or the Save Customer button has been clicked. If the Save Customer button was clicked, the event method invokes the *saveCustomerForm* method. The *saveCustomerForm* method is also called if the user clicks Save on the menu. The *saveCustomerForm* method is where you should put the validation code:

```
private void toolButtonClick(object sender,
    System.Windows.Forms.ToolBarButtonClickEventArgs e)
{
    if (e.Button.Equals(newButton))
    {
        displayCustomerForm();
    }

    if (e.Button.Equals(saveButton))
    {
        saveCustomerForm();
    }
}
```

9   Scroll up to the *saveCustomerForm* method just above the *toolButtonClick* event method. It currently contains a single line of code that displays Customer Saved in the status bar at the bottom of the frame. Make the following changes to the method:

```
private void saveCustomerForm()
{
    CustomerForm cf = (CustomerForm)ActiveMdiChild;
    if (cf.checkTitleAndGender())
    {
        // Save the current customer's details
        statusBar.Text = "Customer saved";
    }
    else
    {
        statusBar.Text = "Errors occurred - correct and " +
            "save again";
    }
}
```

The first statement gets hold of the Customer Details form currently being displayed in the MDI frame (an MDI frame can display multiple forms at the same time). The second statement calls the *checkTitleAndGender* method on this form. If the method returns *true*, the *saveCustomerForm* method displays Customer Saved in the status bar. The *saveCustomerForm* method displays an error message in the status bar if the *checkTitleAndGender* method returns *false*. The actual error itself is still displayed in a message box in the *checkTitleAndGender* method.

Test the application again

1   Run the application. When the Customer Maintenance frame appears, click the New Customer button to display the Customer Details form. Set the Title list box to Mrs, and then click in the first Name text box. This should work without error because the *Validating* event is no longer trapped by the Title list box.

2   Verify that the Male radio button is selected, and then click the Save Customer button. At this point, the *checkTitleAndGender* method is called and the inconsistency is reported.

3   Click OK and notice the text in the status bar of the frame.

4   Select the Female radio button, and then click the Save Customer button on the toolbar. This time no errors are reported and Customer Saved is displayed on the status bar.

5   Exit the application.

Using an *ErrorProvider* Control

Postponing validation is fine and makes the form less frustrating to use. But what happens if there are several validation errors reported when the data is saved? If you use message boxes to present error information, you might end up displaying several of them in succession—one for each error. Additionally, the user will have to remember each error so that it can be corrected. This can get tedious for a user after more than two or three errors are reported. A much better technique is to use an *ErrorProvider* control as shown by the following exercise.

Add an *ErrorProvider* control

1   Return to *CustomerForm* in the Design View window.

2   From the Toolbox, click the *ErrorProvider* control and drop it anywhere on the form. It appears under the form.

ErrorProvider control

3   Click the *errorProvider1* control, and select the Properties window. Change the *(Name)* property to *errorProvider* and verify that the *BlinkStyle* property is set to *BlinkIfDifferentError*.

When an error is reported by a control, an error icon (which you can select by setting the *Icon* property) appears by the control in error and blinks for a short while and then remains static. You can change the *BlinkRate* property if you want to make it blink faster or slower—the default rate is 250 milliseconds (four times a second). If a subsequent error is reported, the icon blinks only if the error is different from the current one. If you want the icon to blink every time, you can set its *BlinkStyle* to *AlwaysBlink*.

4 On *CustomerForm*, select the Title list box. If you look at the Properties window, you discover a new property called *Error on errorProvider*.

If you type a message here (such as Testing), an error icon appears next to the Title list box. If you hold the mouse pointer over the error icon, a ToolTip appears displaying the error message (for example, Testing).

If you leave this property set as it is, the error icon is always displayed, which is not what you want. The icon should be displayed (with a meaningful error message) only in the event of an error, so delete the text "Testing" from the *Error on errorProvider* property. You will write some code to dynamically use the *errorProvider* control shortly.

5 Switch to the Code And Text Editor window for *CustomerForm*. Locate the *checkTitleAndGender* method and replace the statements that call *MessageBox.Show* with invocations of the *errorProvider.SetError* method, as shown here:

```
// Cross check the gender and the title
// to make sure they correspond
public bool checkTitleAndGender()
{
    if (title.Text == "Mr")
    {
        // Check that gender is Male
        if (!male.Checked)
        {
            errorProvider.SetError(gender, "If the title is Mr " +
                "the gender must be male");
            errorProvider.SetError(title, "If the gender is " +
                "female the title must be Mrs, Miss, or Ms");
```

```
                    return false;
            }
    }
    else
    {
        // Check that the gender is Female
        if (!female.Checked)
        {
            errorProvider.SetError(gender, "If the title is Mrs, " +
                "Miss, or Ms the gender must be female");
            errorProvider.SetError(title, "If the gender is male " +
                "the title must be Mr");
            return false;
        }
    }

    // Title and gender match - clear any errors
    errorProvider.SetError(gender, "");
    errorProvider.SetError(title, "");
    return true;
}
```

The *SetError* method of the *ErrorProvider* control specifies which control to mark with an error icon and the message to be displayed as a ToolTip. If you provide an empty string as the second parameter, as the code does at the end of the method, the error icon is removed.

Test the *ErrorProvider* control

1   Compile and run the application. (A finished version is available in the \Microsoft Press\Visual C# Step By Step\Chapter 20\CustomerDetails Complete folder in your My Documents folder, if you need it.)

2   When the application starts, click the New Customer button on the toolbar to display a Customer Details form.

3   Select Mrs in the Title list box, and then verify that the Male radio button is selected.

4   Click the Save Customer button on the toolbar. A message appears in the status bar indicating that the save failed, and error icons are displayed next to the controls that are in error. If you hover the mouse pointer over each of the error icons, you see the error message.

This is a much less intrusive but more reliable and consistent type of validation than the original application contained.

5 Select the Female gender radio button and click the Save button in the toolbar again. As the data is now consistent, you will see the Customer Saved message in the toolbar and the error icons will disappear.

6 Exit the application.

If you want to continue to the next chapter

■ Keep Microsoft Visual Studio .NET running and turn to Chapter 21.

If you want to quit Visual Studio .NET for now

■ On the File menu, click Exit. If you see a Save dialog box, click Yes.

Chapter 20 Quick Reference

To	Do this	Item
Validate the contents of a single control	Use the *Validating* event method. For example: ```\nprivate void titleValidating(\nobject sender,\nSystem.ComponentModel.CancelEventArgs\ne)\n{\n if (!checkTitleAndGender())\n {\n e.Cancel = true;\n }\n}\n```	
Allow the *Validating* event to be raised	Set the *CausesValidation* property of all controls on the form to *true*.	
Validate the contents of multiple controls or an entire form	Use form-level validation. Create a method that validates all the data on the form. Call it when the user indicates that data input is complete, such as when the user clicks the Save Customer button.	
Indicate which values are in error and display error information in a nonintrusive manner	Use an *ErrorProvider* control. Call the *SetError* method of the *ErrorProvider* control to display an error icon and record an error message that can be displayed as a ToolTip when the user holds the mouse over the error icon.	❸ ErrorProvider

Using Complex Controls

In the previous three chapters, you saw how to use the basic controls for creating a Windows Forms application. You now have a solid knowledge of designing and building graphical user interface (GUI) programs using Microsoft Visual C#. In this chapter, you'll learn how to use the *Splitter* control to resize docked controls and how to create forms containing multiple panels by using the *Panel* control. You will see how to use *TreeView* and *ListView* controls for displaying hierarchical data. You will also learn about the *ImageList* control, which is used as a repository for graphics images used by controls, such as the *TreeView* and the *ListView* controls.

The Explorer Interface

The GUI programs you have written so far (Middleshire Bell Ringers Association and Customer Maintenance) have been designed to perform a very specific function—they are both used to input, display, and edit a single data record at a time (either a member of the Middleshire District Bell Ringers Association or a customer). Users often want to be able to search through data and display more than one record at a time. There can also be relationships, either implicit or explicit, between data items, and it helps users to understand the data better if these relationships are made more obvious. For example, in the Middleshire Bell Ringers Association, there is a whole hierarchy of objects and relationships:

- The Middleshire District contains several bell towers.
- Each bell tower has 0 or more bell ringers who are members of the association.
- Each member can ring 0 or more methods.

One way of displaying hierarchical (sometimes referred to as tree-structured) data is to use a *TreeView* control. This is what Windows Explorer does when displaying disk drive, folder, and file information.

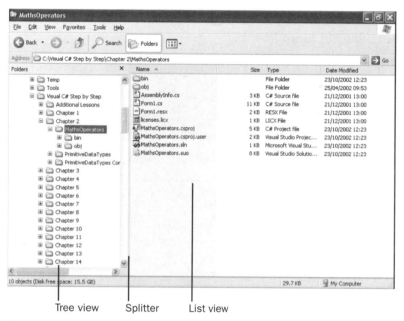

Tree view   Splitter   List view

The Windows Explorer window contains a tree view, a splitter, and a list view, among other controls. The tree view displays the data (in this case, the drives, folders, and files), making the relationships between them clear—you can easily tell which files are in the folders, which folders contain subfolders, and so on. This structure provides a natural way to navigate and search through a large amount of information. Nodes in the tree view can expand or contract as you click the plus sign (+) and the minus sign (–) for each node. The list view displays the contents of the currently selected node, providing more detail if required. The user can right-click the list view, select View from the pop-up menu, and then change how the information in the list view is presented. If the user finds that the tree view provides too much detail, the user can drag the splitter bar that separates the tree view and the list view to the right, making the tree view bigger (and the list view smaller).

This style of interface is very natural, and Microsoft has used it throughout the Microsoft Windows operating system. The Component Services Microsoft Management Console (MMC) also uses this type of interface. Although the MMC is displaying a different type of information than Windows Explorer, the structure of the window includes the tree view, which displays the overall structure; the list view, which presents detailed information; and a splitter bar to use for resizing both views.

Your task for this chapter is to build an application like this for the Middleshire Bell Ringers Association.

Splitter Windows, Docking Controls, and Panels

Before you get too excited, there is a bit of groundwork that you must cover—you need to learn a little bit about the *Splitter* control first. The *Splitter* control allows a user to resize controls on a form (such as the tree view you saw in the Windows Explorer window). A *Splitter* control works with a docked control to resize it. A docked control is a control that is attached (or docked) to one edge of the form that contains it. The *Splitter* control can be used to drag the opposite edge of the control to make the control bigger or smaller. An example will probably help to explain this.

Working with the *Splitter* and Docked Controls

In the following exercise, you will create a test application to show how the *Splitter* control works and to explain more about the *Dock* property of controls.

Create docked controls

1   Using Microsoft Visual Studio .NET, create a new Visual C# project using the Windows Application template. Call it SplitterDemo, and save it in the \Microsoft Press\Visual C# Step By Step\Chapter 21 folder in your My Documents folder.

2   Make sure that Form1 is displayed in the Design View. Using the Toolbox, drag a *CheckedListBox* control to anywhere on the left side of Form1.

3   In the Properties window, select the *Items* property and click the Ellipses button. When the String Collection Editor opens, type some strings of your own (for example, use your name, the name of your pet goldfish, and the names of all the characters in your favorite television program), and then click OK.

4   With the *checkedListBox1* control still selected, locate the *Dock* property in the Properties window. It should currently be set to *None*. Click the drop-down arrow. A diagram appears allowing you to select the edge of the *checkedListBox1* control to which you would like to dock the form.

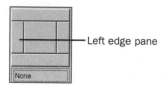
Left edge pane

5   Click the left edge panel in the diagram to indicate that you want to dock the left edge of the *checkedListBox1* control to the form. The *checkedListBox1* control expands to fill the entire left side of the form.

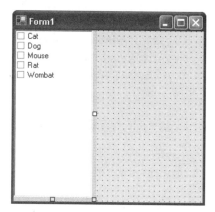

6   In the Toolbox, drag a *TextBox* control to the empty area on the right side of the form. In the Properties window, set the *Multiline* property to *True*.

7   With the *textBox1* control still selected, click the *Lines* property in the Properties window, and then click the Ellipses button. When the Strings Collection Editor opens, type in some more text of your own, and then click OK.

8   In the Properties window, set the *Dock* property for *textBox1* to Fill by clicking in the middle area of the diagram. The text box occupies the right side of the form, filling the area that was left vacant by the *checkedBox1* control.

Add a *Splitter* control

1   In the Toolbox, drag a *Splitter* control and drop it anywhere on the form.

The splitter automatically positions itself between *checkedListBox1* and *textBox1*, appearing as a pair of dotted lines.

2   To make the splitter more visible, set its *BackColor* property to Red.

▶   **Tip**   If you have problems selecting the *Splitter* control on the form, select the control (*splitter1*) from the combo box in the Properties window instead.

3   On the Debug menu, click Start to compile and run the form. When the form runs, position the mouse pointer over the red splitter bar. The cursor changes to the splitter cursor.

4   Drag the splitter cursor to the left and the right. Notice that the selected list box is resized and that the text box adjusts as the selected list box changes size.

5   Close the form and return to Visual Studio .NET.

Splitter Controls and Docking

The position of the *Splitter* control is actually determined by its *Dock* property. By default, the *Dock* property is set to *Left*. This means that it typically attaches its left side to the form. However, if another control (such as *checkedListBox1*) is in the way, the splitter docks to that control instead. At run time, the user dragging the splitter bar causes the resizing of the control that the splitter is docked to. Other controls docked to other edges of the form shrink automatically to make space.

Using a Panel

Using a splitter with a single control is a straightforward exercise, but what happens if the text box in the previous example is replaced with a selection of other controls that do not lend themselves to being resized? This is what we will investigate in the following exercise.

Replace the text box

1   In Visual Studio .NET, delete the *textBox1* control from the form that you created in the previous exercise.

2   In the Toolbox, drag a *Button* control and a *CheckBox* control onto the form, placing them in the empty area on the right side.

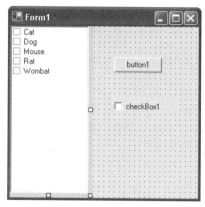

3   Build and run the application. When the form appears, drag the splitter bar to the right. Notice that the button and the check box are unaffected—they do not move (in fact, they get in the way).

4   Close the form and return to Visual Studio .NET.

Docking the Controls

The problem with the button and the check box is that they are not docked. If you looked at the *Dock* property for both controls, you'll see that it is set to None. The *Splitter* control works correctly only with docked controls. It is not convenient in this case to dock the button and the check box. (Try it—the controls will move and get resized.) The solution is to place these controls in a container and dock the container instead. An example of a container is the *Panel* control.

Add a *Panel* control

1   Delete the *button1* and *checkBox1* controls from the form.

2 In the Toolbox, drag a *Panel* control to the empty area on the right of the form.

3 In the Properties window, set the *Dock* property of the *panel1* control to Fill (click the middle region in the diagram). The panel expands to fill the empty space. Set the *BackColor* property of the panel to Yellow so that you can see it.

4 In the Toolbox, drag a *Button* control and a *CheckBox* control to the *panel1* control (which is the yellow area of the form).

5 Build and run the application. Now when you drag the splitter bar, the panel moves, taking the button and check box with it.

6 Close the form.

▶ **Note**   The *Panel* control is used not only for docking. It is useful for grouping related controls together—and in this way is similar to the *GroupBox* control. However, unlike a *GroupBox*, a *Panel* can contain vertical and horizontal scroll bars, making it invaluable for dividing a form into smaller functional areas.

Controls for Navigating Data

Now that we have covered the *Splitter* control in some detail, you can use what you have learned to build the Middleshire Bell Ringers Windows Explorer application in conjunction with some other controls. This section shows you how to build the final Bell Ringers application. You can run the completed version by executing BellRingers.exe, which can be found in the \Microsoft Press\Visual C# Step By Step\Chapter 21\BellRingers Complete\bin\Release folder in your My Documents folder.

The tree view (on the left) allows you to navigate and display the members of the Middleshire Bell Ringers Association, organized by bell tower. The list view (on the right) displays the towers in the Middleshire district. If you expand the Middleshire District node in the tree view (click the plus sign), the tree view expands. If you click one of the towers, Little Mudford for example, the list view changes and displays the members that belong to that tower. If you expand the Little Mudford node in the tree view, you can select any of the members—for example, click Karla Jablonski. The list view changes again to display the methods that Karla can ring. Again if you expand Karla Jablonski, you see these methods in the tree view as well. If you click any of the methods in the tree view, the list view changes again to display only that method. Notice that as you navigate, the list view and the tree view remain synchronized—the list view displays the contents of the selected node in the tree view. The label above the tree view and list view displays the path to the selected node using a \ character as a delimiter between nodes (just like folder names and filenames).

If you select Karla Jablonski in the tree view again and right-click the list view, a pop-up menu appears, allowing you to specify how you want the data in the list view presented. By default, the list view is displayed using large icons. You can switch to small icons (which are more compact), a simple list, or a more detailed view. If there are no additional details available, the list and details views are very similar—the layout is the same but the details view displays a column heading. However, if you select a tower, such as Little Mudford, and display details in the list view, you will see a difference. This time, the list view displays the data for each member of the tower as individual columns.

Working with the *TreeView* Control

In the following exercise, you will start to build the application. Because there is a considerable amount of code involved, some of it has already been written for you—but don't worry; it will all be explained.

Examine the Bell Ringers application

1 In Visual Studio .NET, open the BellRingers project in the \Microsoft Press\Visual C# Step by Step\Chapter 21\BellRingers folder in your My Documents folder. This project contains a form and some pre-written code that you will need to complete this project.

2 In the Solution Explorer, open ExplorerForm.cs in Design View. ExplorerForm.cs currently contains a main menu and a pop-up menu. The main menu appears in the menu bar at the top of the form and only has an Exit command.

3 Switch to the Code And Text Editor window for *ExplorerForm* and scroll to the top of the file. If you look in the *BellRingers* namespace, you see that it contains three types: an enum called *BellRingingInfo*, a struct called *Member*, and the *ExplorerForm* class.

4 Look at the *BellRingingInfo* enumeration. It contains four values. These values correspond roughly to the different node types that are displayed in the tree view—Tower, Member, and Method. There is a fourth value, Empty, that will also be explained shortly.

    ```
    public enum BellRingingInfo {Tower, Member, Method, Empty};
    ```

5 Examine the *Member* structure below the *BellRingingInfo* enumeration. This structure contains fields for the various elements of a member, including an *ArrayList* that holds a list of methods the member can ring. The *ToString* method is provided to allow the structure to be displayed as a string:

```
public struct Member
{
    public string Fname;       // First name
    public string Lname;       // Last name
    public bool Captain;       // Tower captain?
    public int Experience;     // Years of bell ringing experience
    public ArrayList Methods;  // Methods the member can ring

    // The ToString method is used to convert the struct to
    // its string representation
    public override string ToString()
    {
        return Fname + " " + Lname;
    }
}
```

6 Look at the *ExplorerForm* class. This is where you will do most of
your work in the remaining exercises in this chapter. Scroll down to
the *Main* method. There is a set of methods for reading and parsing
an XML file directly below the *Main* method.

▶   **Important**   The name of the XML file is held in the string variable *dataFile-
Path*, created with the other variables at the top of the *ExplorerForm* class. By
default, it is assumed that the file is located in the \Microsoft Press\Visual C#
Step By Step\Chapter 21 folder in your My Documents folder. If you have
installed the application elsewhere, you will need to change this variable; otherwise, the application will not run.

The Middleshire Bell Ringers Association data is held in XML format, and the methods *initializeXmlReader*, *getInfoType*, *getTower-
Name*, *getMemberDetails*, and *getMethodName* are used to read and
extract information from this file. You can ignore how these methods
work for now; you will learn more about how to read and write
XML in Chapter 26.

Following the *getMethodName* method is another batch of methods
that are empty except for comments. These methods are *display-
Towers*, *displayMembers*, *displayMethods*, and *displaySingle-
Method*. These methods are used to display information in the
ListView control.

The *updateListView* method synchronizes the list view with the tree
view as the user navigates.

The remaining methods (which are mainly empty except for some
comments) are used to handle the events raised by the various controls
you will add to the form. You will write the code for these methods.

Lay out the form

1   Return to Design View, displaying *ExplorerForm*. In the Toolbox, click the *Panel* control. Drag it onto the form. Using the Properties window, change its *(Name)* property to panel; set its *Height* property (part of *Size*) to 32; and set its *Dock* property to Top. The panel anchors itself to the top of the form.

2   Set the *BorderStyle* property to FixedSingle. You will use this panel to display a label showing the paths of the nodes in the tree view as the user clicks them.

3   In the Toolbox, drag the *Label* control onto the panel. In the Properties window, change its *(Name)* property to treeLabel; set its *Location* property to 0, 5; set its *Size* property to 680, 23; and set its *Text* property to Path:.

4   In the Toolbox, drag a *TreeView* control onto the form. (Be sure not to place it on the panel.) Change its *(Name)* property to bellRingersTree; set its *Dock* property to Left; and set its *Width* (part of *Size*) to 232. The tree view expands to occupy part of the left side of the form.

TreeView controls can display icons in addition to text in each node. You store icons in an *ImageList* control and then associate the *ImageList* with the *TreeView*.

5   In the Toolbox, drag an *ImageList* control onto the form.

6   The *ImageList* control appears at the bottom of the form. Change its *(Name)* property to treeViewImageList, and then select the *Images* property. Click the Ellipses button. The Image Collection Editor dialog box appears.

7   Click Add to add an image to collection. When the Open File dialog box opens, navigate to the \Microsoft Press\Visual C# Step by Step\Chapter 21 folder in your My Documents folder and double-click the Note.bmp file (this is a bitmap containing an image of a musical note). In the Image Collection Editor dialog box, click Add again and double-click the Bell.bmp file. Repeat this process, adding the Face.bmp and Ring.bmp files, in that order. When you have finished, the image collection should contain four items numbered from zero to three. Click OK to close the Image Collection Editor dialog box.

8   Return to the *bellRingersTree TreeView* control and set its *ImageList* property to treeViewImageList.

9   In the Toolbox, drag a *Splitter* control onto the form. By default, it anchors itself to the right edge of the *bellRingersTree* control. If it doesn't, in the Properties window, set its *Dock* property to Left.

Change its name to *splitter*. The finished form should look something like the following illustration (the illustration shows the form running after you've completed the next exercise that adds code to display the bell images):

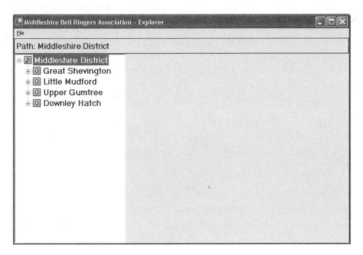

The next stage is to write some code to populate the tree view with data. A file containing the Middleshire Bell Ringers Association members' details already exists. All you need to do is read this file; parse each piece of data; work out whether it is a tower, member, or method; and create nodes and add them to the tree view. Fortunately, as you have already seen, we have supplied you with the code to read and parse the file so that you can concentrate on managing the tree view in this exercise. You will populate the tree view when the form opens.

Handle *TreeView* events

1 In Design View, select the form. In the Properties window, click the Events button. The *Load* event for the form fires when the form first opens, and an event method called *explorerFormLoad* has already been created. Look at the *Load* event—it should be filled in.

2 Change to the Code And Text Editor window, and then locate the *explorerFormLoad* method. The first step is to create the root node for the tree. At the point marked <INSERT 1ST BLOCK OF CODE HERE>, type the following statements:

```
TreeNode rootNode = new TreeNode("Middleshire District",
    DISTRICTIMAGE, DISTRICTIMAGE);
rootNode.Tag = "District";
bellRingersTree.Nodes.Add(rootNode);
```

A tree view contains a hierarchy of *TreeNode* objects—a *TreeNode* contains some data and optionally a collection of child nodes. The first statement creates a *TreeNode* and fills it with the text to be displayed (Middleshire District) and an image to display. The image is actually specified as a number indicating which image from the associated *ImageList* control to use. If you return to the top of the *ExplorerForm* class, you see that *DISTRICTIMAGE* is a constant *int* with the value of 0:

```
private const int DISTRICTIMAGE = 0;
```

This node therefore displays the first image from the *ImageList* control (Note.bmp). When you create a node, you actually have to specify two images because a *TreeNode* can display different icons when it is selected and not selected. In this example, we use the same image for both states.

TreeNode objects (and most controls) have a *Tag* property that you can use to hold any miscellaneous data you want to associate with the control. For reasons that will become clear later, the second statement stores the string "District" in the *Tag* property. The final statement adds the root node to the list of nodes in the *bellRingersTree* control.

3   Compile and run the program. When the form appears, the *TreeView* control contains a single node with the text Middleshire District and a Note icon. Also notice that you can drag the right edge of the tree view to make it bigger or smaller—this is due to the *Splitter* control.

4   Close the form and return to Visual Studio .NET.

5   In Code View, you now need to populate the rest of the tree view. At the point marked <INSERT 2ND BLOCK OF CODE HERE>, add the following variable declarations:

```
TreeNode towerNode = null, memberNode = null, methodNode = null;
```

This code creates three variables that you use for adding the different types of node that will appear in the tree view.

The code immediately following this statement has already been written:

```
Member member = new Member();
member.Methods = new ArrayList();
```

It creates a variable using the *Member* structure you saw previously. As the data file is read, if a member is found, its details are held in this structure and you then add it to the tree view. The member is the only object you need to handle this way because it is the only one that contains additional data—towers and methods are recorded as simple strings.

The event method then calls the *initializeXmlReader* method to open the data file and starts a loop that iterates through the file, parsing it and extracting the next item. The loop finishes when there is no more data (the parser returns the value *BellRingingInfo.Empty*):

```
XmlTextReader reader = initializeXmlReader();
BellRingingInfo infoType;
while ((infoType = getInfoType(reader)) != BellRingingInfo.Empty)
{
    ⋮
}
```

As each item is retrieved, it is examined to see whether it refers to a tower, a member, or a method. The first check looks for a bell tower:

```
if (infoType == BellRingingInfo.Tower)
{
    ⋮
    continue;
}
```

6   In the body of the *if* statement, insert the following statements where indicated (after the comment <INSERT 3RD BLOCK OF CODE HERE>, and before the *continue* statement):

```
string towerName = getTowerName(reader);
towerNode = new TreeNode(towerName, TOWERIMAGE, TOWERIMAGE);
towerNode.Tag = "Tower";
rootNode.Nodes.Add(towerNode);
```

The first statement retrieves the name of the tower from the input stream. The second statement creates a new *TreeNode* using this name and the second image from the *ImageList* control (*TOWER-IMAGE* is a constant with the value of 1). The third statement sets the *Tag* property as Tower, and the final statement adds this new *TreeNode* to the list of nodes directly under the root.

7   Build and run the application again. This time you are able to expand the root node to display a list of bell towers.

8   Close the form and return to Visual Studio .NET.

9   The next block of code in the *explorerFormLoad* method checks for a member rather than a tower:

```
if (infoType == BellRingingInfo.Member)
{
    ⋮
    continue;
}
```

At the point marked <INSERT 4TH BLOCK OF CODE HERE>, add the following code:

```
member = getMemberDetails(reader);
memberNode = new TreeNode(member.ToString(),
    MEMBERIMAGE, MEMBERIMAGE);
towerNode.Nodes.Add(memberNode);
```

These statements are very similar to those you added to create a tower node. They obtain the details of the member from the input stream and create a new *TreeNode*, which contains a string representation of the member (remember that the *ToString* method of the Member structure returns a string containing the member's name) and the third icon from the *ImageList* control (*MEMBERIMAGE* has the value of 2). This node is not added to the root; it is added to the Nodes collection of the current tower.

It is important to realize that the *TreeNode* holds only a string representation of the data. Later, when you add the *ListView* control, you will need to display the other details of each member. These details must therefore be stored somewhere.

10 Add the following statements at the position labeled <INSERT 5TH BLOCK OF CODE HERE>:

```
member.Methods = new ArrayList();
memberNode.Tag = member;
```

This code initializes the list of methods known by the member (they will be discovered in the next block of code), and then stores the member details in the *Tag* property of the *TreeNode*.

11 The final type of *TreeNode* contains bell-ringing methods.

```
if (infoType == BellRingingInfo.Method)
{
    ⋮
}
```

At the point marked <INSERT 6TH BLOCK OF CODE HERE>, type the following statements:

```
string methodName = getMethodName(reader);
methodNode = new TreeNode(methodName, METHODIMAGE, METHODIMAGE);
methodNode.Tag = "Method";
memberNode.Nodes.Add(methodNode);
```

You should be familiar with this idiom by now. The only extra detail worth noting is that the new node is added to the collection held in the current *memberNode*.

12 You must also record the method in the Member structure for the current member. At the point marked <INSERT 7TH BLOCK OF CODE HERE>, type the following statement:

```
member.Methods.Add(methodName);
```

This statement adds the method name to the *Methods ArrayList*.

13 Compile and run the form again. The tree view is now fully populated with tower, member, and method data.

14 Close the form and return to Visual Studio .NET.

The final part of this exercise is to display the paths to the nodes in the *treeLabel* control (which is in the panel at the top of the form) as the user selects them.

15 Switch to Design View, and then click the *bellRingersTree* control. In the Properties window, click the Events button, and then click the *AfterSelect* event. This event occurs immediately after the user has clicked on a node. From the drop-down list, select the *bellRingers-TreeSelect* method. The outline of this method has already been written—you must fill in the blanks.

16 Go back to Code View and find the *bellRingersTreeSelect* event method. It is directly under the *explorerFormLoad* event method that you have just been working on.

The first task is to ascertain exactly which node in the tree the user selected. You are given this vital piece of information in the *Node* property of the *TreeViewEventArgs* parameter (called *e*) passed into this method.

17 Replace the comment <INSERT 8TH BLOCK OF CODE HERE> with the following statement:

```
TreeNode selectedNode = e.Node;
```

TreeNode controls have a property called *FullPath* that returns a string containing the path to the node from the root of the tree view. If you have a *TreeNode*, you can find out where it is in the tree view by querying its *FullPath* property. Use this to fill in the *Text* property of the *TreeLabel* control.

18 Replace the comment <INSERT 9TH BLOCK OF CODE HERE> with the following statement:

```
treeLabel.Text = "Path: " + selectedNode.FullPath;
```

Notice also a thirteenth block of code in this method. Ignore it for now; you will use it in the next exercise.

19 Build and execute the application. This time, when you click the nodes in the tree view, the label at the top of the form tells you where you are. Close the form when you have finished.

Using a *ListView* Control

In the following exercise, you will add the *ListView* control to the form. You will then create the methods needed to display information in this control and keep the information synchronized with the *TreeView* control.

Add a *ListView* control

1 Return to Visual Studio .NET and display *ExplorerForm* in the Design View. In the Toolbox, click the *ListView* control, and then drag it into the empty space on the right side of the form.

2 Change the name of the *ListView* control to *bellRingersList* and change its *Dock* property to Fill. The control will expand to occupy the rest of the form.

Like a tree view, a list view control can also display icons along with text. However, if you examine the properties for the *bellRingersList* control, you see that it contains two image-related properties called *LargeImageList* and *SmallImageList*.

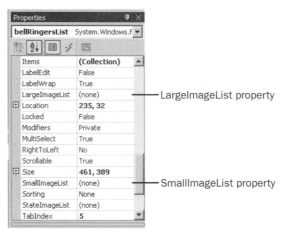

LargeImageList property

SmallImageList property

You might recall that a *ListView* control can present information using several different views—large icons, small icons, list, and details. Icons from the *SmallImageList* are used in the small icons, list, and details views. The *LargeImageList* is used by the large icons view. Use the same icons as the tree view because it confuses the user if they are different.

3   Set the *SmallImageList* property of *bellRingersTree* to *treeViewImage-List*. Another set of images has already been created that you can use for the *LargeImageList* property, but to handle them, you must create another *ImageList* control.

4   In the Toolbox, drag an *ImageList* control onto the form. It appears below the form along with the *treeViewImageList* and the menus. Change its *(Name)* property to largeImageList. Select the *Images* property and click the Ellipses button. When the Image Collection Editor opens, add the following bitmaps from the \Microsoft Press\Visual C# Step by Step\Chapter 21 folder in your My Documents folder, in this order: Large Note.bmp, Large Bell.bmp, Large Face.bmp, Large Ring.bmp. Click OK when you have added them all.

5   Change the *ImageSize* property of the *largeImageList* control to 48, 48. If you leave it at its default setting (16, 16), the icons still appear small.

6   Select the *bellRingersList* control again and set its *LargeImageList* property to largeImageList.

A context (or pop-up) menu, called *listContextMenu*, which you will attach to the *bellRingersList* control, has also been provided for you. If you click the *listContextMenu* control below the form, the caption Context Menu appears on the menu bar of the form, and you are able to display and edit it.

7   Click the Context Menu caption to see the items on *listContext-Menu*. It contains commands allowing the user to change the view presented in the *bellRingersList* control.

8   On the pop-up menu, click Large Icons, and then in the Properties window, click the Events button.

The *Click* event method for the command has already been created and is called *largeIconsClick*—the method is not complete, however, and you will have to write some code to actually change the view shown in the list box. The same is true for the other commands on the pop-up menu.

9   Click the *bellRingersList* control again. Set its *ContextMenu* property to listContextMenu. (You will need to click the Properties button in the Properties window to see the properties.)

10   Build and run the application. The tree view still works as before but you should now see an empty list view as well. It is empty because you haven't yet written any code to fill it in. Still, if you right-click the list view, the pop-up menu appears, although *almost nothing* happens when you click any of the commands. The menu itself changes—a radio button appears next to the selected command the next time the menu is displayed, indicating which view is currently being displayed. The splitter bar still works if you drag the border separating the tree view and the list view.

11 Close the form and return to Visual Studio .NET.

Next you will write the code to synchronize the *bellRingersList* list view with the *bellRingersTree* tree view.

Synchronize the *ListView* and *TreeView* controls

1 In the Code And Text Editor window, locate the *updateListView* method:

```
private void updateListView(TreeNode node)
{
    ⋮
}
```

This method has already been completed but it needs to be explained. Your program should call this method every time the user selects a node in the tree view. The method takes the node that the user has selected as its parameter (node) and then uses it to update the list view.

Remember that there are four different types of nodes that are displayed in the tree view: the *District* (which is the root node at the top of the tree), the *Tower*, the *Members*, and the *Method*. If the user selects the District node in the tree view, the list view must display the towers in the district. If the user selects a Tower, the list view must display the members that ring at that tower. If the user selects a Member, the list view must display all the methods that the member can ring. Finally, if the user selects a method, the list view should just display that single method (there are no further nodes under a method).

How do you know from the node what type of node it is? The answer lies in the *Tag* property. When you created the nodes in the tree view, you set the *Tag* property to indicate the type of each node. The District node, Tower nodes, and Method nodes have a string tag containing the value District, Tower, or Method respectively. Member nodes are a little different. Their tags contain a *Member* struct holding the details of the member. The *if* statement in *updateListView* examines the *Tag* to determine its type:

```
if (node.Tag.GetType().Equals(typeof(System.String)))
{
    // Must be the District, Tower, or Method
    ⋮
}
else
{
    // Must be a Member
    ⋮
}
```

If the *Tag* is a string, a switch statement examines its value and calls the *displayTowers*, *displayMembers*, or *displaySingleMethod* methods as appropriate:

```
switch((string)node.Tag)
{
    case "District":  // Display the Towers in the List View
        displayTowers(node);
        break;

    case "Tower":     // Display the Members in the List View
        displayMembers(node);
        break;

    case "Method":    // Display the current Method in the List
                      // View
        displaySingleMethod(node);
        break;

    default:          // Should never happen!
        break;
}
```

If the *Tag* is not a string, it must be a *Member* struct, and the *display-Methods* method is executed:

```
displayMethods(node);
```

2 Scroll up and locate the *displayTowers* method. There are three pieces of code for you to write here. The first task is to clear the list view—if you don't, anything you display in this method is added to whatever is already there. At the point marked <INSERT 10TH BLOCK OF CODE HERE>, type the following statement:

```
bellRingersList.Clear();
```

Clear is a defined method of the *ListView* class—you do not have to write it.

If the list view is displaying details, data is presented in columns. It is conventional to display a header for each column. In this case, there is only one column.

3   Type the following statement in place of the <INSERT 11TH BLOCK OF CODE HERE> comment:

```
bellRingersList.Columns.Add("Tower", bellRingersList.Width - 4,
    HorizontalAlignment.Left);
```

This line of code adds a column to the list view with the text "Tower" in the column header. The width of the column is set to the same as the width of the list view minus four pixels to allow for the border, and the text in the column is left-justified.

The final step in this method is to actually display the names of all the bell towers. The parameter passed is the District node (which is at the root of the tree view), so all the Tower nodes are directly under it and accessible using its *Nodes* collection.

4   At the point labeled <INSERT 12TH BLOCK OF CODE HERE>, add the following statements:

```
foreach (TreeNode child in node.Nodes)
{
    ListViewItem item = new ListViewItem(child.Text, TOWERIMAGE);
    bellRingersList.Items.Add(item);
}
```

This *foreach* loop iterates through the *Nodes* collection of the District node and creates a new *ListViewItem* object for each node found. In the same way that a *TreeView* control contains a collection of *TreeNode* controls in its *Nodes* property, a *ListView* control contains a collection of *ListViewItems* in its *Items* property. As each *ListViewItem* object is created, it is added to the *Items* collection. The *Text* property of each *ListViewItem* is displayed in the list view along with any icon specified.

You have now written code to update the list view with a list of towers if the user selects the District node at the root of the tree view. You just need to make sure that the *updateListView* method is called.

5   Scroll down to the *bellRingersTreeSelect* event method (you used it in a previous exercise). At the end, you see the comment <INSERT 13TH BLOCK OF CODE HERE>. Replace this comment with a call to *updateListView*, passing in *selectedNode* as the parameter:

```
updateListView(selectedNode);
```

6   Build and execute the application. When the form loads, the root node in the tree view is selected automatically and the list view displays the bell towers using large icons.

If you move around the tree view, the list view does not change, because you have not yet written the code to handle the other types of node (Tower, Member, and Method).

7 Close the form and return to Visual Studio .NET.

Before addressing the remaining items in the list view, it would be nice to get the pop-up menu working so that you can see the different views. Currently you can see only the large icons view.

8 In the Code And Text Editor window, locate the *largeIconsClick* event method under the *bellRingersTreeSelect* method you have just been working on. The statements in this method currently set the *Checked* property of the items in the pop-up menu but little else. At the end of the method, add the following code where indicated (the 14th comment):

```
bellRingersList.View = View.LargeIcon;
TreeNode node = bellRingersTree.SelectedNode;
updateListView(node);
```

The first statement changes the *View* property of the list view—you can probably guess what the value *View.LargeIcon* indicates. The second statement works out which node in the tree view currently has the focus, and the third statement calls the *updateListView* method with this node. As a result, the list view displays the data using large icons (from the *ImageList* control specified by the *Large-ImageList* property).

The other event methods used by the pop-up menu are below the *largeIconsClick* method. They are called *smallIconsClick*, *listClick*, and *detailsClick*.

9 In the *smallIconsClick* method, replace the fifteenth comment with the following statements:

```
bellRingersList.View = View.SmallIcon;
TreeNode node = bellRingersTree.SelectedNode;
updateListView(node);
```

This is the same code as before except that the *View* property of *bell-RingersList* is set to *View.SmallIcon*. Repeat this code for the *list-Click* and *detailsClick* methods (the sixteenth and seventeenth comments) using the values *View.List* and *View.Details*.

10 Compile and execute the application. Right-click the pop-up menu in the list view. You should now be able to change the view and display bell towers using large icons, using small icons, as a list, or with details (the same as list view but with a column header).

11 Close the form and return to Visual Studio .NET.

All that is left to do is write the following methods: *displayMembers* to display members of a tower in the list view; *displayMethods* to display the methods that a member can ring; and *displaySingle-Method* to display the details of a single method.

12 Scroll up through the Code And Text Editor window and locate the *displayMembers* method. If you recall, this method is invoked when the user selects a bell tower in the tree view. The purpose of this method is to display the members that belong to the bell tower. This method is similar to the *displayTowers* method you wrote previously, except that members have more details—first name, last name, captain indicator, and years of experience—requiring four columns. First, though, you must clear the list.

13 At the point marked <INSERT 18TH BLOCK OF CODE HERE>, type the following statement:

```
bellRingersList.Clear();
```

14 Next, add the following statements that add four columns after the 19th comment:

```
bellRingersList.Columns.Add("First Name",
    (bellRingersList.Width - 4)/3, HorizontalAlignment.Left);
bellRingersList.Columns.Add("Last Name",
    (bellRingersList.Width - 4)/3, HorizontalAlignment.Left);
bellRingersList.Columns.Add("Captain",
    (bellRingersList.Width - 4)/6, HorizontalAlignment.Left);
bellRingersList.Columns.Add("Years",
    (bellRingersList.Width - 4)/6, HorizontalAlignment.Right);
```

The Years column is right-justified as is conventional for numeric data. The column widths are calculated to enable them all to fit in the list view without truncating the data (the user can resize the columns at run time if they are too narrow).

15 At the point marked <INSERT 20TH BLOCK OF CODE HERE>, type the following statements:

```
foreach (TreeNode child in node.Nodes)
{
    ListViewItem item;

    if (bellRingersList.View == View.Details)
    {
        // If the List View is showing details then
        // extract full member infomration from
        // the Tag in the child node
        Member member = (Member)child.Tag;
        item = new ListViewItem(member.Fname, MEMBERIMAGE);
        item.SubItems.Add(member.Lname);
        item.SubItems.Add(member.Captain.ToString());
        item.SubItems.Add(member.Experience.ToString());
    }
```

```
else
{
    // Otherwise display the abbreviated member
    // information (name only)
    item = new ListViewItem(child.Text, MEMBERIMAGE);
}
bellRingersList.Items.Add(item);
}
```

As it did for the bell towers list, the code iterates through the list of members contained in the *Nodes* collection of the bell tower node passed in. The complication in this case is that member information is formatted differently depending on the type of view—the details view should display four columns whereas the other views should simply display the member's name.

The *if* statement determines whether the list view is in "details mode." If it is, a *ListViewItem* containing an icon and the member's first name is created. *SubItems* containing the last name, captain indicator, and experience are also created and added to the *ListViewItem*. When the item is displayed, the item itself (the member's first name) appears in the first column. The *SubItems* appear as other columns.

If the list view is not displaying details, the *else* branch of the *if* statement creates a simple *ListViewItem* comprised of the data from the tree view and an icon.

The *ListViewItem* is then added to the *ListView* control and displayed.

16 Build and run the application. Expand the Middleshire District node in the tree view and select the Upper Gumtree tower. The list view displays the members of this tower as large icons. Right-click in the list view and select the Details command in the pop-up menu. The list view shows the details in four columns.

17 Close the form and return to Visual Studio .NET.

18 The *displayMethods* method is almost identical to the *displayTowers* method. The *node* parameter passed in contains a member, and the *Nodes* collection of this parameter contains a list of method names.

Add the following statement to clear the list after the twenty-first comment:

```
bellRingersList.Clear();
```

Create a column for the method names after the twenty-second comment:

```
bellRingersList.Columns.Add("Method",
    bellRingersList.Width - 4, HorizontalAlignment.Left);
```

Loop through the *Nodes* collection of the *node* parameter, create a *ListViewItem* for each method found, and add the following code to the *Items* collection of *bellRingersList* after the twenty-third comment:

```
foreach (string methodName in ((Member)node.Tag).Methods)
{
    ListViewItem item = new ListViewItem(methodName, METHODIMAGE);
    bellRingersList.Items.Add(item);
}
```

19 The *displaySingleMethod* method is the simplest of this set. The node passed in as a parameter contains a method, and all this method does is create a single *ListViewItem* containing this method. The twenty-fourth block of code should clear the list view:

```
bellRingersList.Clear();
```

The twenty-fifth block of code should create a column for displaying the method:

```
bellRingersList.Columns.Add("Method",
    bellRingersList.Width - 4, HorizontalAlignment.Left);
```

The twenty-sixth block of code should create a *ListViewItem* for this method and add it to the list view:

```
ListViewItem item = new ListViewItem(node.Text, METHODIMAGE);
bellRingersList.Items.Add(item);
```

20 Compile and run the application for a final time. As you navigate around the tree view, the list view displays the contents of each node.

21 Close the form when you have finished.

ListView and *TreeView* Synchronization

The completed version of *ExplorerForm* also allows you to navigate using the *ListView* control. If you double-click one of the icons displayed in the list view, the corresponding node in the tree view expands and the list view is updated to display the contents of that node. (This is like clicking a folder in Windows Explorer—the folder expands to show you the files in that folder.) This magic is achieved using the *Activate* event and the *bellRingersListActivate* event method. If you want to know more, look at the code; it is fully commented. There is also a little conundrum for you to puzzle over regarding what happens when the user double-clicks a member in the list view when it is displaying member details rather than icons or a list.

If you want to continue to the next chapter

■   Keep Visual Studio .NET running and turn to Chapter 22.

If you want to quit Visual Studio .NET for now

■   On the File menu, click Exit. If you see a Save dialog box, click Yes.

Chapter 21 Quick Reference

To	Do this	Button
Anchor a control to one edge of its container	Set the *Dock* property for the control to Left, Right, Top, or Bottom.	Left edge pane None
Make a control fill the available space in its container	Set the *Dock* property to Fill.	
Allow docked controls to be resized at run time by the user	Use a *Splitter* control. Set its *Dock* property to attach to the undocked edge of the control that you want to allow the user to resize.	Splitter
Group controls together or subdivide a form into functional areas	Use a *Panel* control. Place the controls to be grouped together on the panel. If the panel moves or is resized, so are all the controls it contains.	Panel
Display hierarchical data	Use a *TreeView* control. Populate the root node of the *TreeView* and add *TreeNode* controls to its *Nodes* collection containing child nodes. Child nodes can contain grandchildren and so on.	TreeView

To	Do this	Button
Determine which node the user has clicked in a *TreeView* control	Use the *AfterSelect* event. The *TreeView-EventArgs* parameter passed into the method contains a reference to the selected node.	
Display a list of complex objects	Use a *ListView* control. Populate the *Items* property with a collection of *ListViewItems* containing the data to be displayed. The *List-View* control supports different presentation styles: large icons, small icons, list, and details.	ListView

Chapter

22

Using the MDI, Windows, and Dialog Boxes

In this chapter, you will learn how to:

- Create multiple document interface (MDI) parent and child forms.

- Dynamically display and hide forms.

- Merge menus on parent and child forms.

- Arrange child forms on a parent form.

- Create modal and modeless dialog boxes and forms.

- Add common dialog boxes to your own applications by using the common dialog controls.

In the previous chapters, you learned how to create Windows Forms applications that comprise a single form or window. You saw how to use the static *Show* method of the *MessageBox* class to open a message or display a warning to a user. Chapter 20 also made use of an MDI form. The example application you worked on in that chapter allowed the user to display a form dynamically. In this chapter, you will learn more about MDI frames and child forms and how to create them. You'll also learn more about dialog boxes, including how to craft your own dialog boxes and display them. Finally, you'll find out about the common dialog controls supplied as part of the Windows Forms library that remove the need for you to create dialog boxes for handling common tasks.

What Is the Multiple Document Interface?

As its name suggests, an application that uses an MDI allows you to display multiple documents at the same time. Each document is displayed in its own window, which is referred to as a *child window*. Child windows are displayed within the bounds of a parent MDI window, in the part of the window called the *MDI client area*. The MDI frame contains the menu bar, status bar, and toolbars for the application—any menus that belong to the child form are displayed in the MDI frame. If the user switches between child windows, the menu changes to the menu used by the child window. The following illustration shows an MDI application and its main features.

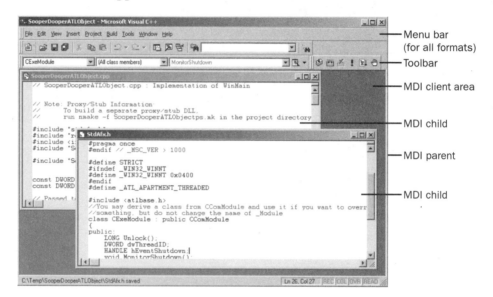

Building an MDI Application

To help you understand a little more about MDI, you are going to build an MDI application. The application is a simple text editor, allowing the user to display multiple text windows at the same time and edit the text.

Create an MDI parent form

1   In Microsoft Visual Studio .NET, create a new project called MDI-Demo in the \Microsoft Press\Visual C# Step By Step\Chapter 22 folder in your My Documents folder. Use the Windows Application template.

2   In the Solution Explorer, change the name of the Form1.cs file to MDIParent.cs. (Right-click Form1.cs in the Solution Explorer and click Rename on the pop-up menu.)

3 Display MDIParent.cs in Design View if it is not already displayed, select it, and then set its properties by using the values in the following table.

Property	Value	Explanation
(Name)	MDIParent	This is the MDI parent form.
IsMDIContainer	True	This property determines that the form is an MDI parent form. The color of the form changes to indicate that it is an MDI parent.
Size	500, 450	Make sure the MDI form is big enough to display the child forms. You could also set the *WindowState* property to *Maximized* if you want to make the MDI form fill the entire desktop when it starts.
Text	MDI Parent Form	This name is more meaningful than *Form1*.

4 In Code View, scroll down to the *Main* method and change the *Application.Run* statement by adding the following code (remember that if you change the name of the main form in an application, you must edit *Main* to use the new name):

```
Application.Run(new MDIParent());
```

5 Return to Design View. In the Toolbox, drag a *MainMenu* control onto the form. Change its name to *mdiMenu*.

6 Click the *MDIParent* form, and then in the Properties window, verify that its *Menu* property is set to *mdiMenu*.

7 Using the menu editor (select the *mdiMenu* control, then click the Type Here caption on the form's menu bar), create a top-level menu containing items labeled &File and &Window. Set their names to *fileItem* and *windowItem*. Add submenu items labeled &New, &Close, and E&xit to the File menu. Name them *newItem*, *closeItem*, and *exitItem*. Insert a separator bar between the Close and Exit items.

The Window menu should not contain any sub-items yet.

8 Create an event handler for the *Click* event of the *exitItem* menu item called *exitItemClick*. (Select the *Exit* item in the menu editor; in the Properties window, click the Events button; select the *Click* event; type **exitItemClick**; and then press Enter. The *exitItemClick* method appears in the Code And Text Editor window.) In the *exitItemClick* method, type the following statement:

```
this.Close();
```

This line of code closes the MDI parent form and the application.

9   Build and run the application just to test it so far. It won't do much yet, but at least you can correct any errors you might have made.

Create an MDI child form

1   Add a child form to the application by clicking Add New Item on the Project menu. When the Add New Item dialog box opens, click the Windows Form template and type **MDIChild.cs** in the Name text box. Click Open to create the form and add it to the project.

2   Display MDIChild.cs in Design View. In the Toolbox, drag a *Text-Box* control onto the form. Change the name of the *textBox1* control to *editData*, set its *Dock* property to Fill (by clicking the middle area of the Dock diagram), set its *Multiline* property to True, and clear the *Text* property.

    The text box fills the entire form. This form acts as the text editor.

3   In the Toolbox, select the *MainMenu* control and drag it onto the *MDIChild* form. Change the name of the menu to *childMenu*. Using the menu editor, add a &File item to the menu called *fileItem*, and add a &Save menu sub-item called *saveItem*. Add a separator after the Save item.

    Set the *MergeType* property of the *fileItem* menu item on the *child-Menu* menu to MergeItems. At run time, the *MainMenu* control of the MDI child form is added to the menu bar of the MDI parent. Rather than having duplicate File menu items, it is better to allow the child form's File menu to be merged with that of the parent form. Setting this property makes the merge process happen automatically.

4   Click the *saveItem* menu item and set its *MergeOrder* property to 1. When menus are merged, the *MergeOrder* property determines the order in which menu items appear. It is possible for several menu items to have the same value for the *MergeOrder* property. When this happens, the order of the items is determined according to the forms containing the menus—the items on the menu of the MDI parent form (which, by default, have a *MergeOrder* value of 0) take precedence over those of the child form and they appear first.

5   Click the separator bar on the child menu and set its *MergeOrder* property to 1. The separator bar needs to appear after the Save menu item on the merged menu.

6   Display the *MDIParent* form in Design View. Click the *fileItem* menu item and set its *MergeType* property to MergeItems.

▶ **Important** When you merge menus, the parent and the child menu items to be merged must both have their *MergeType* properties set to MergeItems; otherwise the menus will not merge correctly.

7 Click the *newItem* menu item. Verify that its *MergeOrder* property is set to 0. Do the same for the *closeItem* menu item. Change the *MergeOrder* property for the *exitItem* menu item to 2.

Recall that you set the *MergeOrder* value for the *saveItem* menu item on the child menu to 1. This means that the Save command is displayed below the Close command but above the Exit command on the File menu at run time.

Display the child form

On the *MDIParent* form, create a *Click* event handler for the *newItem* called *newItemClick* by using Events View in the Properties window. The *newItemClick* event appears in the Code And Text Editor window.

1 In the *newItemClick* event method, type the following code:

```
MDIChild childForm = new MDIChild();
childForm.MdiParent = this;
childForm.Show();
```

This code creates an instance of the *MDIChild* form and displays it in the client area of the MDI parent form. The first statement actually creates the child form. The second statement sets the *MdiParent* property to the current form (the MDI parent running this code). *MdiParent* is a run-time-only property. If you don't set it, the child form is displayed as a freestanding form outside the bounds of the MDI parent. The third statement actually displays the child form.

2 Build and run the application. When the MDI parent form appears, on the File menu click New. A child form appears in the client area and you can type in some text. On the File menu, click New again. Another child form appears. In fact, you can open as many child forms as time, space, and the memory of your computer allow. If you click the File menu, you see the Save command (and the separator bar) lurking between the Close and Exit commands. If you close both child forms, the Save item disappears.

3 On the File menu, click Exit and return to Visual Studio .NET.

If you were inquisitive enough to click the Window menu when the application was running, you would have noticed that not much happens. Traditionally, the

Window menu contains commands for arranging and selecting the child forms. You will add these features in the following procedure.

Fix the Window menu

1   Return to Design View for the *MDIParent* form. Use the menu editor to add to the Window menu the sub-items and *Click* event methods summarized in the following table.

Text	Name	*Click* event method
&Cascade	*cascadeItem*	*cascadeItemClick*
Tile &Horizontal	*horizontalItem*	*horizontalItemClick*
Tile &Vertical	*verticalItem*	*verticalItemClick*

The menu should look like the following illustration:

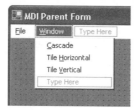

2   In Code And Text Editor window, add the following statement to the body of the *cascadeItemClick* method:

```
this.LayoutMdi(MdiLayout.Cascade);
```

This statement arranges the child forms of the MDI parent in a cascade layout. In the *horizontalItemClick* method, add the following statement:

```
this.LayoutMdi(MdiLayout.TileHorizontal);
```

And in the *verticalItemClick* method, add the following statement:

```
this.LayoutMdi(MdiLayout.TileVertical);
```

3   Display the *MDIParent* form in Design View again, and then select the *windowItem* menu item. In the Properties window, set the *MdiList* property to True.

4   Switch back to Code And Text Editor window displaying MDIParent.cs and locate the *MDIParent* class.

5   Add a private *int* variable called *childCount* to the *MDIParent* class, under the private variables that are near the top of the class but above the *MDIParent* constructor. Initialize *childCount* to 0:

```
private int childCount = 0;
```

6 Locate the *newItemClick* method. Just before the *childForm.Show* statement, add the following code:

```
childCount++;
childForm.Text = childForm.Text + " " + childCount;
```

These two statements modify the title bar text that appears in each child form—each form is numbered so you can distinguish between them.

7 Build and run the application again. Click New on the File menu two times to open a pair of child forms. Click the Window menu—it contains options for arranging the child forms and also displays the title bar text (which is the value of the *Text* property) of each form with a check mark next to the form that currently has the focus. When you select a child form on this menu, that child form has the focus. Click the Cascade, Tile Horizontal, and Tile Vertical commands on the Window menu to rearrange the forms.

8 Close the application and return to Visual Studio .NET.

MDI and Toolbars

You have seen that menus and menu items have properties (*MergeOrder* and *MergeType*) that allow you to specify how to merge them together. This is useful because MDI child forms always display their menus on the menu bar of the MDI parent form. The same is not true for toolbars, however. It is perfectly possible (though uncommon) for a child form to display its own toolbar as part of the child form. If you want to merge toolbars when a child form is displayed, you have to do it programmatically. One technique is to add a *Panel* control to the parent form and display the child toolbar in the panel. You need to be careful about keeping track of which child forms are active, though, and enable or disable toolbar buttons as appropriate.

The Close menu item on the parent form's File menu does not work yet. Its task is to close the child form that currently has the focus.

Close the child form

1   In Design View for the *MDIParent* form, select the *closeItem* menu item in the Properties window. Display the events for the menu, type **closeItemClick** in the *Click* event, and then press Enter.

The *closeItemClick* method appears in the Code And Text Editor window.

2   In the *closeItemClick* method, type the following statements:

```
Form childForm = this.ActiveMdiChild;
if (childForm != null)
{
    childForm.Close();
}
```

The first statement queries the *ActiveMdiChild* property of the MDI parent form. This property returns a reference to the child form that has the focus. The *if* statement checks to make sure that a child form is actually open. If there is no active child form, the *childForm* variable is *null*. If there is an active child form, the form is closed.

3   Build and execute the application. Create some child forms and then click Close on the File menu to close them. When you have finished, exit the application.

Alternatives to MDI

MDI is a useful paradigm if the application you are building contains multiple documents. It is often described as an *application-centered model* because it is the application that drives the different views and documents that are available. However, for many applications, MDI might be too much or otherwise unsuitable.

One alternative to MDI is the Single Document Interface (SDI). In an SDI application, only one document can be open at a time. Microsoft Notepad is an example of an SDI application. An SDI application tends to be easier to use and implements a *document-centered model*, in which the application is driven by the data being presented.

A second alternative to MDI is to use a composite interface, which is a collection of different SDI windows with code to manage and tie them together. Usually one of the SDI windows is a controlling frame that manages the others. Microsoft Visual Basic 4 used this model—the toolbar and menu were in one window, the Properties window was another window, the code editor was a third window, and so on. Each window could be independently minimized, maximized, and closed. If you close the toolbar and menu window in Visual Basic, the application closes because the toolbar and menu window is the controlling frame.

Creating Dialog Boxes

A dialog box is a form that is used to prompt the user, display options, and receive information. For example, an application that uses information held in a file usually prompts the user for the name of the file by using a dialog box. Simpler dialog boxes might be displayed to warn the user about a particular situation or just to display information. Generally speaking, using a dialog box is the recommended way to prompt the user and get information.

Displaying Modal and Modeless Dialog Boxes

Dialog boxes can be classified as modal and modeless. A *modal* dialog box prevents any other window in the application from receiving the focus while the dialog box is displayed. Modal dialog boxes are perfect for situations in which it does not make sense for the application to allow anything else to happen until the user has answered the questions posed by these dialog boxes.

On the other hand, a *modeless* dialog box allows user input to proceed elsewhere in the application while the dialog box is open. The classic example of this situation is the Find And Replace dialog box in Microsoft Word. The user can enter a search string and a replacement, and then use the buttons in the dialog box to seek out and change specific text. However, the user can also continue editing the document without having to close the dialog box—the dialog box loses the focus without closing. The user can return to the Find And Replace dialog box and continue finding and replacing when needed.

In the following exercise, you will see how to create and display a modal dialog box for displaying "About" information in your MDI application.

Create an About form

1   In the MDIDemo project, on the Project menu, click Add Windows Form. The Add New Item dialog box appears. In the dialog box, select the Windows Form template, and in the Name text box, type **About.cs**. Click Open.

The new form will be added to the project and displayed in Design View.

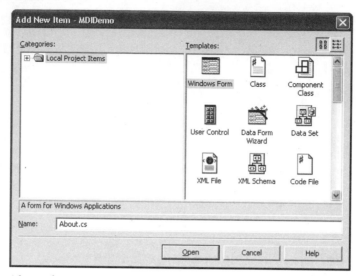

About forms typically do not have Maximize or Minimize buttons, and they often do not have system menus either. Additionally, they should not be resizable.

2   In the Properties window, set the properties of the About form using the information in the following table.

Property	Value	Description
ControlBox	False	Setting this property to False removes the system menu and the Maximize and Minimize buttons.
FormBorderStyle	FixedDialog	This makes the dialog box non-resizable and adds the thick border used in dialog boxes.
Size	300, 184	This dialog box displays only two labels and a button, so it does not need to be very big.
Text	About MDI Demo	The convention for About dialog boxes is that the title bar contains the text "About *<application>*" (where *<application>* is the name of the application).

3   In the Toolbox, add two labels to the About form, side-by-side about halfway down. Clear the *Text* property of the first label (called *label1*), and set its *Image* property by clicking the Ellipses button and selecting the file BEANY.BMP in the \Microsoft Press\Visual C# Step by Step\Chapter 22 folder in your My Documents folder. Set the *Size* property of *label1* to 64, 64 and set its *BorderStyle* property to

FixedSingle. Set the *Text* property of the second label (*label2*) to
MDI Demonstration. It might be necessary to resize the label so that
the text will fit on one line.

4   In the Toolbox, drag a *Button* control onto the form under the two
label controls. Set its *(Name)* property to ok and set its *Text* property
to OK. The completed About form should look like the following
example:

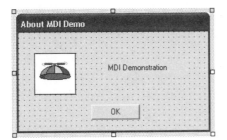

The user clicks the OK button to close the form at run time.

5   On the About form, click OK, and then in the Properties window,
click the Events button. In the *Click* event, type **okClick** and press
Enter. When the *okClick* event method appears in the Code And Text
Editor window, add the following statement:

```
this.Close();
```

A commonly accepted convention is that the About form for an
application should be available from the Help menu on the menu bar
of the main form (in this case, the *MDIParent* form). The Help menu
is typically the rightmost item on the menu bar, just after the Window menu.

Application and System Modal Dialog Boxes

Modal dialog boxes can be further classified as *application modal* or *system
modal*. An application modal dialog box prevents any window in the current
application from getting the focus while the modal dialog box is displayed, but
the user can switch to another application. A system modal dialog box prevents
the user from switching to another application. You should use a system modal
application only to report very, very serious situations that are likely to affect
other applications—for example, that the hard disk is corrupted.

Display the About form

1   Display the *MDIParent* form in Design View.

2   Click the *mdiMenu* control under the form, and then use the menu editor to add another top-level item to the menu. Place the item to the right of the Window item and name it *helpItem*, and set the *Text* property to &Help. Add a sub-item to the Help menu item called *aboutItem*. Set its *Text* property to &About MDI Demo.

The menu should look like the following example:

3   Select *aboutItem* in the menu editor, and then in the Properties window, click the Events button. In the *Click* event, type **aboutItemClick** and press Enter. When the *aboutItemClick* event method is created and displayed in Code View, type the following statements:

```
About aboutDialog = new About();
aboutDialog.ShowDialog();
```

This block of code creates a new instance of the About dialog box called *aboutDialog*. The *ShowDialog* method causes *aboutDialog* to be displayed as a modal dialog box. The method does not finish until the About dialog box is closed, preventing access to other parts of the application (this is a modal dialog).

▶   **Tip**   If you want to display a form as a modeless dialog box, use the *Show* method rather than *ShowDialog*.

4   Build and run the program. When the form appears, on the Help menu, click About MDI Demo. The About dialog box opens.

Notice that you can drag the About dialog box outside the bounds of the MDI Parent Form window.

5   While the About dialog box is open, try to select one of the menu items in the MDI Parent form. You are not able to because of the modal nature of the About dialog box. Click OK to close the About dialog box. Focus returns to the MDI Parent form.

6   Close the form and return to Visual Studio .NET.

Using Common Dialog Controls

There are a number of regular everyday tasks that require the user to specify some sort of information. For example, if the user wants to print a file, the user is usually asked which printer to use, and the user can set additional properties such as the number of copies. You might have noticed that the same Print dialog box is used by many different applications. This is not due to lack of imagination by applications developers; it is just that the requirement is so common that Microsoft has standardized it and made it available as a "common dialog"—a component supplied with the Microsoft Windows operating system that you can use in your own applications.

There are a number of other common dialog boxes available as well, including dialog boxes for opening and saving files, selecting colors and fonts, specifying page formats, and performing print previews. You can use any of these common dialog boxes in Visual Studio .NET through the common dialog controls.

Using the *SaveFileDialog* Control

In the following exercise, you will use the *SaveFileDialog* control. In the MDI Demo application, when the user edits text in a child window, the user will be able to save the text to a file. You will prompt the user for the name of the file by using a *SaveFileDialog* control.

Add a *SaveFileDialog* control

1   Display the *MDIChild* form in Design View.

2   In the Toolbox, drag a *SaveFileDialog* control onto the form. It appears under the form and is given the name *saveFileDialog1*.

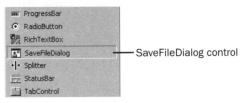
SaveFileDialog control

3   Click the *saveFileDialog1* control and set its properties by using the values specified in the following table.

Property	Value	Description
(Name)	saveFileDialog	The name of the control.
AddExtension	True	Setting this property to *True* allows the dialog box to add the file extension indicated by the *DefaultExt* property to the name of the file specified by the user if the user omits the file extension.
DefaultExt	txt	The default file extension to use.
FileName	Leave blank	The name of the currently selected file. Delete the value if you don't want a file to be selected by default.
InitialDirectory	C:\	The default directory to be used by the dialog box.
OverwritePrompt	True	If this property is *True*, the user is warned when an attempt is made to overwrite an existing file with the same name. For this to work, the *ValidateNames* property must also be set to *True*.
Title	MDI Text Editor	A string that is displayed on the title bar of the dialog box.
ValidateNames	True	This property indicates whether filenames are validated. It is used by some other properties, such as *OverwritePrompt*. If this property is set to *True*, the dialog box also checks to verify that any filename typed in by the user contains only valid characters.

Use the *SaveFileDialog* control

1 In the Code And Text Editor window, add the following *using* statement to the start of MDIChild.cs:

```
using System.IO;
```

This statement is necessary because the *Stream* and *StreamWriter* classes that you are about to use are defined in the *System.IO* namespace.

2 Display the form in Design View. In the menu editor, select the *saveItem* menu item on the *childMenu* menu. In the Properties window, click the Events button, and then select the *Click* event. Type **saveItemClick** and press Enter. The *saveItemClick* method appears in the Code And Text Editor window.

3 In the *saveItemClick* method, type the following statements:

```
DialogResult buttonClicked = saveFileDialog.ShowDialog();
if (buttonClicked.Equals(DialogResult.OK))
{
    Stream saveStream = saveFileDialog.OpenFile();
    StreamWriter saveWriter = new StreamWriter(saveStream);
    foreach (string line in editData.Lines)
    {
        saveWriter.WriteLine(line);
    }
    saveWriter.Close();
}
```

The first statement displays the Save File dialog box by using the *ShowDialog* method (you used this same method when displaying the About dialog box in the previous exercise). The Save File dialog box is modal. Modal dialog boxes have a *DialogResult* property that indicates which button the user clicked (the Save dialog has a Save button and a Cancel button). The *ShowDialog* method returns the value of this *DialogResult* property; if the user clicks Save, the *DialogResult* property will be OK (not Save because there is no such *DialogResult* value).

If the user clicks Save, the *OpenFile* method of the *saveFileDialog* control opens the file that the user selected. The easiest way to write text to the file is to create a *StreamWriter* object and use its *Write* method. The code uses a *foreach* statement to iterate through all the strings the user has typed in the *editData* control (*Lines* is an array property) and writes each string to the *saveWriter StreamWriter* object. When the array has been exhausted, *saveWriter* is closed, which also closes the file.

▶ **Important** Remember that the *SaveFileDialog* control prompts the user for the name of a file to save to, but does not actually do any saving—you still have to write that code yourself.

4 Build and run the application. On the File menu, click New to open a new MDI Child window. Type in several lines of text in the child window. On the File menu, click Save. The Save File dialog box opens and you are asked for the name of the file you want to save.

If you omit the file extension, ".txt" is added automatically when the file is saved. If you pick an existing file, the dialog box warns you before it closes.

5 When you have finished, close the application.

If you want to continue to the next chapter

- Keep Visual Studio .NET running and turn to Chapter 23.

If you want to quit Visual Studio .NET for now

- On the File menu, click Exit. If you see a Save dialog box, click Yes.

Chapter 22 Quick Reference

To	Do this	Button
Make a form a parent MDI window	Set the *IsMDIContainer* property of the form to True.	

Display a child form on an MDI parent form	Set the child form's *MdiParent* property before displaying it. For example:
	
	`childForm.MdiParent =`
	`    this;`
	`childForm.Show();`	

Determine the currently active child form on a parent MDI form	Query the *ActiveMdiChild* property of the parent MDI form. For example:
	
	`Form childForm =`
	`    this.ActiveMdiChild;`	

Merge a child MDI form menu with the MDI parent form's menu	Set the *MergeType* property of the child form's menu item to be included on the parent's menu to MergeItems. Do the same for the parent menu item. Set the *MergeOrder* of the individual submenu items to indicate the order in which they should appear on the parent's menu.	
Display a list of child windows on the parent's Window menu	Set the Window menu's *MdiList* property to *True*. As child windows are created and opened, the text on their title bars is added to the Window menu.	
Programmatically arrange child forms on a parent MDI form	Use the *MdiLayout.Cascade*, *MdiLayout.TileHorizontal*, or *MdiLayout.TileVertical* methods.	
Display a modeless dialog box or form	Use the *Show* method to display the dialog box or form. For example: `childForm.Show();`	
Display a modal dialog box or form	Execute the *ShowDialog* method to display the dialog box or form. For example: `childForm.ShowDialog();`	

To	Do this	Button
Find out which button the user pressed to close a modal dialog box	In the dialog box, set the *DialogResult* property. For example: `this.DialogResult = DialogResult.OK;` In the code that displays the dialog box, use the return value from the *ShowDialog* method: `DialogResult res = childForm.ShowDialog(); if (res.Equals (DialogResult.OK)) { ⋮ }`	
Prompt the user for the name of a file to save	Use a *SaveFileDialog* control. Display the dialog box by using the *ShowDialog* method. When the dialog box closes, the *FileName* property contains the name of the file selected by the user, and you can use the *OpenFile* method of the dialog box to read and write the file.	SaveFileDialog

Creating GUI Components

In this chapter, you will learn how to:

■ Create a user control.

■ Validate data and expose events on a user control.

■ Add a control to the Toolbox.

■ Extend one of the Microsoft .NET Framework control classes to add your own functionality.

■ Subclass an existing user control by using inheritance.

In Part 3 of this book, you learned all about creating components in Microsoft Visual C#—how to define properties, indexers, delegates, and events, and how to define your own operators. In this chapter, you will take these ideas and extend them to graphical user interface (GUI) components. You will create a new Windows Forms control, add it to the Toolbox, and then use it in another project. You will also learn how to use inheritance to subclass an existing control.

Working with User Controls

The *System.Windows.Forms* namespace in the .NET Framework contains a wide variety of controls, including *Button*, *CheckBox*, and *TextBox* controls, which you can drag onto a form. These controls are useful for almost any occasion. If you examine the .NET Framework Software Documentation Kit (SDK) and the .NET Framework Class Library, you will see that these components are all ordinary classes that are descended from the *Control* class. The *Control* class defines the common properties, methods, and events that all controls have. The *Name*, *Location*, and *Size* properties, the *Show* and *Hide* methods, and the *Click* and *Validating* events are some examples that we have already covered, although there are many, many others. The only special aspect of a control is that you can drag it from the Toolbox onto a container of a Windows Forms application. You will see how you can tailor the Toolbox and add controls to it later in this chapter.

Although there is a fine selection of predefined controls already available for you to use, you might find yourself repeating the same actions, writing the same code, and using the same set of controls over and over again. For example, if you are building an application that requires a user to log in to a secure system, you will typically prompt the user for a name and a password. You want to make sure that both the name and the password are filled in and that the password is not displayed as clear text. Take a look at the following example.

When the user clicks the Login button, the user name and password are processed. If they form a valid combination, the user will be allowed to gain access to the rest of the application. If they are invalid, an error message will be raised and the user will be prevented from gaining access. If you are creating several systems, you might find yourself repeatedly writing the same logon information. In a company with a large number of applications, the logon process might be standardized, so you could be tempted to simply cut and paste code from one application to another. However, if the logon procedure changes, you would have a lot of work locating all the applications that use the same information and changing it. It would be much better to define this information in a single place and just reuse it—that is the essence of good design. You can do this by creating a user control.

A user control is a container that can hold other controls, somewhat like a Windows form. A user control derives indirectly from the *Control* class and it contains the common built-in functionality of regular controls (for example, properties such as *BackColor* and *ForeColor*, events such as *Validating*, and methods such as *Show* and *Hide*). However, it does not require you to write any extra code—you simply define any additional properties, methods, and events that you want. A developer employing a user control writes the code setting properties and handling events for the control in much the same way that the developer would for the common controls we have already covered. The beauty of a user control is that, as with ordinary control classes, you can use the same user control across different applications. If you modify the user control, applications that use it can be configured to pick up the modified version of the control automatically without even needing to recompile.

Building the Login User Control

In the following exercises, you will create the *Login* user control that you saw previously.

▶   **Note**   The LoginControl project and the LoginTest project in this chapter use the Windows Control Library template. This template is available on in Visual Studio .NET Professional, Enterprise Developer, or Enterprise Architect editions. It is not in the Standard version of Visual C# .NET 2003, so you won't be able to create the project. The completed projects are, however, installed to the \Microsoft Press\Visual C# Step By Step\Chapter 23 in your My Documents folder. You can load and compile these projects using the Standard version of Visual C# .NET 2003.

Create the Login user control

1   In Visual Studio .NET, create a new project using the Windows Control Library template. Call the project LoginControl, and then set its location as \Microsoft Press\Visual C# Step By Step\Chapter 23 in your My Documents folder.

Creating a user control is much like creating a Windows Forms application. When the project has been created, you are presented with a workspace on which to lay out your controls. By default, this workspace is called UserControl1.

2   In the Solution Explorer, change the filename of UserControl1.cs to LoginControl.cs. Switch to Class View (on the View menu, click Class View) and change the name of the *UserControl1* class to Login. Your blank control should look like the following illustration:

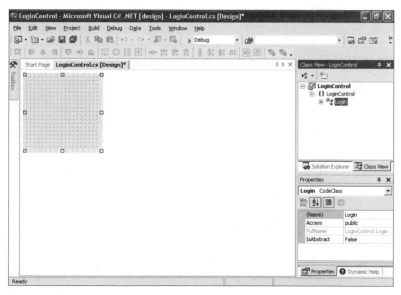

3   Change the *Size* property of the *Login* control to 400, 300.

23

Creating GUI Components

4   In the Toolbox, drag two *Label* controls, two *TextBox* controls, an *ErrorProvider* control, and a *Button* control onto the form. Set their properties by using the values specified in the following table.

Control	Property	Value
label1	*(Name)*	userNameLabel
	Location	32, 48
	Size	100, 23
	Text	user name label
label2	*(Name)*	passwordLabel
	Location	32, 128
	Size	100, 23
	Text	password label
textBox1	*(Name)*	userNameText
	Location	140, 48
	Size	220, 20
	Text	user name
textBox2	*(Name)*	passwordText
	Location	140, 128
	PasswordChar	*
	Size	220, 20
	Text	password
button1	*(Name)*	loginButton
	Location	150, 220
	Size	100, 36
	Text	Login
errorProvider1	*(Name)*	loginError

In the following procedure, you will expose the *Text* property of both labels and the Login button as read/write properties that can be changed when a developer drags a *Login* control onto an application. For security reasons, you will make the *Text* property of both text boxes write-only—a developer can give them default values but cannot gain access to the values that a user enters at run time.

Define properties for the user control

1 In the Class View, right-click the *Login* class, click Add, and then click Add Property on the pop-up menu. When the C# Property Wizard appears, select String from the Property type combo box and type **UserNameLabel** in the Property Name text box. Verify that property access is set to public and that the *get/set* Accessors radio button is selected, and then click Finish.

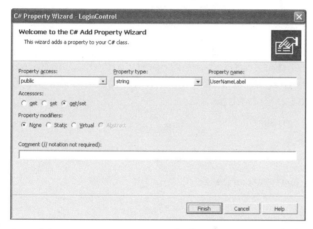

A *public string* property called *UserNameLabel* appears in the Code And Text Editor window.

2 Complete the *UserNameLabel* property by changing the code in the property body as follows:

```
public string UserNameLabel
{
    get
    {
        return userNameLabel.Text;
    }
    set
    {
        userNameLabel.Text = value;
    }
}
```

You can see that this property allows a developer to access the *Text* property of the *userNameLabel* control.

3 Create another *public get/set string* property called *PasswordLabel* in the same way that you created the *userNameLabel* property. Add code to expose the *Text* property of the *passwordLabel* control as shown here:

```
public string PasswordLabel
{
    get
    {
        return passwordLabel.Text;
    }
    set
    {
        passwordLabel.Text = value;
    }
}
```

4   Create a third *public get/set string* property called *LoginButtonText*. Add statements that allow a developer to read and write the *Text* property of the Login button:

```
public string LoginButtonText
{
    get
    {
        return loginButton.Text;
    }
    set
    {
        loginButton.Text = value;
    }
}
```

5   Create a *public* write-only *string* property (with a *set* accessor only) called *UserName*. In the *set* accessor, write the value supplied at run time to the *Text* property of the *userNameText* control. Add a *Browsable(false)* attribute to the property.

By default, any properties that you create for a user control will appear in the Properties window when a developer uses your control at design time. You do not want the *UserName* property to appear because it is write-only. Setting the *Browsable* attribute of a property to *false* prevents it from being displayed:

```
[Browsable(false)]
public string UserName
{
    set
    {
        userNameText.Text = value;
    }
}
```

6   Create another write-only, non-browsable *public string* property
called *Password* that allows the programmer to set a default value
for the *passwordText* control:

```
[Browsable(false)]
public string Password
{
    set
    {
        passwordText.Text = value;
    }
}
```

Validate data and expose events

1   Return to the Design View displaying LoginControl.cs. Click the
Login button and select the Properties window. Click the Events button. In the *Click* event, type **loginClick** and press Enter.

When the user clicks the Login button, your user control will validate
the data entered by the user. If the user has left either the User Name
or the Password text boxes empty, the *loginError* validation control
will display an error icon against the offending control. If the user
has entered values for these controls, your user control will then
employ a secret algorithm to validate the values. If the values are
valid, your user control will raise an event called *LoginSuccess*;
otherwise, the control will fire a different event called *LoginFail*.

2   In the *loginClick* method, add the following statements that make sure
that the user has typed information into both the *userNameText* and
passwordText controls, displaying an error icon if this is not the case:

```
if (userNameText.Text.Length == 0)
{
    loginError.SetError(userNameText,
        "Please enter a user name");
    return;
}

if (passwordText.Text.Length == 0)
{
    loginError.SetError(passwordText,
        "Please enter a password");
    return;
}
```

These checks use the *ErrorProvider* control that we covered in
Chapter 20.

3   Scroll up to the top of the *Login* class and add the following public event definitions:

```
public event System.EventHandler LoginSuccess;
public event System.EventHandler LoginFail;
```

Notice that these two events use the *System.EventHandler* delegate. This delegate is useful if you want to define an event that has no additional data—the event will be passed an empty *System.Event-Args* parameter instead. This delegate is used by many of the Windows Forms controls.

4   Return to the *loginClick* event method. After the code that checks the Password text box, add the following statements to validate the user name and password, and then raise the appropriate event (you will write the *userNameAndPasswordAreValid* method in a moment).

▶   **Note**   You should check first to make sure that there is at least one delegate subscribing to the event before you raise the event; otherwise you will get a null reference error at run time.

```
if (userNameAndPasswordAreValid(userNameText.Text,
    passwordText.Text))
{
    if (LoginSuccess != null)
    {
        LoginSuccess(this, new System.EventArgs());
    }
}
else
{
    if (LoginFail != null)
    {
        LoginFail(this, new System.EventArgs());
    }
}
```

5   All that remains is for you to implement the special, secret, totally uncrackable method that determines whether the user name and password are valid: *userNameAndPasswordAreValid*. There is one slight problem with this—the law prevents the publication of secret algorithms concerning the encryption and decryption of passwords. Therefore, you will have to make do with the following simple implementation. Add this method to the *Login* class:

```
private bool userNameAndPasswordAreValid(string userName,
    string password)
{
    return password.Equals("TrustMe");
}
```

6 On the Build menu, click Build Solution to compile the project.

Using the Login User Control

In the following exercises, you will add the *Login* user control to the Toolbox and then create a simple test application.

Add the Login user control to the Toolbox

1 On the Tools menu, click Add/Remove Toolbox Items. The Customize Toolbox dialog box opens. You can use this dialog box to add COM controls and .NET Framework controls (including user controls) to the toolbar. Click the .NET Framework Components tab (it is selected by default).

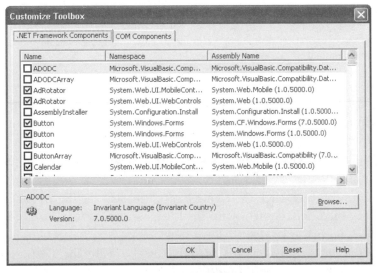

2 Click Browse, and then navigate to the \Microsoft Press\Visual C# Step by Step\Chapter 23\LoginControl\bin\Debug folder in your My Documents folder. Click LoginControl.dll (this is the user control that you have just created), and then click Open. The *Login* control (in the namespace *LoginControl*) will be added to the list of .NET Framework components. Click OK.

3 Switch to Design View, click the Toolbox and then click the General tab. The *Login* control appears.

Create a test application

1 Create a new project using the Windows Application template called LoginTest. Create it in the \Microsoft Press\Visual C# Step by Step\Chapter 23 folder in your My Documents folder. Select the Add To Solution radio button, and then click OK.

▶ **Tip** The Add To Solution option allows you to have more than one project open at the same time in the same session of Microsoft Visual Studio .NET. This ability is very useful for debugging because it allows you to single-step and debug across projects.

2 After the test application has been created, click the Project menu, and select Set As StartUp Project. When you build and execute the application later, this action will cause the LoginTest program to run rather than the user control.

3 Display Form1 in Design View and then change its *Size* property to 456, 360.

4 In the Toolbox, click the General tab. You will see the *Login* control. Drag the *Login* control onto the form. Set its location to 20, 20.

5 Click Form1 in Design View and then change its *BackColor* property to *IndianRed* (this color is available on the Web tab). Change the *ForeColor* property to *LightGray* (also on the Web tab).

The user control automatically picks up the colors of the form and uses them just like any other .NET Framework–defined control. The same behavior applies if you change the *Font* property.

6 Click the *Login* user control (it is called *login1*) and examine its properties in the Properties window. Look at the *LoginButtonText*— this is one of the properties that you defined for the user control. It contains the text Login. This is the default value you set when you designed the control. Change the *LoginButtonText* property to Validate. The text on the Login button will change. Change the *PasswordLabel* property to Password: and the *UserNameLabel* property to Name:. You can also set these properties at run time by using statements such as the following statement:

```
login1.UserNameLabel = "Name:";
```

7 In the Properties window, click the Events button to display the events available for the *login1* control. You will see *LoginFail* and *LoginSuccess* among all the other predefined events. Click the *Login-Fail* event, type **loginFail**, and then press Enter. The *loginFail* event appears in the Code And Text Editor window. Remember that this event will occur if the user's login attempt was unsuccessful. In the *loginFail* method, type the following statement:

```
MessageBox.Show("Login failed", "Fail");
```

8 Return to the Design View for Form1, select the Properties window (which is displaying events), type **loginSuccess** in the *LoginSuccess* event, and then press Enter. Add the following statement when the *loginSuccess* method appears in the Code View:

```
MessageBox.Show("Login succeeded", "Success");
```

9 On the Debug menu, click Start to compile and run the LoginTest application. When the form appears, type your name in the Name text box and type **Hello** in the Password text box. Click Validate. Password validation will fail (the password is TrustMe), the *Login-Fail* event will occur, and the form will run the *loginFail* method. Try again, this time typing **TrustMe** in the Password text box. The *login-Success* method will be run this time because the *LoginSuccess* event will be raised.

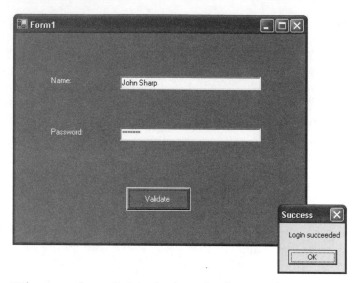

When you have finished, close the form and return to Visual Studio .NET.

Ambient Properties

Properties such as *BackColor*, *ForeColor*, and *Font* are sometimes referred to as the ambient properties. An *ambient* property is a property whose value is governed by the container control (such as a form) on which it has been placed. However, the ambience of a property applies only if the property is not explicitly set when the control is defined. For example, if you explicitly set the *BackColor* property of the *Login* control to Fuchsia (a rather vivid pink) when you define the control, the *BackColor* property will remain set to this shade no matter what color you apply to the container.

Specializing Controls Using Subclassing

User controls give you a powerful mechanism for reusing components. There might be times when a full-blown user control exceeds your requirements. Suppose, for example, you need a toggle button that changes its color and caption when its state changes from selected to unselected, or from unselected to selected.

You could use a check box and set its properties, but if you require the toggle button functionality in several different forms or applications, you will end up writing the same code over and over again. You could create a user control containing a single check box, but that would be a rather heavyweight and inefficient solution. A better technique is to create your own specialized type of check box by using inheritance.

Toggle Buttons

A toggle button is a check box that looks like a button. Unlike a normal button, however, a toggle button retains its state each time you click it. The state then reverts back when you click it again. The simplest example would be an On/Off button. It defaults to the Off state. When you click it, it changes to the On state and remains On until you click it again, at which point it reverts to Off.

Creating a *ToggleButton* Control

In the next set of exercises, you will create a *ToggleButton* control. You will also learn a useful technique for overriding events when subclassing controls.

Create the *ToggleButton* control

1   In Visual Studio .NET, create a new project. Use the Class Library template (*not* the Windows Control Library template). Name the project SubclassedControls, and set the location as the \Microsoft Press\Visual C# Step by Step\Chapter 23 folder in your My Documents folder. Make sure the Close Solution radio button is selected, and click OK.

2   In the Solution Explorer, change the filename of Class1.cs to Toggle-Button.cs. Switch to Class View, click *Class1*, and then change its name to *ToggleButton*.

3   On the Project menu, click Add Reference. The toggle button will be descended from the *CheckBox* class contained in the *System.Windows.Forms* namespace. To use this namespace, you must add a reference to System.Windows.Forms.dll. When the Add Reference dialog box opens, double-click the System.Windows.Forms.dll component. Scroll up through the list of components and double-click System.Drawing.dll as well—you will need the *System.Drawing* namespace because it contains the *Color* class that you will also use. When both namespaces have been selected, click OK.

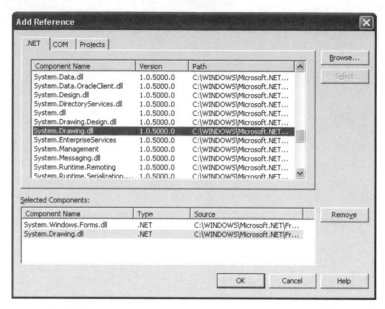

4   In Code View, under the `using System;` statement, add the following two *using* statements that allow you to reference the classes in the *System.Windows.Forms* and *System.Drawing* namespaces directly:

```
using System.Windows.Forms;
using System.Drawing;
```

5   Change the definition of the *ToggleButton* class so that it inherits from the *CheckBox* class:

```
public class ToggleButton : CheckBox
```

6   In the constructor, change the default appearance of the check box to look like a button by adding the following code:

```
public ToggleButton()
{
    this.Appearance = Appearance.Button;
}
```

Define properties for the *ToggleButton* control

1   In the *ToggleButton* class, above the constructor, define two *private string* variables called *checkedText* and *uncheckedText*. These strings will hold the captions to be displayed when the button is in its checked and unchecked states:

```
private string checkedText;
private string uncheckedText;
```

2 Create a *public* read/write property called *CheckedText* (note the uppercase "C"). This property will allow a user to get and set the *private checkedText* (lowercase "c") variable:

```
public string CheckedText
{
    get
    {
        return this.checkedText;
    }

    set
    {
        this.checkedText = value;
    }
}
```

3 Add another *public* read/write property called *UncheckedText* (with an uppercase "U") to allow the user to get and set the *uncheckedText* (lowercase "u") variable:

```
public string UncheckedText
{
    get
    {
        return this.uncheckedText;
    }

    set
    {
        this.uncheckedText = value;
    }
}
```

4 In the constructor, after the statement that sets the *Appearance* property of the check box, initialize the *checkedText* and *uncheckedText* variables by adding the following code:

```
this.checkedText = "Checked";
this.uncheckedText = "Unchecked";
```

5 Add two more *private* variables to the *ToggleButton* class called *checkedColor* and *uncheckedColor*. The type of both variables should be *Color*:

```
private Color checkedColor;
private Color uncheckedColor;
```

6 Create two more read/write properties called *CheckedColor* and *UncheckedColor* that provide *get* and *set* access to the *checkedColor* and *uncheckedColor* variables.

```
public Color CheckedColor
{
    get
    {
        return this.checkedColor;
    }

    set
    {
        this.checkedColor = value;
    }
}

public Color UncheckedColor
{
    get
    {
        return this.uncheckedColor;
    }

    set
    {
        this.uncheckedColor = value;
    }
}
```

7   In the constructor, after initializing the *checkedText* and *unchecked-Text* variables, type the following statements to initialize the *checkedColor* and *uncheckedColor* variables:

```
this.checkedColor = Color.Gray;
this.uncheckedColor = this.BackColor;
```

When the user clicks a toggle button, the *Text* and *BackColor* properties should be set according to the Checked state of the button. The natural place to do this is in the *Click* event. However, keep in mind that you only want to extend the default *Click* event supplied with the *CheckBox* class rather than replace it. If you read the .NET Framework documentation, you will notice that controls typically have a protected *OnXXX* method that raises each event (where *XXX* is the name of the event)—for example, the *Click* event is raised by the *OnClick* method. Controls call these methods when an event occurs. If you want to extend the *Click* event, the trick is therefore to override the *OnClick* method.

Override the *Click* event

1   In the *ToggleButton* class, add a new method called *OnClick*. The method should be protected (you don't want to expose this method to the outside world, but if another developer builds a control that inherits from your *ToggleButton* class, it is only polite to let him or her extend the *Click* event) and marked as override (you are overriding the *OnClick* method inherited from the *CheckBox* class):

```
protected override void OnClick(EventArgs e)
{
}
```

2   In the body of the method, add the following statement that calls the *OnClick* method of the *CheckBox* class:

```
base.OnClick(e);
```

3   Type the following code after the previous statement:

```
if (this.Checked)
{
    this.Text = this.checkedText;
    this.BackColor = this.checkedColor;
}
else
{
    this.Text = this.uncheckedText;
    this.BackColor = this.uncheckedColor;
}
```

This block examines the Checked state and sets the *Text* and *Back-Color* properties of the *ToggleButton* accordingly.

4   On the Build menu, click Build Solution to compile the new control.

Using the *ToggleButton* Control

In the following exercises, you will test the *ToggleButton* user control by building a simple Windows Forms application.

Add the *ToggleButton* control to the Toolbox

1   On the Tools menu, click Add/Remove Toolbox Items.

2   In the Customize Toolbox dialog box, click the .NET Framework Components tab, and then click Browse.

3   Move to the \Microsoft Press\Visual C# Step By Step\Chapter 23\SubclassedControls\bin\Debug folder in your My Documents folder. Select SubclassedControls.dll, and then click Open.

4   The ToggleButton component will appear in the Customize Toolbox dialog box. Click OK.

Test the *ToggleButton* control

1   Create a new project called *ToggleButtonTest* using the Windows Application template. Create it in the \Microsoft Press\Visual C#\Step By Step\Chapter 23 folder in your My Documents folder.

2   Select the Toolbox and look for the *ToggleButton* on the Windows Forms tab. You might be slightly disappointed to find that it's not there. Click the General tab. The *ToggleButton* control appears on this page. To move the *ToggleButton* control to the Windows Forms tab, right-click the *ToggleButton* control, and click Cut. You will be warned that the *ToggleButton* will be removed from the Toolbox— click OK. Select the Windows Forms tab. Right-click any control on this page, and then click Paste.

     The *ToggleButton* control will be appended to the end of the list of controls on this page (don't panic—the control you right-clicked has not disappeared).

3   In the Toolbox, drag the *ToggleButton* control onto the middle of the form (called *Form1*).

4   In the Properties window, change the *Text* property to Off; change the *TextAlign* property to MiddleCenter; set the *Checked* property to False (this is the default value anyway); change the *BackColor* property to Green; and change the *ForeColor* property to White.

5   In the Properties window, set the custom properties that you added to the control: change *CheckedColor* to Red and *CheckedText* to On, *UncheckedColor* to Green and *UncheckedText* to Off.

6   On the Debug menu, click Start to compile and run the test application. When the form appears, the toggle button will be in the Off state and will be colored green.

7   Click the toggle button. It will turn red and be in the On state. Click the toggle button again. It will go back to green and be in the Off state. Close the form and return to Visual Studio .NET.

8   In Design View, select the toggle button, and then in the Properties window, click the Events button. In the *Click* event, type **toggleClick**, and press Enter. The *toggleClick* method appears in the Code And Text Editor window.

9   In the Code And Text Editor window, type the following statement in the body of the *toggleClick* method:

```
MessageBox.Show("Changing state", "Changing");
```

10   Compile and run the program again.

When you click the toggle button, it will still change color, but the event method will also be executed. This behavior occurs because the *ToggleButton* control not only does its own work but calls the *OnClick* method of the base *CheckBox* class as well. If it did not, users wouldn't be able to properly subscribe to the *Click* event.

Close the application.

If you want to continue to the next chapter

■   Keep Visual Studio .NET running and turn to Chapter 24.

If you want to quit Visual Studio .NET for now

■   On the File menu, click Exit. If you see a Save dialog box, click Yes.

Chapter 23 Quick Reference

To	Do this
Create a user control	Use the Windows Control Library template.

Prevent a user control property from being displayed in the Properties window when the control is being used	Prefix the property with the *Browsable(false)* attribute. For example:
	
	`[Browsable(false)]`
	`public string UserName`
	`{`
	   ⋮
	`}`

Add a control to the Toolbox	On the Tools menu, click Add/Remove Toolbox Items, click the .NET Framework Components tab, and then locate the DLL that implements the control. Check the component after it has been added to the list of .NET Framework Components.

To	Do this
Move a control from one tab of the Toolbox to another	Select the control in the Toolbox, right-click the control, and click Cut on the pop-up menu. Move to the destination tab, right-click any control on that tab, and click Paste on the pop-up menu. The control will be appended to the list.
Extend one of the .NET Framework control classes to add your own functionality	Create a Class Library project. Add a reference to the *System.Windows.Forms* namespace and DLL. Use inheritance to subclass the control you want to extend. For example:

```
public class ToggleButton
    : CheckBox
{
    ⋮
}
```

Override and extend an event inherited from a control class	Override the *OnXXX* method (where *XXX* is the name of the event). Call the *OnXXX* method of the base class in the method. For example:

```
protected override
void OnClick(EventArgs e)
{
    base.OnClick(e);
    ⋮
}
```

Managing Data

24

Using a Database

In this chapter, you will learn how to:
■ Create a connection to a database by using the Server Explorer.
■ Retrieve data from a database and browse it graphically in Microsoft Visual Studio .NET.
■ Insert, update, and delete data held in a database.

In Part 4 of this book, you learned how to use Microsoft Visual C# to build user interfaces and present information. In Part 5, you will learn about managing data by using the data access functionality available in Visual Studio .NET and the Microsoft .NET Framework. The first two chapters in this part cover ADO.NET, an updated version of ActiveX Data Objects (ADO) designed and optimized for the .NET common language runtime. In Chapter 26, you will learn how to manipulate XML data.

Using ADO.NET Databases

With the advent of .NET, Microsoft decided to update ActiveX Data Objects (ADO) and created ADO.NET. ADO.NET contains several enhancements over the original ADO architecture, providing improved interoperability and performance. If you are already familiar with ADO, you will notice that the object model of ADO.NET is a little different. For one thing, the *RecordSet* type no longer exists—Microsoft has created the *DataAdapter* and *DataSet* classes that support disconnected data access and operations, allowing greater scalability because you no longer have to be connected to the database all the time. (To be fair, ADO also provided disconnected *RecordSet*s, but they were the exception rather than the rule when used by programmers.) Therefore, your applications can consume fewer resources. With the connection pooling mechanisms of ADO.NET, database connections can be reused by different applications, thereby reducing the need to continually connect to and disconnect from the database, which can be a time-consuming operation.

Using the Northwind Traders Database

▶ **Important**   To perform the exercises in this chapter, you must have access to the Northwind Traders database installed under Microsoft SQL Server 2000 or the Microsoft SQL Server 2000 Desktop Engine. You can set up the SQL Server 2000 Desktop Engine by running Setup.Exe found in the \Program Files\Microsoft Visual Studio .NET 2003\Setup\MSDE folder (this folder and its contents are created when you install Visual Studio .NET). You might need to restart your computer to start the SQL Server service. (The Standard version of Visual C# .NET 2003 does not work with SQL Server 2000. If you've installed the Standard version of Visual C# .NET 2003, please install the Microsoft SQL Server 2000 Desktop Engine.)

To create the Microsoft SQL Server 2000 Desktop Engine version of the Northwind Traders database, open a command prompt window and go to the \Program Files\Microsoft Visual Studio .NET 2003\SDK\v1.1\Samples\Setup folder.

Type the following: **osql –S** *YourServer***\VSdotNET2003 –E –iinstnwnd.sql**.

(Replace *YourServer* with the name of your computer. The osql program is located at \Program Files\Microsoft SQL Server\80\Tools\Binn; you might need to use the PATH command to add this directory to your computer's search path before you execute this command.)

This command runs the instnwnd.sql script. When the script has finished processing (the script will probably run for several minutes), close the command prompt window.

Northwind Traders is a fictitious company that sells edible goods with exotic names to customers. The Northwind database contains a number of tables holding information about the goods that Northwind Traders sells, the customers they sell to, orders placed by customers, suppliers that Northwind Traders obtains goods from to re-sell, shippers that they can use to send goods to customers, and employees that work for Northwind Traders. The following illustration shows all the tables in the Northwind Traders database and how they are related to each other. The tables that you will be using in this chapter are Orders and Products.

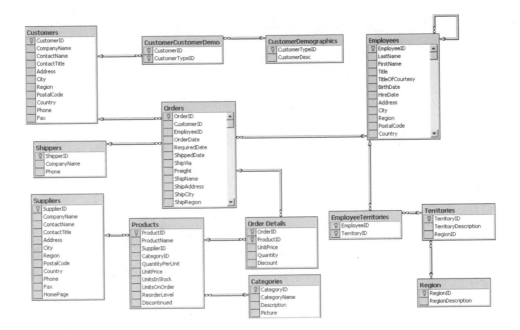

Accessing the Database

In the first set of exercises, you will write a program that connects to the database, retrieves the contents of the Products table, and displays those contents. You will perform these tasks using a Database Project to define a connection to the Northwind database (you will also use this project to browse the database). You will then create a Windows Forms application that uses the database connection to fetch and display the data.

Connect to the database

1   Using Visual Studio .NET, create a new project using the Database Project template. You will find this template in the Database Projects folder under Other Projects. Name the project ListProducts and save it in the \Microsoft Press\Visual C# Step by Step\Chapter 24 folder in your My Documents folder.

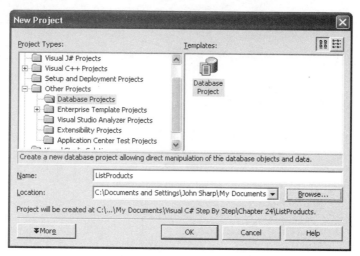

2 When you create the project, the Data Link dialog box appears and prompts you for information about which database to connect to. Click the Provider tab and verify that the Microsoft OLE DB Provider For SQL Server provider is selected (your list of providers might be different from those shown in the following illustration, depending on the other software that you have installed on your computer).

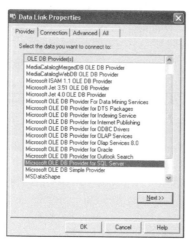

3 Click the Connection tab. Select your SQL Server, and then specify the information needed to log on to the server. If you are using the SQL Server 2000 Desktop Engine, the server name will be *YourServer*\VSdotNET2003, and you should select the Use Windows NT Integrated Security option; otherwise, contact your administrator to find out which user name and password you should use. Set the database name to Northwind.

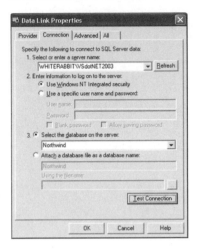

▶ **Tip**   If you have already created a Data Link, you will be prompted with the Add Database Reference dialog box instead. This dialog box will list all the databases that you have used. If this happens, click the Add New Reference button. The Data Link Properties dialog box will then appear.

4   Click Test Connection to verify that you have entered the correct information. If the information is correct, a message box appears. Click OK to close the message box.

5   Click OK to close the Data Link Properties dialog box. The Server Explorer displays your new data connection.

Browse products information

1   In the Server Explorer, expand your data connection, and then expand the Tables folder that appears. A list of all the tables in the database appears. Expand the Products table and a list of all the columns in the table appears.

2   Right-click the Products table and then click Retrieve Data From Table on the pop-up menu.

This command fetches and displays all the data in the Products table. If you want, you can change the data values in the table by typing over them. Behind the scenes, Visual Studio .NET is generating SQL *SELECT* and *UPDATE* statements and submitting them to the database.

▶ **Tip**   You can also delete a row by clicking the row selector bar (the gray bar on the left displaying an arrow indicating the current row) and pressing the Delete key. If you scroll to the bottom of the data, a row marked with an asterisk (*) at the end appears. You can type new values in this row, which are then inserted into the database.

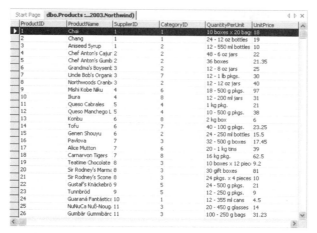

3   Close the window displaying the Products information when you have finished browsing.

Display products data in a Windows Forms application

1   In the Solution Explorer, right-click Solution 'ListProducts'. On the pop-up menu, point to Add, and then click New Project. The Add New Project dialog box opens. This creates a new project and adds it to the ListProducts solution automatically.

2   In the Project Types pane, select Visual C# Projects, and then click Windows Application in the Templates pane. Name the project DisplayProducts, and store it in the \Microsoft Press\Visual C# Step by Step\Chapter 24 folder in your My Documents folder. Click OK. A new project called DisplayProducts is created and the Design View of Form1.cs appears in the Design View window.

3   Rename Form1.cs to ProductsForm.cs and change the name of the *Form1* class to *ProductsForm*.

4   In the Design View window, click the form. In the Properties window, change the *Text* property of *ProductsForm* to Products.

5   Display the Code View for *ProductsForm*. In the Code And Text Editor window, find the *Main* method, and then change the *Application.Run* statement to create and display a *ProductsForm* object rather than *Form1*:

```
Application.Run(new ProductsForm());
```

6   Return to Design View for *ProductsForm*. In the Server Explorer, drag the Products table onto the form. Notice two objects under the form called *sqlConnection1* and *sqlDataAdapter1*.

The *sqlConnection1* object contains properties that specify which database to connect to. You can change this information by modifying the *ConnectionString* property in the Properties window. The type of this object is *SqlConnection*, which is a specialized version of the ADO.NET *Connection* class and is optimized for gaining access to SQL Server databases.

The *sqlDataAdapter1* object holds the SQL commands used to manipulate the data in the Products table, and it uses the *sqlConnection1* object to connect to the database.

7   Select the *sqlDataAdapter1* control and examine the Properties window. Notice the *DeleteCommand*, *InsertCommand*, *SelectCommand*, and *UpdateCommand* properties. These refer to *SqlCommand* objects (which are specialized versions of the ADO.NET *Command* class) used by the adapter to retrieve and manage the data in the Products table.

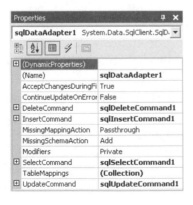

8   Expand the *DeleteCommand* property. Notice the SQL *DELETE* statement that is executed whenever the program wants to delete data in the *CommandText* property and the connection to the database in the *Connection* property.

9   Select the *CommandText* property and click the Ellipses button. The Query Builder dialog box opens and displays the SQL *DELETE* statement in a graphical form with the SQL form underneath (the @ sign in the *WHERE* clause is used to indicate parameters whose values are supplied at run time).

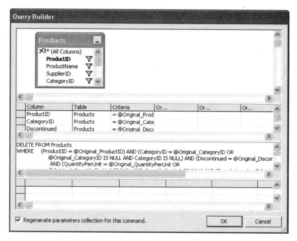

10   Click Cancel. At the bottom of the Properties window, notice three hyperlinks labeled Configure Data Adapter, Generate Dataset, and Preview Data.

The Configure Data Adapter hyperlink displays a wizard that allows you to change the database connection and edit the SQL statements used to fetch and manage the data represented by the *Data-Adapter*—you can experiment with this wizard on your own time. The Preview Data hyperlink opens a dialog box that lets you display the data in the Products table—again, examine this at your leisure. The Generate Dataset hyperlink lets you create a *DataSet* object that is populated with the data returned by executing *SelectCommand* in the *DataAdapter*.

11   Click the Generate Dataset hyperlink. The Generate Dataset dialog box opens.

12   Leave the contents of the Generate Dataset dialog box set to their default values and click OK. Another control, called *dataSet11*, appears under *ProductsForm*. This control represents the *DataSet* you have just created.

13 You have done a lot of work defining the data that you want to see, and all you need to do now is display the data. In the Toolbox, select the *DataGrid* control, and then drag it onto *ProductsForm*.

14 Resize *ProductsForm* to 812, 500 (this should be wide enough to display the full width of the *DataGrid* and a vertical scrollbar). Set the *Dock* property of *dataGrid1* (the new *DataGrid* object you created in the previous step) to *Fill*. The *DataGrid* object fills the entire form. While *dataGrid1* is selected, set its *DataSource* property to *dataSet11.Products* (you will see in Chapter 25 that a *DataSet* object can contain several tables). The *DataGrid* on the form displays the columns from the Products table.

15 Switch back to the Code And Text Editor window displaying ProductsForm.cs and locate the constructor (the method called *Products-Form*). Replace the TODO comment with the following statement:

```
sqlDataAdapter1.Fill(dataSet11);
```

The *Fill* method of an *SqlDataAdapter* object executes the SQL *SELECT* statement specified by its *SelectCommand* property, and populates the *DataSet* passed in as the parameter—*dataSet11*, in this example.

16 Build and execute the program. When the *ProductsForm* appears, the constructor fills the *DataSet*. The *DataGrid* (which uses the *DataSet* as its data source) displays the contents of the Products table.

You can browse the data, type over it, delete rows, and add new rows (using the * row at the bottom). However, none of the changes you make are saved—you need to write a little more code, which is what you will do in the following exercise.

17 Close the form and return to the Visual Studio .NET programming
environment.

Add code to save changes

1 Verify that *ProductsForm* is displayed in Design View. In the Toolbox, drag the *MainMenu* control anywhere onto the form. A new
control called *mainMenu1* appears under the form.

2 Click *mainMenu1*. The caption Type Here is displayed in the menu
bar of *ProductsForm*. Using the techniques described in Chapter 19,
create a File menu item (using the caption &File) containing a submenu item labeled &Save, a menu separator bar, and another submenu item labeled E&xit. Name these menu items *fileItem*,
saveItem, and *exitItem* (do not rename the separator bar).

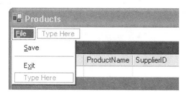

3 In the menu editor, select *exitItem*. In the Properties window, click
the Events button, select the Click event, type **exitItemClick**, and
press Enter. The *exitItemClick* method appears in the Code And Text
Editor window.

4 In the Code And Text Editor window, add the following statement to
the *exitItemClick* method:

```
this.Close();
```

This statement closes the window.

5 Return to Design View and select *saveItem* in the menu editor. In the
Properties window, select the Click event, type **saveItemClick**, and
press Enter. The *saveItemClick* method appears in the Code And
Text Editor window.

6 In the Code And Text Editor window, add the following statements
to the *saveItemClick* method:

```
try
{
    DataSet changedData = dataSet11.GetChanges();
    if (changedData != null)
    {
        int numRows = sqlDataAdapter1.Update(changedData);
        MessageBox.Show("Database updated " + numRows +
```

```
            " rows successfully", "Success");
        dataSet11.AcceptChanges();
    }
    else
    {
        MessageBox.Show("Nothing to save", "No changes");
    }
}
catch(Exception ex)
{
    MessageBox.Show("An error occurred updating the database: " +
        ex.Message, "Error", MessageBoxButtons.OK,
        MessageBoxIcon.Error);
    dataSet11.RejectChanges();
}
```

This code saves the changes made to the *DataSet* back to the database. The *GetChanges* method of *dataSet11* returns a new *DataSet* called *changedData* containing all the rows that have been modified in some way (updated, deleted, or inserted). If the user has not made any changes, *GetChanges* returns a null *DataSet*. The *if* statement checks whether *changedData* is null. If it is, a message box appears stating that there is nothing to save. If *changedData* is not null, the *Update* method of *sqlDataAdapter1* is used to propagate the changes back to the database.

The *Update* method takes a *DataSet* containing modified data as a parameter and iterates through it. For each row in each table in the *DataSet* (remember that a *DataSet* can contain more than one table), the *Update* method determines whether the row is new, marked for deletion, or has been updated. It then runs the SQL statement indicated by the appropriate property of *sqlDataAdapter1* (*InsertCommand*, *DeleteCommand*, or *UpdateCommand*), passing the data in each row as parameters to these SQL statements. When it finishes, the *Update* method returns an integer indicating how many rows were affected. The block of code shown in the *saveItemClick* method uses this information to display a message to the user. Finally, the *AcceptChanges* method of the *DataSet* marks all the modified rows as having been saved—if you did not do this, a subsequent call to the *GetChanges* method would return a *DataSet* containing the rows you have just updated as well as any newly modified rows.

▶ **Note** When dealing with multi-user databases, you should be aware that errors can occur when modifying data, and you must be prepared to handle them. For example, two users could try to update the same data at the same time, or one user might delete a row that another is updating. There is also the possibility of integrity errors—what happens if you try to set the SupplierID column for a product to a supplier that does not exist? The database traps this problem and reports an error to the application requesting the update. If any sort of error occurs while updating the database, the *Update* method of *sqlDataAdapter1* generates an exception. For this reason, the update logic is held in a *try/catch* block. If an exception is raised, a message box appears informing you of the problem. The *RejectChanges* method of the *DataSet* is then used to discard the modifications you made to the *DataSet*. This is a simple (somewhat Draconian) but robust technique. In the Chapter 25, you will see how to handle errors more gracefully.

7   Build and run the application. When the Products form appears, change the SupplierID of the first row to 4. Change the UnitPrice of the second row to 50. Move down to the third row (you have to move away from a row before its changes are saved), and then on the File menu, click Save. You will be rewarded with the Success message box indicating that two rows were modified. Click OK to close the message box.

8   Click the gray selector (containing the arrow) to the left of the third row and press Delete. Row 3 disappears from view. On the File menu, click Save.

The operation fails because there are outstanding orders in the database for this product and the integrity rules of the database do not let you delete it without removing those orders first. An error message appears.

9   Click OK to close the message box. Notice that row 3 reappears in the *DataGrid*. This occurs because the *RejectChanges* method is called.

10   On the File menu, click Exit to close the application and return to the Visual Studio .NET programming environment.

Using ADO.NET Programmatically

In the following set of exercises, you will write your own code to access the database rather than dragging controls from the Server Explorer. The aim of the exercise is to help you learn more about ADO.NET and understand the object model implemented by ADO.NET by programming it manually. In many cases, this is what you will have to do in real life—the drag-and-drop approach is fine for creating prototypes, but on many occasions you will want more control over how data is fetched and manipulated.

The application you are going to create will generate a simple report displaying information about customers' orders. The program will prompt the user for a CustomerID and then display the orders for that customer.

Connect to the database

1   Create a new project called ReportOrders using the Console Application template. Save it in the \Microsoft Press\Visual C# Step By Step\Chapter 24 folder in your My Documents folder and click OK.

2   In the Solution Explorer, change the name of Class1.cs to Report.cs. In the Properties window, change the name of the *Class1* class to *Report*.

3   In the Code And Text Editor window add the following statement under the using System; statement:

```
using System.Data.SqlClient;
```

The *System.Data.SqlClient* namespace contains the specialized ADO.NET classes used to gain access to SQL Server.

4   Locate the *Main* method of the *Report* class. Add the following *try/catch* block in the body of the *Main* method. All the code that you will write for gaining access to the database goes inside the *try* part of this block—remember that you must be prepared to handle exceptions whenever you use a database.

```
try
{
// You will add your code here in a moment
}
catch(Exception e)
{
    Console.WriteLine(
        "An error occurred accessing the database: "
        + e.Message);
}
```

5   Replace the comment in the *try* block with the following code that connects to the database:

```
SqlConnection dataConnection = new SqlConnection();
dataConnection.ConnectionString = "Integrated Security=true;" +
    "Initial Catalog=Northwind;" +
    "Data Source=YourServer\\VSdotNET2003";
dataConnection.Open();
```

▶   **Important**   In the *ConnectionString* property, replace *YourServer* with the name of your computer or the computer running SQL Server. If you are using a version of SQL Server 2000 other than the Desktop Engine, you should also omit the \\VSdotNET2003 suffix.

SqlConnection is a subclass of the ADO.NET *Connection* class. It is designed to handle connections to SQL Server databases only. You can either specify the details of the database you want to connect to as a parameter to the constructor or you can set the *Connection-String* property after you have created the *SqlConnection* object (the previous code uses the latter approach).

The contents of the *ConnectionString* property are important. The example specifies integrated security (this is the preferred method of access because you do not have to prompt the user for any form of user name or password, and you are not tempted to hard-code user names and passwords into your application). The Initial Catalog indicates which database to use and the Data Source specifies the server on which SQL Server is running (if you are running SQL Server on your own computer, you can replace the name of the server with localhost). Notice that a semicolon separates all the parameters in the *ConnectionString*.

▶ **Important** If your administrator has not granted your user account trusted access to SQL Server, you have to use the *User ID* and *Password* parameters instead—ask your administrator for a user name and password you can use. For example:

```
myConnection.ConnectionString =
    "User ID=John;Password=GillinghamFC;
Initial Catalog=Northwind;Data Source=localhost";
```

However, don't do this unless it is absolutely necessary because it is a poor practice and not secure. Anyone reading your code will be able to see your password. An alternative is to display a form prompting the user for his or her name and password.

There are also many other parameters that you can encode in the *Connection-String*. See the .NET Framework SDK documentation for details.

The next step is to prompt the user for a CustomerID and then query the database to find all of the orders for that customer.

Query the Orders table

1 Add the following statements after the code that opens the database connection:

```
Console.Write("Please enter a CustomerID (5 characters): ");
string customerId = Console.ReadLine();
```

These statements prompt the user for a CustomerID and get the user's response in the string variable *customerId*.

2   Type the following statements after the code you just entered:

```
SqlCommand dataCommand = new SqlCommand();
dataCommand.Connection = dataConnection;
dataCommand.CommandText = "SELECT OrderID, OrderDate, " +
    "ShippedDate, ShipName, ShipAddress, ShipCity, " +
    "ShipCountry ";
dataCommand.CommandText += "FROM Orders WHERE CustomerID='" +
    customerId + "'";
Console.WriteLine("About to execute: " + dataCommand.CommandText);
```

The first statement creates an *SqlCommand* object. Like *SqlConnection*, this is a specialized version of an ADO.NET class, *Command*, that has been designed for gaining access to SQL Server. A *Command* object is used to execute a command against a data source. In the case of a relational database, the text of the command is an SQL statement.

The second line of code sets the *Connection* property of the *SqlCommand* object to the database connection you opened in Step 1. The next two statements populate the *CommandText* property with an SQL *SELECT* statement that retrieves information from the Orders table for all orders that have a CustomerID that matches the value in the *customerId* variable (you could do this in a single statement, but it has been split over two lines to make it easier to read). The *Console.WriteLine* statement just repeats the command about to be executed to the screen.

The fastest way to get data from a SQL Server database is to use the *SqlDataReader* class. This class extracts rows from the database as fast as your network allows and deposits them in your application.

3   Add the following statement after the code you just entered:

```
SqlDataReader dataReader = dataCommand.ExecuteReader();
```

The next task is to iterate through all the orders (if there are any) and display them.

Fetch data and display orders

1   Add the *while* loop shown below after the statement that creates the *SqlDataReader* object:

```
while (dataReader.Read())
{
    // Code to display the current row
}
```

The *Read* method of the *SqlDataReader* class fetches the next row from the database. It returns *true* if another row was retrieved successfully; otherwise, it returns *false*, usually because there are no more rows. The *while* loop you have just entered keeps reading rows from the *dataReader* variable and finishes when there are no more rows.

2   Add the following statements to the body of the *while* loop you created in the previous step:

```
int orderId = dataReader.GetInt32(0);
DateTime orderDate = dataReader.GetDateTime(1);
DateTime shipDate = dataReader.GetDateTime(2);
string shipName = dataReader.GetString(3);
string shipAddress = dataReader.GetString(4);
string shipCity = dataReader.GetString(5);
string shipCountry = dataReader.GetString(6);
Console.WriteLine("Order {0}\nPlaced {1}\nShipped {2}\n" +
    "To Address {3}\n{4}\n{5}\n{6}\n\n", orderId, orderDate,
    shipDate, shipName, shipAddress, shipCity, shipCountry);
```

This process is how you read the data from an *SqlDataReader* object. An *SqlDataReader* object contains the most recent row retrieved from the database. You can use the *GetXXX* methods to extract the information from each column in the row—there is a *GetXXX* method for each common type of data. For example, to read an *int* value, you use the *GetInt32* method; to read a string, you use the *GetString* method; and you can probably guess how to read a *DateTime* value. The *GetXXX* methods take a parameter indicating which column to read: 0 is the first column, 1 is the second column, and so on. The previous code reads the various columns from the current Orders row, stores the values in a set of variables, and then prints out the values of these variables.

Firehose Cursors

One of the major drawbacks in a multi-user database application is locked data. Unfortunately, it is common to see applications retrieve rows from a database and keep those rows locked to prevent another user from changing the data while the application is using them. In some extreme circumstances, an application can even prevent other users from reading data that it has locked. If the application retrieves a large number of rows, it locks a large proportion of the table. If there are many users running the same application at the same time, they can end up waiting for each other to release locks and it all leads to a slow running and frustrating mess.

The *SqlDataReader* class has been designed to remove this drawback. It fetches rows one at a time and does not retain any locks on a row after it has been retrieved. It is wonderful for improving concurrency in your applications. The *SqlDataReader* class is sometimes referred to as a "firehose cursor." (The term *cursor* is an acronym that stands for "current set of rows.")

When you have finished using a database, it's good practice to release any resources you have been using.

Disconnect from the database

1   In the Code pane, add the following statements after the *while* loop:

```
dataReader.Close();
dataConnection.Close();
```

These statements close the *SqlDataReader* object and the connection to the database. You should always close an *SqlDataReader* when you have finished with it because you are not able to use the current *SqlConnection* object to run any more commands until you do. It is also considered good practice to do it even if all you are going to do next is close the *SqlConnection*.

2   Build the application and then, on the Debug menu, click Start Without Debugging to run the application.

By default, the Start Without Debugging command runs the application and then prompts you before it closes the Console window so that you get a chance to read the output. The Start command doesn't give you the same chance.

3   At the prompt, type the CustomerID **VINET**. The SQL *SELECT* statement appears, followed by the orders for this customer.

4   Run the application again, and then type **BONAP** when prompted for a CustomerID.

Some rows appear, but then an error message is displayed. The problem is that relational databases allow some columns to contain null values. A null value is a bit like a null variable in C#. It doesn't have a value and, if you try to use it, you get an error. Null values are used in databases to indicate that data in a column or in a row does not have a value. In the Orders table, the ShippedDate column can contain null if the order has not yet been shipped. You will correct this error in the final exercise.

Closing Connections

In many earlier applications, you might notice a tendency to open a connection when the application starts and not close the connection until the application terminates. The rationale behind this strategy was that opening and closing database connections was an expensive and time-consuming operation. This strategy had an impact on the scalability of applications because each user running the application had a connection to the database open while the application was running, even if the user went to lunch for a couple of hours. Most databases have a limit on the number of concurrent connections that they allow. (Sometimes this is because of licensing reasons, but more often it's because each connection consumes a certain amount of resources on the database server and these resources are not infinite.) Eventually the database would hit a limit on the number of users that could operate concurrently.

Most modern OLE DB providers (including the SQL Server provider) implement *connection pooling*. Database connections are created and held in a pool. When an application requires a connection, the OLE DB provider extracts the next available connection from the pool. When the application closes the connection, it is returned to the pool and made available for the next application that wants a connection. This means that opening and closing a database connection is no longer an expensive operation. Closing a connection does not disconnect from the database; it just returns the connection to the pool. Opening a connection is simply a matter of obtaining an already open connection from the pool. Therefore, you should not hold on to connections longer than you need to—open a connection when you need it and close it as soon as you have finished with it.

You should note that the *ExecuteReader* method of the *SqlCommand* class, which creates an *SqlDataReader*, is overloaded. You can specify a *CommandBehavior* parameter that closes the connection used by the *SqlDataReader* automatically when the *SqlDataReader* is closed. For example:

```
SqlDataReader dataReader =
    dataCommand.ExecuteReader(CommandBehavior.CloseConnection);
```

When you read the data from the *SqlDataReader* object, you should check that the data you are reading is not null.

Handle null database values

1 In the Code And Text Editor window, locate the *while* loop that iterates through the rows retrieved by using the *dataReader* variable. Change the body of the *while* loop as shown here:

```
while (dataReader.Read())
{
    int orderId = dataReader.GetInt32(0);
    if (dataReader.IsDBNull(2))
    {
        Console.WriteLine("Order {0} not yet shipped\n\n", orderId);
    }
    else
    {
        DateTime orderDate = dataReader.GetDateTime(1);
        DateTime shipDate = dataReader.GetDateTime(2);
        string shipName = dataReader.GetString(3);
        string shipAddress = dataReader.GetString(4);
        string shipCity = dataReader.GetString(5);
        string shipCountry = dataReader.GetString(6);
        Console.WriteLine("Order {0}\nPlaced {1}\nShipped{2}\n" +
            "To Address {3}\n{4}\n{5}\n{6}\n\n", orderId, orderDate,
            shipDate, shipName, shipAddress, shipCity, shipCountry);
    }
}
```

The *if* statement uses the *IsDBNull* method to determine whether the OrderDate column is null. If it is null, no attempt is made to fetch it (or any of the other columns, which should also be null if there is no OrderDate value); otherwise the columns are read and printed as before.

2   Compile and run the application again. Type **BONAP** for the CustomerID when prompted. This time you do not get any errors, but you receive a list of orders that have not yet been shipped.

If you want to continue to the next chapter

■   Keep Visual Studio .NET running and turn to Chapter 25.

If you want to quit Visual Studio .NET for now

■   On the File menu, click Exit. If you see a Save dialog box, click Yes.

Chapter 24 Quick Reference

To	Do this
Create a connection to a database graphically in Visual Studio .NET	Use a Database Project. The Data Link Wizard prompts you for the details of the connection to create.
Browse data in Visual Studio .NET	Use the Server Explorer. Select the connection to use, and then expand the Tables folder. Right-click the table you want to browse and then click Retrieve Data From Table.
Use a database connection in a Visual Studio .NET Windows Forms application	Use the Server Explorer. Drag the table that you want to use onto the form. An *SqlConnection* object and an *SqlDataAdapter* object are added to the form.
Generate a *DataSet* that you can use for retrieving data from an *SqlDataAdapter*	In the Design View of the Code pane, select the *SqlDataAdapter* object. In the Properties window, click the Generate Dataset hyperlink below the properties. In the Generate Dataset dialog box, click OK.
Display data in a *DataSet* by using a *DataGrid*	Use the *DataGrid* control. Set its *DataSource* property to the *DataSet* to be used. Populate the *DataSet* by using the *Fill* method of the *SqlDataAdapter*. For example: `SqlDataAdapter1.Fill(dataSet11);`
Save changes made to data in a *DataSet*	Write a *GetChanges* method to create a new *DataSet* containing only the modified data. Make sure that there are actually changes to be made to the database. Call the *Update* method of an *SqlDataAdapter* object passing the *DataSet* as the parameter. If successful, call *AcceptChanges* to commit the changes in the *DataSet*; otherwise, call *RejectChanges* to undo the changes in the *DataSet*.

To	Do this
Programmatically connect to a database	Create an *SqlConnection* object, set its *ConnectionString* property with details specifying the database to use, and call the *Open* method.
Create and execute a database query in code	Create an *SqlCommand* object. Set its *Connection* property to a valid *SqlConnection* object. Set its *CommandText* property to a valid SQL *SELECT* statement. Call the *ExecuteReader* method to run the query and create an *SqlDataReader* object.
Fetch data using an *SqlDataReader* object	Make sure the data is not null by using the *IsDBNull* method. If the data is not null, use the appropriate *GetXXX* method (such as *GetString* or *GetInt32*) to retrieve the data.

Chapter

25

Working with Data Binding and *DataSets*

In this chapter, you will learn how to:

■ Bind a property of a control to a data source at design time or run time by using simple binding.

■ Bind a control to a list of values from a data source by using complex binding.

■ Create and use disconnected *DataSets* to retrieve data and reduce the load on your database.

■ Validate the changes the user has made to the data in a disconnected *DataSet* and update a database with the changed values.

In Chapter 24, you learned the essentials of using Microsoft ADO.NET for executing queries and updating databases. You used a *DataSet* generated by Microsoft Visual Studio .NET to retrieve data from the Products table and display it in a *DataGrid* control. You then updated the database by using SQL commands executed by an *SqlDataAdapter* object. You also learned how to use ADO.NET programmatically by writing code to create an *SqlConnection* object to connect to the database, execute a query using an *SqlCommand* object, and retrieve data by using an *SqlDataReader* object.

In this chapter, you'll learn more about data binding—linking a control property and a data source. The *DataGrid* control introduced in Chapter 24 is an example of a data-bound control. You will learn how to dynamically bind properties of controls to a *DataSet* by using simple data binding. You will also learn how to use complex data binding with the *ComboBox* control. You will then learn how to use *DataSet*s in an efficient manner, by disconnecting them from the database after you have fetched the data you need and then reconnecting them to update the database after you have made changes.

Windows Forms Controls and Data Binding

Many properties of most Windows Forms controls can be attached, or bound, to a data source. After they are bound, the value in the data source changes the value of the bound property and vice versa. You have already seen data binding in action by using a *DataGrid* in the DisplayProducts project in Chapter 24. The *DataGrid* on the form was bound to a *DataSet* containing records from the Products table in the database. You achieved this by setting the *DataSource* property of the *DataGrid*.

At run time, when you changed the value of any column in any row in the *Data-Grid*, the data in the *DataSet* was updated. Later on, these changes were propagated back to the database.

Windows Forms controls support two types of data binding: simple and complex. *Simple data binding* allows you to attach a property of a control or form to a single value in a data source, and *complex data binding* is specifically used to attach a control to a list of values.

Using Simple Data Binding

You use simple data binding to utilize a value from a data source. A data source can be almost anything, from a column in a row in a *DataSet* to the value of a property of another control to a simple variable. You can perform simple data binding at design time using the *DataBindings* property of a control, but for maximum flexibility, you can perform simple data binding dynamically at run time. In the exercises that follow, you will build an application that demonstrates two different ways of using simple data binding: you will bind data to the *Text* property of a *TextBox* control and to a column in a *DataSet* (the application is not intended to be pretty!).

▶ **Note**   The Standard version of Visual C# .NET 2003 does not work with SQL Server 2000. If you've installed the Standard version of Visual C# .NET 2003, please install the Microsoft SQL Server 2000 Desktop Engine and create the Microsoft SQL Server 2000 Desktop Engine version of the Northwind Traders database as described in Chapter 24.

Bind to the *Text* property of a *TextBox* control

1   In Visual Studio .NET, create a new project called DataBindingDemo in the \Microsoft Press\Visual C# Step by Step\Chapter 25 folder in your My Documents folder using the Windows Application template.

2   In the Toolbox, drag the *Button* control onto the form. Set its *Location* property to 16, 16.

3   In the Toolbox, drag a *TextBox* control onto the form. Set its *Location* property to 112, 16, which is to the right of the button.

4   Switch to the Code And Text Editor window displaying Form1.cs, and then locate the *Form1* constructor. After the call to the *Initialize-Component* method, add the following statement (be sure not to put quotes around *textBox1*):

```
button1.DataBindings.Add("Text", textBox1, "Text");
```

Every control that you can drag onto a form has a *DataBindings* collection. This collection lets you associate a property of the control with a value. If the value changes, the property is updated automatically, and if the property changes, the bound value is likewise updated automatically. The line of code you have just added binds the *Text* property (the first parameter of the *Add* method) of the button to the *Text* property (the third parameter) of the *textBox1* control (the second parameter).

▶ **Tip**   The data source referenced by the second parameter of the *DataBindings.Add* method can be one of a variety of different types. The .NET Framework SDK documentation mentions that *Add* expects an *Object* as the second parameter. This arrangement means that you can supply any type of object and the code will compile correctly, but the code might not run unless the specified object is capable of acting as a data source.

5   Return to Design View and double-click the *button1* control. This action displays the default event handler for the control (and creates it if necessary). In the case of a *Button* control, the default event is the *Click* event. Visual Studio .NET creates a method called *button1_Click* and displays it in Code View.

6   Add the following statement to the *button1_Click* method:

```
button1.Text = "Hello";
```

This statement changes the caption that appears on the button.

7   Build and run the application. When the form first appears, the caption of the button is set to *textBox1*, which is the same as the text in the *textBox1* control. Click the *TextBox* control (displaying textBox1) and type **Goodbye**. As you type, the caption on the button changes. The simple data binding updates the bound property of the button.

8   Click the button. The caption changes to "Hello." Click the text box. The contents change to "Hello" as well. The data binding causes any changes you make to the bound property to be propagated back to the original data source.

9   Close the form and return to the Visual Studio .NET programming environment.

Bind to a column in a *DataSet*

In this exercise, you will bind to a value retrieved from the database using a *DataSet*. You will use the Visual Designer rather than writing code to perform the simple data binding.

1   In Visual Studio .NET, display *Form1* in the Design View window. On the View menu, click Server Explorer to display the Server Explorer. The data connection (machinename\VSdotNET2003 .Northwind.dbo, where machinename is the name of your Microsoft SQL Server computer) you created in Chapter 24 appears. Expand the data connection, and then expand the Tables folder. Click and drag the Orders table onto the form.

An *SqlConnection* object called *sqlConnection1* and an *SqlData-Adapter* object called *sqlDataAdapter1* appear below the form.

2   Click *sqlDataAdapter1*. In the Properties window (make sure it is displaying properties rather than events), expand the *Select-Command* property. You should recall that this contains the SQL *SELECT* statement that is executed to retrieve data from the database. Click the *CommandText* property, and then click the Ellipses button. The Query Builder window appears.

3   In the SQL pane, replace the *SELECT* statement with the following code:

```
SELECT COUNT(*) AS NumOrders
FROM Orders
```

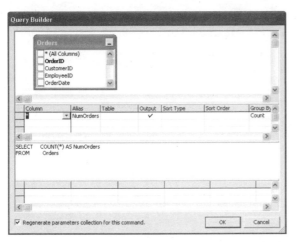

This query returns the number of rows in the Orders table and names the expression NumOrders.

▶ **Important** Simple data binding binds only a single value to a property of a control. The original SQL *SELECT* statement would have returned all the columns for every row in the Orders table (probably more than one value), and only the first value (the OrderID of the first row) could actually be used for simple binding. It is far more common to use simple binding for SQL *SELECT* statements that return a single value, such as a count of the number of rows in a table.

4 Click the OK button in the Query Builder window to save the changes you made.

5 With the *sqlDataAdapter1* object still selected, click the Generate Dataset hyperlink at the bottom of the Properties window. When the Generate Dataset dialog box opens, click OK to create the new *DataSet*. The new *DataSet* object called *dataSet11* appears under the form.

6 In the Toolbox, drag a *Label* control onto the form below *button1*, and then set its *Location* property to 16, 72.

7 While the *Label* control is still selected, go to the Properties window and expand the *(DataBindings)* property. Select the *(Advanced)* property, and then click the Ellipses button. The Advanced Data Binding dialog box opens. You can use this dialog box to perform simple data binding to most of the properties of the control.

8 Scroll down to the *Text* property and click the drop-down arrow. A list of available data sources appears: DataSet11 and None. Expand the DataSet11 folder by clicking the plus sign (+). The Orders table appears. Expand the Orders table and the NumOrders expression appears. Click NumOrders and click Close to save the changes.

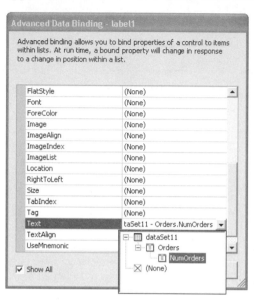

9   Switch to the Code And Text Editor window, and return to the constructor for the *Form1* class. Under the statement you added in the previous exercise (setting the *DataBindings* property for the *button1* control), type the following statements:

```
sqlConnection1.Open();
sqlDataAdapter1.Fill(dataSet11);
```

These two statements open the connection to the database and populate the *DataSet* by running the SQL statement defined by the *SelectCommand* property of *sqlDataAdapter1*. You edited this SQL statement to return a count of the number of rows in the Orders table.

10 Compile and run the application again. The *Label* control displays the number of rows in the Orders table (probably 830 if you have not changed any of the data since the database was created).

11 Close the form, and return to the Visual Studio .NET programming environment.

Using Complex Data Binding

You have seen how to use simple data binding for attaching the property of a control to a single value in a data source. Complex data binding is useful if you want to display a list of values from a data source. In the following exercises, you will use complex data binding to display the names of products in a list box and then retrieve the ProductID of a product that the user selects.

▶ **Tip** The *ComboBox* and *CheckedListBox* controls also support complex data binding using the same techniques that you will see in these exercises.

Create the form

1 In Visual Studio .NET, create a new project called ComplexBinding-Demo in the \Microsoft Press\Visual C# Step by Step\Chapter 25 folder in your My Documents folder using the Windows Application template.

2 Display the Server Explorer (on the View menu, click Server Explorer). The data connection you used in the previous exercise will still be visible.

3 In the Server Explorer, drag the Products table in the Tables folder onto the form. As before, an *SqlConnection* object called *sqlConnection1* and an *SqlDataAdapter* object called *sqlDataAdapter1* appear below the form.

4 In the Toolbox, drag a *TextBox* control onto the form, and then set its *Location* property to 16, 32. Clear its *Text* property.

5 In the Toolbox, drag a *ListBox* control onto the form and set its *Location* property to 16, 72. Set its *Size* property to 256, 186.

Create and configure a data source

This application will only query the database. You will create a data source that retrieves only the columns needed (ProductName and ProductID) and does not generate Data Manipulation Language (DML) statements to modify the database.

1 Select the *sqlDataAdapter1* object displayed under the form. Click the Configure Data Adapter hyperlink at the bottom of the Properties window. The Data Adapter Configuration Wizard opens.

2 On the wizard, click Next. The Choose Your Data Connection page appears. Use the default connection (which should be the same as the one that was created when you dragged the Products table onto the form), and then click Next. The Choose A Query Type page appears.

3 Make sure that the Use SQL Statements option is selected and then click Next. The Generate the SQL Statements page appears. Change the *SELECT* statement to this:

```
SELECT ProductID, ProductName
FROM Products
```

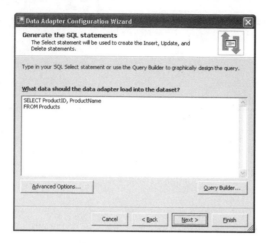

▶   **Tip**   If you want to use a more complex *SELECT* statement and cannot remember SQL syntax, click the Query Builder button to create the query graphically.

4   When you're finished, click Advanced Options. The Advanced SQL Generation Options dialog box appears.

In the wizard, clear the Generate Insert, Update, And Delete Statements option. The other options, which relate to the mechanisms used by a *DataAdapter* for identifying the rows to be updated and deleted in the database, and for re-querying after performing an Insert, are disabled. Click OK to return to the Generate The SQL Statements page.

5   In the wizard, click Next.

6   The View Wizard Results page is displayed, informing you that *sqlDataAdapter1* was successfully configured. If you do not get this result, use the Back button to go back through the wizard and correct any errors—you might have mistyped the *SELECT* statement!

7   Click Finish to close the wizard.

▶   **Tip**   If you look at the properties for *sqlDataAdapter1*, notice that the *Insert-Command*, *DeleteCommand*, and *UpdateCommand* properties are now null (displayed as (none) in the Properties window). You should also recognize text in the *CommandText* property of the *SelectCommand* property. If you prefer, you can edit these properties directly rather than using the wizard.

8   While *sqlDataAdapter1* is still selected, click the Generate Dataset hyperlink at the bottom of the Properties window. When the Generate Dataset dialog box opens, accept the default values and then click OK. The *DataSet* is generated and a new object, *dataSet11*, appears under the Form1 window in Design View.

Bind the *ListBox* to the *DataSet*

1   In Design View, click *listBox1*. In the Properties window, click the *DataSource* property and select *DataSet11.Products* from the drop-down list.

2   Click the *DisplayMember* property and select ProductName from the drop-down list. This is the data that will be displayed in the list box.

3   Click the *ValueMember* property and select ProductID from the drop-down list. When the user selects an item in the list box, this is the value that is associated with the item.

4   In the Properties window, click Events. Click the *SelectedIndex-Changed* event, type **itemSelected**, and press Enter. The *itemSelected* method appears in the Code And Text Editor window. Add the following code to the *itemSelected* method:

```
textBox1.Text = listBox1.SelectedValue.ToString();
```

The *SelectedValue* property returns the *ValueMember* of the currently selected row—this is the ProductID of the row that the user selects. It is returned as an object, so you must use *ToString* if you want to treat it as a string.

5   In the *Form1* constructor, after the call to the *InitializeComponent* method, type the following statements to open the connection to the database and populate the *DataSet*:

```
sqlConnection1.Open();
sqlDataAdapter1.Fill(dataSet11);
```

6   Compile and run the application. On the form, the first row in the list box is selected by default and the ProductID is displayed in the text box. As you select different ProductName items in the list box, the corresponding ProductID appears in the text box.

7 When you have finished, close the form and return to the Visual Studio .NET programming environment.

Disconnected *DataSets*

Databases are intended to support multiple concurrent users but, as you have already seen, resources such as the number of concurrent connections allowed might be limited. In an application that fetches and displays data, you never know quite how long the user will be browsing the data, and it is not a good practice to keep a database connection open for an extended period of time. Instead, a better approach is to connect to the database, fetch the data into a *DataSet* object, and then disconnect again. The user can browse the data in the *DataSet* and make any changes required. After the user finishes, the program can reconnect to the database and submit any changes. Of course, there are complications that you need to consider—such as what happens if two users have queried the same data and both users update the same data, changing it to different values. In the following set of exercises, you will see how to handle these situations.

Creating a Disconnected *DataSet*

You are going to create an application that can manage sales territories in the Northwind database (Northwind Traders groups their sales by territory for analysis purposes). Territory information is held in the Territories table.

Examine the Territories table

1 In the Server Explorer, select the Territories table in the data connection you have been using for the previous exercises. Right-click the Territories table, and on the pop-up menu, click Retrieve Data From Table. You are presented with a list of territories.

2 Examine the data. Notice that the table has columns called TerritoryID, TerritoryDescription, and RegionID. (If you look at the data in the Region table, you will see that there are four regions called Northern, Southern, Eastern, and Western.) When you have finished browsing the Territories table, close the window.

Create the application

1   Create a new project called ManageTerritories in the \Microsoft Press\Visual C# Step by Step\Chapter 25 folder in your My Documents folder using the Windows Application template. Form 1.cs appears in the Design View window.

2   In the Solution Explorer, change Form1.cs to TerritoriesForm.cs. In the Properties window, change the *(Name)* property of *Form1* to TerritoriesForm. Set the *Text* property to Manage Territories, and change its *Size* property to 304, 408. In the Code And Text Editor window, locate the *Main* method and change the *Application.Run* statement:

```
Application.Run (new TerritoriesForm());
```

3   Switch back to the Design View window. In the Toolbox, drag a *DataGrid* control onto the form. Rename the *DataGrid* control as *territoriesGrid*. Set its *Location* property to 8, 8 and its *Size* property to 280, 328.

4   Add two *Button* controls to the form below *territoriesGrid* and set their *Location* properties to 48, 344 and 176, 344. Rename them as *queryButton* and *saveButton*. Change the *Text* property of each button to Query and Save, respectively.

Create and bind to the *DataSet*

1   In the Server Explorer, select the Territories table in your data connection and drag it onto the form. After *sqlConnection1* and *sqlDataAdapter1* have been created, rename them *territoriesConnection* and *territoriesAdapter*.

2   Select *territoriesAdapter*. In the Properties window, expand the *SelectCommand* property, and verify that the *CommandText* property is the following:

```
SELECT TerritoryID, TerritoryDescription, RegionID
FROM Territories
```

▶   **Tip**   If the *CommandText* property is different, you probably dragged the wrong table onto the form (an easy mistake to make). Delete the *territoriesConnection* and *territoriesAdapter* objects, and use the Server Explorer to drag the correct table onto the form.

3   With *territoriesAdapter* still selected, click the Generate Dataset hyperlink at the bottom of the Properties window. When the Generate Dataset dialog box opens, type **territoriesDataset** in the New text box (the default is DataSet1), and click OK to generate the default *DataSet*.

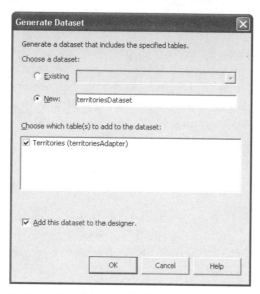

A *DataSet* object called *territoriesDataset1* is added at the bottom of the form.

4   In Design View, select the *territoriesGrid* control. In the Properties window, set the *DataSource* property of *territoriesGrid* to *territoriesDataset1.Territories*. The TerritoryID, TerritoryDesc, and RegionID columns appear in the grid.

Typed *DataSets*

When you use the Generate Dataset dialog box to create a new *DataSet*, you are actually creating a new type. If you look in the ManageTerritories folder on your disk using Windows Explorer, you will see a file called territoriesDataSet.cs. This file contains a class called *territoriesDataset* that descends from *System.Data .DataSet*. It is a specialized subclass, designed to handle data for a specific table—the Territories table, in this case. It contains properties that are peculiar to the Territories table, for example, the *TerritoryIDColumn* property to retrieve the value of the TerritoryID, and the *RegionIDColumn* property to retrieve the value of the RegionID. Similarly, it contains events such as *Territories-*

RowChanged and *TerritoriesRowDeleted*, and methods such as *AddTerritories-Row* and *FindByTerritoryID*.

The general idea is that this is a self-contained *DataSet* that a programmer can use for accessing Territories data. The names of the methods, properties, and events appear automatically in the IntelliSense feature of Visual Studio .NET, and the strong type-checking features of the .NET run time prevents a developer from trying to use this *DataSet* for the wrong data (for example, you could not accidentally use it to try and query the Products table).

Retrieve the data and disconnect

1 In the Design View window, select the Query button. In the Properties window, click Events. Create a *Click* event handler called *queryClick*.

2 In the Code And Text Editor window, add the following code to the *queryClick* method:

```
try
{
    territoriesConnection.Open();
    territoriesAdapter.Fill(territoriesDataset1);
    territoriesConnection.Close();
}
catch (Exception ex)
{
    MessageBox.Show("Error retrieving data: " + ex.Message,
        "Error", MessageBoxButtons.OK, MessageBoxIcon.Error);
}
```

This code is very similar to the statements you have been using previously. It connects to the database and then uses the *Fill* method of the *SqlDataAdapter* object to populate the *DataSet*. It differs in that it closes the connection to the database after the data has been retrieved. The data is buffered in memory in the *DataSet* instead.

The other difference between this code and the code used previously is that you have used a *try/catch* block to trap any exceptions raised—you never know, something might have happened to the database making it impossible to query the table.

3 Build and run the program. When the form first appears, it initially displays a single row of null values in the *DataGrid*.

4 On the form, click Query to retrieve all the rows from the Territories table and display them. Remember that although you can modify

data that is displayed in the grid, you have not written the code for the Save button yet, so your changes are not saved.

5   Close the form and return to the Visual Studio .NET programming environment.

Handling Updates with a Disconnected *DataSet*

Saving changes made to the data in the *DataGrid* involves reconnecting to the database, performing any required *INSERT*, *UPDATE*, and *DELETE* statements, and then disconnecting from the database. You must also be prepared to handle any errors that might occur.

Validate the changes

1   In the Design View window, select the Save button. In the Properties window, click Events. Create a *Click* event handler called *saveClick*.

2   In the Code And Text Editor window, add the following *try/catch* block to the *saveClick* method:

```
try
{
    DataSet changes = territoriesDataset1.GetChanges();
    if (changes == null)
    {
        return;
    }

    // Check for errors

    // If no errors then update the database, otherwise tell the user
}
catch(Exception ex)
{
    MessageBox.Show("Error: " + ex.Message, "Errors",
        MessageBoxButtons.OK, MessageBoxIcon.Error);
    territoriesDataset1.RejectChanges();
    territoriesConnection.Close();
}
```

This block of code uses the *GetChanges* method of the *DataSet* to create a new *DataSet* that contains only the rows that have changed. Although this code is not strictly necessary, it makes performing the updates to the database (which you will do shortly) quicker because the update routines do not have to calculate which rows have changed and which ones haven't. If there are no changes (the *DataSet* is null), the method finishes; otherwise the method checks for errors in the data and updates the database. If an exception occurs while doing the updates, the application displays a message to the user, cancels the changes in the *DataSet* using the *RejectChanges* method, and closes the connection to the database. (You do not need to check the connection state because it is safe to close an already closed connection.)

▶ **Tip** You can examine the current state of an *SqlConnection* object to determine whether it is currently connected to the database by querying its *State* property. The *State* property uses the *ConnectionState* enumeration and can be *Broken*, *Closed*, *Connecting*, *Executing*, *Fetching*, or *Open*. For example:

```
if (territoriesConnection.State == ConnectionState.Open)
{
    // Connection is open
}
```

Before updating the database, you should make sure that the data is valid. After all, you don't want to waste a round-trip over the network to the database and all those database resources if the operation is going to fail.

The *SqlDataAdapter* class has a *FillError* event that you can also use to trap errors that occur when the *Fill* method runs. The *FillError* event delegate takes a *FillErrorEventArgs* parameter that has properties that allow you to determine the cause of the event. It also has a *Continue* property that you can set to true if you decide that the error is not serious enough to cancel the *Fill* method.

Retrieving Large *DataSets*

Retrieving all the data from a table is fine for small *DataSets* (such as 100 or 200 rows) but is not recommended for larger *DataSets*. The likelihood of a user really wanting to examine more than 200 rows at a time is quite small (no matter what users say), and retrieving a large volume of data that is not going to be used wastes the bandwidth of your network.

Fortunately, the *Fill* method used by the *SqlDataAdapter* class is overloaded, and one version allows you to limit the number of rows retrieved. You can also specify a starting point indicating from which row the *Fill* method should start. The following statement fetches 200 rows starting with row 400 in the database:

```
int numRows = myAdapter.Fill(myDataSet, 400, 200, "MyTable");
```

The final parameter, *MyTable*, indicates which table in the *DataSet* you want to populate—you must specify this even if there is only one table. By using this version of the *Fill* method, you can retrieve data from the database in chunks that are more manageable.

Handle the errors

1 In the Code And Text Editor window, locate the // *Check for errors* comment in the *saveClick* method and replace it with the following code:

```
DataTable dt = changes.Tables[0];
DataRow [] badRows = dt.GetErrors();
```

The first statement extracts the first table in the changed *DataSet*. (A *DataSet* can contain several tables; it just so happens that the *DataSets* you have been using contain only one table.) The *GetErrors* method of a *DataTable* object returns an array of all the rows in the table that have one or more validation errors. If there are no errors, *GetErrors* returns an empty array.

2 Locate the // *If no errors then update the database, otherwise tell the user* comment and replace it with the following code block:

```
if (badRows.Length == 0)
{
    // Update the database
}
else
{
    // Find the errors and inform the user
}
```

There are several strategies you can use for reporting errors to the user. One useful technique is to find all the errors and report them in a single (but possibly long) message.

3 Replace the // *Find the errors and inform the user* comment in the *saveClick* method with the following statements:

```
string errorMsg = null;
foreach (DataRow row in badRows)
{
    foreach (DataColumn col in row.GetColumnsInError())
    {
        errorMsg += row.GetColumnError(col) + "\n";
    }
}
MessageBox.Show("Errors in data: " + errorMsg,
    "Please fix", MessageBoxButtons.OK,
    MessageBoxIcon.Error);
```

This code iterates through all the rows in the *badRows* array. Each row may have one or more errors, and the *GetColumnsInError* method returns a collection containing all the columns with bad data. The *GetColumnError* method retrieves the error message for an individual column. Each error message is appended to the *errorMsg* string. When all the bad rows and columns have been examined, the application displays a message box showing all the errors. The user should be able to use this information to correct the changes and then resubmit them.

Integrity Rules and *DataSets*

In this example, which uses a simple, single table *DataSet*, you are unlikely to get any validation errors reported by *GetErrors*. When the *territoriesDataset* class was generated, it also included information about primary key columns, data types for each column, integrity rules, and so on. This information was retrieved from the adapter class when the *territoriesDataset* class was created (the adapter in turn obtained this information from the database). When the user makes any changes, or adds rows, integrity checks are performed, and, if there is any attempted data violation (for example, the user tries to give two rows the same primary key value), the *DataSet* itself displays a message to the user.

There might be times when a *DataSet* cannot perform all the required validation rules until the user submits the changes. For example, if the *DataSet* comprises several tables that have a foreign key/primary key relationship, it would be annoying if the user was forced to input data in a particular sequence. This situation is when the *GetErrors* method comes into its own—the method assumes that the user has finished entering data so that it can perform any complex cross-checking and trap any errors.

Having said all of this, you never know when the user is going to enter something so unusual that you haven't even contemplated it. It is good practice, therefore, to write defensive code. Put in your own explicit checks as well as use those built into the generated *DataSet* class.

Update the database

1   Once you are certain that the data seems to be correct, you can send it to the database. Locate the *// Update the database* comment in the *saveClick* method and replace it with the following statements:

```
territoriesConnection.Open();
int numRows = territoriesAdapter.Update(changes);
territoriesConnection.Close();
```

```
MessageBox.Show("Updated " + numRows + " rows", "Success");
territoriesDataset1.AcceptChanges();
```

This code reopens the connection to the database and posts the changes using the *Update* method of the *territoriesAdapter* object. When the changes have been completed, the connection is closed, the user is told how many rows were affected, and the *AcceptChanges* method marks the changes as permanent in the *DataSet*. Notice that this code is all encapsulated within a *try/catch* block to handle any errors.

2   Build and run the program. When the Manage Territories form appears, click Query to fetch and display all the territories. Change the values in the TerritoryDescription column of the first two territories, and then click Save. The changes are made to the database and a message tells you that two rows were updated.

3   Close the form and run the application again. Click Query. The new descriptions for the first two rows appear, proving that the data was saved to the database.

4   Close the form and return to the Visual Studio .NET programming environment.

DataSet Update Events

When you run the *Update* method of an *SqlDataAdapter*, there is a whole new set of errors that can occur—another user might have already deleted a row you want to update or inserted a row containing a primary key that you have also used. As before, you should write your code defensively and be prepared to handle almost any type of error.

To help you, the *SqlDataAdapter* class contains two events called *RowUpdating* and *RowUpdated*. The *RowUpdating* event occurs as the change is about to be made in the database. The delegate for this event takes an *SqlRowUpdatingEventArgs* parameter, which contains properties that allow you to examine the SQL command about to be executed, the DataRow being used as the source of the update, and a *Status* property that you can modify to prevent the update from occurring. You can set the *Status* property to one of the following values: *Continue* (the *SqlDataAdapter* continues processing rows), *ErrorsOccurred* (the *Update* operation stops and raises an exception), *SkipAllRemainingRows* (no more rows are processed but it does not raise an exception), and *SkipCurrentRow* (the current row is ignored and processing continues with the next row).

The *RowUpdated* event is very similar, except that it occurs after the update has been performed in the database. It uses an *SqlRowUpdatedEventArgs* parameter (which is very similar to *SqlRowUpdatingEventArgs*), and you can examine its *Status* property to ascertain whether the update was successful. The *Errors* property gives you access to any error that occurred during the update.

If you want to continue to the next chapter

■ Keep Visual Studio .NET running and turn to Chapter 26.

If you want to quit Visual Studio .NET for now

■ On the File menu, click Exit. If you see a Save dialog box, click Yes.

Chapter 25 Quick Reference

To	Do this
Use simple binding to bind a property of a control to a data source at design time	Expand the *DataBindings* property of the control. Click Advanced, and then in the Advanced Data Binding dialog box, specify the property and the data source.
Use simple binding to bind a property of a control to a data source at run time	Use the *Add* method of the *DataBindings* property. Specify the property to bind to and the data source. For example, to bind the *Text* property of the *Button* control named *button1* to the *Text* property of the *textBox1* control, use the following code: ``` Button1.DataBindings.Add("Text", textBox1, "Text"); ```
Use complex binding to bind a control to a list of values from a data source	Set the *DataSource* property of the control. Specify the data to be displayed using the *DisplayMember* property, and then specify the data to be used as the value of the control by using the *ValueMember* property.
Modify the properties of an *SqlDataAdapter* object	Select the *SqlDataAdapter* object and click the Configure Data Adapter hyperlink at the bottom of the Properties window. Use the Data Adapter Configuration Wizard to change the *SELECT* statement used to retrieve data and to indicate whether the *SqlDataAdapter* object can be used for modifying the database.

To	Do this

Create a disconnected *DataSet*	Open the connection to the database, populate the *DataSet* using the *Fill* method of an *SqlDataAdapter*, and then close the database connection. For example:
	
	``
	myConnection.Open();
	myAdapter.Fill(myDataSet);
	myConnection.Close();
	``

Validate the changes the user has made to the data in a disconnected *DataSet*	For each *DataTable* in the *DataSet*, call the *GetErrors* method to find all of the rows containing errors. For each row found, use the *GetColumnsInError* method to iterate through all the columns that contain errors, and for each column, call the *GetColumnError* method to obtain the details of the error for that column.
Update the database with the information in a disconnected *DataSet*	Reconnect to the database. Run the *Update* method of the *SqlDataAdapter* object passing the *DataSet* as the parameter. When the Update method has completed, close the *SqlConnection* object. If the updates were successful, call *AcceptChanges* on the *DataSet*; otherwise call *RejectChanges*.

Handling XML

In this chapter, you will learn how to:

■ Create and write an XML document.

■ Read an XML document and process XML data.

■ Use an XML schema to validate an XML document.

XML is becoming increasingly important as the standard format for data inter-change. In this chapter, you'll learn how to use the XML classes of the Microsoft .NET Framework to read, write, and manipulate XML documents.

Why XML?

XML, or Extensible Markup Language, is a language used for describing data. The aim of XML is to provide a standard format that different applications running on different hardware can read, process, and write. Having read that last sentence, you might be getting a feeling of déjà vu. After all, aren't these also the problems that SQL was designed to address? The answer is both yes and no.

The purpose of SQL is to provide an English-like programming language that allows you to query and maintain data in a relational database. SQL is parsed and executed by a database management system that actually manages the raw data. Many different database systems can use SQL, but internally they tend to define their own unique data structures for storing the data. This is what gives one database vendor a perceived advantage over another. The first vendor can claim that, as a result of some incredible set of algorithms, their system operates 10 times faster than any other system. What this means is that, if you have a database from vendor A, you cannot necessarily use vendor B's tools to access that data unless you use some bridging piece of middleware, such as an OLE DB driver. And you should also consider that not all data is held in relational databases—there are many other sources as well.

To complicate matters further, the types of distributed applications that you are building these days are very different from those that were prevalent in the mid-1980s, when the SQL standardization effort was in full swing. For one thing, you might want to transmit data over the Internet. The application at the other end could be anything from a simple HTML browser to a complex e-commerce system. Because of this type of complexity, it is widely recognized that a standard data format is not only useful but also essential for building modern, extensible, networked applications. This brings us to the World Wide Web Consortium.

The Goals of XML

In 1996, the World Wide Web Consortium (or W3C, as it is known) set about the task of devising a standard format for data. It had several goals.

One goal was that this format should be able to represent any form of structured data. This means that, in addition to specifying the data itself, XML should also indicate in a clear and unambiguous manner how the data is organized. Another goal was to ensure that the format was both portable and usable over the Internet. This was important because there could be any number of applications in different locations needing to process the data. Additionally, the format would make it as easy as possible for developers to write programs that consume and produce XML; after all, if it were too complex, no one would want to use it. W3C has published documents (called Recommendations) describing the structure and processing of XML documents. (For more information about W3C, go to *www.w3c.org*.)

The Structure of XML

To meet the requirements for portability and openness, XML uses plain text to represent data embedded in tags, which describe the structure of the data. For example, the data in the Shippers table (shippers ship orders to customers) in the Northwind SQL Server database can be depicted as shown in the following example:

```
<?xml version="1.0"?>
<Shippers>
  <Shipper>
    <ID>1</ID>
```

```
    <Name>Speedy Express</Name>
    <Phone>(503) 555-9831</Phone>
  </Shipper>
  <Shipper>
    <ID>2</ID>
    <Name>United Package</Name>
    <Phone>(503) 555-3199</Phone>
  </Shipper>
  <Shipper>
    <ID>3</ID>
    <Name>Federal Shipping</Name>
    <Phone>(503) 555-9931</Phone>
  </Shipper>
</Shippers>
```

The XML tags are the elements embedded between angle brackets (<, >). The first element (<?xml version="1.0"?>) indicates the version of XML that this document conforms to. (You can ignore it for now.) The rest of the document contains the data.

A valid, well-formed XML document must conform to a number of criteria. There must be a single root element acting as a container for all the data. This root element is shown in the preceding code as the Shippers element, which contains all the individual shippers as nested subelements. For each "start" element (for example, <Shipper>), there must be a corresponding "end" element (</Shipper>) that indicates the end of the data for that item. Given this description, you can quite easily observe that this document contains the details of three shippers and you can see the ID, name, and phone number of each one.

▶ **Tip** Indentation and line breaks are not significant in XML, but you can use them to make the document easier to read.

XML Schemas

This is all very well, but there are other ways of structuring the Shippers data in XML. A second instance, using XML attributes rather than elements, is shown in the following example:

```
<?xml version="1.0"?>
<Shippers>
  <Shipper ID="1" Name="Speedy Express" Phone=" (503) 555-9831" />
  <Shipper ID="2" Name="United Package" Phone=" (503) 555-3199" />
  <Shipper ID="3" Name="Federal Shipping" Phone=" (503) 555-9931" />
</Shippers>
```

If application A sends Shippers data to application B, which format should it use and how will application B recognize the format? Application A should use an XML schema. A *schema* describes the structure of an XML document and can include additional information such as validation rules and checks. An XML schema can be used to validate the structure and the data in an XML document, as you will see later in this chapter.

The schema for the Shippers XML document would contain a rule that forbids negative values for the Shipper ID. The following schema is for the second version of the Shippers XML document:

```
<xs:schema id="Shippers " targetNamespace="
  http://tempuri.org/Shippers2.xsd"
  xmlns="http://tempuri.org/Shippers2.xsd"
  xmlns:xs="http://www.w3.org/2001/XMLSchema"
  xmlns:msdata="urn:schemas-microsoft-com:xml-msdata"
  attributeFormDefault="qualified"
  elementFormDefault="qualified">
    <xs:element name="Shippers" msdata:IsDataSet="true"
      msdata:EnforceConstraints="False">
      <xs:complexType>
        <xs:choice maxOccurs="unbounded ">
          <xs:element name="Shipper">
            <xs:complexType>
              <xs:attribute name="ID " form="unqualified"
              type="xs:integer" use="required" />
                <xs:attribute name="Name" form="unqualified"
                  type="xs:string" use="required" />
                <xs:attribute name="Phone" form="unqualified"
                  type="xs:string" use="required" />
            </xs:complexType>
          </xs:element>
        </xs:choice>
      </xs:complexType>
    </xs:element>
</xs:schema>
```

As long as the two applications agree on which schema to use, they should understand that any data passed between them should conform to this schema. Many organizations are developing standard schemas to describe common data requirements across various industries, enabling applications that are based on these schemas to interoperate freely (at least, that's the theory).

XML Schemas and DTDs

The original XML specifications included the use of document type definitions (DTD) for specifying the structure of an XML document. DTDs have their own grammar and are not designed to be used for specifying data integrity rules or for validating data. XML schemas are intended to be used as a replacement for DTDs. XML schemas use XML rather their own syntax. (There is actually an XML schema available that defines the structure of an XML schema.) Most modern implementations of the W3C recommendations, such as the .NET Framework, use XML schemas rather than DTDs.

XML as a Transport Format and Protocol

XML can also be used as a format for transmitting data over a network. An application that sends data, possibly a complex object, can convert the information into an XML document and transmit it. At the other end of the connection, the receiving application can read the XML and convert it back into a complex object. This act of converting to and from XML for transmission is known as serialization and is widely used throughout the .NET Framework when building distributed applications (for example, the data in a *DataSet* is transmitted as XML).

An extension of this idea is to convert procedure calls into XML documents using an agreed-upon schema and transmit them to a server process that can read the request, perform the appropriate service, and return any values (also as an XML document). This is the basic idea behind Simple Object Access Protocol (SOAP). SOAP is used to send requests and receive replies from Web services. You will learn more about SOAP and Web services in Chapter 31 and Chapter 32.

XML APIs and the .NET Framework

It was stated previously that a goal of W3C was to devise a format (XML) that is easy to program and use. Various APIs have been developed for handling XML; the two most common are the Document Object Model (DOM) and the Simple API for XML (SAX). The DOM is also the work of W3C (SAX is not); it has been through several iterations and is still being updated as technology and requirements evolve.

Microsoft has taken many of the programmatic features of the DOM and exposed them through the *XmlDocument* class in the *System.Xml* namespace in the .NET Framework class library. Microsoft has also added some extensions to the functionality of the implementation. In the rest of this chapter, you will learn how to create an XML schema and use the classes of the *System.Xml* namespace for creating and processing XML documents. This chapter only scratches the surface of performing XML processing in Microsoft Visual C#— there are many other classes and methods beyond those described in this chapter.

The Employee Timesheet System

To illustrate an example of producing and consuming an XML document, you will build part of a timesheet system used by employees for tracking their time spent on various projects. The Employee Timesheet System will consist of two applications. The first application will allow an employee to record the time spent on her activities during a working day. This application will write information to an XML file. The second application will read the XML file and print a summary of some of the key information. These applications will be kept simple so that you can focus on the XML aspects.

Creating an XML Schema

The first task is to define the XML schema that the applications will use. The information that you will store in the XML file will be the employee's ID and name, and for each activity the employee has performed, you will record an activity ID, an activity name or description, and the amount of time spent performing the activity.

Define the XML schema

1   In Microsoft Visual Studio .NET, create a new Windows application called RecordTimesheets in the \Microsoft Press\Visual C# Step By Step\Chapter 26 folder in your My Documents folder.

2   When the project has been created, on the Project menu, click Add New Item. In the Add New Item dialog box, select XML Schema in the Templates list, and then type **Timesheet.xsd** for the name. Click Open to create the new schema. A blank schema is added to your project and appears in the Design View window.

3   With Timesheet.xsd (which is currently empty) selected in the Design View window, click the XML button at the bottom of the window. The XML representation of the schema is displayed.

Click the Schema button to return to Design View.

4 Click the Toolbox. It contains an XML Schema tab that contains the items you can add to an XML schema.

5 The employee ID and the activity ID data will both be non-negative integers. In the Toolbox, drag a *simpleType* element onto the schema in the Design View window. An element called *simpleType1* is created.

6 Change the name of *simpleType1* to *IDType*. Click the type (displaying a string by default) and select NonNegativeInteger from the list of available types.

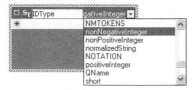

26

Handling XML

> ▶ **Tip**   You can also set these properties in the Properties window.

7   The actual timesheet data entered by each employee will be a list of records. Each record will contain the activity ID, the description of the activity, and the time spent on that activity. In the Toolbox, drag the *complexType* element onto the schema in the Design View window.

8   Change the name of the element to *TimesheetRecords*. Click next to the asterisk (*) in the row under the name. This creates a new attribute. Click the drop-down arrow that appears, and then select sequence. A group element called *group1* is added to the *TimesheetRecords* element.

9   Select the *group1* group element. Click the row under the name, and then select Element from the drop-down list.

10   Change the name of the new element from *Element1* to *ActivityID*. Change its type from *string* to *IDType*. Click the row under the *ActivityID* element and select Element from the drop-down list to create another element. Set the new element's name to *ActivityName* and its type to *string*. Add one more element called *ActivityDuration*. Set its type to *decimal*.

11   A daily timesheet for an employee will contain the employee ID, the employee name, and one or more *TimesheetRecords* structures (an employee will perform at least one activity in a day, and might perform several). In the Toolbox, drag another *complexType* element onto the schema in Design View. Change the name of the *complexType* element to *DailyTimesheetInfo*. Add three elements to the *DailyTimesheetInfo* structure: an *IDType* called *EmployeeID*, a string called *EmployeeName*, and a *TimesheetRecords* element called *TimesheetData*.

After you add the third element and set its type, a copy of the *TimesheetRecords* and *group1* structure appears and is linked to the *DailyTimesheetInfo* structure.

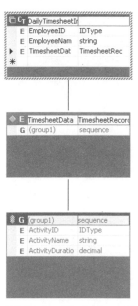

12 Click the *TimesheetData* element. In the Properties window, set its *minOccurs* property to 1 and type **unbounded** in the *maxOccurs* property.

You have now defined the data types needed for recording timesheet information. The next step is to define how the XML file will use these data types. In this example, the XML file will consist of a single element containing a *DailyTimesheetInfo* structure.

13 In the Toolbox, drag an *element* element onto the schema in the Design View window.

14 Change the name of the element from *Element1* to *Timesheet*. Change its type to *DailyTimesheetInfo*. The elements and the group that consists of a *DailyTimesheetInfo* structure appear automatically.

15 Click the XML button at the bottom of the Design View window. The following completed definition of the schema in XML format is displayed:

```
<?xml version="1.0" encoding="utf-8" ?>
<xs:schema id="Timesheet "
  targetNamespace="http://tempuri.org/Timesheet.xsd"
  elementFormDefault="qualified"
  xmlns="http://tempuri.org/Timesheet.xsd"
  xmlns:xs="http://www.w3.org/2001/XMLSchema">
    <xs:simpleType name="IDType">
      <xs:restriction base="xs:nonNegativeInteger" />
    </xs:simpleType>
    <xs:complexType name="TimesheetRecords">
```

```
            <xs:sequence>
              <xs:sequence>
                <xs:element name="ActivityID" type="IDType" />
                <xs:element name="ActivityName" type="xs:string" />
                <xs:element name="ActivityDuration"
                   type="xs:decimal" />
              </xs:sequence>
            </xs:sequence>
          </xs:complexType>
          <xs:complexType name="DailyTimesheetInfo">
            <xs:sequence>
              <xs:element name="EmployeeID" type="IDType" />
              <xs:element name="EmployeeName" type="xs:string" />
              <xs:element name="TimesheetData"
                 type="TimesheetRecords" minOccurs="1"
                 maxOccurs="unbounded" />
            </xs:sequence>
          </xs:complexType>
          <xs:element name="Timesheet" type="DailyTimesheetInfo">
        </xs:element>
      </xs:schema>
```

16 On the File menu, click the Save All command to save the schema
and other project files.

One way to test the schema is to create an XML file that uses it and input some
test data.

Test the XML schema

1 On the Project menu, click Add New Item. Select XML File from the
list of templates, and then name the file TestData.xml. Click Open to
create the file. An XML file containing only an XML declaration is
created and displayed in the Design View window:

```
<?xml version="1.0" encoding="utf-8" ?>
```

2 In the Properties window, change the *targetSchema* property to *http:/
/tempuri.org/Timesheet.xsd*. This is the fully qualified namespace
that the Schema Editor created for your Timesheet schema. A
Timesheet element is added to the XML file specifying this
namespace.

```
<?xml version="1.0" encoding="utf-8" ?>
<Timesheet xmlns=http://tempuri.org/Timesheet.xsd>

</Timesheet>
```

3 Click the Data button at the bottom of the XML window. The Data View window appears. You can use this view to enter data.

4 Click the EmployeeID column. Replace the *(null)* value with 99. Change the EmployeeName value to your own name. Click the plus sign (+) that appears in the status column to the left of the row. A hyperlink appears that you can click to enter *TimesheetData* information.

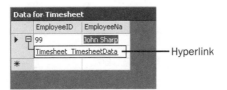 —— Hyperlink

5 Click the hyperlink. The Data View window changes to allow you to type information about activities performed by the employee.

6 Add an activity with an ActivityID of 1, an ActivityName of Writing Books, and an ActivityDuration of 2.5 hours. Add a second activity with an ActivityID of 2, an ActivityName of Programming, and an ActivityDuration of 5 hours.

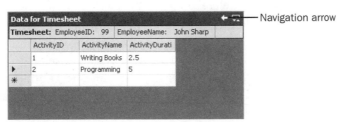 —— Navigation arrow

7 Click the navigation arrow in the upper-right corner of the Data View. You are returned to the Employees view in the Data View window.

8 Click the XML button at the bottom of the Data View window. The following XML representation of the data you have just entered is displayed:

```xml
<?xml version="1.0" encoding="utf-8" ?>
<Timesheet xmlns="http://tempuri.org/Timesheet.xsd">
    <EmployeeID>99</EmployeeID>
    <EmployeeName>John Sharp</EmployeeName>
    <TimesheetData>
        <ActivityID>1</ActivityID>
        <ActivityName>Writing Books</ActivityName>
        <ActivityDuration>2.5</ActivityDuration>
    </TimesheetData>
    <TimesheetData>
```

26

Handling XML

```
          <ActivityID>2</ActivityID>
          <ActivityName>Programming</ActivityName>
          <ActivityDuration>5</ActivityDuration>
      </TimesheetData>
  </Timesheet>
```

9 Now that you know the schema works, you no longer need the XML
   file. In the Solution Explorer, right-click TestData.xml. On the pop-
   up menu, click Delete. Click OK to confirm the delete. On the File
   menu, click Save All to save the project and the schema.

Building the Timesheet Recording Application

Now that you have defined the XML schema to be used, you can build the
timesheet recording application.

Examine the form

1 In the RecordTimesheets project, right-click Form1.cs in the Solution
   Explorer, and then click Delete to remove the form from the project.
   Click OK to confirm the delete.

2 On the Project menu, click Add Existing Item. In the Add Existing
   Item dialog box, navigate to the \Microsoft Press\Visual C# Step By
   Step\Chapter 26 folder in your My Documents folder, select
   TimesheetForm.cs, and then click Open. The TimesheetForm form is
   added to your project. Display TimesheetForm in the Design View
   window.

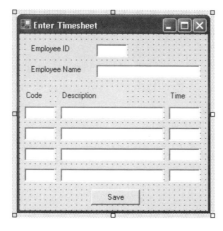

This form allows a user to enter up to four rows of timesheet information for each employee. When the user clicks Save, the data is saved as an XML file using the Timesheet schema, which you are now going to write.

Save timesheet data as XML

1 Display the Code And Text Editor window for TimesheetForm. Add the following *using* statement to the code at the start of the form:

```
using System.Xml;
```

The *System.Xml* namespace contains many of the classes used to process XML data.

2 Create an event method for the *Click* event of the *saveButton* control. Name the method *saveClick*. This is the method that will create the XML file.

3 In the *saveClick* method, add the following statements:

```
XmlTextWriter writer = new XmlTextWriter("Timesheet.xml", null);
writer.Formatting = Formatting.Indented;
writer.WriteStartDocument();
```

An *XmlTextWriter* is used to write XML data to an output stream, in this case a file called Timesheet.xml. The *null* parameter indicates that the writer does not perform any special character encoding. Setting the *Formatting* property to *Formatting.Indented* causes the writer to write the XML data in an indented and more readable manner. The *WriteStartDocument* method actually creates the XML document and outputs the following line when it is executed:

```
<?xml version="1.0" encoding="utf-8" ?>
```

4 Add the following statements to create the *Timesheet* element at the root of the document and specify the Timesheet.xsd schema:

```
writer.WriteStartElement("Timesheet");
writer.WriteAttributeString("xmlns", null,
    "http://tempuri.org/Timesheet.xsd");
```

This writes the following line when the code runs:

```
Timesheet xmlns="http://tempuri.org/Timesheet.xsd"
```

5 Add the following block of code:

```
writer.WriteStartElement("EmployeeID");
writer.WriteString(empID.Text);
writer.WriteEndElement();
writer.WriteStartElement("EmployeeName");
```

```
writer.WriteString(empName.Text);
writer.WriteEndElement();
```

These statements create the *EmployeeID* and *EmployeeName* elements of the document using the information supplied by the user in the two text boxes at the top of the form. The *WriteStartElement* method writes the opening tag for an element. Each *WriteStartElement* method call should have a corresponding *WriteEndElement* call that writes the closing tag for the element. The result of this code is to generate the following lines:

```
<EmployeeID>99</EmployeeID>
<EmployeeName>John Sharp</EmployeeName>
```

These lines assume that the user typed 99 for the *EmployeeID* and John Sharp for the *EmployeeName*.

6   Below the Employee ID and Employee Name text boxes is a set of additional text boxes where the user can enter up to four lines of timesheet activity information. The form makes these text boxes available in the arrays called *code*, *name*, and *duration* (each array contains four text boxes). The following code iterates through these text boxes, stopping when all four rows of data have been processed or when an empty row is found. Each row is added to the XML document as a *TimesheetData* element. Append this code to the *saveClick* method, after the statements you have already added:

```
for(int i = 0; i < codes.Length; i++)
{
    string code = codes[i].Text;
    if (code.Equals(""))
        break;

    writer.WriteStartElement("TimesheetData");

    string name = descriptions[i].Text;
    string duration = durations[i].Text;
    writer.WriteStartElement("ActivityID");
    writer.WriteString(code);
    writer.WriteEndElement();
    writer.WriteStartElement("ActivityName");
    writer.WriteString(name);
    writer.WriteEndElement();
    writer.WriteStartElement("ActivityDuration");
    writer.WriteString(duration);
    writer.WriteEndElement();

    writer.WriteEndElement();
}
```

Notice how the *ActivityID*, *ActivityName*, and *ActivityDuration* elements are nested inside the *TimesheetData* element. The XML output by this block of code will look similar to the following code:

```
<TimesheetData>
  <ActivityID>1</ActivityID>
  <ActivityName>Book writing</ActivityName>
  <ActivityDuration>2.5</ActivityDuration>
</TimesheetData>
<TimesheetData>
  <ActivityID>2</ActivityID>
  <ActivityName>Programming</ActivityName>
  <ActivityDuration>3</ActivityDuration>
</TimesheetData>
<TimesheetData>
  <ActivityID>3</ActivityID>
  <ActivityName>Email</ActivityName>
  <ActivityDuration>2</ActivityDuration>
</TimesheetData>
```

7   The final steps are to finish the *Timesheet element* (the root element holding all the data), close the XML document, and flush the XML output stream to make sure everything is written to disk. The following three statements achieve this goal. Add them to the end of the method, after the *for* loop's block of code:

```
writer.WriteEndElement();
writer.WriteEndDocument();
writer.Close();
```

Test the application

1   Build and run the application. When the form appears, type in some values of your choosing. (Make the data meaningful because you will be using the XML file that is created in the next exercise.)

2   Click Save to generate the XML file and then close the form.

3   In Windows Explorer, navigate to the \Microsoft Press\Visual C# Step By Step\Chapter 26\RecordTimesheets\bin\Debug folder in your My Documents folder. Find the file Timesheet.xml. This is the file you just created. Double-click the file to start Microsoft Internet Explorer and display the file in the Internet Explorer window.

4   Close Internet Explorer and return to the Visual Studio .NET programming environment.

Creating the Timesheet Analysis Application

You will now create the application that analyzes timesheet information. It will read the XML file you created in the previous exercise, validate it against the Timesheet schema (to make sure the file actually contains timesheet data), and display the names of each activity performed and the total number of hours worked by the employee.

Validate the XML data

1   In Visual Studio .NET, open the AnalyzeTimesheets project in the \Microsoft Press\Visual C# Step By Step\Chapter 26\Analyze-Timesheets folder in your My Documents folder.

This is a console application that you will use to validate and examine an XML timesheet file. At the top of the Analyze.cs file, you will see the following *using* statements:

```
using System;
using System.IO;
using System.Xml;
using System.Xml.Schema;
```

The *System.IO* namespace contains classes for reading and writing files. The *System.Xml* namespace has classes for processing XML (you used this namespace in the previous exercise). The *System.Xml.Schema* namespace contains classes for handling XML schemas.

Examine the *Analyze* class. It contains two methods: *Main* and *valHandler*. The *Main* method expects the user to supply the name of an XML file on the command line as a parameter. If the filename is missing, an error message is displayed and the program terminates. If the user provides a filename, the code that you are about to write in the *try/catch* block will open the file and verify that it is an XML file in the correct format. The *valHandler* method is an event handler. You will use it to report any validation errors that occur when you parse the XML file.

2   In the *try* block in *Main*, type the following statements to open the file specified by the user and create an *XmlTextReader* object that you can use to read contents of the file:

```
StreamReader stream = new StreamReader(args[0]);
XmlTextReader reader = new XmlTextReader(stream);
```

3 Add the following statements after the code you just entered:

```
XmlSchemaCollection schemaColl = new XmlSchemaCollection();
schemaColl.Add(null, "Timesheet.xsd");
XmlValidatingReader valReader = new XmlValidatingReader(reader);
valReader.ValidationType = ValidationType.Schema;
valReader.Schemas.Add(schemaColl);
valReader.ValidationEventHandler +=
    new ValidationEventHandler(valHandler);
```

The first two statements create and populate an *XmlSchemaCollection*. An *XmlSchemaCollection* caches XML schemas, which can then be used to validate XML data as it is read. In this example, the schema in the Timesheet.xsd file is loaded. The third statement creates an *XmlValidatingReader* based on the *XmlTextReader* you instantiated in the previous step. An *XmlValidatingReader* is similar to an *XmlTextReader*, except that you can associate an *XmlSchema-Collection* with it.

As the XML file is read, the data will be automatically validated against the XML schemas in the collection. If an unexpected tag is found, a *ValidationEvent* is raised. You can trap this event using the *ValidationEventHandler* property. Statements four through six set the properties of the *XmlValidatingReader* to validate data against the cached Timesheet.xsd schema and invoke the *valHandler* event method if the validation fails.

4 Create the following *while* loop. The *Read* method of an *XmlValidatingReader* extracts the next element from the XML stream. It returns *true* if an element was found, otherwise it returns *false*.

```
while (valReader.Read())
{
    // Do nothing - just validate the data
}
```

You can see that this loop simply iterates over the XML stream but does not do any additional processing. As each element is read, the *XmlValidatingReader* compares it to the expected input specified by the associated schema, invoking the *valHandler* method if an unexpected element is found.

5 The following statements display a message and close the readers and the stream. Add these statements after the *while* loop:

```
Console.WriteLine("File processed");
valReader.Close();
reader.Close();
stream.Close();
```

6   Build the application. Open a command window and navigate to the
\Microsoft Press\Visual C# Step By Step\Chapter 26\Analyze-
Timesheets\bin\Debug folder in your My Documents folder.

In this folder, find the executable program you just built, a copy of
the schema you defined previously (Timesheet.xsd), and two XML
files (Timesheet.xml and BadTimesheet.xml).

7   Use Notepad to examine the two XML files. You will notice that
Timesheet.xml contains data that conforms to the Timesheet.xsd
schema, but BadTimesheet.xml does not.

8   Run the AnalyzeTimesheets program using Timesheet.xml as the
parameter. A File Processed message is displayed. Run Analyze-
Timesheets again, using BadTimeshcct.xml as the parameter. The following message is displayed:

```
Validation failed: Element 'http://tempuri.org/Timesheet.xsd:
 TimesheetData' has invalid child element
 'http://tempura.org/Timesheet.xsd:ActivityID'.
 An error occurred at (9, 6).
File processed.
```

If you edit the BadTimesheet.xml file, you will see that the first point
that the structure of the data diverges from the schema is at line 9,
column 6.

9   Return to the AnalyzeTimesheets application in the Visual Studio
.NET programming environment.

You have seen how to read and validate an XML file. Now you need to process
the data as you read it. In the following exercise, you will report the name of
each activity performed and the total number of hours worked.

Summarize the XML data

1   In the *Main* method, create a decimal variable called *hours* before the
while loop that reads the XML file and initialize it to zero:

```
decimal hours = 0;
```

2   In the body of the *while* loop, delete the comment and add the following *if* statement:

```
if (valReader.LocalName.Equals("ActivityName"))
{
    Console.WriteLine("Activity: " + valReader.ReadString());
}
```

As each element is read by the *XmlValidatingReader*, its name is made available in the *LocalName* property. The previous *if* statement examines the name of the current element to see if it is an *ActivityName* element. If it is, the *ReadString* method is used to extract the value of the element, and it is printed out.

3 Add the following *if* statement to the body of the *while* loop, below the first *if* statement:

```
if (valReader.LocalName.Equals("ActivityDuration"))
{
    hours += Decimal.Parse(valReader.ReadString());
}
```

The logic here is similar to the first *if* statement; if the *XmlValidatingReader* has found an *ActivityDuration* element, it reads the value, converts it to a decimal, and adds it to the *hours* variable.

4 Change the *Console.WriteLine* statement after the *while* loop to print out the total number of hours worked:

```
Console.WriteLine("File processed. Number of hours " +
    "worked - {0}", hours);
```

5 Compile the program. Switch to the command window in the \Microsoft Press\Visual C# Step By Step\Chapter 26\Analyze-Timesheets\bin\Debug folder in your My Documents folder. Run the AnalyzeTimesheets program using Timesheet.xml as the parameter. You will see the following output:

```
Activity: Book writing
Activity: Programming
Activity: Email
File processed. Number of hours worked - 7.5
```

Run the program again, using BadTimesheet.xml as the parameter. You will see the following output:

```
Activity: Book writing
Validation failed: Element 'http://tempuri.org/Timesheet.xsd:
 TimesheetData' has invalid child element
 'http://tempura.org/Timesheet.xsd:ActivityID'.
 An error occurred at (9, 6).
Activity: Programming
Activity: Email
File processed. Number of hours worked - 7.5.
```

You can see that if you supply a *ValidationEventHandler* for an *XmlValidatingReader*, the event handler will run when a validation exception is detected. After the event handler has completed, the error is considered "handled" and execution continues. If you want to end the XML processing, you must throw an exception in the event handler.

If you want to continue to the next chapter

■   Keep Visual Studio .NET running and turn to Chapter 27.

If you want to quit Visual Studio .NET for now

■   On the File menu, click Exit. If you see a Save dialog box, click Yes.

Chapter 26 Quick Reference

To	Do this
Create an XML schema	On the Project menu, click Add New Item. Select the XML Schema template. Use the Toolbox to add types, elements, and groups to the schema in Design View.
Create an XML file	On the Project menu, click Add New Item. Select the XML File template.
Associate an XML file with an XML schema	Set the *targetSchema* property of the XML file to the fully qualified name of the schema.
Write an XML file	Create an *XmlTextWriter* object. Call the *WriteStartDocument* method to write the XML declaration at the start of the file. Use the *WriteStartElement* and *WriteEndElement* methods to append elements to the file; they might be nested. Call the *WriteEndDocument* method to finish writing the file.
Validate an XML file	Create an *XmlValidatingReader* to read the XML file. Associate it with the schema to be used to validate the data. Provide a *ValidationEventHandler* method to trap any validation exceptions.
Read an XML file	Iterate through the file using an *XmlTextReader* or *XmlValidatingReader* object. Call the *Read* method to extract the next element from the file. Use the *LocalName* property to determine the name of the current element, and use *ReadString* to get its value.

Building Web Applications

Introducing ASP.NET

In this chapter, you will learn how to:

- Create simple Microsoft ASP.NET pages.
- Build applications that can be accessed from a Web browser.
- Use ASP.NET Server controls efficiently.

In the previous sections of this book, you have seen how to build Microsoft Visual C# applications that run in the Microsoft Windows environment on the desktop. These applications typically allow a user to gain access to a database by using ADO.NET and possibly use XML as a standard format for sharing data with other applications. In this final part of the book, you will consider the world of Web applications. These are applications that are accessed over the Internet. Rather than using your desktop, Web applications rely on a Web browser to provide the user interface.

In the first four chapters of this part, you will examine the classes provided by the Microsoft .NET Framework for building Web applications. These classes constitute an XML Web service that uses ASP.NET. You will learn about the architecture of ASP.NET, Web forms, and Server controls. You will see that the structure of applications that execute over the Web are different from those that run on the desktop, and you will be shown some best practices for building efficient, scalable Web applications.

In the final two chapters in this part, you'll learn about XML Web services. XML Web services allow you to build distributed applications composed of components that can be spread across the Internet (or an intranet). You will see how to create an XML-based Web service and understand how XML Web services are built on the Simple Object Access Protocol (SOAP). You will also study the techniques that a client application can use to consume an XML Web service.

Understanding the Internet as an Infrastructure

You have heard all the hype about the Internet, and so none of it will be repeated here. However, you should consider a few points. The Internet is a big network (alright—a *really* big network) and, as a result, the information and data that you can access over it can be quite remote. This should have an impact on the way you design your applications. For example, you might get away with locking data in a database while a user browses it in a small, local desktop application, but this strategy will not be feasible for an application accessed over the Internet. Resource use impacts scalability much more for the Internet than for local applications.

Network bandwidth itself is also a scarce resource that should be used sparingly. You might notice variations in the performance of your own local network according to the time of day (networks always seem to slow down on a Friday afternoon just when you are trying to get everything done before the weekend), the applications that users in your company are running, and many other factors. But, no matter how variable the performance of your own local network is, the Internet is far more unpredictable. You are dependent on any number of servers routing your requests from your Web browser to the site you are trying to access, and the replies can get passed back along an equally tortuous route. The network protocols and data presentation mechanisms that underpin the Internet reflect the fact that networks can be (and at times most certainly will be) unreliable and that an application running on a server can be accessed by a user running one of many different Web browsers on one of many different operating systems.

Understanding Web Server Requests and Responses

A user gaining access to an application over the Internet by using a Web browser uses the Hypertext Transfer Protocol (HTTP) to communicate with the application. Applications are usually hosted by some sort of Web server that reads HTTP requests and determines which application should be used to respond to the request. The term "application" in this sense is a very loose term—the Web server might invoke an executable program to perform an action, or it might process the request itself using its own internal logic or other means. However the request is processed, the Web server will send a response to the client, again by using HTTP. The content of an HTTP response is usually presented as a Hypertext Markup Language (HTML) page; this is the language that most browsers understand and know how to display.

▶ **Note**   Applications run by users that access other applications over the Internet are often referred to as clients or client applications. The applications being accessed are usually called servers or server applications.

Managing State

HTTP is a connectionless protocol. This means that a request (or a response) is a stand-alone packet of data. A typical exchange between a client and an application running on a Web server might involve several requests. For example, the user can display a page, enter data, click some buttons, and expect the display to change as a result, allowing the user to enter more data, and so on. Each request sent by the client to the server is separate from any other requests sent both by this client and any other clients using the same server (and maybe running the same application) simultaneously. The problem is that a client request often requires some sort of context or state.

For example, consider the following common scenario. A Web application allows the user to browse goods for sale. The user can select various items and add them to a virtual shopping cart. The user might want to buy several items, placing each one in the shopping cart. A useful feature of such an application is the ability to display the current contents of the shopping cart.

Where should the contents of the shopping cart (the client's state) be held? If this information is held on the Web server, the Web server must be able to piece together the different HTTP requests and determine which requests come from one client and which come from others. This is feasible but might require additional processing to reconcile client requests against state information and, of course, it would require some sort of database to persist that state information between client requests. A complication with this technique is that the Web server has no guarantee, once the state information has been preserved, that the client will submit another request that uses or removes the information. If the Web server saved every bit of state information for every client that used it, it could need a very big database indeed!

An alternative is to store state information on the client machine. The *Cookie Protocol* was developed to allow Web servers to cache information in cookies (small files) on the client computer. The disadvantages of this approach are that the application has to arrange for the data in the cookie to be transmitted over the Web as part of every HTTP request so that the Web server can access it. The application also has to ensure that cookies are of a limited size. Perhaps the most significant drawback of cookies is that users can disable them and prevent the Web browser from storing them on their computers, which will cause any attempt to save state information to fail.

Understanding ASP.NET

Any framework for building and running Web applications has a number of items that it should address. It must do the following:

- Support the standard HTTP
- Manage client state efficiently
- Provide tools allowing for the easy development of Web applications
- Generate applications that can be accessed from any browser that supports HTML
- Be responsive and scalable

Microsoft originally developed the Active Server Pages model in response to many of these issues. Active Server Pages allowed developers to embed application code in HTML pages. A Web server such as Microsoft Internet Information Services (IIS) could execute the application code and use it to generate an HTML response. However, Active Server Pages did have its problems: you had to write a lot of application code to do relatively simple things, such as display a page of data from a database; mixing application code and HTML caused readability and maintenance issues; and performance was not always what it could be because Active Server Pages had to interpret application code in an HTML request every time the request was submitted, even if it was the same code each time.

With the advent of the .NET platform, Microsoft updated the Active Server Pages framework and created ASP.NET. The main features of ASP.NET include the following:

- A rationalized program model, using Web forms that contain presentation logic and code files that separate out the business logic. You can write code in any of the supported .NET languages, including C#. ASP.NET Web forms are compiled and cached on the Web server to improve performance.

- Server controls that support server-side events but are rendered as HTML to allow them to operate correctly in any HTML-compliant browser. Microsoft has also extended many of the standard HTML controls as well, allowing you to manipulate them in your code.

- Powerful Data controls for displaying, editing, and maintaining data from an ADO.NET data source.

- Options for caching client state using cookies on the client's computer, in a special service (the ASP.NET State service) on the Web server, or in a Microsoft SQL Server database. The cache is easily programmable using code.

In the remainder of this chapter, you will learn more about the structure of an ASP.NET application that uses Server and HTML controls.

Creating Web Applications with ASP.NET

A Web application that uses ASP.NET typically consists of one or more ASP.NET pages or Web forms, code files, and configuration files.

A Web form is held in an .aspx file, which is essentially an HTML file with some Microsoft .NET–specific tags. An .aspx file defines the layout and appearance of a page. Each .aspx file often has an associated code file containing the application logic for the components in the .aspx file, such as event handlers and utility methods. A *tag*, or directive, at the start of each .aspx file specifies the name and location of the corresponding code file. ASP.NET also supports application-level events, which are defined in Global.asax files.

Each Web application also has a configuration file called Web.config. This file, which is in XML format, contains information regarding security, cache management, page compilation, and so on.

Building an ASP.NET Application

In the following exercise, you will build a simple ASP.NET application that uses Server controls to gather input from the user about the details of the employees of a fictitious company. The application will show you the structure of a typical Web application.

▶ **Important**   To perform the exercises in this part of the book, IIS must be running on your computer. You can check that it is running by using the Services tool. On the taskbar, click Start and then click Control Panel. (If your computer is running Microsoft Windows XP with the Windows XP theme, in the Control Panel, click Performance And Maintenance.) Click Administrative Tools, and then double-click Services. In the Services tool, look for the World Wide Web Publishing Service and verify that its status is Started. If it is not, start it. Close the Services tool.

▶ **Note**   The solutions supplied for this part of the book, which you can find with this book's sample files, require that you "Web Share" the folders containing the solutions using the correct URL. After installing the solutions, use Windows Explorer to navigate to the \Microsoft Press\Visual C# Step By Step\Chapter 27 folder in your My Documents folder. Right-click the EmployeeInfo Complete 1 folder and select Sharing (select Sharing And Security under Windows XP) from the menu. Click the Web Sharing tab in the EmployeeInfo Complete 1 Properties dialog box and click the Share This Folder radio button. In the Edit Alias dialog box, click OK to accept the defaults. (If you change the alias name or the permissions, the Web application might not work.) Click OK in the EmployeeInfo Complete 1 Properties dialog box.

You should repeat this process for all the solutions in Chapters 28, 29, 30, 31, and 32 except for the EmployeeInfo solution in Chapter 28. Use the default alias name and permissions each time—the solution folders have been named to avoid any clashes.

Create the Web application

1   In the Microsoft Visual Studio .NET programming environment, create a new ASP.NET Web application. Set the location to *http://localhost/EmployeeInfo*.

An application is created consisting of a number of files, including WebForm1.aspx (the file containing the Web form), Global.asax (the Web application code file), and Web.config (the configuration file). WebForm1.aspx will be displayed in the Design View window.

2   In the Properties window, change the *File Name* property of WebForm1.aspx to EmployeeForm.aspx.

3   In the Class View window, expand the *EmployeeInfo* namespace and change the name of the *WebForm1* class to *EmployeeForm*.

4   Click the HTML tab at the bottom of the form to view the HTML format of the form. In Design View, you can drag controls onto the Web form from the Toolbox, and Visual Studio .NET will generate the appropriate HTML for you. This is the HTML that you see when you view the form in HTML View. You can also edit the HTML directly if you want.

Lay out the Web form

1   Click the Design tab at the bottom of the form to return to Design View. In the Properties window, change the title property of the *DOCUMENT* object to Employee Information.

2   Click inside the Design View window and then on the Format menu, click Document Styles. The Document Styles dialog box opens. This dialog box allows you to create a style for the form. (A *style* specifies the default font, color, layout, and other attributes for the Web form and its controls.) You will use this dialog box to create a style sheet for the form.

3   In the Document Styles dialog box, click the Add Style Sheet button to create a new style sheet. A <STYLE> tag appears in the dialog box.

4   In the Document Styles dialog box, select the <STYLE> tag and click the Add Style Rule button. The Add Style Rule dialog box opens.

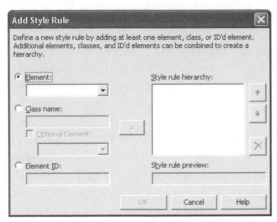

5 Verify that the Element option is selected, select BODY from the drop-down list, and then click OK. A BODY element is added to the Document Styles dialog box. You use the BODY element to specify the default font, color, background image, and so on, for the Web form.

6 In the Document Styles dialog box, select the BODY element, and then click the Build Style button. The Style Builder dialog box opens.

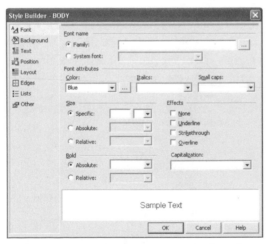

7 In the Font Name section, verify that the Family option is selected, and then click the Ellipses button on the right side. In the Font Picker dialog box that opens, select Arial in the Installed Fonts list, and then click the > button to add it to the Selected Fonts list. Click OK to return to the Style Builder dialog box.

8 In the Color drop-down list, select Blue.

9   In the left pane of the dialog box, click Background. The Background page is displayed. Select the Transparent check box.

10   Using Windows Explorer, copy the file \Microsoft Press\Visual C# Step By Step\Chapter 27\computer.bmp in your My Documents folder to the folder C:\Inetpub\wwwroot\EmployeeInfo. This folder is the home directory of the EmployeeInfo application on which you are currently working.

11   Return to the Style Builder dialog box in the Visual Studio .NET programming environment. In the Image text box, type **computer.bmp**. Click OK to return to the Document Styles dialog box, and then close the Document Styles dialog box. The Web form will contain a transparent background image of a computer.

12   Open the Toolbox and make sure that the Web Forms tab is displayed.

The Toolbox contains tabs holding controls that you can drop onto ASP.NET forms. These controls are similar, in many cases, to the controls you have been using to build Windows forms. The difference is that these controls have been designed to operate in an HTML environment, and they are rendered as regular HTML at run time.

13   In the Toolbox, add four *Label* controls and three *TextBox* controls to the Web form. Notice how the controls pick up the font and color specified by the Web form's style. Set the properties of these controls to the values shown in the following table.

Control	Property	Value
Label1	*Font Bold* (expand the *Font* property)	True
	Font Name	Arial Black
	Font Size	X-Large
	Text	Honest John Software Developers
	Height	36px
	Width	630px
Label2	*Text*	First Name
TextBox1	*Height*	24px
	Width	230px
	(ID)	FirstName
Label3	*Text*	Last Name
TextBox2	*Height*	24px

Control	Property	Value
	Width	**230px**
	(ID)	**LastName**
Label4	*Text*	**Employee Id**
TextBox3	*Height*	**24px**
	Width	**100px**
	(ID)	**EmployeeId**

14 Move the labels and text boxes to the positions shown on the form in the following illustration:

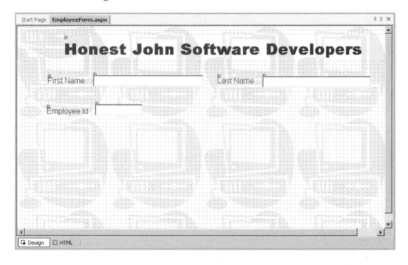

▶ **Tip** You can align and space controls by using the commands on the Format menu. To align a set of controls, select them all and then, on the Format menu, click Align and select the appropriate alignment (Left, Center, Right, Top, Middle, Bottom). Similarly, you can space controls by selecting them and then using the Horizontal Spacing or Vertical Spacing command on the Format menu.

15 Switch to the HTML View. The HTML should look like similar to the following code (the positions of the controls might vary slightly on your form):

```
<%@ Page language="c#" Codebehind="EmployeeForm.aspx.cs"
 AutoEventWireup="false" Inherits="EmployeeInfo.EmployeeForm" %>
<!DOCTYPE HTML PUBLIC "-//W3C//DTD HTML 4.0 Transitional//EN" >
<HTML>
  <HEAD>
    <title>Employee Information</title>
    <meta name="GENERATOR" Content="Microsoft Visual Studio 7.0">
    <meta name="CODE_LANGUAGE" Content="C#">
```

```
<meta name="vs_defaultClientScript"
  content="JavaScript (ECMAScript)">
<meta name="vs_targetSchema" content=
  "http://schemas.microsoft.com/intellisense/ie5">
<STYLE>BODY {
  BACKGROUND-IMAGE: url(computer.bmp); COLOR: blue;
  FONT-FAMILY: Arial; BACKGROUND-COLOR: transparent }
</STYLE>
</HEAD>
<body MS_POSITIONING="GridLayout">
  <form id="Form1" method="post" runat="server">
    <asp:Label id="Label1" style="Z-INDEX: 101; LEFT: 96px;
      POSITION: absolute; TOP: 24px" runat="server"
      Font-Bold="True" Font-Names="Arial Black"
      Font-Size="X-Large" Width="712px" Height="46px">
      Honest John Software Developers
    </asp:Label>
    <asp:Label id="Label2" style="Z-INDEX: 102; LEFT: 62px;
      POSITION: absolute; TOP: 104px" runat="server">First Name
    </asp:Label>
    <asp:Label id="Label3" style="Z-INDEX: 103; LEFT: 414px;
      POSITION: absolute; TOP: 104px" runat="server">Last Name
    </asp:Label>
    <asp:Label id="Label4" style="Z-INDEX: 107; LEFT: 62px;
      POSITION: absolute; TOP: 167px" runat="server">Employee Id
    </asp:Label>
    <asp:TextBox id="FirstName" style="Z-INDEX: 104; LEFT: 156px;
      POSITION: absolute; TOP: 101px" runat="server"
      Width="230px" Height="24px">
    </asp:TextBox>
    <asp:TextBox id="LastName" style="Z-INDEX: 105; LEFT: 507px;
      POSITION: absolute; TOP: 101px" runat="server"
      Width="230px" Height="24px">
    </asp:TextBox>
    <asp:TextBox id="EmployeeId" style="Z-INDEX: 106;
      LEFT: 160px; POSITION: absolute; TOP: 161px"
      runat="server" Width="100px" Height="24px">
    </asp:TextBox>
  </form>
</body>
</HTML>
```

16 Return to the Design View.

17 Add another *Label* control and four *RadioButton* controls to the Web form. Set the properties of these controls to the values listed in the following table.

Control	Property	Value
Label5	*Text*	Position
RadioButton1	*Text*	Worker
	TextAlign	Left
	GroupName	PositionGroup
	Checked	True
	(ID)	WorkerButton
RadioButton2	*Text*	Boss
	TextAlign	Left
	GroupName	PositionGroup
	Checked	False
	(ID)	BossButton
RadioButton3	*Text*	Vice President
	TextAlign	Left
	GroupName	PositionGroup
	Checked	False
	(ID)	VPButton
RadioButton4	*Text*	President
	TextAlign	Left
	GroupName	PositionGroup
	Checked	False
	(ID)	PresidentButton

The *GroupName* property determines how a set of radio buttons are grouped—all buttons with the same value for *GroupName* are in the same group and will be mutually exclusive.

18 Align these controls so that your Web form looks like the following illustration:

19 Add another *Label* control and a *DropDownList* control to the Web form. Set their properties to the values shown in the following table.

Control	Property	Value
Label6	*Text*	**Role**
DropDownList1	*Width*	**230px**
	(ID)	**PositionRole**

The *PositionRole* drop-down list will display the different positions that an employee can have within the company. This list will vary according to the position of the employee in the company, and you will write code to populate this list dynamically.

20 Place the controls so that the form looks like the following illustration:

21 Add two *Button* controls and another *Label* control to the form. Set their properties to the values shown in the following table.

Control	Property	Value
Button1	*Text*	Save
	(ID)	SaveButton
Button2	*Text*	Clear
	(ID)	ClearButton
Label7	*Text*	(blank)
	Height	48px
	Width	680px
	(ID)	InfoLabel

Position the controls so that the form looks like the following illustration:

You will write event handlers for these buttons in a later exercise. The Save button will collate the information entered by the user and display it in the *InfoLabel* label at the bottom of the form. The Clear button will clear the text boxes and set other controls to their default values.

Test the Web form

1   On the Debug menu, click Start. This will start Microsoft Internet Explorer and run your Web form.

2   Enter some information for a fictitious employee. Test the radio buttons to verify that the buttons are all mutually exclusive. Click the drop-down arrow in the Role list; the list will be empty. Click Save and Clear. At first glance, the radio buttons might not appear to do anything but, if you look closely, you will see that they actually cause the form to be redisplayed. Close Internet Explorer and return to the Visual Studio .NET programming environment.

Understanding Server Controls

The Web Forms controls you added to the form are collectively known as Server controls. Server controls are similar to the standard HTML components that you can use on an ordinary Web page, except that they are more programmable. Most Server controls expose event handlers, methods, and properties that code running on the server can execute and modify dynamically at run time. In the following exercises, you will learn more about programming Server controls.

Examine a Server control

1   In the Visual Studio .NET programming environment, display EmployeeForm.aspx in the HTML View window.

2   Examine the HTML code for the form. Notice that it contains the definitions for each of the controls. Look at the first *Label* control in more detail (the code won't look exactly like the following listing):

```
<asp:Label id="Label1" style="Z-INDEX: 101; LEFT: 96px;
  POSITION: absolute; TOP: 24px" runat="server"
  Font-Bold="True" Font-Names="Arial Black"
  Font-Size="X-Large" Width="630px" Height="36px">
  Honest John Software Developers
</asp:Label>
```

There are a couple of things to observe. First, look at the type of the control: *asp:Label*. All Web forms controls live in the "asp" namespace because this is the way they are defined by Microsoft. The second noteworthy item is the *runat="server"* attribute. This attribute indicates that the control can be accessed programmatically by code running on the Web server—code that can query and change the values of any of the properties of this control (for example, change its text).

3 Return to the Design View window.

The EmployeeForm.aspx page requires several event handlers: a set of handlers to populate the *PositionRole* drop-down list when the user selects a position (Worker, Boss, Vice President, President); another handler to save the information entered when the user clicks the Save button; and a final handler to clear the form when the user clicks the Clear button.

HTML Controls

ASP.NET also supports HTML controls. If you click the HTML tab in the Toolbox, you are presented with a list of controls. These are the controls that Microsoft supplied with the original Active Server Pages model. They are provided so that you can port existing ASP pages into ASP.NET more easily. However, if you are building an application from scratch, you should use the Web Forms controls instead.

HTML controls also have a *runat* attribute, allowing you to specify where event handling code should be executed for these controls. Unlike Web Forms controls, the default location for HTML controls to execute code is in the browser rather than on the server—assuming that the user's browser supports this functionality.

Write event handlers

1 On the View menu, click Code. The display changes to the Code And Text Editor window and displays a file called EmployeeForm.aspx.cs. This file contains the entire C# code for the form and is very similar to the code for a Windows form. Unlike Windows forms, however, this code is held in a file separate from the logic that defines the layout. If you momentarily return to the EmployeeForm.aspx file and switch to HTML View, you will see the following line at the top:

```
<%@ Page language="c#" Codebehind="EmployeeForm.aspx.cs ... %>
```

This directive specifies the file containing the program code for the Web form and the language in which it is written, in this case, C#. The other supported languages are Microsoft Visual Basic .NET and Microsoft JScript .NET.

2   Return to the EmployeeForm.aspx.cs file. At the top of the file, there is a set of *using* statements. Note that this file makes heavy use of the *System.Web* namespace and its sub-namespaces—this is where the ASP.NET classes reside. Also, notice the code itself is in a class called *EmployeeForm* that descends from *System.Web.UI.Page*; this is the class from which all Web Forms descend.

3   Add a method called *initPositionRole* to the *EmployeeForm* class:

```
private void initPositionRole()
{
}
```

You will use this method to initialize the *PositionRole* drop-down list to its default set of values.

4   Add the following statements to this method:

```
PositionRole.Items.Clear();
PositionRole.Enabled = true;
PositionRole.Items.Add("Analyst");
PositionRole.Items.Add("Designer");
PositionRole.Items.Add("Developer");
```

The first statement clears the list. The second statement enables the list (you will write some code shortly that disables it under certain circumstances). The remaining statements add the three roles that are applicable to the workers.

5   Locate the *Page_Load* method. This method is called when the page is first displayed. Add a call to the *initPositionRole* method to populate the *PositionRole* drop-down list with its default values:

```
initPositionRole();
```

6   Switch to the EmployeeForm.aspx file, and change to Design View for the form. Select the *WorkerButton* radio button. In the Properties window, click the Events button. In the *CheckChanged* event, type **WorkerChecked** and press Enter. This event occurs when the user clicks the radio button and its value changes.

7   In the *WorkerChecked* event method, add the following statement:

```
initPositionRole();
```

The default values for the *PositionRole* drop-down list are those for a worker.

8 Switch to EmployeeForm.aspx. Select the *BossButton* radio button, and use the Properties window to create an event method called *BossChecked* for the *CheckedChanged* event. When the form is displayed in Code View, type the following statements in the *BossChecked* method:

```
PositionRole.Items.Clear();
PositionRole.Enabled = true;
PositionRole.Items.Add("General Manager");
PositionRole.Items.Add("Project Manager");
```

These are the roles that a manager can fulfill.

9 Create an event handler for the *CheckedChanged* event for the *VPButton* (Vice President) radio button, called *VPChecked*. Add the following statements to the *VPChecked* method:

```
PositionRole.Items.Clear();
PositionRole.Enabled = true;
PositionRole.Items.Add("VP Sales");
PositionRole.Items.Add("VP Marketing");
PositionRole.Items.Add("VP Production");
PositionRole.Items.Add("VP Human Resources");
```

10 Create a final event handler for the *CheckedChanged* event for the *President* radio button, called *PresidentChecked*. Add the following code to the *PresidentChecked* method:

```
PositionRole.Items.Clear();
PositionRole.Enabled = false;
```

Roles do not apply to the president of the company, so the drop-down list is disabled.

11 Create an event handler for the *Click* event of the Save button. Call the method *SaveClick*. The *SaveClick* method would usually be used to save the information to a database, but to keep this application simple, the method will just echo some of the data in the *InfoLabel* control instead. Add the following statements to the *SaveClick* method:

```
string position = "";

if (WorkerButton.Checked)
    position = "Worker";
if (BossButton.Checked)
    position = "Manager";
if (VPButton.Checked)
    position = "Vice President";
if (PresidentButton.Checked)
    position = "President";
```

```
InfoLabel.Text = "Employee: " + FirstName.Text + " " +
    LastName.Text + "    Id " +
    EmployeeId.Text + "    Position " +
    position;
```

The   character is a non-blanking space in HTML; ordinary white space characters will be ignored by the browser.

12 Create an event method for the *Click* event of the Clear button called *ClearClick*. Type the following block of code in this method:

```
FirstName.Text = "";
LastName.Text = "";
EmployeeId.Text = "";
WorkerButton.Checked = true;
initPositionRole();
InfoLabel.Text = "";
```

This code clears the information entered by the user and then resets the role to Worker (the default value).

Test the Web form again

1 On the Debug menu, click Start to run the Web form again. Internet Explorer starts and displays the form.

2 Type in an employee's name and ID number (make them up). Click the Role drop-down list. The list of roles for a worker is displayed.

3 Change the position of your fictitious employee to Vice President, and then click the Role drop-down list box. Notice that the list has not changed and still displays the roles for a worker. The list hasn't changed because the *CheckedChanged* event for the Vice President radio button has not fired.

4 Close Internet Explorer and return to the Visual Studio .NET programming environment.

5 Display EmployeeForm.aspx in the Design View window, and then select the *WorkerButton* radio button. In the Properties window, set the *AutoPostBack* property to True.

When the user clicks this radio button, the form will be sent back to the server for processing, the *CheckedChanged* event will fire, and the form can be updated to display the roles for this radio button.

6 Set the *AutoPostBack* property to *True* for the other radio buttons: *BossButton*, *VPButton*, and *PresidentButton*.

7 Run the Web form again. This time you will find that when you click the radio buttons, there is a slight flicker while the form is submitted to the server, the event handler runs, the drop-down list is populated, and the form is displayed again.

8 On the View menu, click Source to display the source of the HTML page being displayed in the browser. Notepad starts and displays HTML similar to the following:

```
<!DOCTYPE HTML PUBLIC "-//W3C//DTD HTML 4.0 Transitional//EN" >
<HTML>
  <HEAD>
    <title>Employee Information</title>
    <meta name="GENERATOR" Content="Microsoft Visual Studio 7.0">
    <meta name="CODE_LANGUAGE" Content="C#">
    <meta name="vs_defaultClientScript" content="JavaScript">
    <meta name="vs_targetSchema"
      content="http://schemas.microsoft.com/intellisense/ie5">
    <STYLE>BODY { BACKGROUND-IMAGE: url(computer.bmp);
      COLOR: blue; FONT-FAMILY: Arial;
      BACKGROUND-COLOR: transparent }
    </STYLE>
  </HEAD>
  <body MS_POSITIONING="GridLayout">
    <form name="Form1" method="post"
      action="EmployeeForm.aspx" id="Form1">
    <input type="hidden" name="__EVENTTARGET" value="" />
    <input type="hidden" name="__EVENTARGUMENT" value="" />
    <input type="hidden" name="__VIEWSTATE"
      value="dDwtMjgyMzQ5Nzgz0 3Q8O2w8aTwxPjs+O2w8dDw7bDxpPDE3P
jtpPDE5PjtpPDIxPjtpPDIzPjtpPDI3Pjt pPDI5Pjs+O2w8dDxwPHA8bDxDaGV
ja2Vk0z47bDxvPGY+Oz4+Oz47Oz47dDxwPHA 8bDxDaGVja2Vk0z47bDxvPGY+Oz
4+Oz47Oz47dDxwPHA8bDxDaGVja2Vk0z47bD xvPHQ+Oz4+Oz47Oz47dDxwPHA8b
DxDaGVja2Vk0z47bDxvPHQ+Oz4+Oz47Oz47dDx0P HA8cDxsPEVuYWJsZWQ7Pjts
PG88dD47Pjt0PGk8Mz47QDxBbmFFseXN0O0Rlc21nb mVyO0RldmVsb3Blcjs
+O0A8QW5hbHlzdDtEZXNpZ25lcjtEZXZlbG9wZXI7Pj47P js7Pjt0PHA8cDxsPF
RleHQ7PjtsPFxlOz4+Oz47Oz47Pj47Pj47bDxQcmVzaWRlb nRCdXR0b247UHJlc
21kZW50QnV0dG9uO1ZQQnV0dG9uO1ZQQnV0dG9uO0Jvc3NCdX R0b247V29ya2Vy
QnV0dG9uOz4+" />
    <script language="javascript">
<!--
    function __doPostBack(eventTarget, eventArgument) {
      var theform = document.Form1;
      theform.__EVENTTARGET.value = eventTarget;
      theform.__EVENTARGUMENT.value = eventArgument;
      theform.submit();
    }
// -->
</script>
```

```
<span id="Label1" style="font-family:Arial Black;
  font-size:X-Large;font-weight:bold;height:36px;width:630px;
  Z-INDEX: 101; LEFT: 46px; POSITION: absolute; TOP: 19px">
  Honest John Software Developers
</span>
<input name="FirstName" type="text" id="FirstName"
  style="height:24px;width:230px;Z-INDEX: 102; LEFT: 120px;
  POSITION: absolute; TOP: 81px" />
<input name="LastName" type="text" id="LastName"
  style="height:24px;width:230px;Z-INDEX: 103; LEFT: 455px;
  POSITION: absolute; TOP: 81px" />
<input name="EmployeeId" type="text" id="EmployeeId"
  style="height:24px;width:100px;Z-INDEX: 104; LEFT: 120px;
  POSITION: absolute; TOP: 123px" />
<span id="Label3" style="Z-INDEX: 105; LEFT: 367px;
  POSITION: absolute; TOP: 81px">Last Name</span>
<span id="Label4" style="Z-INDEX: 106; LEFT: 24px;
  POSITION: absolute; TOP: 125px">Employee Id</span>
<span id="Label2" style="Z-INDEX: 107; LEFT: 33px;
  POSITION: absolute; TOP: 81px">First Name</span>
<span id="Label5" style="Z-INDEX: 108; LEFT: 53px;
  POSITION: absolute; TOP: 168px">Position</span>
<span style="Z-INDEX: 109; LEFT: 132px;
  POSITION: absolute; TOP: 302px">
  <label for="PresidentButton">President</label>
  <input id="PresidentButton" type="radio"
    name="PositionGroup" value="PresidentButton"
    onclick="__doPostBack('PresidentButton','')"
    language="javascript" />
</span>
<span style="Z-INDEX: 110; LEFT: 96px; POSITION: absolute;
  TOP: 268px"><label for="VPButton">Vice President</label>
  <input id="VPButton" type="radio" name="PositionGroup"
  value="VPButton" onclick="__doPostBack('VPButton','')"
  language="javascript" />
</span>
<span style="Z-INDEX: 111; LEFT: 163px;
  POSITION: absolute; TOP: 234px">
  <label for="BossButton">Boss</label>
  <input id="BossButton" type="radio" name="PositionGroup"
    value="BossButton" checked="checked"
    onclick="__doPostBack('BossButton','')"
    language="javascript" />
</span>
<span style="Z-INDEX: 112; LEFT: 148px;
  POSITION: absolute; TOP: 200px">
  <label for="WorkerButton">Worker</label>
  <input id="WorkerButton" type="radio" name="PositionGroup"
  value="WorkerButton" checked="checked"
```

```
    onclick="__doPostBack('WorkerButton','')"
    language="javascript" />
</span>
<span id="Label6" style="Z-INDEX: 113; LEFT: 411px;
  POSITION: absolute; TOP: 168px">Role
</span>
<select name="PositionRole" id="PositionRole"
  style="width:230px;Z-INDEX: 114; LEFT: 455px;
  POSITION: absolute; TOP: 168px">
  <option value="Analyst">Analyst</option>
  <option value="Designer">Designer</option>
  <option value="Developer">Developer</option>

</select>
<span id="InfoLabel" style="height:48px;width:680px;
  Z-INDEX: 115; LEFT: 16px; POSITION: absolute;
  TOP: 368px">
</span>
<input type="submit" name="SaveButton" value="Save"
  id="SaveButton" style="Z-INDEX: 116; LEFT: 304px;
  POSITION: absolute; TOP: 325px" />
<input type="submit" name="ClearButton" value="Clear"
  id="ClearButton" style="Z-INDEX: 117; LEFT: 396px;
  POSITION: absolute; TOP: 323px" />
</form>
</body>
</HTML>
```

Notice that there is no mention of any "asp:" Server controls in this file and no C# code. Instead, the Server controls and their contents have been converted to the equivalent HTML controls (and some JavaScript). This is one of the basic features of the Server controls—you access them programmatically like ordinary .NET objects, with methods, properties, and events. When they are rendered by the Web server, they are converted into HTML, allowing you to use any browser to view ASP.NET Web forms at run time.

9 Close Notepad.

10 Click Save. The *InfoLabel* control displays the details of the new employee. If you examine the source, you will see that the HTML for the *InfoLabel* control (rendered as an HTML span with an ID of "InfoLabel") contains this text.

11 Click Clear. The form resets to its default values.

12 Close Internet Explorer and return to the Visual Studio .NET programming environment.

Event Processing and Round-Trips

Server controls are undoubtedly a very powerful feature of ASP.NET, but they come with a price. You should remember that although events are raised by the Web client, the event code is executed on the Web server and that each time an event is raised, an HTTP request (or post-back) is sent over the network to the Web server. The task of the Web server is to process this request and send a reply containing an HTML page to be displayed. In the case of many events, this page will be the same as the one that issued the original request. However, the Web server also needs to know what other data the user has entered on the page so that when it generates the HTML response, it can preserve these values in the display. (If the Web server only sent back the HTML that composed the original page, any data entered by the user would disappear.) If you look at the HTML source of a page generated by a Web form, you will notice a hidden input field in the form. The example shown previously had this hidden field:

```
<input type="hidden" name="__VIEWSTATE"
value="dDwxNDk0MzA1NzE003Q802w8aTwxPjs+02w8dDw7bDxpPDE3PjtpPDE5
PjtpP DIxPjtpPDI3PjtpPDMzPjs+02w8dDxwPHA8bDxDaGVja2VkOz47bDxvPH
Q+0z4+0z 470z47dDxwPHA8bDxDaGVja2VkOz47bDxvPGY+0z4+0z470z47dDxw
PHA8bDxDaGVja2 VkOz47bDxvPGY+0z4+0z470z47dDx0PDt0PGk8Mz47QDxBbm
FseXN000R1c21nbmVy00 R1dmVsb3B1cjs+00A8QW5hbH1zdDtEZXNpZ25lcjtE
ZXZ1bG9wZXI7Pj47Pjs7Pj t0PHA8cDxsPFR1eHQ7PjtsPFx10z4+0z470z47Pj
47Pj47bDxQZW9uQnV0dG9u01BIQ kJ1dHRvbjtQSEJCdXR0b247V1BCdXR0b247
V1BCdXR0b247UHJ1c21kZW50QnV0dG9u0 1ByZXNpZGVudEJ1dHRvbjs+Pg==" />
```

This information is the content of the controls, or view state, in an encoded form. It is sent to the Web server whenever any event causes a post-back. The Web server will use this information to repopulate the fields on the page when the HTML response is generated.

All of this has an impact on scalability. The more controls you have on a form, the more state information has to be passed between the browser and Web server during the post-back processing, and the more events you use, the more frequently this will happen. In general, to reduce network overhead, you should keep your Web forms relatively simple and avoid excessive use of server events.

If you don't want the state of a control to be preserved across post-backs, you can set the *EnableViewState* property of the control to *False* (the default setting is *True*).

If you want to continue to the next chapter

- Keep Visual Studio .NET running and turn to Chapter 28.

If you want to quit Visual Studio .NET for now

- On the File menu, click Exit. If you see a Save dialog box, click Yes.

Chapter 27 Quick Reference

To	Do this
Create a Web application	Use the ASP.NET Web Application template.
View and edit definition of a Web form	Switch to HTML View.
Create a style for a Web form	On the Format menu, click Document Styles. In the Document Styles dialog box, click the Add Style Sheet button. Add style rules to the new style sheet.
Add Server controls to a Web form	In the Toolbox, click the Web Forms tab. Drag controls onto the Web form.
Add HTML controls to a Web form	In the Toolbox, click the HTML tab. Drag controls onto the Web form.
Create an event handler for a Server control	In Design View, select the control on the Web form. In the Properties window, click the Events button. Locate the event you want to use and type the name of an event handler method. In Code View, write the code for the event.
View the HTML source code for a Web form at run time	On the View menu in Internet Explorer, click Source. The HTML source will be displayed in Notepad.

Understanding Validation Controls

In this chapter, you will learn how to:

- Validate user input in a Microsoft ASP.NET Web form.
- Use the ASP.NET validation controls.
- Determine whether to perform user input validation at the client or the Web server.

As with Windows Forms applications, validating user input in a Web Forms application is an important part of any system. With Windows forms, you have a limited choice of where the validation should be performed—you check that the user's input makes sense, using events attached to the controls and forms of the application itself. With Web forms, there is an additional complication that you must consider: should you perform validation at the client (the browser) or at the server? In this chapter, you will examine this question and discover the options that are available to you.

Comparing Server and Client Validations

Consider the EmployeeForm.aspx page of the EmployeeInfo application again. The user is expected to enter the details of an employee: the name, employee ID, position, and role. All the text boxes should be mandatory. The employee ID should be a positive integer.

In a Windows Forms application, you would use the *Validating* event to make sure the user typed something into the First Name and Last Name text boxes and that the employee ID value was numeric. Web forms do not have a *Validating* event, which means that you cannot use the same approach.

Server Validation

If you examine the *TextBox* class, you will notice that it publishes the *Text-Changed* event. This event runs the next time the form is posted back to the server after the user changes the text typed in the text box.

> ▶   **Important**   Notice that the *TextChanged* event only runs the next time the form is posted to the server. By default, to save network bandwidth, *TextBox* controls do not notify the server when they are changed. If you want the *TextChanged* event to run immediately, you must set the *AutoPostBack* property of the *TextBox* control to True.

Like all Web controls events, this event runs at the Web server. This involves the transmission of data from the Web browser to the server, processing the event at the server to validate the data, and then packaging up any validation errors as part of the HTML response sent back to the client. If the validation being performed is complex, such as possibly requiring crosschecking against a database or some other data source, this might be an acceptable technique. But if you are simply inspecting the data in a single text box in isolation, this type of validation could impose an unacceptable overhead.

Client Validation

The Web Forms model provides for client-side validation through the use of validation controls. If the user is running a browser such as Microsoft Internet Explorer 4 or later, which supports dynamic HTML, these controls generate Microsoft JScript code that runs in the browser and avoids the need to perform a network round-trip to the server. If the user is running an earlier browser, the validation controls generate server-side code instead. The key point is that the developer creating the Web form does not have to worry about this; all the browser detection and code generation features are built into the validation controls. The developer simply drops a validation control onto the Web form, sets its properties (using either the Properties window or code), and specifies the validation rules to be performed and any error messages to be displayed.

There are five types of validation controls supplied with ASP.NET:

- *RequiredFieldValidator*   Use this control to ensure that the user has entered data into a control.

- *CompareValidator*   Use this control to compare the data entered against a constant value, the value of a property of another control, or a value retrieved from a database.
- *RangeValidator*   Use this control to check the data entered by a user against a range of values, checking that the data falls either inside or outside a given range.
- *RegularExpressionValidator*   Use this control to check that the data input by the user matches a specified regular expression, pattern, or format (such as a telephone number, for example).
- *CustomValidator*   Use this control to define your own custom validation logic and attach it to a control to be validated.

Although each control performs a single well-defined type of validation, you can use several of them in combination. For example, if you want to make sure that the user enters a value into a text box and that this value falls within a particular range, you can attach a *RequiredFieldValidator* control and a *Range-Validator* control to the text box.

These controls can work in conjunction with a *ValidationSummary* control to display error messages. You will use some of these controls in the following exercises.

Implementing Client Validation

Returning to the EmployeeForm.aspx Web form, you can probably see that *RequiredFieldValidator* controls will be required for the First Name, Last Name, and Employee Id text boxes. The employee ID must also be numeric and should be a positive integer. In this application, you will specify that the employee ID must be between 1 and 5000. This is where a *RangeValidator* control is useful.

Add *RequiredFieldValidator* controls

1   In the Microsoft Visual Studio .NET programming environment, open the EmployeeInfo project (on the File menu, point to Open, and then click Project From Web).

▶   **Tip**   If you followed the instructions in Chapter 27 sequentially, you will have no problem accessing the source files for the exercises in this chapter. If you are having difficulties, verify that you have access to the files needed. The project solution (.sln) file must be available; by default, it is created in a project folder under the Visual Studio Projects folder under My Documents. Also, you must "Web Share" the folder containing the all project files (as described in

Chapter 27 on page 505) as *http://localhost/<project name>* where *<project name>* is the name of the project. Open the Visual Studio project from the solution file to reset any paths, rebuild, and save the project again.

The Open Project From Web dialog box opens.

2   Type **http://localhost/EmployeeInfo** and then click OK. The Open Project dialog box opens.

3   Select EmployeeInfo.csproj, and then click Open. The project loads.

4   In the Solution Explorer, right-click EmployeeForm.aspx, and then click View Designer to display the Web form in Design View.

5   In the Toolbox, drag the *RequiredFieldValidator* control onto the form just below the First Name text box. A control called *RequiredFieldValidator1* is added to the form, and the text Required-FieldValidator appears in red under the First Name text box.

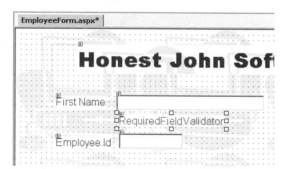

6   With *RequiredFieldValidator1* selected, click the Properties window. Set the *ControlToValidate* property to *FirstName*. Type **You must enter a first name for the employee** in the *ErrorMessage* property.

This is the message that will be displayed if the control to be validated (the First Name text box) is left blank. Notice that this message replaces the red text on the form.

7   Add two more *RequiredFieldValidator* controls to the form. Place the first control under the Last Name text box, set its *ControlToValidate* property to LastName, and type **You must enter a last name for the employee** in its *ErrorMessage* property. Place the second *RequiredFieldValidator* control under the Employee Id text box; set its *ControlToValidate* property to EmployeeId, and type **You must specify an employee id** in its *ErrorMessage* property.

8   Run the form to test it. When it first appears in Microsoft Internet Explorer, all the required text boxes will be empty. Click Save. The error messages belonging to all three *RequiredFieldValidator* controls are displayed.

Notice that the *Click* event for the Save button did not run; the label at the bottom of the form did not display the data summary (and the screen did not even flicker). This behavior is because the validation controls prevented the post-back to the server, and they will continue to block posts back to the server until all the errors have been corrected.

9 Type a name in the First Name text box. As soon as you move away from the text box, the error message disappears. If you return to the First Name text box, erase the contents, and then move to the next text box, the error message is displayed again. All this functionality is being performed in the browser and no data is being sent to the server over the network.

10 Enter values in the First Name, Last Name, and Employee Id text boxes, and then click Save. This time the *Click* event runs and the summary is displayed in the *InfoLabel* control at the bottom of the form.

11 Close the form and return to the Visual Studio .NET programming environment.

Currently, you can type anything into the Employee Id text box. In the following exercise, you will use a *RangeValidator* control to restrict the values entered to integers in the range of 1 through 5000.

Add a *RangeValidator* control

1 In the Toolbox, drag a *RangeValidator* control onto the form under the *RequiredFieldValidator* control below the Employee Id text box.

2 With the *RangeValidator* control selected, click the Properties window. Change the *ControlToValidate* property to EmployeeId. Type **Id must be between 1 and 5000** in the *ErrorMessage* property. Set the *MaximumValue* property to 5000, the *MinimumValue* property to 1, and the *Type* property to Integer.

3 Run the form again. Enter a first name and a last name, but leave the employee ID blank. Click Save. An error message telling you that you must supply an employee ID is displayed.

4 Type **AAA** in the Employee Id text box, and then click Save. An error message telling you that the employee ID must be between 1 and 5000 is displayed.

5   Type **101** in the Employee Id text box, and then click Save. This time the data is valid, the form is posted back to the server, the *Click* event of the Save button runs, and a summary of the information entered in the *InfoLabel* label appears at the bottom of the form.

6   Experiment with values that are out of range. Try -1 and 5001 to check that the *RangeValidator* control works as expected.

7   Close the form and return to the Visual Studio .NET programming environment.

Disabling Client Validation

If you want, you can suppress client validation and force all checks to be performed at the server. To do this, set the *EnableClientScript* property of the validation control to False. You might find it useful to do this under certain circumstances, such as those involving custom validations (using the *CustomValidator* control) that are complex or require access to data that is available only on the server. In addition, the *CustomValidator* control also has a *ServerValidate* event that can be used to perform validation explicitly on the server, even if *EnableClientScript* is set to True.

Remember that, if the browser does not support dynamic HTML, all validations will be performed by code generated on the server anyway.

You have seen how validation controls can validate the data that the user enters, but the error message display is not very pretty. In the following exercise, you will use a *ValidationSummary* control to change the way that the error information is presented to the user.

Add a *ValidationSummary* control

1   In the EmployeeForm.aspx Web form, select the *RequiredFieldValidator1* control under the First Name text box. In the Properties window, set the *Text* property to *.

The message, You Must Enter A First Name For The Employee, changes to an asterisk (*) because the validation controls display the *Text* property on the form. If no value is specified for the *Text* property, it takes the value of the *ErrorMessage* property.

2 Move the *RequiredFieldValidator1* control, placing it to the right of the First Name text box. Now, if a validation error occurs, you will see a red asterisk appear next to the text box with the error.

3 Select the *RequiredFieldValidator2* control, set its *Text* property to *, and then move it to the right of the Last Name text box.

4 Select the *RequiredFieldValidator3* control, set its *Text* property to *, and then move it to the right of the Employee Id text box. Do the same for the *RangeValidator1* control. The Web form should look like the following illustration:

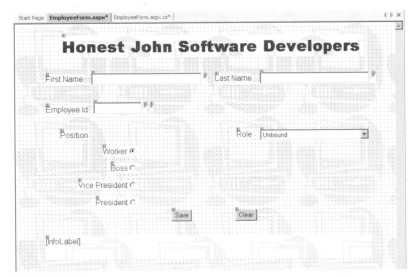

5 In the Toolbox, drag the *ValidationSummary* control onto the form in the space above the button controls and to the right of the radio buttons. A *ValidationSummary* control displays the *ErrorMessage* values for all of the validation controls on the Web form.

6 Leave the *ValidationSummary* control set to its default size. Verify that the *ShowSummary* property is set to True.

7 Run the Web form. When the form appears, leave the First Name, Last Name, and Employee Id text boxes blank, and then click Save. Red asterisks appear next to each of the text boxes, and the corresponding error messages are displayed in the *ValidationSummary* control at the bottom of the form.

8   Enter a first name, a last name, and then type **AAA** in the Employee Id text box. As you move from text box to text box, the asterisks disappear from the First Name and Last Name text boxes, but another asterisk appears next to the Employee Id text box.

9   Click Save. The error message displayed by the *ValidationSummary* control changes.

10 Type **101** in the Employee Id text box, and then click Save. All error messages and asterisks disappear and a summary of the data you entered appears in the *InfoLabel* control as before.

11 Close the form and return to the Visual Studio .NET programming environment.

Dynamic HTML and Error Messages

If you have a browser that supports dynamic HTML, you can display the validation summary data in a message box rather than on the Web form. To do this, set the *ShowMessageBox* property of the *ValidationSummary* control to True. At run time, if any validation errors occur, the error messages will be displayed in a message box.

If you want to continue to the next chapter

■   Keep Visual Studio .NET running and turn to Chapter 29.

If you want to quit Visual Studio .NET for now

■   On the File menu, click Exit. If you see a Save dialog box, click Yes.

Chapter 28 Quick Reference

To	Do this	Button
Perform server-side validation of user input	Use events belonging to server controls; for example, the *TextChanged* event of the *TextBox* control.	
Perform client-side validation of user input	Use a *Validation* control. Set the *ControlToValidate* property to the control to be validated and the *ErrorMessage* property to an error message to be displayed. Verify that the *EnableClientScript* property is set to True.	
Force the user to enter a value in a text box	Use a *RequiredFieldValidator* control.	RequiredFieldValidator
Check the type and range of data values entered into a text box	Use a *RangeValidator* control. Set the *Type*, *MaximumValue*, and *MinimumValue* properties as required.	RangeValidator
Display a summary of validation error messages	Use a *ValidationSummary* control. Verify that the *ShowSummary* property is set to True.	ValidationSummary

Accessing Data with Web Forms

29

Web Forms

In this chapter, you will learn how to:

■ Use Forms-based authentication to secure access to a Web application.

■ Create Web Forms that present data from a database using a *DataGrid* control.

■ Update a database from a Web form.

■ Build applications that need to display potentially large volumes of data while minimizing resource use.

In the previous two chapters, you saw how to build a simple Web application that allowed the user to enter information and validate the data that was entered. In this chapter, you'll learn about creating applications that display data from a database and update the database with any changes made by the user. You will see how to do this in an efficient manner that minimizes use of shared resources, such as the network and the database.

Security is always an important issue, especially when building applications that can be accessed over the Internet. Therefore, you will also see how to configure a Web Forms application to use Forms-based security to verify the identity of the user.

Using the Web Forms *DataGrid* Control

When you looked at accessing databases in previous chapters, you learned how to use the Windows Forms *DataGrid* control. There is also a Web Forms *DataGrid* control, which is similar but has some subtle differences because

Microsoft designed it to be used in a Microsoft ASP.NET environment. One difference is related to fetching and displaying large volumes of data. In a Web Forms application, it is very likely that the client application (or the browser) will be remote from the database that is being used. It is imperative that you use network bandwidth wisely (this has been stated several times already, but it is very important and worth repeating), and you should not waste resources retrieving vast amounts of data that the user does not want to see. The Web Forms *DataGrid* control supports *paging*, which allows you to fetch data on demand as the user scrolls up and down through a *DataSet*.

Like the Windows Forms *DataGrid* control, the Web Forms *DataGrid* control can be used while it is disconnected from the database. You can create an *SqlConnection* object to connect to a database, use an *SqlDataAdapter* to populate a *DataSet*, bind the *DataSet* to the *DataGrid* control, and then disconnect from the database. Unlike a Windows Forms *DataGrid* control, the information in a Web Forms *DataGrid* control is presented in a grid of read-only text (rendered as an HTML table in the browser). However, properties of the Web Forms *DataGrid* control allow a user to enter edit mode, which changes a selected row into a set of text boxes that the user can use to modify the data that is presented. You will use this technique in the exercises in this chapter.

Managing Security

Applications built using the Microsoft .NET Framework have a range of mechanisms available for ensuring that the users who run those applications have the appropriate privileges. Some of the techniques available rely on identifying users based on some form of identifier and password, whereas others are based on the integrated security features of Microsoft Windows. If you are creating a Web application that will be accessed over the Internet, using Windows integrated security is probably not an option—users are unlikely to be members of any domain recognized by the Web application and might be running an operating system other than Windows, such as UNIX. Therefore, the best option to use is Forms-based security.

Understanding Forms-Based Security

Forms-based security allows you to verify the identity of a user by displaying a login form that prompts the user for an ID and a password. After the user has been authenticated, the various Web Forms that comprise the application can be accessed, and the user's security credentials can be examined by code on any page if additional authorization is needed (a user might be able to log in to the system but might not have access to every part of the application).

To use ASP.NET Forms-based security, you must configure the Web application by making some changes to the Web.config file, and you must also supply a form to validate the user. The security form will be displayed whenever the user tries to gain access to any page in the application if the user has not already been validated. The user will be able to proceed to the requested page only if the logic in the login form verifies the user's identity.

▶ **Important**   It might seem, to the uninitiated, that ASP.NET Forms-based security is excessive. It's not. Don't be tempted to create a login form that acts as an entry point to your application and assume that users will always access your application through it. Browsers can cache forms and URLs locally on users' computers. Another user might be able to gain access to the browser cache depending on how the computer itself is configured, find the URLs of the sensitive parts of your application, and navigate directly to them, bypassing your login form. You have control over your Web server (hopefully) but you have almost no control over the user's computer. The ASP.NET Forms-based mechanism is pretty robust and, assuming that your Web server is secure, it should be adequate for most of your applications.

Implementing Forms-Based Security

In the first set of exercises in this chapter, you will create and configure a Web application that uses Forms-based security to verify the user's credentials.

Create the application

1   In the Microsoft Visual Studio .NET programming environment, create an ASP.NET Web application called CustomerInfo on your local Web server (localhost).

2   In Solution Explorer, change the name of WebForm1.aspx to CustomerData.aspx. In the Class View, change the name of the *WebForm1* class to *CustomerData*.

3   In the Toolbox, drag a *Label* control onto the middle of the *CustomerData* form. Type **This form will be implemented later** in the *Text* property of the label.

Build the login form

1   The login form is displayed whenever a user who has not been validated attempts to gain access to your application. When configured to use Forms-based security, the ASP.NET run time will redirect calls to your application to the login form. On the Project menu, click

Add Web Form. The Add New Item dialog box opens. Make sure the Web Form template is selected and type **LoginForm.aspx** for the name. Click Open to create the form.

2   Make sure that LoginForm.aspx is displayed in the Design View window. Using the Toolbox, add three *Label* controls, two *TextBox* controls, and a *Button* control to LoginForm.aspx. Set the properties of these controls using the values shown in the following table.

Control	Property	Value
Label1	Text	User Name:
Label2	Text	**Password:**
Label3	ID	**Message**
	Text	Leave blank
	ForeColor	**Red**
TextBox1	ID	**UserName**
TextBox2	ID	**Password**
	TextMode	**Password**
Button1	ID	**LoginButton**
	Text	**Login**

3   Click the HTML tab. Change the *POSITION*, *LEFT*, and *TOP* properties of the style attribute for each of the *Label* and *TextBox* controls, as shown in the following code:

```
<asp:Label id="Label1" style="LEFT: 183px;
  POSITION: absolute; TOP: 76px" runat="server">User Name:
</asp:Label>
<asp:Label id="Label2" style="LEFT: 183px;
  POSITION: absolute; TOP: 133px" runat="server">Password:
</asp:Label>
<asp:Label id="Message" style="LEFT: 183px;
  POSITION: absolute; TOP: 288px" runat="server" ForeColor="Red">
</asp:Label>
<asp:TextBox id="UserName" style="LEFT: 305px;
  POSITION: absolute; TOP: 71px" runat="server">
</asp:TextBox>
<asp:TextBox id="Password" style="LEFT: 305px;
  POSITION: absolute; TOP: 128px" runat="server"
  TextMode="Password">
</asp:TextBox>
```

4   Change the *LEFT*, *TOP*, and *POSITION* properties of the style attribute, and the *Width* attribute of the *Button* control, as shown in the following code:

```
<asp:Button id="LoginButton" style="LEFT: 305px;
  POSITION: absolute; TOP: 210px" runat="server"
  Text="Login" Width="78px" Height="24px">
</asp:Button>
```

5   Switch to Design View. The form should look like the following illustration:

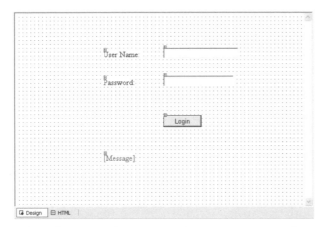

6   Select the Login button. In the Properties window, click Events and create an event handler for the *Click* event called *loginButtonClick*. In the Code And Text Editor window that is displaying Login-Form.aspx.cs, add the following *using* statement to the list at the top of the form:

```
using System.Web.Security;
```

This namespace contains classes and methods for handling security in Web applications—the *FormsAuthentication* class that you will use in the next step, for example.

7   Type the following statements in the *loginButtonClick* method:

```
private void loginClick(object sender, System.EventArgs e)
{
    if (UserName.Text.Equals("John")
        && Password.Text.Equals("JohnsPassword"))
    {
        Message.Text = "";
        FormsAuthentication.RedirectFromLoginPage(UserName.Text,
            true);
    }
    else
    {
        Message.Text = "Invalid username or password";
    }
}
```

This code performs a very simple validation check; the only supported user is *John*, with the password of *JohnsPassword*. (In a commercial system, expect to use a database of user names and passwords rather than hard-coded values.) If the user name and password match, the static *RedirectFromLoginPage* method of the *FormsAuthentication* class will create a persistent cookie containing the user name, store it, and then proceed to the page the user was originally trying to access.

Configure the application to use Forms-based security

1   In Solution Explorer, double-click Web.config to display the application configuration file.

2   Locate the <authentication> tag. It will indicate that Windows authentication is being used:

```
<authentication mode="Windows" />
```

Change the <authentication> tag as shown in the following code:

```
<authentication mode="Forms">
  <forms name="logincookie" loginUrl="LoginForm.aspx"
    protection="All" timeout="30" />
</authentication>
```

This code specifies that, if a user who has not been validated attempts to gain access to a page in the application, the user will be redirected to the LoginForm.aspx page. If the login is successful, a cookie called logincookie will be created and stored on the user's computer. This cookie provides access to the rest of the application. The cookie will be encrypted using Triple DES but will expire after 30 minutes if the user is inactive, forcing the user to log in again.

3   Modify the <authorization> tag as shown in the following code:

```
<authorization>
  <deny users="?" />
</authorization>
```

The <authorization> tag specifies which users can gain access to which resources in the application. Specifying a <deny> tag with "?" denies access to anonymous (or unauthorized) users.

▶   **Important**   Without the <authorization> tag, any user can gain access to any page in the application without being validated.

4   On the File menu, click Save All.

5   On the Build menu, click Build Solution.

6 Start Microsoft Internet Explorer, and type **http://localhost/CustomerInfo/CustomerData.aspx** in the Address text box. Rather than the *CustomerData* form appearing, you are redirected to the LoginForm.

If you type in a random user name and password and then click Login, the Invalid User Name Or Password message appears in red. If you type John and JohnsPassword, and then click Login, you are redirected to the CustomerData form, which displays the This Form Will Be Implemented Later message.

7 Close Internet Explorer. Start Internet Explorer again and navigate to *http://localhost/CustomerInfo/CustomerData.aspx*. As long as you have not spent more than 30 minutes between closing Internet Explorer and opening it again, your cookie is still valid and you go straight to the CustomerData page without being asked to log in again.

8 Close Internet Explorer and return to the Visual Studio .NET programming environment.

Querying Data

Now that you can control access to your application, you can turn your attention to querying and maintaining data. You will use Microsoft ADO.NET controls to connect to the database, query data, and maintain the data, just as you did in the Windows Forms applications you built earlier.

▶ **Important** The security model used by the ASP.NET service prevents it from being able to use SQL Server databases unless the account used by the ASP.NET service is granted access. ASP.NET must be able to use the SQL Server for you to perform the exercises in the remainder of the book.

If you have installed and configured the QuickStart samples that are included in Visual Studio .NET 2003 as part of the Microsoft .NET Framework SDK 1.1, the account used by ASP.NET will already have been granted access to the Northwind database. If you have not already installed the QuickStart samples, you can grant access to the ASP.NET service using the steps that follow.

In the following exercise, you will learn how to grant access to the ASP.NET service.

Grant access to the ASP.NET service

1 From the Windows Start menu, point to All Programs, point to Accessories, and then click Command Prompt. A command prompt window opens.

2   In the command prompt window, type **osql -E
-S<*your_computer*>\VSdotNET2003** where <*your_computer*> is the
name of your computer. This command starts the osql query tool,
allowing you to enter SQL commands. You will see the prompt 1>.

3   At the prompt, type **exec sp_grantlogin N'**<your_computer>**ASP-
NET'** where <*your_computer*> is the name of your computer, and
press Enter. Make sure that you type the N and the single quotes
exactly as shown.

4   When the 2> prompt appears, type **go** and press Enter. The following
message appears: Granted login access to <*your_computer*>\ASPNET.

5   At the 1> prompt, type **exec sp_defaultdb N'**<*your_computer*>**ASP-
NET', N'Northwind'** and press Enter.

6   At the 2> prompt, type **go** and press Enter. The following message
appears: Default database changed.

7   At the 1> prompt, type **use Northwind** and press Enter.

8   At the 2> prompt, type **go** and press Enter.

9   At the 1> prompt, type **exec sp_grantdbaccess
N'**<your_computer>**ASPNET', N'ASPNET'** and press Enter.

10 At the 2> prompt, type **go** and press Enter. The following message
appears: Granted database access to '<*your_computer*>\ASPNET.

11 At the 1> prompt, type **exit** and press Enter. You are returned to the
command prompt.

12 Close the command prompt window.

Displaying Customer Information

In the following exercises, you will fetch all of the rows in the Customers table
in the Microsoft SQL Server Northwind Traders database and display them in a
DataGrid.

Lay out the *CustomerData* form

1   Display the CustomerData.aspx page in Design View. Delete the
label displaying This Form Will Be Implemented Later.

2   In the Toolbox, click the *DataGrid* control. Drag it onto the form. A
DataGrid is added to the form and displays placeholder data. Resize

the *DataGrid* so that it fills most of the form (it does not have a *Dock* property, unlike its Windows Forms counterpart).

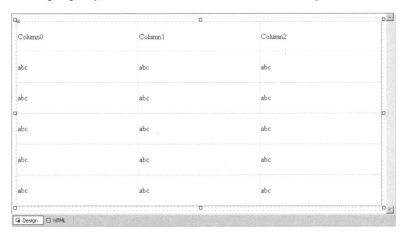

3   Right-click the *DataGrid*, and then click AutoFormat in the pop-up menu. The Auto Format dialog box opens. This dialog box lets you pick from one of the predefined color schemes and layouts for the *DataGrid*. Select the Colorful 1 scheme, and then click OK.

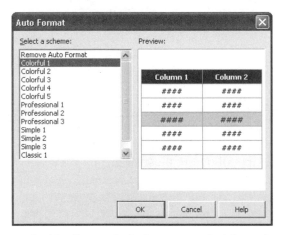

4   In the Toolbox, click the Data tab. This tab contains ADO.NET controls. Drag an *SqlDataAdapter* control onto the form. When the Data Adapter Configuration Wizard opens, use the information in the following table to answer the prompts on each page of the wizard.

29

Web Forms

Page	Prompt	Response
Welcome To The Data Adapter Configuration Wizard		Click Next.
Choose Your Data Connection	Which data connection should the data adapter use?	If you completed the exercises in Chapter 24, accept the default data connection, and then click Next. If you did not, create a new data connection by clicking the New button and following the instructions in the section entitled "Accessing the Database" in Chapter 24. Then click Next.
Choose a Query Type	How should the data adapter access the database?	Select Use SQL Statements (the default), and then click Next.
Generate The SQL Statements	What data should the data adapter load into the dataset?	Type the following code, and then click Next:

```
SELECT *
FROM Customers
```

Page	Prompt	Response
View Wizard Results		Verify that the data adapter was configured successfully and click Finish. If there are any errors, click Back and correct the SQL statement.

An *SqlDataAdapter* object called *sqldataAdapter1* is added to the bottom of the form, along with an *SqlConnectionObject* called *sqlConnection1*.

5   In the Toolbox, drag the *DataSet* control onto the form. When the Add Dataset dialog box opens, select Untyped Dataset and click OK. A *DataSet* control called *dataSet1* is added below the form. Your form should look like the following illustration:

6 Select the *DataGrid* control. In the Properties window, set the *Data-Source* property to *dataSet1*. This action binds the *DataGrid* to the *DataSet*; any data in the *DataSet* will be displayed in the *DataGrid*.

DataGrid Styles

You can also change the styles of the elements of a *DataGrid* manually by using the properties in the Properties window. *BackColor, BorderStyle, Border-Width, FooterStyle, HeaderStyle,* and *ItemStyle* are the most commonly modified properties.

Alternatively, you can right-click the *DataGrid*, and then click Property Builder. This command displays the DataGrid Properties dialog box. Click the Format tab. You can change the layout, font, and color of most elements of the *DataGrid*.

Populate the *DataGrid* and display data

1 On the View menu, click Code to display the CustomerData.aspx.cs file. This file contains the code behind the form.

2 In the *CustomerData* class, create a private method called *bindGrid* after the *Page_Load* method.

This method will open the connection to the database and populate the *DataSet*. The *DataBind* method of the *DataGrid* control notifies the *DataGrid* that the *DataSet* has changed, causing the *DataGrid* to display the information held in the *DataSet* (it will generate columns automatically). After the data has been fetched, the connection to the database is closed to conserve resources.

```
private void bindGrid()
{
    sqlConnection1.Open();
    sqlDataAdapter1.Fill(dataSet1);
    DataGrid1.DataBind();
    sqlConnection1.Close();
}
```

3 Locate the *Page_Load* method. This method is called every time the page is displayed. Add the following statements:

```
if (!IsPostBack)
{
    bindGrid();
}
```

The *IsPostBack* property of a form determines whether the form is being displayed for the first time or is being rendered as the result of a postback (possibly because a user clicked a button on the form). If the form is being displayed for the first time, the *bindGrid* method will retrieve the data from the database and display it. In the event of a postback, the data is already present in the *DataGrid* and does not need to be fetched again.

4   Save the application and use Start on the Debug menu to run it. Internet Explorer will start. On the CustomerData page, the *Data-Grid* containing every row from the Customers table in the database is displayed.

    If you click Source on the View menu in Internet Explorer, you will see that the *DataGrid* is rendered as an HTML table (and contains a large amount of state data).

5   After you finish browsing the customers, close Internet Explorer and return to the Visual Studio .NET programming environment.

Retrieving Data on Demand

Fetching the details of every customer is very useful, but suppose that there are a large number of rows in the Customers table. It is highly unlikely that a user would actively want to browse thousands of rows, so fetching them all would be a waste of time and network bandwidth. Instead, it would be far better to fetch data in chunks and allow the user to page through that data. This is what you will do in the following set of exercises.

Modify the *DataGrid* to use paging

1   Ensure that CustomerData.aspx is displayed in the Design View window. Right-click the *DataGrid* control on the form, and then click Property Builder. The DataGrid1 Properties dialog box opens. Click the Paging button on the left to display the Paging properties.

2   Select the Allow Paging check box. Change the *Page Size* property to 8 rows. Verify that the Show Navigation Buttons option is selected, and that the *Position* property is set to Bottom. Change the *Mode* property to Page Numbers to allow the user to go directly to a particular page without navigating through all the preceding pages. Set the *Numeric Buttons* property to 20—this is the maximum number of page numbers that will be displayed at the bottom of the grid.

3 Click OK to close the dialog box and save your changes. The paging area appears at the bottom of the data grid and displays a pair of placeholder page numbers.

Column0	Column1	Column2
abc	abc	abc
abc	abc	abc
abc	abc	abc
abc	abc	abc
abc	abc	abc
abc	abc	abc
abc	abc	abc
abc	abc	abc
	1 2	

▶ **Tip** You can also modify some paging properties available in the DataGrid Properties dialog box using code. Look at the *PagerStyle* compound property in the Properties window to see the attributes that you can change.

Fetch a page of data

1 When the user clicks a page number in the paging area of the *Data-Grid* control, the *PageIndexChanged* event is raised. This event determines which page of data the user wants to see and then displays that page. With the *DataGrid* control still selected, click Events in the Properties window. Create an event method for the *PageIndex-Changed* event called *changePage*.

2 In the Code And Text Editor window, add the following statements to the *changePage* method:

```
DataGrid1.CurrentPageIndex = e.NewPageIndex;
bindGrid();
```

The *DataGridEventArgs* parameter, *e*, contains information about the new page to be displayed, including the new page number (which is in the *NewPageIndex* property). Changing the *CurrentPageIndex* property of the *DataGrid* control to this page will display the new page. You must also rebind the *DataGrid* to the *DataSet*, which is what the call to the *bindGrid* method does.

29

Web Forms

3   Save and run the application. When the CustomerData form appears, the first 8 rows of data and a set of page numbers are displayed.

4   Click the page numbers at the bottom of the grid to move from page to page.

5   Close Internet Explorer and return to the Visual Studio .NET programming environment when you have finished browsing the data.

Optimizing Data Access

Your application no longer wastes network bandwidth across the Internet, but it is still wasteful when it accesses the database. Every time you display a page of data, the *bindGrid* method retrieves every customer in the database. It would be better to fetch the customer information only once, and cache it in the Web application.

Web Applications and Caching

You have to make a decision at this point when designing Web applications. If you want to ensure that the data is completely up-to-date when it is displayed, you should not cache data. The cost is repeated access to the database. The larger the set of data you are using, the more expensive repeated access becomes and the more attractive caching becomes, at least in theory. However, you ought to be aware of how caching is performed and how the cache is stored.

The cache is held in memory on the Web server, in the process that services ASP.NET requests on behalf of the client. In a Web server farm, where client requests can be directed to any of a number of different server processes, the administrator can configure the system to store cached information in "global" memory using the ASP.NET State service. In both cases, if you are caching large data sets, you must make certain that you have sufficient memory available to handle all concurrent requests. The administrator can also configure the cache to use a SQL Server database. In this situation, the benefits of the cache are further diminished because your application will be using a database again, although it is a different one.

To summarize, caching is not necessarily a guarantee of improved performance. Use it wisely.

Use a cache object

1 Display Customer.aspx.cs in the Code And Text Editor window. Locate the *Page_Load* method and change it as shown in the following code:

```
private void Page_Load(object sender, System.EventArgs e)
{
    if (!IsPostBack)
    {
        sqlConnection1.Open();
        sqlDataAdapter1.Fill(dataSet1);
        Cache["CustomerData"] = dataSet1;
        bindGrid();
        sqlConnection1.Close();
    }
}
```

This method connects to the database and populates the *DataSet*. It then caches the *DataSet*. The *Cache* object is a collection that is built into ASP.NET. It can contain any type of data. You index the cache using a string value of your own choosing; in this example, it is *CustomerData*. The *bindGrid* method (which you will amend in a moment) will retrieve the *DataSet* from the cache and bind it to the *DataGrid*. Finally, the connection to the database is closed.

2 Locate the *bindGrid* method and modify it as follows:

```
private void bindGrid()
{
    dataSet1 = (DataSet)Cache["CustomerData"];
    DataGrid1.DataBind();
}
```

You can see that the *bindGrid* method no longer gains direct access to the database. All calls made to *bindGrid* (for example, in the *changePage* method) will use the cached data instead.

▶ **Note** The *Cache* object has Web application scope and as such is shared by clients executing the same Web application. This type of cache is useful if multiple clients need to access the same data. Each client also has its own unique *Session* cache (accessed using the *Session* object with indexer notation), and two clients can both have their own private cached objects indexed using the same string. The *Cache* and *Session* objects will work in a Web farm environment, and so are useful when building scalable applications.

3   Save and run the Web application again. It should still work, and it might be slightly faster. You might not notice much change, but remember that you are using a local database, and you are probably the only user accessing it. If the database were being stressed more heavily, you would notice a difference as you moved from page to page.

As an experiment, to prove that the cache is being used, you could try stopping SQL Server after the first page has been displayed. You will still be able to move from page to page and display the data.

Be sure to restart SQL Server before you continue with the following exercise.

Editing Data

You have seen how to use a *DataGrid* control to fetch and browse data. The following set of exercises concentrate on deleting and modifying data using a *DataGrid* control.

Deleting Rows

The *DataGrid* control allows you to add buttons to the grid to indicate that a command should be performed. You can add your own custom buttons and commands, but Visual Studio .NET supplies some predefined buttons for deleting and editing data. In the following exercise, you will add a Delete button to the *DataGrid* and write code to delete the current row from the database when the user clicks it.

Create the Delete button

1   Ensure that CustomerData.aspx is displayed in the Design View window. Right-click the *DataGrid* control, and then click Property Builder. When the DataGrid1 Properties dialog box opens, click the Columns button on the left.

2   Expand the Button Column node in the Available Columns tree view. Select the Delete button and click the > button to copy it into the Selected Columns list. In the lower part of the dialog box displaying the ButtonColumn properties, change the *Button Type* property to PushButton, but leave the other properties set to their default values.

Notice that the *Command Name* property is set to Delete—this is important. If you change the property, the *Command Name* is passed in the parameter to the *ItemCommand* event of the *DataGrid* (this feature is useful if you are defining your own custom buttons). However, if you leave the *Command Name* property set to Delete, clicking the Delete button at run time raises the *DeleteCommand* event instead.

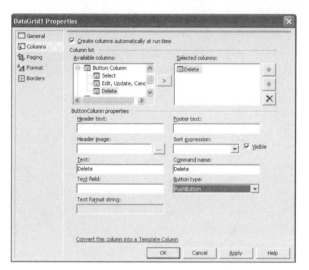

3   Click OK to save the changes. A Delete button is added to every row in the *DataGrid*.

	Column0	Column1	Column2
Delete	abc	abc	abc
Delete	abc	abc	abc
Delete	abc	abc	abc
Delete	abc	abc	abc
Delete	abc	abc	abc
Delete	abc	abc	abc
Delete	abc	abc	abc
Delete	abc	abc	abc
	1 2		

Delete a row

1   To delete a row, you must subscribe to the *DeleteCommand* event. Move the *DataGrid* control down, and then add a *Label* control to the form. Place it above the *DataGrid* control. Change its *ID* prop-

erty to ErrorMessage, and clear its *Text* property. Set its *Height* property to 40px and its *Width* property to 760px.

2   Select the *DataGrid* control on the form, click Events in the Properties window, and then create an event method for the *Delete-Command* event called *deleteRow*.

3   In the Code And Text Editor window displaying Customer-Data.aspx.cs, add the following *using* command to the list at the top of the file:

```
using System.Data.SqlClient;
```

If you recall, the *SqlClient* namespace contains the ADO.NET classes for gaining access to SQL Server.

4   Type the following statements in the *deleteRow* method:

```
try
{
    ErrorMessage.Text = "";
    SqlCommand delCommand = new SqlCommand();
    delCommand.Connection = sqlConnection1;
    delCommand.CommandText = "DELETE FROM Customers " +
        "WHERE CustomerID = '" + e.Item.Cells[1].Text + "'";
    delCommand.CommandType = CommandType.Text;
    sqlConnection1.Open();
    delCommand.ExecuteNonQuery();
    sqlDataAdapter1.Fill(dataSet1);
    Cache["CustomerData"] = dataSet1;
    bindGrid();
    sqlConnection1.Close();
}
catch (Exception ex)
{
    ErrorMessage.Text = ex.Message;
}
```

Much of this code should be familiar to you. It creates an *SqlCommand* object containing a *DELETE* statement. The code then opens the connection to the database and runs the SQL statement. The *DataSet* used by the *DataGrid* is repopulated and cached to reflect the changes, and the *DataGrid* is rebound to the *DataSet* before closing the database connection. If an error occurs, the *ErrorMessage* label displays the reason for the error.

The key point is the use of the parameter *e*. This parameter has the type *DataGridCommandEventArgs*. This type has an *Item* property that references the current row in the *DataGrid* control. The *Item* property contains a *Cells* collection—one cell for each column in the current row. The first cell (*Cells[0]*) contains the Delete button, and the second cell (*Cells[1]*) contains the Customer ID. The *Text* property of this cell returns the value of the Customer ID.

5   Save and run the application. Go to Page 3 of the data and delete the customer with the ID of FISSA. This should be successful. Try to delete customer FAMIA. This will fail with an error because this customer has outstanding orders; the referential integrity rules of the Northwind Traders database forbid you from deleting a customer that has outstanding orders.

6   Close the form and return to the Visual Studio .NET programming environment.

Updating Rows

You can also add an Edit button to a *DataGrid* to allow a user to change the data in a selected row in the *DataGrid*. The row changes into a set of *TextBox* controls when the user clicks the Edit button. The user can save the changes or discard them. This is achieved using two additional buttons: Update and Cancel. In the following set of exercises, you will add these buttons to the CustomerData form and write code to maintain the database.

Create the Edit, Update, and Cancel buttons

1   Display the CustomerData.aspx form in Design View. Right-click the *DataGrid*, and then click Property Builder. In the DataGrid1 Properties dialog box, click Columns, expand the Button Column node in the Available Columns tree view, select Edit, Update, Cancel, and then click the > button. Set the *Button* type to PushButton.

2   Click OK to save your changes. Another column containing an Edit button is added to the *DataGrid*.

The following exercise will show you how to modify a row and update a database. Here's what it will entail. When the user clicks the Edit button, the selected row should switch into edit mode. Edit mode involves displaying the contents of the row as a series of *TextBox* controls. You achieve this by trapping the *EditCommand* event to set the *EditItemIndex* property of the *DataGrid* control to the index of the item that is being edited. This will also cause the Update and Cancel buttons to appear. If the user clicks the Cancel button, you use the *CancelCommand* event to undo any changes made and return to browse mode. If the user clicks the Update button, you use the *UpdateCommand* event to propagate the changes to the database.

Modify a row and update the database

1   Select the *DataGrid* control. In the Properties window, click the Events button and create an event method called *editRow* for the *EditCommand* event. In the *editRow* method, add the following statements:

```
DataGrid1.EditItemIndex = e.Item.ItemIndex;
bindGrid();
```

Setting the *EditItemIndex* property of a *DataGrid* control to a row number causes that row to be displayed as a set of text boxes. The *ItemIndex* property of the *Item* property of the *DataGridCommand-EventArgs* parameter, *e*, contains the index of the current row in the *DataGrid*. You must rebind the *DataGrid* to the *DataSet* before the row will be rendered properly.

2   Locate the *deleteRow* method. Modify the statement that sets the *CommandText* property of the *delCommand* variable to refer to *e.Item.Cells[2]*:

```
delCommand.CommandText = "DELETE FROM Customers " +
    "WHERE CustomerID = '" + e.Item.Cells[2].Text + "'";
```

This is necessary because you have inserted a new column by adding the Edit button.

3   Create an event method called *cancelChange* for the *Cancel-Command* event of the *DataGrid* control. Add the following statements to the *cancelChange* method:

```
DataGrid1.EditItemIndex = -1;
bindGrid();
```

Setting the *EditItemIndex* property of a *DataGrid* control to -1 causes all rows to be displayed as labels and discards any changes made while in edit mode.

4   Create a final event method called *updateRow* for the *Update-Command* event of the *DataGrid* control. Type the following statements in the *updateRow* method:

```
try
{
    ErrorMessage.Text = "";
    SqlCommand updCommand = new SqlCommand();
    updCommand.Connection = sqlConnection1;
    updCommand.CommandText = "UPDATE Customers SET CompanyName = '"
        + ((TextBox)e.Item.Cells[3].Controls[0]).Text
        + "', ContactName = '"
        + ((TextBox)e.Item.Cells[4].Controls[0]).Text
```

```
                          + "', ContactTitle = '"
                          + ((TextBox)e.Item.Cells[5].Controls[0]).Text
                          + "', Address = '"
                          + ((TextBox)e.Item.Cells[6].Controls[0]).Text
                          + "', City = '"
                          + ((TextBox)e.Item.Cells[7].Controls[0]).Text
                          + "', Region = '"
                          + ((TextBox)e.Item.Cells[8].Controls[0]).Text
                          + "', PostalCode = '"
                          + ((TextBox)e.Item.Cells[9].Controls[0]).Text
                          + "', Country = '"
                          + ((TextBox)e.Item.Cells[10].Controls[0]).Text
                          + "', Phone = '"
                          + ((TextBox)e.Item.Cells[11].Controls[0]).Text
                          + "', Fax = '"
                          + ((TextBox)e.Item.Cells[12].Controls[0]).Text + "'"
                          + " WHERE CustomerID = '"
                          + ((TextBox)e.Item.Cells[2].Controls[0]).Text + "'";
            updCommand.CommandType = CommandType.Text;
            sqlConnection1.Open();
            updCommand.ExecuteNonQuery();
            sqlDataAdapter1.Fill(dataSet1);
            Cache["CustomerData"] = dataSet1;
            DataGrid1.EditItemIndex = -1;
            bindGrid();
            sqlConnection1.Close();
        }
        catch (Exception ex)
        {
            ErrorMessage.Text = ex.Message;
        }
```

This code is similar to the *deleteRow* method you created earlier; the main difference is that the SQL statement that is generated and executed is an *UPDATE* statement. Also notice that when the *DataGrid* is in edit mode, you gain access to the contents of the row slightly differently. Rather than reading the *Text* property of each cell, you must use the Controls collection, casting it to the appropriate control. (In this case, each row is rendered as a set of *TextBox* controls.) In some circumstances, cells can contain several controls, hence the use of a collection.

5   Save and run the application. Click the Edit button on the first row.

Notice that the first row changes into a collection of *TextBox* controls, and the Edit button is replaced with an Update button and a Cancel button. (This is an example of a cell containing multiple controls.)

6 Modify the ContactName and ContactTitle columns, and then click Update. The database is updated, the row reverts back to a set of labels, the Edit button reappears, and the new data is displayed in the row.

▶ **Tip** In an ideal solution, you would not be allowed to modify the Customer ID because this is the primary key used to identify the row to be updated. If you do change it, you will find the change is discarded when you click the Update button. The Microsoft ASP.NET QuickStart Tutorial shows a technique for making a column read-only, but it relies on using statically created columns in the *Data-Grid*. (You have been using automatically generated columns in this chapter.) For more information, see Server-side Data Access under ASP.NET Web Forms in the ASP.NET QuickStart Tutorial.

If you want to continue to the next chapter

■ Keep Visual Studio .NET running and turn to Chapter 30.

If you want to quit Visual Studio .NET for now

■ On the File menu, click Exit. If you see a Save dialog box, click Yes.

Chapter 29 Quick Reference

To	Do this	Button
Use Forms-based security	Create a login form to validate the user. Edit the Web.config file, setting the <authentication> and <authorization> elements to redirect the user to the login form if the user attempts to access any other form in the application without first being validated. For example:	

```
<authentication mode="Forms">
  <forms name="logincookie"
    loginUrl="LoginForm.aspx"
    protection="All"
    timeout="30" />
</authentication>
<authorization>
  <deny users="?" />
</authorization>
```

To	Do this	Button
Display multiple rows from a data source on a Web form	Use a *DataGrid* control. Populate a *DataSet* with the data to be displayed, set the *DataSource* property of the *DataGrid* to the *DataSet*, and run the *DataBind* method of the *DataGrid* to display the data.	DataGrid
Retrieve data on demand rather than all at once	Use paging with the *DataGrid* control. Select the Allow Paging property and set the other paging properties (for example, *Page Size* and *Mode*). Use the *PageIndexChanged* event to determine the page that the user wants to display, and fetch the data.	

Cache frequently accessed data to avoid having to re-fetch it from the database	Use the ASP.NET Cache object to store data in memory on the server. For example:
	
	`Cache["CustomerData"] =`
	`    dataSet1;`	

Delete rows using a *DataGrid* control	Add a *Button Column* to the *Data-Grid* containing a Delete button, with the *Command Name* property set to Delete. Use the *DeleteItem* event of the *DataGrid* to identify the row to be deleted and remove it.	
Edit and update rows using a *Data-Grid* control	Add a *Button Column* to the *Data-Grid* containing Edit, Update, and Cancel buttons. Use the *EditCom-mand* event to set the *EditItemIndex* property of the *DataGrid* and render the edited row as a set of *TextBox* controls. Use the *UpdateCommand* event to send changes to the database, and then use the *CancelCommand* event to discard any changes made by setting the *EditItemIndex* property of the *DataGrid* to -1.	

29

Web Forms

Building ASP.NET Applications

In this chapter, you will learn how to:

■ Make more advanced use of a *DataGrid* control.

■ Use templates for customizing the layout of a *DataGrid* control.

■ Navigate between Web forms and pass data from one Web form to another.

You already learned how to retrieve data from a database and display it in a Web form using a *DataGrid* control, and how to update a database with changes captured from the client in a *DataGrid* control. In this chapter, you'll learn about some additional features of the *DataGrid* control that can be used for formatting and presenting data. Additionally, you'll learn how to pass information from one Web form to another and how to navigate between forms using hyperlinks and other controls.

Additional Features of the *DataGrid* Control

The *DataGrid* control has several features that you can use to help the user analyze the data that is presented. The two most commonly used features are the ability to dynamically sort data and the capacity to change the way in which data is presented by using Column templates.

Sorting a *DataGrid*

Although you can sort data as it is retrieved from a data source (for example, by using an *ORDER BY* clause with an SQL *SELECT* statement), you waste resources by continuing to fetch the same data just to reorder it. Unless you really need to refresh the data, it is far more efficient to sort the data already buffered in a *DataSet*. The *DataGrid* control provides a property and an event to help you sort data in any column quickly and easily—however, you need to use a *DataView* component to sort and display the data. This is what you will do in the following exercise.

Create the SupplierInfo application

1   Create a Microsoft ASP.NET Web application. Set the location to *http://localhost/SupplierInfo*.

2   In Solution Explorer, change the name of WebForm1.aspx to Supplier.aspx. In the Class View, change the name of the *WebForm1* class to *Supplier*. In the Properties window, update the *Title* property of the *DOCUMENT* object to *Suppliers*.

3   In Server Explorer, expand the SQL Servers node for your server, expand the node for your local Microsoft SQL Server computer, open the Northwind database, and then locate the Suppliers table. Drag the Suppliers table onto the Web form.

By now you should be familiar with this technique for creating Microsoft ADO.NET objects for accessing a database. This technique creates an *SqlConnection* object called *sqlConnection1* and an *SqlDataAdapter* called *sqlDataAdapter1*.

4   In the Toolbox, click the Data tab. Drag the *DataSet* control onto the Web form. When the Add Dataset dialog box opens, select Untyped Dataset and click OK. The *dataSet1* object is added underneath the form.

5   In the Toolbox, click the Web Forms tab. Drag a *DataGrid* control onto the Web form. With the *DataGrid* control selected, click the Auto Format link underneath the Properties window. In the Auto Format dialog box, select the Professional 2 Scheme and click OK. When you have completed these tasks, the form will look like the following illustration:

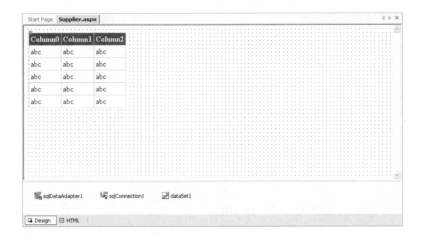

Bind the *DataGrid* and display the data

1 Switch to the Code And Text Editor window displaying Supplier.aspx.cs. Add a private *void* method called *bindGrid* to the *Supplier* class:

```
private void bindGrid()
{
    sqlConnection1.Open();
    sqlDataAdapter1.Fill(dataSet1);
    DataGrid1.DataSource = dataSet1;
    DataGrid1.DataBind();
    Cache["SupplierData"] = dataSet1;
    sqlConnection1.Close();
}
```

This code should be familiar to you. It opens the connection to the database, populates the *DataSet* with the contents of the Suppliers table, and binds the *DataGrid* to the *DataSet*, thereby displaying the Suppliers data. The *DataSet* is cached (you will use it again later) and the connection to the database is closed.

2 Find the *Page_Load* method, and add the following statements to invoke the *bindGrid* method if the Web form is being displayed for the first time:

```
if (!IsPostBack)
{
    bindGrid();
}
```

Add the sort functionality

1 Return to the Design View for Supplier.aspx. Select the *DataGrid1* control on the Web form. In the Properties window, set the *Allow-Sorting* property to True.

Enabling this property causes the header of each column to be displayed as a hyperlink at run time. When the user clicks the hyperlink, the *SortCommand* event is raised. You can trap this event and use it to sort the selected column.

2 In the Properties window, click the Events button. Create an event handler for the *SortCommand* event of the *DataGrid1* control, called *sortSuppliers*.

A new event method is created that takes a *DataGridSortCommandEventArgs* parameter. This parameter contains information about the column that the user clicked.

3 Add the following statements to the *sortSuppliers* method:

```
dataSet1 = (DataSet)Cache["SupplierData"];
DataView sortView = new DataView(dataSet1.Tables["Suppliers"]);
sortView.Sort = e.SortExpression;
DataGrid1.DataSource = sortView;
DataGrid1.DataBind();
```

This code retrieves the cached *DataSet* and uses it to create a *Data-View* object. A *DataView* can be used as a data source, and it allows you to filter the data that is displayed and to specify a sort sequence. The *DataView* used displays all the rows in the Suppliers table in the *DataSet*. Setting the *Sort* property sorts the data in the *DataView*—the *DataGridSortCommandEventArgs* parameter, *e*, has a property called *SortExpression* that indicates which column to sort. The *Data-View* is used as the data source for the *DataGrid*, and the *DataBind* method redisplays the sorted data.

▶ **Tip**   The *Sort* property is a string containing the name of the column to sort. By default, data is displayed in ascending order of the data in the sort column. You can append the text DESC to the end of the sort expression to display the data in descending order. You can also sort by multiple columns by setting the *Sort* property of the *DataView* to a string containing a comma-separated list of column names.

4   On the Debug menu, click Start to run the application. On the Suppliers form, notice how the column titles in the *DataGrid* appear as hyperlinks.

5   Click the CompanyName column. The data is displayed in ascending order, according to the name of the company.

6   Close the form and return to the Microsoft Visual Studio .NET programming environment.

Using Column Templates

You can apply a template to change the layout and appearance of a *DataGrid* control. A template describes the HTML that is used to render parts of the control. The *DataGrid* control allows you to specify a template for laying out the *Header*, *Footer*, and *Pager* elements of the control as well as for formatting the individual items that are displayed or edited.

▶ **Important**   It is important to understand the differences between a style and a template. A *style* is used to change the appearance of elements within a control. You can indicate which font, color, text size, and other attributes to modify when using a style, as you did in the previous chapter. A *template*, on the other hand, changes the layout of the control itself. You can include other controls as part of a template, and you can arrange for the template to be applied to selected elements of the control. For example, the default layout used by the *DataList* control is tabular (rows and columns of text data), but by using a template, you can change this layout to a multi-column display that presents data in each cell using a variety of HTML controls (for example, images).

Column templates are useful when you want to display data using a format other than a text field. For example, the Discontinued column in the Products table would be better displayed as a check box. You will see how to do this in the next exercise.

Create the Product Info application

1   Create an ASP.NET Web application. Set the location to *http://localhost/ProductInfo*.

30

ASP.NET Applications

2   Change the name of the WebForms1.aspx file to Product.aspx, update the name of the *WebForm1* class to *Product*, and change the title of the *DOCUMENT* object to *Products*.

3   In Server Explorer, expand the SQL Servers node for your server, expand the node for your local SQL Server computer, open the Northwind database, and locate the Products table. Expand the Products table, and then click the ProductID column. Press Ctrl and then click the ProductName, CategoryID, QuantityPerUnit, UnitPrice, and Discontinued columns to select all of these columns simultaneously.

4   Drag one of the selected columns onto the Web form. An *SqlConnection* object (*sqlConnection1*) and an *SqlDataAdapter* object (*sqlDataAdapter1*) are added to the form. However, the *SqlDataAdapter* only fetches the selected columns from the Products table.

▶   **Note**   If you drag the table onto the form, you get all the columns.

5   In the Toolbox, click the Data tab. Drag the *DataSet* control onto the Web form. When the Add Dataset dialog box opens, select Untyped Dataset, and then click OK. As before, the *dataSet1* object is added underneath the form.

6   Drag a *DataGrid* control from the Web Forms page of the Toolbox onto the Web form. Click the Auto Format link underneath the Properties window. In the Auto Format dialog box, select the Professional 2 scheme and click OK. In the Properties window, set the *DataSource* property for *DataGrid1* to *dataSet1*.

Because this form will not be sorting the data, you will not make use of a *DataView* object, and the *DataSet* can be directly attached to the *DataGrid*.

Bind the *DataGrid*

1   Display the Code And Text Editor window for Product.aspx.cs. Create the *bindGrid* method in the *Product* class as shown:

```
private void bindGrid()
{
    sqlConnection1.Open();
    sqlDataAdapter1.Fill(dataSet1);
    DataGrid1.DataBind();
    sqlConnection1.Close();
}
```

2   Find the *Page_Load* method, and then add the following statements that invoke the *bindGrid* method if the Web form is being displayed for the first time:

```
if (!IsPostBack)
{
    bindGrid();
}
```

3   Save and run the application. When the Web form appears, you will see the selected details for each product, with each item displayed as a label, including the Discontinued column.

4   Close the form and return to the Visual Studio .NET programming environment.

Display the Discontinued column as a check box

1   Display Product.aspx in the Design View window. Select the *Data-Grid* control. Click the Property Builder link underneath the Properties window. The DataGrid1 Properties dialog box opens.

2   Click the Columns button on the left. Select Template Column from the Available Columns list, and then click the > button to transfer it into the Selected Columns list.

Click OK. When the *DataGrid* control is redisplayed on the form, you will see an additional narrow column on the left side of the control.

3   Right-click the *DataGrid* control on the Web form, point to Edit Template, and then click Columns[0]. (If you had created more than one Column template, they would all be listed here.)

The *DataGrid* displayed on the Web form switches to Edit Template mode, allowing you to modify the contents of the column header and footer, as well as the column itself, while it is displayed and being edited.

4   In the Toolbox, drag the *CheckBox* control onto the Item Template area of the *DataGrid* control. Click in the blue area marked as the Header Template and type **Discontinued**.

5   Right-click the *DataGrid* control again, and then click End Template Editing. The *DataGrid* returns to its normal display, but now contains a check box column titled Discontinued as the first column.

30

ASP.NET Applications

6   Click the HTML tab at the bottom of the Design View window. Notice the <Columns> tag that is part of the *<asp:DataGrid>* element. This tag has subelements describing the Header and Item templates for the new column. The *<ItemTemplate>* element includes the *<asp:CheckBox>* control.

7   Change the *CheckBox* element as shown in the following code:

```
<asp:CheckBox id="CheckBox1" runat="server"
  Checked='<%# DataBinder.Eval(Container.DataItem,
  "Discontinued") %>'>
</asp:CheckBox>
```

This code sets the *Checked* property of the *CheckBox* using a data binding expression. The expression between <%# and %> is evaluated as each row is returned from the database and displayed in the *DataGrid*; this occurs when the *DataBind* method of the *DataGrid* runs. The *DataBinder* class is used to evaluate expressions that bind data to ASP.NET server controls. The static *Eval* method parses and evaluates an expression dynamically at run time. The first parameter (*Container.DataItem*) is the object against which the expression (Discontinued) is evaluated. In this case, the *Container* object is the *DataGrid* holding the Template column. The *DataItem* property of a *DataGrid* refers to the current row. The expression *DataBinder.Eval(Container.DataItem, "Discontinued")* therefore extracts the value of the Discontinued column in the current row of the *DataGrid* control.

8   Run the application again. There are now two Discontinued columns: a *CheckBox* appearing as the first column and the original text column on the right side. Notice how each *CheckBox* is checked when the value in the Discontinued column is *True*.

9   Close the form and return to the Visual Studio .NET programming environment.

To take more control of the order in which columns in a *DataGrid* are displayed, you need to prevent them from being generated automatically and create them yourself. The next exercise shows you how to do this.

Reorganize the *DataGrid* columns

1   Display Product.aspx in the Design View window. Select the *DataGrid* control. Click the Property Builder link underneath the Properties window to open the *DataGrid1* Properties dialog box. Click Columns and clear the Create Columns Automatically At Run Time check box. Add five more Template Columns to the Selected Columns list. Select the first Template Column in the list, and then click the down-arrow to move it to the end of the list. Click OK to save the changes.

   The *DataGrid* on the form is updated. It still contains the Discontinued column, but it now also has five blank columns.

2   Right-click the *DataGrid* control, point to Edit Template, and then click Columns[0]. Type **Product ID** in the Header Template text box. Click the Item Template text box, and then in the Toolbox, drag a *Label* control onto the Item Template.

3   Right-click the *DataGrid* control again, point to Edit Template, and then click Columns[1]. Type **Product Name** in the Header Template text box, and then add a *Label* control to the Item Template. Repeat this process for the remaining columns (2, 3, and 4), typing **Category ID**, **Quantity Per Unit**, and **Unit Price** in each column's Header Template text box, respectively. After you have edited the Template Column for Columns[4], right-click the *DataGrid* control, and then click End Template Editing. The templates are applied to the *DataGrid* control.

Product ID	Product Name	Category ID	Quantity Per Unit	Unit Price	Discontinued
Label	Label	Label	Label	Label	□
Label	Label	Label	Label	Label	□
Label	Label	Label	Label	Label	□
Label	Label	Label	Label	Label	□
Label	Label	Label	Label	Label	□

4   Click the HTML button at the bottom of the Design View window. In the *DataGrid* control, locate the *<ItemTemplate>* element for the Product ID Template Column. Change the *asp:Label* control to display

30

ASP.NET Applications

the ProductID for the current row in the *DataGrid* control by replacing the Label text with the data binding expression, as shown here:

```
<asp:Label id="Label1" runat="server">
  <%# DataBinder.Eval(Container.DataItem, "ProductID") %>
</asp:Label>
```

5   Change the *asp:Label* control for the Product Name template using the following code:

```
<asp:Label id="Label2" runat="server">
  <%# DataBinder.Eval(Container.DataItem, "ProductName") %>
</asp:Label>
```

6   Change the *asp:Label* control for the Category ID template using the following code:

```
<asp:Label id="Label3" runat="server">
  <%# DataBinder.Eval(Container.DataItem, "CategoryID") %>
</asp:Label>
```

7   Change the *asp:Label* for the Quantity Per Unit template using the following code:

```
<asp:Label id="Label4" runat="server">
  <%# DataBinder.Eval(Container.DataItem, "QuantityPerUnit") %>
</asp:Label>
```

8   Change the *asp:Label* for the Unit Price template using the following code:

```
<asp:Label id="Label5" runat="server">
  <%# DataBinder.Eval(Container.DataItem, "UnitPrice") %>
</asp:Label>
```

9   Save and run the application again. The columns in the *DataGrid* should now appear in the expected sequence.

10   Close the form and return to the Visual Studio .NET programming environment.

Navigating Between Forms

Another key aspect of Web Forms applications is the ability to navigate from one form to another by clicking a hyperlink or button. In addition to moving between forms, you often need to pass information between forms. The following illustration shows a *DataGrid* control displaying a list of the different product categories from the Northwind Traders database. The *DataGrid* contains a Template Column displaying an *ImageButton* control.

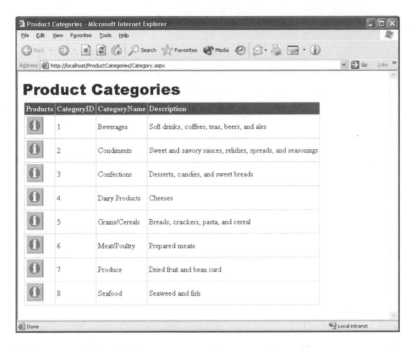

If the user clicks the button, another page that allows users to view the products in the selected category is displayed.

The Web Forms model supports the standard HTTP mechanisms for moving between URLs and handling parameters through the *Server* and *Request* objects of ASP.NET.

Using Buttons and Hyperlinks

In the following exercise, you will build the application shown in the previous images. You will create a Web form containing a *DataGrid* for displaying data from the Categories table in the Northwind Traders database. You will add a Template Column to the *DataGrid* holding the *ImageButton* control. When the user clicks the button, another form will appear showing the products in the selected category.

Create the Product Categories application

1 Create a new ASP.NET Web application. Set the location to *http:// localhost/ProductCategories*. Change the name of the WebForm1.aspx file to Category.aspx. Likewise, update the name of the *WebForm1* class to *Category*, and then change the *Title* property of the *DOCUMENT* object to Product Categories.

2   Add a *Label* control to the top left corner of the form. Set the *Text* property of this control to Product Categories. Change the *Font Name* property to Arial Black, and then set the *Font Size* property to X-Large.

3   In Server Explorer, locate the Categories table in the Northwind database on your local SQL Server. Select the CategoryID, CategoryName, and Description columns (using Ctrl+click), and then drag the CategoryID column onto the Web form to create an *SqlConnection* object and an *SqlDataAdapter* object.

4   Add a *DataSet* object from the Data page in the Toolbox to the form. In the Add Dataset dialog box, select Untyped Dataset. Drag a *DataGrid* control from the Web Forms page onto the form, and place it underneath the *Label* control. Click the Auto Format hyperlink in the Properties window. In the Auto Format dialog box, select the Professional 2 scheme for the *DataGrid* and click OK. Set the *DataSource* property of the *DataGrid* to *dataSet1*.

5   In the Code And Text Editor window for Category.aspx.cs, create the *bindGrid* method in the Category class:

```
private void bindGrid()
{
    sqlConnection1.Open();
    sqlDataAdapter1.Fill(dataSet1);
    DataGrid1.DataBind();
    sqlConnection1.Close();
}
```

6   Add the following code to the *Page_Load* method:

```
if (!IsPostBack)
{
    bindGrid();
}
```

7   Save and run the application to test it. The form displays a list of product categories.

8   Close the form and return to the Visual Studio .NET programming environment.

Add the Navigation button

1   Select the *DataGrid* control in the Design View window. Click the Property Builder hyperlink below the Properties window. When the DataGrid1 Properties dialog box opens, click Columns and add a Template Column to the Selected columns list. Type **Products** in the

Header Text text box and click OK. The new column is added to the *DataGrid* control.

2 Using Windows Explorer, copy the image file named info.gif from the \Microsoft Press\Visual C# Step By Step\Chapter 30 folder in your My Documents folder to C:\Inetpub\wwwroot\ProductCategories. This is the folder that is hosting your Web application. The bitmap file info.gif contains an Information icon.

3 In the Visual Studio .NET programming environment, right-click the *DataGrid* control, point to Edit Template, and then click Columns[0] – Products. The *DataGrid* switches to Edit Template mode.

4 Using the Toolbox, add an *ImageButton* control to the Item Template. Click the *ImageButton* control and use the Properties window to set the *ImageUrl* property of this button to **info.gif**. This sets the Information symbol as the image for the button.

When the user clicks the button, the user is taken to another form that displays a list of products for the selected category. However, you cannot use the standard *Click* event handler for buttons created in Template Columns. This is because the compiler attempts to connect the event handling method to the button when the form is first created, and the button does not exist at that time because buttons are created dynamically—if you try to use the standard *Click* event handler, you will get a Null Object Reference exception when the form starts. Instead, you must use the *ItemCommand* event of the *DataGrid* control.

The *ItemCommand* event is raised whenever any button in the *Data-Grid* is clicked. A button has a *CommandName* property that can be set to a unique string for each button. The parameter to the *Item-Command* event will contain this *CommandName* property so that the event handler can identify which button was clicked if there is more than one button. A button can also pass additional information by setting the *CommandArgument* property.

5 Set the *CommandName* property of the *ImageButton* control to *Get-ProductDetails*. Click the HTML button to display the form in HTML format. Find the *ItemTemplate* property for the *ImageButton* control and add a *CommandArgument* that dynamically extracts the CategoryID for the selected row:

```
<asp:ImageButton id=ImageButton1 runat="server"
  CommandArgument='<%# DataBinder.Eval(Container.DataItem,
  "CategoryID") %>' ImageUrl="info.gif"
  CommandName="GetProductDetails">
</asp:ImageButton>
```

6   Click the Design button. The *DataGrid* containing the image button controls appears in the first column.

Products	Column0	Column1	Column2
🛈	abc	abc	abc
🛈	abc	abc	abc
🛈	abc	abc	abc
🛈	abc	abc	abc
🛈	abc	abc	abc

7   Create an event handler for the *ItemCommand* event of the *Data-Grid* control. Name the method *processCommand*. In the *process-Command* method, type the following statements:

```
if (e.CommandName.Equals("GetProductDetails"))
{
    Server.Transfer("ProductForm.aspx?CategoryID=" +
        e.CommandArgument.ToString());
}
```

The parameter *e* to the *processCommand* method is a *DataGrid-CommandEventsArgs* object. This object has a number of important properties, two of which are used by this code. The *CommandName* property contains the *CommandName* string of the button that was clicked, and the *CommandArgument* property contains a copy of the *CommandArgument* value specified for the button. This code creates an HTTP query string that invokes the ProductForm.aspx page passing the CategoryID value as a parameter. The *Server.Transfer* method will navigate to this URL.

Create the Products Web form

1   On the Project menu, click Add Web Form. In the Add New Item dialog box, select the Web Form template. Type **ProductForm.aspx** and click Open.

2   Add a *Label* control to the top left corner of the new form. Clear the *Text* property. Set the *Font Name* property to Arial Black, and set the *Font Size* property to X-Large.

3 In the Toolbox, drag a *HyperLink* control onto the form underneath the *Label* control. Type **Return to Categories** in the *Text* property of the *HyperLink* control. Set its *NavigateUrl* property to Category.aspx.

4 In Server Explorer, open the Products table in the Northwind database on your local SQL Server. Select the ProductID, ProductName, CategoryID, QuantityPerUnit, and UnitPrice columns. Drag the ProductID column onto the Web form to create an *SqlConnection* object and an *SqlDataAdapter* object.

5 Select the *sqlDataAdapter1* object below the Web form. In the Properties window, expand the *SelectCommand* composite property. Select the *CommandText* property and click the Ellipses button to open the Query Builder dialog box. Clear the Output check box in the CategoryID row in the grid. In the Criteria column for CategoryID, type the following statement:

```
= @CategoryID
```

This statement restricts the query to return only those products that match the value of the *@CategoryID* expression; this is a parameter that you will provide at run time (parameter names always start with an @ sign). This statement will also cause a WHERE clause to be added to the SQL SELECT statement.

Verify that the Regenerate Parameters Collection For This Command check box is selected, and then click OK.

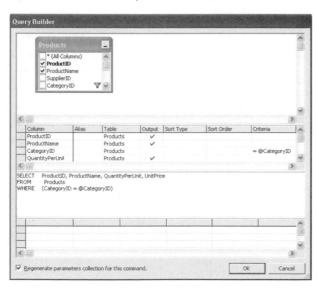

6   In the Toolbox, add a *DataSet* control (select Untyped Dataset) and a *DataGrid* control to the form. Place the *DataGrid* control underneath the *HyperLink* control you added previously. In the Auto Format dialog box, set the layout of the *DataGrid* to the Professional 2 scheme. Set the *DataSource* property of the *DataGrid* to *dataSet1*.

Display products that match the specified category

1   Display ProductForm.aspx.cs in the Code And Text Editor window. Locate the *Page_Load* method and add the following statements:

```
int catID = Int32.Parse(Request.Params["CategoryID"]);
Label1.Text = "Products in Category " + catID;
sqlDataAdapter1.SelectCommand.Parameters[
    "@CategoryID"].Value = catID;
sqlConnection1.Open();
sqlDataAdapter1.Fill(dataSet1);
DataGrid1.DataBind();
sqlConnection1.Close();
```

Remember that this page is invoked from the Categories page. The selected CategoryID is passed as a parameter to the page using an HTTP query string. The *Request* property of the current page provides access to information about the request, in particular to the parameters passed across. These are available in the params array that you can index either by number or by the name of the parameter.

The first line of code retrieves the *CategoryID* parameter from the *Request* property, converts it to an integer, and saves it in the *catID* variable. The second statement displays the CategoryID in the label on the form. The next statement populates the @*CategoryID* parameter of the *SelectCommand* of the *SqlDataAdapter* with the Category ID. The remaining statements connect to the database, fetch the matching products, display them in the data grid, and then close the database connection.

2   Save and run the application. When the Product Categories form appears, click the Information button for the Dairy Products category (row 4).

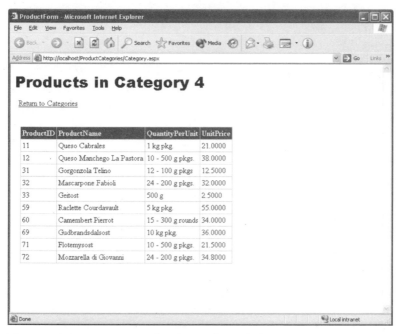

The ProductForm page displays a list of cheeses.

3   Click the Return to Categories hyperlink. In the Product Categories form, select another category and click the Information button. The products in that category are displayed.

4   When you have finished browsing, close the form and return to the Visual Studio .NET programming environment.

Other Data Controls

The *DataGrid* control is ideally suited to presenting data in a tabular format. However, if you want to use some other layout, you are better off using one of the other data controls, either the *Repeater* or the *DataList* control.

The *Repeater* control has no default layout and relies entirely on templates to define how to display data. It specifies *HeaderTemplate*, *ItemTemplate*, *AlternatingItemTemplate* (applied to every alternate row if specified), *SeparatorTemplate* (appearing between rows), and *FooterTemplate* elements. You can place almost any HTML or ASP.NET Server control in these templates, which gives you a great deal of flexibility. However, the *Repeater* control cannot be used to update a data source. One other drawback is that the *Repeater* control has no graphical builder for defining its layout; you have to type in the HTML yourself.

30

ASP.NET Applications

The *DataList* control, on the other hand, is slightly less flexible in its display capabilities, but it supports updates.

The *Repeater* and the *DataList* controls can be bound to a *DataSet* in exactly the same way as a *DataGrid* control. You can use data binding expressions and the *DataBinder.Eval* method to extract values from the *DataSet* as the data is fetched and as the display builds.

If you want to continue to the next chapter

■ Keep Visual Studio .NET running and turn to Chapter 31.

If you want to quit Visual Studio .NET for now

■ On the File menu, click Exit. If you see a Save dialog box, click Yes.

Chapter 30 Quick Reference

To	Do this
Enable sorting in a *Data-Grid*	Set the *AllowSorting* property of the *DataGrid* to True. Create an event method to trap the *SortCommand* event. In the *SortCommand* method, create a *DataView* based on the table to be sorted, and then set the *Sort* property to the *SortExpression* property of the *DataGridSortCommandEventArgs* parameter that is passed in. Set the *DataSource* property of the *DataGrid* to the *DataView*. Run the *DataBind* method of the *DataGrid* to update the display. For example: ```DataView sortView = new DataView(\n dataSet1.Tables["Suppliers"]);\nSortView.Sort = e.SortExpression;\nDataGrid1.DataSource = sortView;\nDataGrid1.DataBind();```
Display information in a format other than ordinary text in a *DataGrid*	Create a Column template for the *DataGrid*. Add the control (or controls) that you want to use to the Item template. Add any header information you require to the Header template. In the HTML View, use a data binding expression to populate the properties of these controls using information from the underlying *DataSet*.

To	Do this
Control the order in which columns are displayed in a *DataGrid*	In the Property Builder dialog box, clear the Create Columns Automatically check box. Create Column templates for each column you want to display. Using the Template Editor, add controls to each Column template to display the data. In the HTML View, create data binding expressions to populate the controls with data from the *DataSet*.
Navigate from one Web form to another	You can do one of the following: run the *Server.Transfer* method, specifying the URL of the destination Web form, or create a *HyperLink* object and set its *NavigateUrl* property to the URL of the destination form.
Pass data from one Web form to another	Use the *Server.Transfer* method and pass the data using an HTTP query string. For example:

```
Server.Transfer(
    "ProductForm.aspx?CategoryID=2");
```

In the receiving form, read the data from the *Params* collection in the *Request* property. For example
:

```
int catID = Int32.Parse(
    Request.Params["CategoryID"]);
```

Chapter

31

Building an XML Web Service

In this chapter, you will learn how to:

- Create an XML Web service that exposes simple Web methods.

- Test a Web service using Microsoft Internet Explorer.

- Design classes that can be passed as parameters or returned from an XML Web service.

The previous chapters showed you how to create Web forms and build interactive Web applications using Microsoft ASP.NET. Although this approach is appropriate for applications where the client is a Web browser, you will increasingly encounter situations where it is not. As mentioned in previous chapters, the Internet is just a big network. It is possible to build distributed systems that use elements that are spread across the Internet—databases, security services, financial components, and so on. The aim of this chapter is to show you how to design, build, and test components that can be accessed over the Internet and integrated into larger applications.

What Is an XML Web Service?

You can think of an XML Web service as a component, or black box, that provides some useful facility to clients, or consumers. Just as Distributed Component Object Model (DCOM) is thought of as "COM with a longer wire," an XML Web service can be thought of as a component with a truly global reach.

However, unlike DCOM, Remote Method Invocation (RMI), Internet Inter-ORB Protocol (IIOP), or any of the other object-model–specific protocols in common use, a consumer gains access to an XML Web service using a standard, accepted, and well-understood protocol (HTTP) and data format that is based on XML.

RMI and IIOP

RMI is the protocol used by the Java platform for communicating between Java components. It is Java-specific. IIOP is also used by Java to allow Java components to communicate with non-Java components that conform to the CORBA model. CORBA is the Common Object Request Broker Architecture. It is a scheme defined by the Object Management Group (OMG), designed to allow distributed components that are built using different languages to communicate with each other.

A Web service can be implemented in a variety of languages. Currently, Microsoft Visual C++, Microsoft Visual C#, Microsoft Visual J#, and Microsoft Visual Basic .NET are supported with the Microsoft .NET Framework, and it is likely that there will be others in the future. In the Microsoft .NET platform, the Web services are XML-based Web services. As far as the consumer is concerned, however, the language used by the Web service, and even how the Web service performs its tasks, is not important. The consumer's view of an XML Web service is as an interface that exposes a number of well-defined methods. All the consumer needs to do is call these methods using the standard Internet protocols, passing parameters in XML format and receiving responses also in XML format.

One of the driving forces behind the .NET Framework is the concept of the "programmable Web." The idea is that, in the future, systems will be constructed using the data and services provided by multiple XML Web services. XML Web services provide the basic elements for systems, the Web provides the means to gain access to them, and developers glue them together in meaningful ways.

XML Web services can be application-specific and possibly even developed in-house by an organization. However, you might find a number of common, horizontal services useful across applications. Examples include Microsoft .NET Passport, which provides a single sign-in facility across multiple Web sites; and Microsoft .NET Alerts, which allows businesses to notify subscribing customers about offerings and events. There is also a market for third-party vertical XML Web services that implement some functionality common to a particular business segment (for example, finance and manufacturing). If this sounds familiar, it should. It is the basis for building business-to-business (B2B) and business-to-consumer (B2C) applications.

The Role of SOAP

Simple Object Access Protocol (SOAP) is the protocol used by consumers for sending requests to, and receiving responses from, XML Web services.

SOAP is a lightweight protocol built on top of HTTP. It is possible to exchange SOAP messages over other protocols but, currently, only the HTTP bindings for SOAP have been defined. It defines an XML grammar for specifying the names of methods that a consumer wants to invoke on an XML Web service; for defining the parameters and return values; and for describing the types of parameters and return values. When a client calls an XML Web service, it must specify the method and parameters by using this XML grammar.

SOAP is being adopted as an industry standard. Its function is to improve cross-platform interoperability. The strength of SOAP is its simplicity and also the fact that it is based on other industry standard technologies: HTTP and XML.

The SOAP specification defines a number of things. The most important are the following:

- The format of a SOAP message
- How data should be encoded
- How to send messages (method calls)
- How to receive responses

For example, consider an XML Web service called ProductService.asmx (in the .NET Framework, URLs for XML-based Web services have the suffix .asmx) that exposes methods for accessing the Products table in the Northwind Traders database (you will build this XML Web service later in this chapter). One such method called *HowMuchWillItCost* allows a client to supply the name of a product and a quantity. The method queries the unit price in the database to calculate the total cost of buying the specified quantity of the product. The SOAP request sent by the client might look like this:

```
POST /NorthwindServices/ProductService.asmx HTTP/1.1
Host: localhost
Content-Type: text/xml; charset=utf-8
Content-Length: 633
SOAPAction: "http://www.contentmaster.com/webservices/HowMuchWillItCost"

<?xml version="1.0" encoding="utf-8"?>
<soap:Envelope xmlns:xsi="http://www.w3.org/2001/XMLSchema-instance"
```

XML Web Service

31

```
xmlns:xsd="http://www.w3.org/2001/XMLSchema" xmlns:soap="http://schemas.xml-
soap.org/soap/envelope/">
  <soap:Body>
    <HowMuchWillItCost xmlns="http://www.contentmaster.com/webservices">
      <productName>Chai</productName>
      <howMany>39</howMany>
    </HowMuchWillItCost>
  </soap:Body>
</soap:Envelope>
```

The request contains two parts: a header comprising everything to the
<soap:Body> tag, and the actual body of the message in the <soap:Body> tag.
You can see how the body encodes parameters—in this example, the name of
the product is Chai and the quantity is 39.

The Web server will receive this request, identify the XML Web service and
method to run, run the method, obtain the results, and send them back to the
client as the following SOAP result:

```
HTTP/1.1 200 OK
Content-Type: text/xml; charset=utf-8
Content-Length: 515

<?xml version="1.0" encoding="utf-8"?>
<soap:Envelope xmlns:xsi="http://www.w3.org/2001/XMLSchema-instance"
xmlns:xsd="http://www.w3.org/2001/XMLSchema" xmlns:soap="http://schemas.xml-
soap.org/soap/envelope/">
  <soap:Body>
    <HowMuchWillItCostResponse xmlns=
      "http://www.contentmaster.com/webservices">
      <HowMuchWillItCostResult>529</HowMuchWillItCostResult>
    </HowMuchWillItCostResponse>
  </soap:Body>
</soap:Envelope>
```

The client can then extract the result from the body of this message and process
it.

What Is the Web Services Description Language?

The body of a SOAP message is XML. The Web server expects the client to use
a particular set of tags for encoding the parameters for the method. How does a
client know which schema to use? The answer is that, when asked, an XML
Web service is expected to supply a description of itself. A client can submit a
request to an XML Web service with the query string wsdl appended to it:

```
http://localhost/NorthwindServices/ProductService.asmx?wsdl
```

The XML Web service will reply with a description like this:

```xml
<?xml version="1.0" encoding="utf-8"?>
<definitions xmlns:s="http://www.w3.org/2001/XMLSchema"
  xmlns:http="http://schemas.xmlsoap.org/wsdl/http/"
  xmlns:mime="http://schemas.xmlsoap.org/wsdl/mime/"
  xmlns:tm="http://microsoft.com/wsdl/mime/textMatching/"
  xmlns:soap="http://schemas.xmlsoap.org/wsdl/soap/"
  xmlns:soapenc="http://schemas.xmlsoap.org/soap/encoding/"
  xmlns:s0="http://www.contentmaster.com/webservices"
  targetNamespace="http://www.contentmaster.com/webservices"
  xmlns="http://schemas.xmlsoap.org/wsdl/">
<types>
  <s:schema attributeFormDefault="qualified"
    elementFormDefault="qualified"
    targetNamespace="http://www.contentmaster.com/webservices">
  <s:element name="HowMuchWillItCost">
    <s:complexType>
      <s:sequence>
        <s:element minOccurs="1" maxOccurs="1"
          name="productName" nillable="true" type="s:string" />
        <s:element minOccurs="1" maxOccurs="1"
           name="howMany" type="s:int" />
      </s:sequence>
    </s:complexType>
  </s:element>
  <s:element name="HowMuchWillItCostResponse">
    <s:complexType>
      <s:sequence>
        <s:element minOccurs="1" maxOccurs="1"
          name="HowMuchWillItCostResult" type="s:decimal" />
      </s:sequence>
    </s:complexType>
  </s:element>
  <s:element name="decimal" type="s:decimal" />
  </s:schema>
</types>
  ⋮
data omitted
  ⋮
<message name="HowMuchWillItCostSoapIn">
  <part name="parameters" element="s0:HowMuchWillItCost" />
</message>
<service name="Service1">
  <port name="Service1Soap" binding="s0:Service1Soap">
    <soap:address location=
      "http://cheshirecat/WebService1/Service1.asmx" />
  </port>
```

```
    <port name="Service1HttpGet" binding="s0:Service1HttpGet">
      <http:address location=
        "http://cheshirecat/WebService1/Service1.asmx" />
    </port>
    <port name=
      "Service1HttpPost" binding="s0:Service1HttpPost">
      <http:address location=
        "http://cheshirecat/WebService1/Service1.asmx" />
    </port>
  </service>
</definitions>
```

This is known as the Web Service Description (a large chunk in the middle has been omitted to save space), and the schema used is called Web Services Description Language (WSDL). This description provides enough information to allow a client to construct a SOAP request in a format that the Web server should understand. The description looks complicated but, fortunately, Microsoft Visual Studio .NET contains tools that can parse the WSDL for an XML Web service in a mechanical manner, and then use it to create a proxy object that a client can use to convert method calls into SOAP requests. You will do this in the following chapter. For now, you can concentrate on building an XML Web service.

Building the ProductService Web Service

In this chapter, you will create the ProductService Web service. This XML Web service will expose two Web methods. The first method will allow the user to calculate the cost of buying a specified quantity of a particular product in the Northwind Traders database, and the second method will take the name of a product and return all the details for that product.

Creating the ProductService Web Service

In the first exercise, you will create the ProductService Web service and implement the *HowMuch WillItCost* Web method. You will then test the Web method to ensure that it works as expected.

Create the Web service

1   Create a new project using the ASP.NET Web Service template. Call the project NorthwindServices, and create it on your local Web server.

2   In Solution Explorer, change the name of the Web service class file from Service1.asmx to ProductService.asmx.

3   In Class View, rename the *Service1* class to *ProductService*.

4   Select the class, and then on the View menu, click Code to display the Code And Text Editor window for ProductService. Notice that it is held in a file called ProductService.asmx.cs.

5   Examine the *ProductService* class; it is descended from *System. Web. Services. WebService*. Scroll to the bottom of the class. A method has been commented out because this is just a sample Web method.

```
namespace NorthwindServices
{
    /// <summary>
    /// Summary description for Service1.
    /// </summary>
    public class ProductService : System.Web.Services.WebService
    {
        public ProductService()
        {
            //CODEGEN: This call is required by the ASP.NET Web Services Designer
            InitializeComponent();
        }

        Component Designer generated code

        /// <summary>
        /// Clean up any resources being used.
        /// </summary>
        protected override void Dispose( bool disposing )
        {
        }

        // WEB SERVICE EXAMPLE
        // The HelloWorld() example service returns the string Hello World
        // To build, uncomment the following lines then save and build the project
        // To test this web service, press F5

//      [WebMethod]
//      public string HelloWorld()
//      {
//          return "Hello World";
//      }
    }
}
```

6   Add the following *WebService* attribute to the *ProductService* class. This attribute indicates the namespace used to identify the XML Web service:

```
[WebService
    (Namespace="http://www.contentmaster.com/NorthwindServices")]
public class ProductService : System.Web.Services.WebService
{
    ⋮
}
```

Web Service Namespaces

An XML Web service should use a unique namespace to identify it so that client applications can distinguish it from other services on the Web. By default, XML Web services created with Visual Studio .NET use *http://tempuri.org*. This is fine for XML Web services that are under development, but you should create your own namespace when you publish the Web service. A common convention is to use your company's URL as part of the namespace, together with some other form of identifier. You should note that the namespace does not have to be an existing URL—its purpose is only to uniquely identify the Web service.

Define the *HowMuchWillItCost* Web method

1   Delete the sample Web method (HelloWorld, which is commented out) in the *ProductService* class. In its place, add the following method:

```
[WebMethod]
public decimal HowMuchWillItCost(string productName,
    int howMany)
{
}
```

All methods exposed by an XML Web service must be tagged with the *WebMethod* attribute. This method will expect the client to pass in the name of a product found in the Products table in the Northwind Traders database and a quantity of that product. The method will use the information in the database to calculate the cost of supplying this quantity of the product and pass it back as the return value of the method.

2   Add the following *using* statement to the top of the file:

```
using System.Data.SqlClient;
```

This is the namespace that contains the Microsoft ADO.NET classes for gaining access to the Microsoft SQL Server computer.

3   In the *HowMuchWillItCost* Web method, type the following statements:

```
try
{
    SqlConnection sqlConn = new SqlConnection(
        "data source=YourServer\\VSdotNET2003;" +
        "initial catalog=Northwind;integrated security=true");
    SqlCommand sqlCmd = new SqlCommand();
    sqlCmd.CommandText = "SELECT UnitPrice FROM Products " +
        "WHERE ProductName = '" + productName + "'";
    sqlCmd.Connection = sqlConn;
    sqlConn.Open();
    decimal price = (decimal)sqlCmd.ExecuteScalar();
    sqlConn.Close();
```

```
    return price * howMany;
}
catch(Exception e)
{
    throw new Exception("Error calculating cost: " + e.Message);
}
```

This code connects to the Northwind Traders database and runs an SQL *SELECT* statement to retrieve the UnitPrice column for the selected product in the Products table. The *ExecuteScalar* method is the most efficient way of running a *SELECT* statement that returns a single value. The UnitPrice column is stored in the *price* variable, which is then multiplied by the *howMany* parameter that is passed in to calculate the cost.

Although the Web service uses a *try...catch* block to trap any database access errors, it does not validate the parameters passed in (for example, the client might supply a negative value for the *howMany* parameter). You should add the necessary code yourself.

4   On the Build menu, click Build Solution to compile the XML Web service.

Test the Web method

1   Start Internet Explorer and go to the URL *http://localhost/North-windServices/ProductService.asmx*. The ProductService test page is displayed.

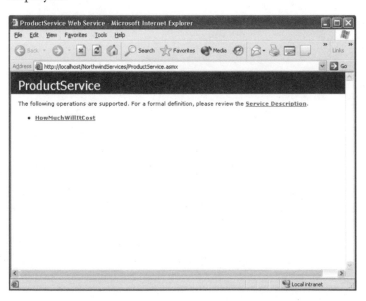

The test page allows you to view the WSDL description by clicking the Service Description hyperlink or to test individual Web methods (in this example, there is only one: *HowMuchWillItCost*).

▶ **Tip**   You can also test the XML Web service by clicking the Start command from the Debug menu, which starts Internet Explorer and moves to the URL of the Web service. Using the Debug menu gives you the advantage of being able to set breakpoints and trace the execution of the Web method.

2   Click the Service Description hyperlink. The URL changes to *http://localhost/NorthwindServices/ProductService.asmx?WSDL*, and Internet Explorer displays the WSDL description of your XML Web service.

3   Click the Back button in the Toolbar to return to the test page. Click the HowMuchWillItCost hyperlink. Internet Explorer generates another page that allows you to input the parameters and test the *HowMuchWillItCost* method. The page also displays sample SOAP requests and responses.

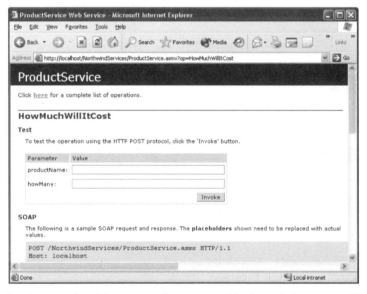

4   In the *productName* text box, type **Chai,** and then type **23** in the *howMany* text box. Click Invoke. The Web method runs, and a second Internet Explorer window opens and displays the response in SOAP format.

5   Close both Internet Explorer windows and return to the Visual Studio .NET programming environment.

Handling Complex Data

SOAP also allows you to pass complex data structures between a client and an XML Web service as input parameters, output parameters, or return values. To do this, the data structures themselves are serialized into an external format. For example, in the following exercise, you will build a class that holds information about a product in the Northwind Traders database. The class will contain many properties, including *ProductID*, *ProductName*, *SupplierID*, and *CategoryID*. You will then create a Web method that returns an instance of this class. The SOAP serialization process will convert the class into XML, send the serialized version across the network using SOAP, and reconstruct the class from the XML at the other end (a very simple marshalling technique). The following structure shows an example of how the class will be serialized for transmission:

```
<?xml version="1.0" encoding="utf-8"?>
<Product xmlns:xsi="http://www.w3.org/2001/XMLSchema-instance"
  xmlns:xsd="http://www.w3.org/2001/XMLSchema"
  xmlns="http://www.contentmaster.com/webservices">
  <ProductID>1</ProductID>
  <ProductName>Chai</ProductName>
  <SupplierID>4</SupplierID>
  <CategoryID>1</CategoryID>
  <QuantityPerUnit>10 boxes x 20 bags</QuantityPerUnit>
  <UnitPrice>23</UnitPrice>
  <UnitsInStock>39</UnitsInStock>
  <UnitsOnOrder>0</UnitsOnOrder>
  <ReorderLevel>10</ReorderLevel>
  <Discontinued>false</Discontinued>
</Product>
```

The serialization process is automatic and largely transparent as long as you follow a few simple rules when defining the class. In particular, serialization can marshal only public fields and properties. If an object contains private members that do not have corresponding *get* and *set* properties, it will not transfer correctly; the private data will not be initialized at the receiving end. Also note that all properties must have both *get* and *set* accessors, even if they are logically read-only. This is because the XML serialization process must be able to write this data back to the object after it has been transferred. Additionally, the class must have a default (with no parameters) constructor.

It is common to design classes used for SOAP purely as containers for transmitting data. You can then define additional functional classes that act as facades providing the business logic for these data structures. Users and applications would gain access to the data by using these business facades.

If you want, you can customize the serialization mechanism using the various SOAP attribute classes of the *System.Xml.Serialization* namespace or define your own XML serialization mechanism by implementing the *ISerializable* interface of the *System.Runtime.Serialization* namespace.

Define the *Product* class

1 In the NorthwindServices project, on the Project menu, click Add Class. In the Add New Item dialog box, click the Class template, and then type **Product.cs** for the name of the new class. Click Open to create the class.

2 Add the following private variables to the *Product* class, above the constructor. There is one variable for each of the columns in the Products table:

```
private int productID;
private string productName;
private int supplierID;
private int categoryID;
private string quantityPerUnit;
private decimal unitPrice;
private short unitsInStock;
private short unitsOnOrder;
private short reorderLevel;
private bool discontinued;
```

3 Create a read/write property called *ProductID* below the constructor. The property provides access to the private *productID* variable:

```
public int ProductID
{
    get
    {
        return this.productID;
    }

    set
    {
        this.productID = value;
    }
}
```

4 Add properties to provide read/write access to the remaining variables:

```
public string ProductName
{
```

```csharp
        get
        {
            return this.productName;
        }

        set
        {
            this.productName = value;
        }
    }

    public int SupplierID
    {
        get
        {
            return this.supplierID;
        }

        set
        {
            this.supplierID = value;
        }
    }

    public int CategoryID
    {
        get
        {
            return this.categoryID;
        }

        set
        {
            this.categoryID = value;
        }
    }

    public string QuantityPerUnit
    {
        get
        {
            return this.quantityPerUnit;
        }

        set
        {
            this.quantityPerUnit = value;
        }
    }
```

```csharp
public decimal UnitPrice
{
    get
    {
        return this.unitPrice;
    }

    set
    {
        this.unitPrice = value;
    }
}

public short UnitsInStock
{
    get
    {
        return this.unitsInStock;
    }

    set
    {
        this.unitsInStock = value;
    }
}

public short UnitsOnOrder
{
    get
    {
        return this.unitsOnOrder;
    }

    set
    {
        this.unitsOnOrder = value;
    }
}

public short ReorderLevel
{
    get
    {
        return this.reorderLevel;
    }

    set
    {
        this.reorderLevel = value;
    }
```

```
    }

    public bool Discontinued
    {
        get
        {
            return this.discontinued;
        }

        set
        {
            this.discontinued = value;
        }
    }
}
```

▶ **Tip** Although it is a commonly accepted practice to give properties and private fields the same name that differ only in the case of the initial letter, you should be aware of one drawback. Examine this code:

```
public int CategoryID
{
    get
    {
        return this.CategoryID;
    }

    set
    {
        this.CategoryID = value;
    }
}
```

This code will compile perfectly well, but it results in the program hanging whenever the *CategoryID* property is accessed. This is because the *get* and *set* accessors reference the property (upper-case C) rather than the private field (lower-case c), which causes an endless recursive loop. This sort of bug is very difficult to spot!

Create the *GetProductInfo* Web method

1 Return to the ProductService.asmx.cs file. In the Code And Text Editor window, add a second Web method called *GetProductInfo* that takes a product name (a string) as its parameter and returns a *Product* object:

```
[WebMethod]
public Product GetProductInfo(string productName)
{
}
```

2 Add the following statements to the *GetProductInfo* method:

```
Product product = new Product();
try
{
    SqlConnection sqlConn = new SqlConnection(
        "data source=YourServer\\VSdotNET2003;" +
        "initial catalog=Northwind;integrated security=true");
    SqlCommand sqlCmd = new SqlCommand();
    sqlCmd.CommandText = "SELECT * FROM Products " +
        "WHERE ProductName = '" + productName + "'";
    sqlCmd.Connection = sqlConn;
    sqlConn.Open();
    SqlDataReader productData = sqlCmd.ExecuteReader();
    if (productData.Read())
    {
        product.ProductID = productData.GetInt32(0);
        product.ProductName = productData.GetString(1);
        product.SupplierID = productData.GetInt32(2);
        product.CategoryID = productData.GetInt32(3);
        product.QuantityPerUnit = productData.GetString(4);
        product.UnitPrice = productData.GetDecimal(5);
        product.UnitsInStock = productData.GetInt16(6);
        product.UnitsOnOrder = productData.GetInt16(7);
        product.ReorderLevel = productData.GetInt16(8);
        product.Discontinued = productData.GetBoolean(9);
    }
    else
    {
        throw new Exception ("Product " + productName +
            " not found");
    }
    productData.Close();
    sqlConn.Close();
    return product;
}
catch(Exception e)
{
    throw new Exception("Error finding product: " +
        e.Message);
}
```

These statements use ADO.NET to connect to the Northwind Traders database and retrieve the details for the specified product from the database. If no such product exists, the code raises an exception; otherwise, it populates an instance of the *Product* class with the data found and returns it.

▶ **Tip** Notice that the *Product not found* exception will actually be caught and thrown again by the *catch* block. In this way, it is treated exactly like any other exception thrown in the *try* block when accessing the database. This is a common technique.

3 Build and run the XML Web service. When Internet Explorer displays the test page, click the GetProductInfo hyperlink. The GetProductInfo test page appears, allowing you to test the *GetProductInfo* method.

4 In the productName text box, type **Chai** and then click Invoke. The Web method runs, fetches the details for Chai, and returns a *Product* object. The *Product* object is serialized as XML and displayed in Internet Explorer.

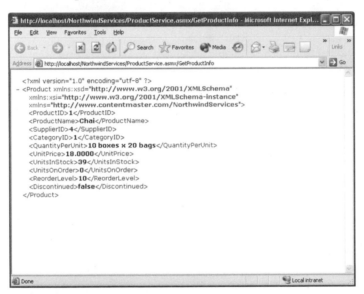

5 Close Internet Explorer.

If you want to continue to the next chapter

■ Keep Visual Studio .NET running and turn to Chapter 32.

If you want to quit Visual Studio .NET for now

■ On the File menu, click Exit. If you see a Save dialog box, click Yes.

Chapter 31 Quick Reference

To	Do this
Create an XML Web service	Use the ASP.NET Web Service template. Use the *Web-Service* attribute to specify the namespace used to uniquely identity the Web service to the outside world. Tag each method you want to expose with the *WebMethod* attribute.
Test an XML Web service	Use Internet Explorer to navigate to the XML Web service URL and display the test page. Click the link corresponding to the Web method you wish to run. On the Web method test page, enter values for the parameters and click Invoke. The Web method will run and generate a SOAP response that will be displayed in Internet Explorer.
Pass complex data as Web method parameters and return values	Define a class to hold the data. Ensure that each item of data is accessible either as a public field or through a public property that provides *get* and *set* access. Make sure that the class has a default constructor (which might be empty).

Consuming a Web Service

In this chapter, you will learn how to:

■ Create a reference to an XML Web service in a client application.

■ Invoke a Web method.

■ Execute a Web method asynchronously.

In Chapter 31, you learned how to create a Web service exposing a pair of Web methods. You tested the Web service using the test page displayed in Microsoft Internet Explorer. In the real world, the methods exposed by an XML Web service will be used by applications rather than by users running a browser. In this chapter, you'll learn how to construct an application that uses the methods exposed by an XML Web service.

Web Services, Clients, and Proxies

In the previous chapter, you saw that a Web service uses SOAP to provide a mechanism for receiving requests and sending back results. SOAP uses XML to format the data being transmitted, which rides on top of the HTTP protocol used by Web servers and browsers. This is what makes XML Web services so powerful—HTTP and XML are well understood (in theory anyway) and are the subjects of several standards committees. SOAP itself is going through the standardization process and has been adopted by most companies that want to make their services available over the Web. A client that "talks" SOAP can communicate with an XML Web service. The client and the XML Web service can be implemented in totally different languages, running on otherwise incompatible systems. For example, a Microsoft Visual Basic client running on a handheld device can communicate with an XML Web service being hosted on an IBM 390 mainframe running UNIX.

So how does a client "talk" SOAP? There are two ways: the difficult way and the easy way.

Talking SOAP: The Difficult Way

In the difficult way, the client application must perform a number of steps:

1   Determine the URL of the XML Web service running the Web method.

2   Perform a Web Services Description Language (WSDL) inquiry using the URL to obtain a description of the Web methods available, the parameters used, and the values returned. This is an XML document. (You saw an example in the previous chapter.)

3   Convert each Web method call into the appropriate URL and serialize each parameter into the format described by the WSDL document.

4   Submit the request, along with the serialized data, to the URL using HTTP.

5   Wait for the Web service to reply.

6   Using the formats specified by the WSDL document, de-serialize the data returned by the XML Web service into meaningful values that your application can then process.

This is a lot of work to just invoke a method, and it is potentially error-prone.

Talking SOAP: The Easy Way

The bad news is that the easy way to use SOAP is not much different from the difficult way. The good news is that the process can be automated because it is largely mechanical. Many vendors supply tools that can generate proxy classes based on a WSDL description. The proxy hides the complexity of using SOAP and exposes a simple programmatic interface based on the methods published by the Web service. The client application calls Web methods by invoking methods with the same name in the proxy. The proxy converts these local method calls into SOAP requests and sends them to the Web service. The proxy waits for the reply, de-serializes the data, and then passes it back to the client just like the return from any simple method call.

Consuming the ProductService Web Service

In Chapter 31, you created a Web service called ProductService that exposed two Web methods: *GetProductInfo* to return the details of a specified product and *HowMuchWillItCost* to determine the cost of buying *n* items of product *x* from Northwind Traders. In this chapter, you will use this XML Web service and create an application that consumes these methods. You'll start with the *GetProductInfo* method.

Create a Web service client application

1   In the Microsoft Visual Studio .NET programming environment, create a new project using the Windows Application template. Name the project ProductInfo and save it in the \Microsoft Press\Visual C# Step By Step\Chapter 32 folder in your My Documents folder.

2   Change the size of the form to 392, 400. Set its *Text* property to Product Details.

3   Add 10 labels to the form, evenly spaced down the left side. From top to bottom, set the *Text* property of each label using the following values: Product Name, Product ID, Supplier ID, Category ID, Quantity Per Unit, Unit Price, Units In Stock, Units On Order, Reorder Level, and Discontinued.

4   Add nine text boxes to the form next to the first nine labels. Clear the *Text* property for each text box. Set the name of each text box from top to bottom using the following values: *productName, productID, supplierID, categoryID, quantityPerUnit, unitPrice, unitsInStock, unitsOnOrder,* and *reorderLevel*.

5   Add a check box to the form next to the *Discontinued* label and below the *reorderLevel* text box. Set its name to *discontinued*, and then clear its *Text* property.

6   Add a button to the form to the right of the *productName* text box. Change the name of the button to *getButton*, and then set its *Text* property to *Get*.

The completed form should look like the following illustration:

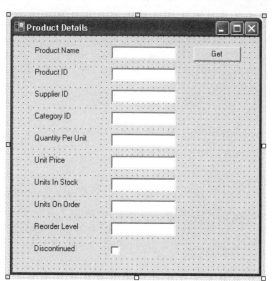

Add a reference to the XML Web service

1 On the Project menu, click Add Web Reference. The Add Web Reference dialog box opens.

   This dialog box allows you to browse for XML Web services and examine the WSDL descriptions.

2 You can either type the URL of a Web service in the Address text box at the top of the dialog box if you know it, or if the XML Web service is hosted on your local Web server, you can click the Web Services On The Local Machine hyperlink in the left pane of the dialog box. Click this link now.

   A list of XML Web services is displayed. (Your list might vary from the one shown in the following illustration, depending on what is installed on your computer and whether you have configured the QuickStart tutorials supplied with Visual Studio .NET.)

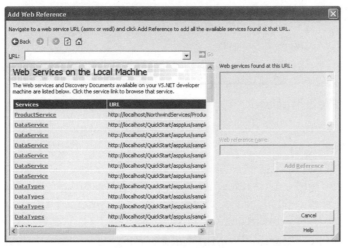

3 Click the ProductService Web service in the list in the left pane. The pane will display the operations available in the ProductService Web service, in the same format used by Internet Explorer in the previous chapter. The URL will also change to *http://localhost/NorthwindServices/ProductService.asmx*.

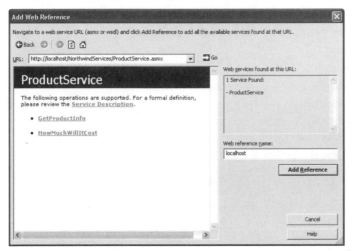

4 In the right pane of the dialog box, click the Add Reference button. A reference to the Web service will be created and added to the project.

5 Look at the Solution Explorer. A new folder called Web References has been added and contains an item called localhost (if the Web service is on a different server, the item will be named after that server).

6   Click the localhost item and examine its properties in the Properties window. You will notice the Web Reference property, which contains the URL of the Web service.

Execute a Web method

1   Display Form1.cs in the Code And Text Editor window. Add the following *using* statement to the list at the top of the file:

```
using ProductInfo.localhost;
```

When you add a Web reference to a project, the proxy generated by the Web service is placed in a namespace that is named after the Web service host—in this case, *localhost*.

2   Create an event method for the *Click* event of *getButton* called *getButtonClick*. In the *getButtonClick* method, create the following variable:

```
ProductService productService = new ProductService();
```

ProductService is the proxy class that provides access to the XML Web service (the proxy will always be named after the Web service). It resides in the *localhost* namespace. To gain access to the Web service, you must create an instance of the proxy, which is what this code does.

3   Execute the XML Web service from the *getButtonClick* method. You are probably aware of how unpredictable networks are, and this applies doubly to the Internet. Create a *try/catch* block below the statement that creates the *productService* variable. (The Web service you will be using will also throw an exception if you try to access a non-existent product.)

```
try
{
    // Code goes here in the next steps
}
catch (Exception ex)
{
    MessageBox.Show("Error fetching product details: " +
        ex.Message, "Error", MessageBoxButtons.OK,
        MessageBoxIcon.Error);
}
```

4   Add the following statement to the *try* block:

```
Product prod = productService.GetProductInfo(productName.Text);
```

GetProductInfo is the name of the Web method that returns the product details for a named product (see Chapter 31 to refresh your memory). The proxy object (*productService*) makes the call to the Web method look like an ordinary local method call. The information returned by the *GetProductInfo* method is assembled into an instance of the *Product* class (you also defined the *Product* class in Chapter 31 as part of the Web service). The WSDL description of the Web service provides enough information to define the structure of this class, and you can use it in your client application as shown here.

5 Add the following statements, which extract the details from the *Product* object and display them on the form:

```
productID.Text = prod.ProductID.ToString();
supplierID.Text = prod.SupplierID.ToString();
categoryID.Text = prod.CategoryID.ToString();
quantityPerUnit.Text = prod.QuantityPerUnit;
unitPrice.Text = prod.UnitPrice.ToString();
unitsInStock.Text = prod.UnitsInStock.ToString();
unitsOnOrder.Text = prod.UnitsOnOrder.ToString();
reorderLevel.Text = prod.ReorderLevel.ToString();
discontinued.Checked = prod.Discontinued;
```

Test the application

1 Build and run the project. When the Product Details form appears, type **Chai** in the Product Name text box and click Get.

After a short delay while the client instantiates the proxy, the proxy marshals the parameter and sends the request to the XML Web service. The Web service reads the database, creates a *Product* object, marshals it as XML, and then sends it back to the proxy. The proxy unmarshals the XML data and creates a copy of the *Product* object, and then passes this copy to your code in the *getButtonClick* method. The details for Chai then appear in the form as shown on the following page.

2   Type **Tofu** in the Product Name text box, and then click Get. You will probably find that the details are displayed more quickly this time.

3   Type **Sticky Toffee** in the Product Name text box, and then click Get once more. Because this product does not exist, the Web service will throw an exception that is passed back to your application. If you look closely, you will see the Product Sticky Toffee Not Found message.

4   Click OK to acknowledge the error. Close the Product Details form and return to the Visual Studio .NET programming environment.

Web Services, Anonymous Access, and Authentication

When you create a Web Service client using Visual Studio .NET, the client application executes Web services using anonymous access by default. By default, a Web service created using Visual Studio .NET is configured to permit anonymous access. This might be fine for some Web services, but under some circumstances you might want to restrict access to authenticated clients only.

You can configure the authentication mechanism for a Web service using the Internet Information Services console. (Under the Windows XP scheme, from the Start menu, click Control Panel, Performance And Maintenance, Administrative Tools, and finally double-click the Internet Information Services shortcut. Under other Windows XP schemes or under Windows 2000, from the Start menu, click Settings, Control Panel, Administrative Tools, and finally double-click the Internet Services Manager shortcut.) If you expand the Default Web Site node, select your Web service, and click Properties from the Action menu, you can change the Directory Security settings by clicking the Edit button under Anonymous Access And Authentication Control. Check the Anonymous Access box to permit unauthenticated access—the accepted convention is to use the local IUSR account for such access; the Web service will execute using this identity, which must be granted access to any resources used by the Web service, such as SQL Server databases.

The alternative to using anonymous access is using authenticated access. If you clear the Anonymous access check box and select one or more of the authenticated mechanisms (Digest, Basic, Integrated Windows), you can restrict access to clients that supply a valid user name and password. For more information on the differences between the authenticated access modes, consult the Internet Information Services documentation (click Help in the Authentication Methods dialog box).

You can supply the information needed to authenticate the client application by setting the *Credentials* property of the Web service proxy at run time. This property is a *NetworkCredential* object (the *NetworkCredential* class is located in the *System.Net* namespace). The following code creates a *NetworkCredential* object for the user "John," with the password "JohnsPassword" and sets the *Credentials* property of the *productService* Web service proxy:

```
using System.Net;
⋮
private void getButtonClick(...)
{
    ProductService productService = new ProductService();
    try
    {
        NetworkCredential credentials =
            new NetworkCredential("John", "JohnsPassword");
        productService.Credentials = credentials;
        Product prod = productService.GetProductInfo(...);
        ⋮
    }
    ⋮
}
```

The user name and password must be valid for the Windows domain (a different Windows domain can be specified as an optional third parameter to the *NetworkCredential* constructor), and the specified account must be granted access to the various resources used by the Web service if it is to function correctly.

Executing a Web Method Asynchronously

It was pointed out in the previous exercise that invoking a Web method might take a significant amount of time. If you are building applications that need to be responsive, it is not good for them to stop responding or "freeze" while Web methods are running. Fortunately, the proxy class generated by Visual Studio .NET contains methods that allow you to invoke a Web method asynchronously so that while the Web method is running, your application can do other things.

If you look at the proxy class generated for an XML Web service, you will see that each Web method has two additional methods associated with it. These are called *BeginXXX* and *EndXXX* (where *XXX* is the name of the Web method). You call the *BeginXXX* method to initiate the Web method, and use *EndXXX* to obtain the results that are passed back. Running a Web method in this way usually involves creating a delegate that can run when the Web method completes.

In the following exercise, you will invoke the *HowMuchWillItCost* method asynchronously.

Create another XML Web service client application

1   In the Visual Studio .NET programming environment, create a new project using the Windows Application template. Call the project OrderCost, and save it in the \Microsoft Press\Visual C# Step By Step\Chapter 32 folder in your My Documents folder.

2   Change the *Text* property of Form1 to Order Cost.

3   Add three labels, two text boxes, a *NumericUpDown* control, and a button to the form. Set the properties of these controls using the values in the following table.

Control	Property	Value
label1	Text	Product Name
	Location	16, 40
label2	Text	Number Required
	Location	16, 80
label3	Text	Total Cost
	Location	16, 200
textBox1	Name	ProductName
	Location	128, 40
	Text	Leave blank
numericUpDown1	Name	NumberRequired
	Location	128, 80
textBox2	Name	TotalCost
	Location	128, 200
	Text	Leave blank
button1	Name	HowMuchButton
	Location	16, 136
	Text	How Much

The form should look like the following illustration:

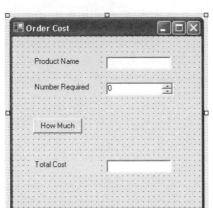

4   On the Project menu, click Add Web Reference. In the Add Web reference dialog box, type **http://localhost/NorthwindServices/Product-Service.asmx** in the URL text box and press Enter. This will display the test page for the ProductService Web service.

5   Click Add Reference. The localhost Web Reference will be added to the project.

Invoke a Web method asynchronously

1   In the Code And Text Editor window for Form1.cs, add the following *using* statement:

```
using OrderCost.localhost;
```

2   Create the following method in the Form1 class:

```
private void howMuchCallback(IAsyncResult ar)
{
    try
    {
        // Code will go here in the next step
    }
    catch (Exception ex)
    {
    MessageBox.Show("Error getting response: " + ex.Message,
        "Error", MessageBoxButtons.OK, MessageBoxIcon.Error);
    }
}
```

This method is the callback that will run when the *HowMuch WillIt-Cost* Web method completes. The *IAsyncResult* parameter will contain information about the data returned by the Web method.

3 Type the following statements in the *try* block of the *howMuchCall-back* method:

```
ProductService productService = (ProductService)ar.AsyncState;
decimal totCost = productService.EndHowMuchWillItCost(ar);
totalCost.Text = totCost.ToString();
```

The parameter *ar* contains a property called *AsyncState* that holds a reference to the proxy object that ran the XML Web service. This code retrieves the proxy object and calls the *EndHowMuch WillIt-Cost* method, which passes back the return value of the Web method (in this case, the total cost of the order). This cost is then displayed in the form.

4 Create an event method for the *Click* event of the How Much button called *howMuchClick*. This method will invoke the Web method. Type the following code in the body of this method:

```
ProductService productService = new ProductService();
try
{
    AsyncCallback callback = new AsyncCallback(howMuchCallback);
    IAsyncResult running =
        productService.BeginHowMuchWillItCost(productName.Text,
        Int32.Parse(numberRequired.Text), callback,
        productService);
}
catch (Exception ex)
{
    MessageBox.Show("Error sending request: " + ex.Message,
        "Error", MessageBoxButtons.OK, MessageBoxIcon.Error);
}
```

This code instantiates a proxy object. The *try* block creates a delegate that refers to the *howMuchCallback* method you wrote in the previous step. The *BeginHowMuch WillItCost* method of the proxy object initiates a call to the XML Web service. The first two parameters (the product name and the number required) are the parameters to the Web method. The third parameter is the delegate to run when the Web method completes, and the final parameter is passed as the parameter to the *howMuchCallback* delegate.

5 Build and run the application. When the Order Cost form appears, type **Tofu** for the product name and set the number required to 5. Click How Much.

The total cost (116.25) appears after a short delay. Notice that once the Web method starts running, the form will be responsive. There's a short delay while the proxy is instantiated and the Web method is invoked, but after that you can tab through the controls. In this example, the duration between the Web method starting and finishing is small, but the more processing a Web method performs, the more you will notice the delay.

Monitoring Web Method Execution

You can monitor the progress of the Web method by querying the *IsCompleted* property of the *IAsyncResult* object returned by the *BeginXXX* method of the proxy object. While this property is *false*, the Web method is running. When it becomes *true*, the Web method has completed.

Chapter 32 Quick Reference

To	Do this
Add a Web reference to an application and create a proxy class	On the Project menu, click Add Web Reference. Either type the URL of the Web service in the Address text box at the top of the dialog box, or click the Web References On Local Web Server link and locate the Web service. Click Add Reference to create the Web service proxy.
Invoke a Web method synchronously	Create an instance of the proxy class; it will reside in a namespace named after the Web server hosting the Web service. Run the Web method using the proxy class.
Invoke a Web method asynchronously	Create a method to act as a callback to be invoked when the Web method finishes. In this callback method, call the *EndXXX* method of the Web method proxy to obtain any results returned by the Web method. To call the Web method, create a delegate that refers to the callback. Run the *BeginXXX* method of the Web service proxy, passing in any Web method parameters, the delegate, and the proxy object.
Determine whether an asynchronous Web method has completed	Examine the *IsCompleted* property of the *IAsyncResult* object created when invoking the *BeginXXX* method of the proxy object. If this property is *true*, the Web method has completed.

Index

Symbols and Numbers

About the Authors

John Sharp is a principal technologist at Content Master Ltd., a technical authoring company in the United Kingdom. He develops and delivers instruction on everything from C#, J#, ASP.NET, and .NET development to UNIX and Java programming. John is deeply involved with Microsoft .NET development, writing courses, building tutorials, and delivering conference presentations covering Microsoft Visual C# development and Microsoft ASP.NET. He lives in Tetbury, Gloucestershire, in the United Kingdom.

Jon Jagger is a technology specialist for Content Master Ltd., specializing in C#, C++, Java, C, patterns, design, and general programming. Jon is a UK C++ standards panel member and regular contributor to the *ACCU Overload* journal. His interests include training excellence, design, simplicity, problem solving, and Monty Python (which he says is required knowledge for all software developers). Jon, his wife Natalie, and their three small children (Ellie, Penny, and Patrick) live in a delightful 104-year-old house overlooking a 7-acre field of barley in a village called Trull (population 300).

Keyhole Saw

Saws have been in use since prehistoric times. One dating from 1450 B.C., taken from an Egyptian tomb, doesn't look much different from some saws in use today. Different saws fill different needs. For cutting holes, there is the compass saw or the shorter, thinner-bladed **keyhole saw**, which as the name implies is used to cut keyholes.*

At Microsoft Press, we use tools to illustrate our books for software developers and IT professionals. Tools very simply and powerfully symbolize human inventiveness. They're a metaphor for people extending their capabilities, precision, and reach. From simple calipers and pliers to digital micrometers and lasers, these stylized illustrations give each book a visual identity, and a personality to the series. With tools and knowledge, there's no limit to creativity and innovation. Our tagline says it all: *the tools you need to put technology to work*.

*__The Great Tool Emporium__. © 1979 by David X. Manners. Published by Book Division, Times Mirror Magazines, Inc.

The manuscript for this book was prepared and submitted to Microsoft Press in electronic form. Pages were composed by Microsoft Press using Adobe FrameMaker+SGML for Windows, with text in Sabon and display type in ITC Franklin Gothic. Composed pages were delivered to the printer as electronic pre-press files.

Cover designer:	Methodologie, Inc.
Interior Graphic Designer:	James D. Kramer
Principal Compositor:	Kerri DeVault
Interior Graphic Artist:	James D. Kramer
Principal Proofreader:	Victoria Thulman
Indexer:	Lee Ross and Tony Ross

Get a **Free**
e-mail newsletter, updates,
special offers, links to related books,
and more when you

register on line!

Register your Microsoft Press® title on our Web site and you'll get
a FREE subscription to our e-mail newsletter, *Microsoft Press Book
Connections.* You'll find out about newly released and upcoming books
and learning tools, online events, software downloads, special offers
and coupons for Microsoft Press customers, and information about
major Microsoft® product releases. You can also read useful additional
information about all the titles we publish, such as detailed book
descriptions, tables of contents and indexes, sample chapters, links to
related books and book series, author biographies, and reviews by other
customers.

Registration is easy. Just visit this Web page and fill in your information:

http://www.microsoft.com/mspress/register

Microsoft®

Proof of Purchase

Use this page as proof of purchase if participating in a promotion or rebate offer on
this title. Proof of purchase must be used in conjunction with other proof(s) of
payment such as your dated sales receipt—see offer details.

Microsoft® Visual C#® .NET Step by Step—Version 2003
0-7356-1909-3

CUSTOMER NAME

Microsoft Press, PO Box 97017, Redmond, WA 98073-9830

MICROSOFT LICENSE AGREEMENT

Book Companion CD

IMPORTANT—READ CAREFULLY: This Microsoft End-User License Agreement ("EULA") is a legal agreement between you (either an individual or an entity) and Microsoft Corporation for the Microsoft product identified above, which includes computer software and may include associated media, printed materials, and "online" or electronic documentation ("SOFTWARE PRODUCT"). Any component included within the SOFTWARE PRODUCT that is accompanied by a separate End-User License Agreement shall be governed by such agreement and not the terms set forth below. By installing, copying, or otherwise using the SOFTWARE PRODUCT, you agree to be bound by the terms of this EULA. If you do not agree to the terms of this EULA, you are not authorized to install, copy, or otherwise use the SOFTWARE PRODUCT; you may, however, return the SOFTWARE PRODUCT, along with all printed materials and other items that form a part of the Microsoft product that includes the SOFTWARE PRODUCT, to the place you obtained them for a full refund.

SOFTWARE PRODUCT LICENSE

The SOFTWARE PRODUCT is protected by United States copyright laws and international copyright treaties, as well as other intellectual property laws and treaties. The SOFTWARE PRODUCT is licensed, not sold.

1. **GRANT OF LICENSE.** This EULA grants you the following rights:

   a. **Software Product.** You may install and use one copy of the SOFTWARE PRODUCT on a single computer. The primary user of the computer on which the SOFTWARE PRODUCT is installed may make a second copy for his or her exclusive use on a portable computer.

   b. **Storage/Network Use.** You may also store or install a copy of the SOFTWARE PRODUCT on a storage device, such as a network server, used only to install or run the SOFTWARE PRODUCT on your other computers over an internal network; however, you must acquire and dedicate a license for each separate computer on which the SOFTWARE PRODUCT is installed or run from the storage device. A license for the SOFTWARE PRODUCT may not be shared or used concurrently on different computers.

   c. **License Pak.** If you have acquired this EULA in a Microsoft License Pak, you may make the number of additional copies of the computer software portion of the SOFTWARE PRODUCT authorized on the printed copy of this EULA, and you may use each copy in the manner specified above. You are also entitled to make a corresponding number of secondary copies for portable computer use as specified above.

   d. **Sample Code.** Solely with respect to portions, if any, of the SOFTWARE PRODUCT that are identified within the SOFTWARE PRODUCT as sample code (the "SAMPLE CODE"):

      i. **Use and Modification.** Microsoft grants you the right to use and modify the source code version of the SAMPLE CODE, *provided* you comply with subsection (d)(iii) below. You may not distribute the SAMPLE CODE, or any modified version of the SAMPLE CODE, in source code form.

      ii. **Redistributable Files.** Provided you comply with subsection (d)(iii) below, Microsoft grants you a nonexclusive, royalty-free right to reproduce and distribute the object code version of the SAMPLE CODE and of any modified SAMPLE CODE, other than SAMPLE CODE, or any modified version thereof, designated as not redistributable in the Readme file that forms a part of the SOFTWARE PRODUCT (the "Non-Redistributable Sample Code"). All SAMPLE CODE other than the Non-Redistributable Sample Code is collectively referred to as the "REDISTRIBUTABLES."

      iii. **Redistribution Requirements.** If you redistribute the REDISTRIBUTABLES, you agree to: (i) distribute the REDISTRIBUTABLES in object code form only in conjunction with and as a part of your software application product; (ii) not use Microsoft's name, logo, or trademarks to market your software application product; (iii) include a valid copyright notice on your software application product; (iv) indemnify, hold harmless, and defend Microsoft from and against any claims or lawsuits, including attorney's fees, that arise or result from the use or distribution of your software application product; and (v) not permit further distribution of the REDISTRIBUTABLES by your end user. Contact Microsoft for the applicable royalties due and other licensing terms for all other uses and/or distribution of the REDISTRIBUTABLES.

2. **DESCRIPTION OF OTHER RIGHTS AND LIMITATIONS.**

   - **Limitations on Reverse Engineering, Decompilation, and Disassembly.** You may not reverse engineer, decompile, or disassemble the SOFTWARE PRODUCT, except and only to the extent that such activity is expressly permitted by applicable law notwithstanding this limitation.

   - **Separation of Components.** The SOFTWARE PRODUCT is licensed as a single product. Its component parts may not be separated for use on more than one computer.

   - **Rental.** You may not rent, lease, or lend the SOFTWARE PRODUCT.

- **Support Services.** Microsoft may, but is not obligated to, provide you with support services related to the SOFTWARE PRODUCT ("Support Services"). Use of Support Services is governed by the Microsoft policies and programs described in the user manual, in "online" documentation, and/or in other Microsoft-provided materials. Any supplemental software code provided to you as part of the Support Services shall be considered part of the SOFTWARE PRODUCT and subject to the terms and conditions of this EULA. With respect to technical information you provide to Microsoft as part of the Support Services, Microsoft may use such information for its business purposes, including for product support and development. Microsoft will not utilize such technical information in a form that personally identifies you.

- **Software Transfer.** You may permanently transfer all of your rights under this EULA, provided you retain no copies, you transfer all of the SOFTWARE PRODUCT (including all component parts, the media and printed materials, any upgrades, this EULA, and, if applicable, the Certificate of Authenticity), **and** the recipient agrees to the terms of this EULA.

- **Termination.** Without prejudice to any other rights, Microsoft may terminate this EULA if you fail to comply with the terms and conditions of this EULA. In such event, you must destroy all copies of the SOFTWARE PRODUCT and all of its component parts.

3. **COPYRIGHT.** All title and copyrights in and to the SOFTWARE PRODUCT (including but not limited to any images, photographs, animations, video, audio, music, text, SAMPLE CODE, REDISTRIBUTABLES, and "applets" incorporated into the SOFTWARE PRODUCT) and any copies of the SOFTWARE PRODUCT are owned by Microsoft or its suppliers. The SOFT-WARE PRODUCT is protected by copyright laws and international treaty provisions. Therefore, you must treat the SOFTWARE PRODUCT like any other copyrighted material **except** that you may install the SOFTWARE PRODUCT on a single computer provided you keep the original solely for backup or archival purposes. You may not copy the printed materials accompanying the SOFTWARE PRODUCT.

4. **U.S. GOVERNMENT RESTRICTED RIGHTS.** The SOFTWARE PRODUCT and documentation are provided with RESTRICTED RIGHTS. Use, duplication, or disclosure by the Government is subject to restrictions as set forth in subparagraph (c)(1)(ii) of the Rights in Technical Data and Computer Software clause at DFARS 252.227-7013 or subparagraphs (c)(1) and (2) of the Commercial Computer Software—Restricted Rights at 48 CFR 52.227-19, as applicable. Manufacturer is Microsoft Corporation/One Microsoft Way/Redmond, WA 98052-6399.

5. **EXPORT RESTRICTIONS.** You agree that you will not export or re-export the SOFTWARE PRODUCT, any part thereof, or any process or service that is the direct product of the SOFTWARE PRODUCT (the foregoing collectively referred to as the "Restricted Components"), to any country, person, entity, or end user subject to U.S. export restrictions. You specifically agree not to export or re-export any of the Restricted Components (i) to any country to which the U.S. has embargoed or restricted the export of goods or services, which currently include, but are not necessarily limited to, Cuba, Iran, Iraq, Libya, North Korea, Sudan, and Syria, or to any national of any such country, wherever located, who intends to transmit or transport the Restricted Components back to such country; (ii) to any end user who you know or have reason to know will utilize the Restricted Components in the design, development, or production of nuclear, chemical, or biological weapons; or (iii) to any end user who has been prohibited from participating in U.S. export transactions by any federal agency of the U.S. government. You warrant and represent that neither the BXA nor any other U.S. federal agency has suspended, revoked, or denied your export privileges.

DISCLAIMER OF WARRANTY

NO WARRANTIES OR CONDITIONS. MICROSOFT EXPRESSLY DISCLAIMS ANY WARRANTY OR CONDITION FOR THE SOFTWARE PRODUCT. THE SOFTWARE PRODUCT AND ANY RELATED DOCUMENTATION ARE PROVIDED "AS IS" WITHOUT WARRANTY OR CONDITION OF ANY KIND, EITHER EXPRESS OR IMPLIED, INCLUDING, WITHOUT LIMITA-TION, THE IMPLIED WARRANTIES OF MERCHANTABILITY, FITNESS FOR A PARTICULAR PURPOSE, OR NONINFRINGEMENT. THE ENTIRE RISK ARISING OUT OF USE OR PERFORMANCE OF THE SOFTWARE PRODUCT REMAINS WITH YOU.

LIMITATION OF LIABILITY. TO THE MAXIMUM EXTENT PERMITTED BY APPLICABLE LAW, IN NO EVENT SHALL MICROSOFT OR ITS SUPPLIERS BE LIABLE FOR ANY SPECIAL, INCIDENTAL, INDIRECT, OR CONSEQUENTIAL DAM-AGES WHATSOEVER (INCLUDING, WITHOUT LIMITATION, DAMAGES FOR LOSS OF BUSINESS PROFITS, BUSINESS INTERRUPTION, LOSS OF BUSINESS INFORMATION, OR ANY OTHER PECUNIARY LOSS) ARISING OUT OF THE USE OF OR INABILITY TO USE THE SOFTWARE PRODUCT OR THE PROVISION OF OR FAILURE TO PROVIDE SUPPORT SERVICES, EVEN IF MICROSOFT HAS BEEN ADVISED OF THE POSSIBILITY OF SUCH DAMAGES. IN ANY CASE, MICROSOFT'S ENTIRE LIABILITY UNDER ANY PROVISION OF THIS EULA SHALL BE LIMITED TO THE GREATER OF THE AMOUNT ACTUALLY PAID BY YOU FOR THE SOFTWARE PRODUCT OR US$5.00; PROVIDED, HOWEVER, IF YOU HAVE ENTERED INTO A MICROSOFT SUPPORT SERVICES AGREEMENT, MICROSOFT'S ENTIRE LIABILITY REGARDING SUPPORT SERVICES SHALL BE GOVERNED BY THE TERMS OF THAT AGREEMENT. BECAUSE SOME STATES AND JURISDICTIONS DO NOT ALLOW THE EXCLUSION OR LIMITATION OF LIABILITY, THE ABOVE LIMITATION MAY NOT APPLY TO YOU.

MISCELLANEOUS

This EULA is governed by the laws of the State of Washington USA, except and only to the extent that applicable law mandates govern-ing law of a different jurisdiction.

Should you have any questions concerning this EULA, or if you desire to contact Microsoft for any reason, please contact the Microsoft subsidiary serving your country, or write: Microsoft Sales Information Center/One Microsoft Way/Redmond, WA 98052-6399.

PN 097-0002296